EqualBITE

Gender equality in
higher education

EqualBITE

Gender equality in higher education

Edited by:
Judy Robertson
Alison Williams
Derek Jones
Lara Isbel
Daphne Loads

Illustrated by:
Elspeth Maxwell

Designed by:
Alan J. Tait

SENSE PUBLISHERS
ROTTERDAM/BOSTON/TAIPEI

A C.I.P. record for this book is available
from the Library of Congress.

978-94-6351-141-4 (paperback)
978-94-6351-142-1 (hardback)
978-94-6351-143-8 (e-book)

Published by:
Sense Publishers
P.O. Box 21858
3001 AW Rotterdam
The Netherlands
www.sensepublishers.com

Printed on acid-free paper

"The ivory tower, like other stately homes in the UK, might present a grand façade to the world but closer inspection reveals a dark, spidery basement full of inequalities."

The Wellcome Trust, with the Francis Crick Institute and GlaxoSmithKline, have recently come together to create EDIS—Equality and Diversity in Science and Health. Underlying our vision is the fact that tough scientific problems do not get solved by monolithic thinking: their solutions require diversity of experience, thought and approach. This is why we were so pleased to see this new guide to one aspect of diversity—gender equality—and to see how good it is: the book is comprehensive; it is raw, honest and personal; and it is very well written. It is a book both for reading cover-to-cover and for dipping into, and it will be enormously influential.

One of the great strengths of the book is that the contributors address the practical issues that frequently thwart attempts to make higher education more diverse and inclusive. In particular, although EqualBITE's editors included common topics such as unconscious bias and representation on committees, they went beyond these to consider issues that at first sight may be less significant. The short contribution *What have you done to my squash courts!* uses humour to show that the changes institutions make in relation to gender equality won't always be popular—indeed they might frustrate us personally—but they are all part of making universities and institutes more inclusive. Elsewhere, the different formats of the contributions, including articles, practical 'recipes' for gender equality, and illustrations drawn by students at Edinburgh College of Art, make for a read that is as enjoyable as it is informative.

Whether you are an individual scientist wishing to be a better ally for women colleagues, a lab head keen to understand how to make your lab meetings more inclusive, or an individual struggling with how to raise your profile on a grant application, you will find something useful in this book. For us at the Wellcome Trust, the chapters on defining excellence and becoming a better scientific evaluator will support our own efforts to make research more diverse and inclusive.

Jim Smith
Director of Science,
Wellcome Trust

Gemma Tracey
Diversity & Inclusion Programme
Manager – Science & Research,
Wellcome Trust

Contents

Gender and language

Gender and leadership

Gender, change and the future

A list of URLs associated with footnotes can be found at
https://www.ed.ac.uk/equality-diversity/innovation-development/equal-bite/webrefs, organised by article

Foreword

I am delighted to write a foreword to this EqualBITE book. The contributions in this book have been generated by staff, students and friends of the University of Edinburgh and report practical strategies to improve equality and inclusion in higher education. The contributions are diverse, ranging from recipes to articles, to artwork, to instructions, to personal reflections on experience. The common theme running through them is the crucial role that equality and inclusion plays in the life of the University. The values of equality and inclusion are important to staff and to the University itself. As an institution, we are very proud of our equality awards and charter mark participation (including institutional Athena SWAN Silver award and membership of the Race Equality Charter). None of this would have achieved without the support and hard work of very many people throughout the University.

The contributions demonstrate many examples of great practice, both by individuals and by the institution, that contribute positively to equality and inclusion. They also provide inspiration for further work to make Edinburgh (and other higher education institutions) an even better place to work and study.

I am very grateful to everyone who has contributed so enthusiastically to this book, and to the editorial team Judy Robertson, Alison Williams, Derek Jones, Lara Isbel and Daphne Loads. I hope that other readers enjoy it as much as I have.

Jane Norman
Vice-Principal People & Culture
The University of Edinburgh

Edinburgh, July 2017

Acknowledgements

Our thanks go to the many students and staff of the University of Edinburgh who participated in this project through survey responses, workshops, focus groups, interviews, data-gathering and inspiring conversations, including – but not limited to – Catherine Burns (Research Support Office), Gerard Lerpiniere (Director of Lothian Equal Access Programme), Denise Boyle (University HR Services), Ann MacDonald, Harvey Dingwall, Jean Grier, Gin Lowdeen, Jenny Leeder, Andrew Clausen and Gail Burton.

We have had the invaluable support of the Institute for Academic Development – technical, practical, and moral, in particular from Jon Turner, Sara Shinton, Lucy Ridley and Silje Graffer. The Steering Committee (Jane Norman, Jon Turner, Simon Clark and Caroline Wallace), have been an unfailing source of challenge, wisdom and connections to the wider University and have provided contributions to the content.

Our thanks go to our colleagues at Edinburgh University Students' Association: Sarah Moffat, Paul Bradley, Chris Belous and Jenna Kelly for their perspectives and contributions, and access to the Unapologetically Me exhibition and exhibitors.

This project has not happened in a vacuum – it has run in parallel with other University of Edinburgh gender initiatives (past and ongoing) including the Playfair Steps Initiative (Information Services), Edinburgh Interdisciplinary Feminism and Gender Reading Group, Hoppers (Informatics), Ingenious Women (Institute for Academic Development), Aurora (Leadership Foundation for Higher Education), Inspiring Women (Equality and Diversity), Dangerous Women (Institute for Advanced Studies in Humanities) and many others.

Special thanks are due to the sixty-seven contributors of articles and papers, recipes, photographs and illustrations. Thanks also to our back office team - Vince Robbins proofreader, Jane Read indexer, and the design team of Elspeth Maxwell and Alan Tait who have brought the book to life and opened up levels of clarity and interpretation hitherto unseen. And finally to all the EqualBITE editors for the collaborative, collegiate and continuously fun and challenging way we work together.

Introduction

_____

In September 2015, a group of University of Edinburgh senior staff met with the editorial team to explore how the University might reflect on its progress towards gender equality. How could the insights, the frustrations, the excellent practice, and the sheer complexity of it all be captured and shared? The outcome was a remit to delve into the gap between policy and practice, to reflect, sometimes humorously, sometimes critically, and always constructively, on how things actually are. We set out to edit a book, for an audience of university communities worldwide, containing stories to inform, entertain and inspire people to achieve gender equality.

EqualBITE: Gender equality in higher education is the culmination of this two-year project, gathering and sharing experiences of the University of Edinburgh's progress towards gender equality that have relevance far beyond this immediate institution, and indeed beyond academia into wider society.

The stories are presented as articles and as 'recipes', a conceptual metaphor (explored in full shortly) that provides people with an opportunity to share and adapt practical advice. The recipes and articles inform: they encapsulate wisdom hard-won through challenges, mistakes, and triumphs, and through small changes that add up to wider progress. The recipes, in particular, entertain: the authors' voices come strongly through the text, along with descriptions of sometimes funny, sometimes absurd, situations. The recipes and papers will, we intend, inspire other people, other departments and other institutions to try out what they contain. Most recipes have been included because we have found the practices they describe to be reliable, well-tested within or beyond the University of Edinburgh or – an essential part of the BITE approach – evidenced in the literature. Others have been included because they offer personal insights into what it is like to be an individual within the current academic climate.

EqualBITE is values-driven. The very first thing we did when starting the project was to agree what values should inform it, and how they would be reflected in our own behaviour and decision-making. Our initial statement affirmed our understanding "that by embracing differences we create a more vibrant and rigorous intellectual, supportive and learning context for all our community."

EqualBITE has a vision. With the writer bell hooks, we ask you to imagine:

> living in a world where there is no domination [...] but where a vision of mutuality is the ethos shaping our interaction. Imagine living in a world where we can all be who we are, [...] able to create beloved community, to live together, realising our dreams of freedom and justice, living the truth that we are all "created equal". (bell hooks, 2000, p. x).

Our position is that women and men are intellectually equal, and can be equally capable in all higher education roles; and that the University of Edinburgh as an organisation, and we as individuals within it, are responsible for creating an environment in which all staff and students can flourish whatever their gender. Gender bias can make it more challenging for women to succeed in higher education, despite having the same levels of talent and ambition, the same potential for outstanding and worthwhile contributions, and the same aspirations for success. We have worked from the understanding that gender equality is not a zero-sum game in which men lose if women gain; rather that when it's better for women it's better for everyone. We recognise that values and approaches which are often labelled as feminine or masculine are not necessarily gender-specific, and neither are the different aspirations and definitions of success, or of leadership. We believe that policies and practices designed to promote a positive working environment and career progression for women should benefit all.

EqualBITE is not an academic text and the editorial team are not specialists in gender studies. Our individual and collective approach to the project is, as with the other contributors, experiential. While the book does have a certain academic flavour (and a commitment to, and respect for, research evidence) it is also a representation of people's experiences. It is intended to be a frank exploration of the messy reality which is reflected in some of the clusters of recipes and papers where differing views and multiple readings of reality (Charmaz, 2000) are presented. At heart, it is pragmatic and positive, and a catalyst for creating a culture which is better for everyone.

Project parameters

Although we initially set out the project parameters, we promptly found that we had to keep revisiting and revising them as our understanding of the complexity of the subject grew exponentially through the conversations we had with contributors and through our own personal and professional reflections. For example, we were swiftly disabused of our original decision to exclude all non-academic aspects of university life after conversations with students and Edinburgh University Students' Association staff. We therefore include gendered aspects of sport and exercise, social and club life that students raised, but not life in residences, which they did not.

We have kept to our original aim that content should be contributed by University of Edinburgh students, members of staff groups and academic staff. Keeping the material within one university creates a coherence that, paradoxically, enables the learning to be more widely applied; to university communities worldwide, and beyond academia.

The project is about culture change in academic institutions, as observed within this particular one, but the situated examples and stories, almost without exception, are relevant in other institutions; Edinburgh-specific content and context is added where appropriate.

Why a recipe book?

In BITE: Recipes for Remarkable Research (2014), the first book in this series, we were faced with the challenge of approaching and making sense of a complex research landscape, and making it accessible to a diverse audience.

As Derek Jones wrote:

> The recipe was clearly a conceptual metaphor that the group shared [...] it is an instantly recognisable form and this matters a great deal. [...] By using metaphors to translate elements of information and knowledge, recipes allow summaries of research and observation. Looking at the recipe components, Background can provide context, experiential reporting, observations, positioning, proposing, relevance, and importance – all the things one might, in fact, expect as the necessary preconditions for some piece of research in context. Ingredients can describe elements, artefacts, items, and other things, and can include conceptual elements such as attitudes, approaches, and ideas. [...] Method can provide steps for replication, recreation or simply description. More importantly, since this is a recipe metaphor, it can also allow for 'maybes' and 'possibilities' – not simply the definite elements. (Jones, 2014, pp. 12-13)

We found this experience repeated in the writing workshops we ran at the start of the EqualBITE project – the power of the metaphor was such that people immediately grasped it. Participants, given a simple template, were able to capture their initial thoughts quickly, making changes to the structure as required by their own particular story. And as the project developed it became once again clear that the recipe is a powerful tool for thinking. Recipes are fun to do – something that for busy and overworked people is a great motivator, and for the editors so much easier to invite than a full paper. And we have enjoyed the wonderful paradox of using a recipe – such a symbol of domesticity – to help improve the position of women in the professional world.

Our contributors

There are seventy-one recipes, papers, and editorial articles, and eighteen student photographs and drawings, from sixty-seven authors and contributors (of whom five wish to remain anonymous). Of the named sixty-two contributors, there are forty-six women and sixteen men; thirty-eight are University staff, twenty-two are students, and two are from outside the University.

Our aim, from the start of this project, has been to gather material in a diagonal slice across the institution – from students and academic and professional staff at all levels and across the three Colleges.

We reached staff (and many fewer students than we would have liked) through a series of workshops, which spread awareness of the EqualBITE project, generating our first tranche of recipes, and creating a base and a website from which to move forward. Active support from the Steering Committee and especially from the Institute for Academic Development facilitated senior leaders' conversations (see *Leadership perspectives on gender equality*) and ensured engagement at a senior level from both academic and professional services viewpoints. We used our internal and external networks to broaden our reach, and to invite papers from specialists.

We found engaging with the student population more difficult. Fewer than ten students in all attended the workshops; a postcard campaign across the campuses raised awareness, but while it invited contributions there were no returns. An online survey, sent to the entire student body by the students association, received only four responses. In talking to Edinburgh University Students' Association (EUSA) staff, and to student groups, we realised there were two main barriers: a mistrust of 'the University' and its hierarchy, and the language we had used. Students did not connect with 'gender equality' and only when we met with student groups (a Gender Studies class, Edinburgh College of Art (ECA) Illustration students, EUSA) and invited them to talk about things in their everyday experience, did they connect the phrase 'gender equality' with issues of everyday sexism.

Many of the students we spoke to seemed initially unaware of the issues with which women staff struggled. We did, however, find that female students working in bars and clubs were very aware of sexism and sexist comments and pressures: maybe gender inequalities are more apparent when one enters the world of work.

The two main student contribution sets came from EUSA's Unapologetically Me exhibition of photographs and accompanying text, and from drawings made by third-year ECA students in response to a workshop discussion (see *Perspectives from students*).

Our final challenge was to engage men in the project. Around a quarter of the authors are male, most of them members of our internal networks. Only one male students turned up at an initial workshop, subsequently contributing a recipe and a short article; and one of the drawings was contributed by a male ECA student. As the project progressed, we started to invite colleagues with specific expertise to contribute, which in some cases introduced additional men to the project.

Most of the recipes and articles are illustrated. The illustrator's intention was to develop a visual language for the book by creating a compelling illustration for each recipe; we have found that they add another layer of meaning, revealing aspects of the content that had not been obvious at first.

The editorial team

Creating this book by drawing together so many contributions required a fairly large editorial team. There are five of us. We have backgrounds in science, humanities, arts and social science. We work in academic departments, professional services and one of us is (in theory) retired. We span three decades in age. Some of us are on flexible contracts and work odd hours (some of us just work odd hours anyway). We frequently disagree about whether phrases like "ecosophical gestalt analysis" belong in a recipe (obviously not). Some of us are parents, one of us is a man, and we have varying views on Wonder Woman. Most of all: we are a team. There is no way that a single editor could have brought this book together. It has emerged from our lengthy discussions, disagreements, difficult decisions, dogged persistence and occasional flashes of collective brilliance. Judy, Lara and Daphne are employed directly by the University of Edinburgh, Alison is an academic consultant, and Derek is our much needed critical friend from the Open University. Our Steering Committee consists of Jane Norman, Jon Turner, Simon Clark and Caroline Wallace who have all been thoroughly supportive throughout. Indeed, this project happened because of Jon Turner's openness to new ideas and thrived because of his unwaveringly positive attitude.

> ...the University of Edinburgh is a place where we can have conversations about challenging topics. In some cases, students (within the Students' Association) start the conversations which will disrupt and challenge tradition, and the University will engage in the debate, adding academic depth and long experience to passionate personal convictions...

The University of Edinburgh has stood up to the scrutiny of this book unflinchingly; it has willingly invested in collecting a set of experiences which were always intended to capture the gap between aspiration and reality. The University even set aside the corporate brand for the integrity of design of the volume. Of course, a university is not a single entity. It is a loose coalition of thousands of individuals with differing perspectives and experiences. All the individuals who volunteered to contribute or who we approached to fact check or give alternative perspectives have been creative and generous in sharing their expertise and have been open to criticism. The University of Edinburgh is a place where we can have conversations about challenging topics. In some cases, students (within the Students' Association) start the conversations which will disrupt and challenge tradition, and the University will engage in the debate, adding academic depth and long experience to passionate personal convictions.

The structure of the book

The opening section positions the book within contexts of academia in the UK and in the University of Edinburgh. We present a model for change, derived from the project and the literature, that suggests how individuals and leaders can address gender bias as a remediable habit. The recipes and articles that follow focus on gendered aspects of academia, including curriculum, journals and seminars, the gendered aspects of the REF (Research Excellence Framework), and the need to be sceptical when researchers claim sex differences. A cluster of recipes tackles career issues, including women and competition, and the challenges of balancing work and family responsibilities.

A further cluster of recipes and articles portray the student perspective, dealing with difficult topics including the complex question of harassment, from differing and complementary points of view, and through different media. We hear from students, academic and professional staff, and EUSA, in photographs, a paper and response, and student drawings. The next sections focus, first, on the power of language to maintain or change bias, and the responsibility we have as individuals and as colleagues and mentors to use words mindfully and constructively, and then, on the key intersection of gender and leadership. Multiple readings of reality are shared in the section on the University of Edinburgh's Sport & Exercise facilities, and in an examination of how the physical environment can support

equitable thoughts and behaviours. Finally, we listen in to a conversation with senior University leaders, and finish by reviewing the themes and putting forward recommendations that have emerged over the two years of the project.

There are recipes and articles that describe processes for real personal change – for example, *Catalyst* where a student reflects on how involvement in EqualBITE has changed his personal and professional perspective. There are recipes for initiating and sustaining change within teams and groups – for example, very practical steps towards running and contributing to meetings in which every voice is heard and valued, and bias – implicit or explicit – is called out (*How to run more equal meetings* and *Becoming visible in meetings*). And there are papers that explore real change at an institutional level – for example, *A model for change* and *Asking for equitable buildings*.

Other recipes and images share the author's or maker's sense of what it is like to be them; for example, to be a young woman researcher caught by an early period in a campus without sanitary provision (*Rose surprise*), or a student who has to decide each morning whether they look too masculine to go safely into a women-only toilet (*Perspectives from students*), or a male post-graduate speaking out when he hears sexist language (*Allies in the classroom*). Recipes share pivotal moments, they provide illuminating facts, the articles explore topics in depth, introduce new topics, explain why an issue exists in the first place, and shine theory onto the everyday. Recipes are grounded in the authors' experience, referenced in the literature and linked, separately and where appropriate, to the University of Edinburgh's processes and procedures.

The glossary of terms will help the reader, as compiling it has helped us, to navigate the sometimes opaque waters of gender equality terminology.

We invite you to read this book in whatever way makes sense to you. You might want to skip through the recipes, gathering insights and taking comfort and inspiration. You might be in a position of influence and looking for research evidence to support your case for change, or you might be mulling over a particular quandary and needing a sense of no longer being alone.

Whatever approaches you take, we invite you to bear in mind the uniqueness of each author's voice, and your own situation, seen through the lens of the EqualBITE values, and take what is pertinent and useful.

As editors we position gender equality in the context of human rights, agreeing with Eleanor Roosevelt that:

> Where, after all, do universal human rights begin? In small places, close to home – so close and so small that they cannot be seen on any maps of the world. Yet they are the world of the individual person; the neighbourhood [...] the school or college [...] the factory, farm or office. Such are the places where every man, woman and child seeks equal justice, equal opportunity, equal dignity without discrimination. Unless these rights have meaning there, they have little meaning anywhere. (Roosevelt, 1958)

The book is intended to be practical and inspirational. Our hope is that you can take the learning, adapt it, and apply it in your own situation, 'in the small places, close to home'.

Gender in higher education: the current landscape in the UK

Judy Robertson

The UK aspires to have a world-leading higher education system, striving both to provide high quality education to students from all over the world and conduct world leading research. It is also committed to ensuring that research has an economic or social impact, and that access to higher education is widened.

There are 164 universities in the UK in receipt of public funds, educating 2.28 million students, and employing 201,380 academic and 208,750 non-academic staff [1]. The ambitions for the sector are reasonably well founded – currently 400,000 international students have chosen to study here and in terms of research, the 4.1% of the world's researchers based in the UK produce 16% of the world's most highly cited articles.

Higher education in this country, however, is subject to a set of complex political and economic pressures which impact the working lives of staff and impact students. Life in the ivory tower is not altogether peaceful and productive. Furthermore, on peering through the windows of the ivory tower, we do not see equal proportions of men and women on each floor. The structure was built with glass ceilings, glass basements and all manner of other architectural barriers for women.

University students

More women than men study at UK universities; there is a 12% gap in favour of women (up to 15% in Scotland, the part of the UK in which the University of Edinburgh is based). The proportion of women students varies by discipline, from as low as 17% women on engineering and technology-based courses to 81% women in subjects allied to medicine [2]. There is also a slightly higher proportion of men who are unable to continue with their studies. Women also perform better in terms of their final degree outcomes – in every subject (apart from social studies) women achieve a higher proportion of first class and 2:1 degrees. It is heartening that women are no longer in the minority at universities, although the widened gap does give some concern for the educational chances of men from disadvantaged backgrounds [3] (see *Educated Pass: engaging young males from low socio-economic status backgrounds with learning*).

Education really does enable women to improve their financial circumstances. Women graduates earn up to three times the income of women without degrees whereas graduate men earn twice the salary of male non-graduates [4]. The gender difference in the graduate premium is mostly because non-graduate wages for women are so low.

According to the Equal Pay Act 1970 and the Equality Act 2010, it is illegal to discriminate against people for their sex, race or other protected characteristics [5]. Despite this, there is an 18% gender pay gap in the UK which the government is leisurely committed to eliminating in a generation [6]. After all, as women have been waiting for pay equality for hundreds of years, what does a few decades matter? The government attributes the gender pay gap to a complex set of overlapping factors including the fact that women are less likely to progress up the career ladder, that more women work part-time and that "a higher proportion of women choose occupations that offer less financial reward (e.g. administration). Many high paying sectors are disproportionately

made up of male workers (e.g. information and communications technology)." However, data suggests that even within jobs in the same sector, women are under-rewarded.

Analysis of the government's Longitudinal Earnings Outcome data [7] tells us that while education helps women gain prosperity, there is still a troubling gender pay gap which begins after graduation and continues to grow [8]. For example, the median difference in pay between male and female computer science graduates is already £4,400 five years after leaving university. So although it is true that there are proportionally fewer women (14%) employed in the technology sector, women who are employed there are under-compensated. Gaps exist even in professions which have been traditionally female dominated such as education and nursing. There are further inequalities relating to intersectionalities; Pakistani, Bangladeshi, and Black Caribbean women graduates earn less than white women graduates. Universities, it would appear, have some work to do in helping their women students prepare to take their place in the financially unfair world of work (see *Salary negotiation*). Employers have even more work to do to ensure that they they are treating their female employees equitably.

University is not just a place to get a degree and then arrange a job. It is a place to learn, to make friends, to seek new experiences, to live. Unfortunately, studies suggest that women students can experience an unpleasant and harassing environment at university. In an online survey of 2,156 university students conducted by the National Union of Students [9], 25% of students overall (and 37% of the women in the sample) had suffered unwelcome sexual advances, including inappropriate touching and groping. The same proportion had endured sexual comments about their body, and one-third had been made uncomfortable by overtly sexual conversations about them. About 30% of respondents had experienced verbal harassment, and two-thirds had heard jokes about rape when on campus. Two-thirds of respondents had witnessed fellow students experience sexual comments and conversations. The National Union of Students found in a later study that new students in their first week at university were particularly at risk, but that 61% of them were unsure how to report the incidents to their university [10].

Such figures reflect the experiences of women in the wider public in the UK, where 64% of women have experienced unwelcome sexual attention and 35% have endured unwanted touching [11]. It would also seem that students report a good environment on university campuses (5.8 on a 7-point scale, slightly higher than in the community as a whole [12]). The harassment seems to be largely student to student, and in social or sporting places rather than within the classroom. The incidence and extent of staff-student harassment is not yet well documented.

A taskforce led by Universities UK has issued a set of recommendations about how universities can deal with sexual harassment [13], calling for institutions to work closely with their student unions to "take an institution-wide approach to tackling violence against women, harassment and hate crime". An account of the University of Edinburgh's work relating to sexual harassment in partnership with the Edinburgh University Students' Union can be found later in the book.

Women students are likely to have witnessed or experienced harassment at some point during their studies, and may often experience conversations in which women are objectified or denigrated, or their personal appearance is scrutinised. Furthermore, women students are more likely to report mental health problems than men (34% of women students, 19% of male students) [14], including anxiety, depression and eating disorders. LGBT students are also disproportionately likely to suffer from mental health difficulties. The article about the Unapologetically Me project led by the Edinburgh University Students' Association gives some insight into what it is like to be a female or transgender person at university today.

There is much to be done to support all of our students to have positive experiences of universities. We want men to have opportunities to study and succeed at university, regardless of their socio-economic background. We want women's academic excellence to be rewarded with job opportunities with equal chances of promotion and fair pay. We want all students to have positive mental health, and no one to experience harassment on campus or in wider communities. This must be accomplished in society as a whole, but universities can lead the way through educating graduates to be agents of change and by creating positive environments for learning (see *Creating a safe space for classroom discussions*).

University staff

Although the majority of staff in higher education institutions in the UK are women (44.6% of academic staff), they are over-represented in lower pay grades and under-represented in higher pay grades [15]. For example, women are considerably less likely to be promoted to professor than men (only 23% of professors are women [16]), and only 20% of university principals are women. Women are also more likely to work part-time: 76.0% of men employed by universities work full-time compared with 58.3% of women. In terms of job security, a lower proportion of women are on open-ended contracts (61.5% compared to 66.5%).

Although universities in the UK use a jointly negotiated pay scale across institutions, a pay gap still exists in the sector. The gap is primarily caused by the lower proportions of women in senior grades (where the salary scale has more flexibility for discretionary increments), and is worse in elite institutions. The gender pay gap in universities currently stands at 12% [17], which is less than the pay gap across all sectors in the UK (18%).

University staff in the UK are under pressure. In a 2014 study conducted by the UCU (University and College Union), 79% of the 6439 respondents agreed or strongly agreed that they find their job stressful [18]. Academics are not alone in suffering from stress – the Health and Safety Executive calculate that stress accounts for 45% of working days lost due to ill-health across the UK [19]. Public service industries including education tend to have higher levels of stress. In fact, UCU members reported lower levels of well-being than average across all sectors in the Health and Safety Executive's stressor categories [20]. The Health and Safety Executive data also shows that more women than men suffer from stress across a wide age range, across the workforce.

High workload is one factor associated with stress at universities. In the UCU survey, more than a quarter of respondents found their workload unmanageable all or most of the time. Two-thirds found their workloads unmanageable at least half of the time. This is in spite of working long hours: 41% of people on full-time contracts reported working in excess of 50 hours per week (although standard contracts specify working hours in the range of 35-40 hour week), and one in ten report working 60 hours or more per week. According to the UCU, staff in higher education and FE are working an average of more than two days unpaid every week, with professors (56.1 hours), principal research fellows (55.7 hours) and teaching assistants (54.9 hours) reporting the highest average full-time hours per week. There is not a gender difference in working hours for staff on full time contracts, but women who work part-time with small fractions (one to two days per week) tend to work longer unpaid additional hours than men in the same position. This is why it is particularly important for managers to ensure that the workload for staff on part-time or flexible contracts is carefully planned and managed (see *Flexible working: being realistic*). In response to the findings of these and similar surveys, the University and College Union and the National Union of Students have produced a joint statement [21] calling on university employers to monitor staff workload to ensure that staff are not overloaded and unable to spend sufficient time with students to offer high quality education.

The UCU data from successive surveys confirms that academics are now working in a rapidly changing work environment, with expanded roles and greater administrative responsibilities. There are two major, potentially contradictory, demands on staff in the form of the Research Excellence Framework (REF) and now the Teaching Excellence Framework (TEF). (It is worth noting that many Scottish universities, including Edinburgh, opted out of the TEF [22] on the grounds that there is already an effective way of reviewing and enhancing HE (higher education) teaching in Scotland). Universities must invest considerable time and attention to ensuring high standards in these areas because they both have large funding and reputation implications. Many universities are trying to wrestle with the demands of maintaining research and teaching excellence, which is difficult to achieve as the success of both enterprises commonly rely on the efforts of the same individuals. "How can I keep my research going and still do my best teaching?" is surely a familiar refrain for academics the world over but it is brought to an excruciating head by the relentlessly high standards and exacting data gathering of the excellence frameworks. Factor in a highly competitive environment both between staff and between institutions, and it is no wonder that stress levels among academics are so high, workplace satisfaction has plummeted, and reports of personal harassment and bullying have increased [23].

There is reason to believe that women are more vulnerable to such HE workplace pressures because of widespread unconscious bias. With respect to research, studies of the REF indicate that women were less likely than their male colleagues to have work submitted to the REF [24] (51% of the available pool of women compared to 67% of the available pool of men had their work submitted for review), which has the potential to damage morale and promotion prospects for women. (See Emily

Yarrow's *Gender and the Research Excellence Framework* for an in-depth consideration of this.) Furthermore, evidence is mounting internationally and across disciplines that because of implicit bias, women academics are less likely to receive invitations to review papers (Lerback, 2017), are invited to speak at conferences less frequently (Nature, 2016), and have lower grant success rates (RCUK, 2016). These topics are tackled in more depth in *Gender balancing your scholarly journal, Gender balancing your seminar speakers* and *How to become a better scientific evaluator*. Again, being subject to the steady "drip drip" of unconscious bias has an impact on career progression and self-efficacy (see *Dealing with imposter syndrome*). Moreover, when teaching is evaluated by student satisfaction scores (which is one measure used in TEF), women will potentially be disadvantaged due to unconscious bias of (male) students against female teachers (Boring, 2017; MacNell, et al., 2014).

In summary, there are persistent gender inequalities in UK higher education. Women staff are less likely to be promoted to higher grades, are less likely to have permanent contracts, and are paid less. Women in general are also more likely to suffer from workplace stress, and it is known that the HE sector in the UK is a particularly stressful place to work at the moment. Two of the major factors which contribute to workload and stress in HE – measurements of research and teaching excellence – can perpetuate gender inequalities through implicit bias.

Athena SWAN

In spite of the the bleak picture of higher education in the UK, there is good reason to be cheerful: Athena SWAN [25]. This charter, started in 2005 by the Equality Challenge Unit, aims to remove barriers to progression and success for all. The scheme started with a focus on the experiences of women students and academic staff in the STEMM disciplines (science, technology, engineering, medicine and mathematics), but since 2015 has been expanded to include arts, humanities, social sciences, business and law (AHSSBL) as well as professional services and support staff. It now considers the perspectives of men

(where appropriate) and also trans people. The scheme has been extended to include the Republic of Ireland, and a similar scheme is under consideration in Australia [26]. By its tenth anniversary, 143 institutions had joined Athena SWAN, holding 669 awards between them. In applying for an award, departments must show quantitative evidence relating to the representation of women, the progression of students into academia, career progression and working environment. Since 2015, the charter has also committed to tackling the gender pay gap, addressing the consequences of short-term contracts on career progression, tackling discriminatory treatment against trans people, and to using an approach of intersectionality to consider individuals whose experiences are shaped by the intersection of gender and race, and other protected characteristics.

Athena SWAN awards are hard won. Higher education institutions in the UK can apply for Athena SWAN awards at Bronze, Silver or Gold level, as can individual departments within each institution. For a Bronze award, the department must show evidence of a solid foundation towards dismantling discrimination and fostering an inclusive culture. Silver award holders have a significant record in promoting and achieving equality. To achieve Gold, there must be sustained progress, and the responsibility to be a beacon of achievement, and a champion of good practice to other institutions. Bronze applications have a success rate of 64%, new Silver awards are 33% successful, upgrades from Bronze to Silver applications are 50% successful and Gold awards are only 33% successful. The awards must be renewed regularly, and the success of the Athena SWAN charter in terms of meeting its aims is also subject to review and evaluation.

An evaluation of the Athena SWAN scheme in 2013 (Fox, 2014). found evidence of sustainable culture and attitude changes within the award-holding departments. While the report indicated further work is needed in supporting undergraduate and postgraduate students, and that the process of preparing for a submission was considered by some to be burdensome, there was considerable evidence that Athena

SWAN is a valuable driver for improving gender diversity (MacNell, et al., 2014). Staff who work in a department which "lives the Athena SWAN life" appear to be more satisfied with their work environment.

It is possible to argue that Athena SWAN can be a mechanical box-ticking exercise but in a sense, it does not matter if this is how it starts: models of behavioural change indicate that external motivation can be a driver for internalising change (see *A model for change*). As the Pro Vice Chancellor of Cambridge University put it: "Athena SWAN provides a stimulus because universities and their staff are competitive; they like recognition and prizes. It gives us a framework to help improve processes and behaviours, and it is also a good mechanism for sharing expertise and good practice" [27]. What matters is that the Athena SWAN awards are a true reflection of the institutional culture rather than a metallic veneer over deep-rooted inequalities. A recently published evaluation of the working culture of a well-known UK university which holds an institutional Silver award [28], illustrates that this might not always be the case. Researchers external to the university, using a qualitative action inquiry approach, found that the institutional culture of individualised excellence in research was to the detriment of the well-being of staff and students and many examples of bullying and discrimination were described. It is vital that the Equality Challenge Unit considers this sort of contradiction as part of its ongoing self-evaluation. Documenting staff satisfaction is one way to approach this.

Athena SWAN has created and responded to pressures from the wider research infrastructure in the UK. In 2011, the Department of Health linked some future National Institute for Health Research funding to achievement of an Athena SWAN silver award, resulting in a healthy (and probably hasty) increase in applications from medical and dental schools [29]. Research Councils UK (RCUK) has stopped short of requiring Athena SWAN accreditation [30] but have muttered darkly about requiring it in the future "if there is no evidence of improvement". RCUK are no doubt focusing

their energies on improving their own woeful equality track record RCUK (2016). For their part, Athena SWAN will now require departments to consider RCUK data on success rates as part of departmental Athena SWAN submissions. If giving out shiny metal badges for success is a good carrot for competitive academics, threatening to cut off research funding is an excellent motivational stick. A cynic might suggest these tactics are what will really make gender equality more than "a ladies' problem".

Conclusion

The ivory tower, like other stately homes in the UK, might present a grand façade to the world but closer inspection reveals a dark, spidery basement full of inequalities. Men from disadvantaged social backgrounds might never make it to the ivory tower in the first place, and men who do get there are less likely to do well. Women students are more likely than men to suffer from mental health problems and encounter sexual harassment during their university lives, and even as graduates will earn less pay for the work they do during the course of their careers. Women staff are less likely to have permanent contracts, and considerably fewer of them ascend the career staircase of the ivory tower to professorial or senior management levels. Those who do make it there are paid less than men. The occupants of the ivory tower no longer sip port and think deep thoughts. Instead they drink Red Bull and fill in spreadsheets. They work long hours under stress to serve conflicting, crushing governmental agendas of excellence.

Yet, being an academic is still a privilege. It is a joy to teach and learn from young minds, and to draw on the wisdom and experience of colleagues. Academia offers an unparalleled opportunity to think and generate knowledge (in between completing spreadsheets). It is also our chance to persuade each of our graduates to go out and tackle inequalities wherever they find them. Change may happen slowly, but Athena SWAN is surely making it happen. Every Athena SWAN award is a little candle in a window of the ivory tower.

Online references

1 http://www.universitiesuk.ac.uk/facts-and-stats/Pages/higher-education-data.aspx

2 http://www.ecu.ac.uk/wp-content/uploads/2015/11/Equality-in-HE-statistical-report-2015-part-2-students.pdf

3 http://www.hepi.ac.uk/wp-content/uploads/2016/05/Boys-to-Men.pdf

4 https://www.ifs.org.uk/publications/7998

5 https://www.gov.uk/discrimination-your-rights/types-of-discrimination

6 https://www.gov.uk/government/news/uk-gender-pay-gap

7 https://www.gov.uk/government/statistics/graduate-outcomes-longitudinal-education-outcomes-leo-data

8 http://wonkhe.com/blogs/why-is-there-such-a-large-gender-pay-gap-for-graduates/

9 https://www.nus.org.uk/Global/20140911 Lad Culture FINAL.pdf

10 https://www.nus.org.uk/en/news/two-thirds-of-freshers-not-aware-of-sexual-harrassment-reporting-procedures-at-university/

11 http://www.universitiesuk.ac.uk/policy-and-analysis/reports/Documents/2016/changing-the-culture.pdf

12 https://www.timeshighereducation.com/news/times-higher-education-student-experience-survey-2015-results/2019564.article

13 http://www.universitiesuk.ac.uk/policy-and-analysis/reports/Documents/2016/changing-the-culture.pdf

14 https://yougov.co.uk/news/2016/08/09/quarter-britains-students-are-afflicted-mental-hea/

15 http://www.ecu.ac.uk/wp-content/uploads/2015/11/Equality-in-HE-statistical-report-2015-part-1-staff.pdf

16 https://www.ucu.org.uk/media/7959/Holding-down-womens-pay-Feb-16/pdf/ucu_IWDpayreport_mar16.pdf

17 https://www.ucu.org.uk/media/8620/The-gender-pay-gap-in-higher-education-201516---full-report-May-17/pdf/ucu_2015-16genderpaygapreort_full_may17.pdf

18 https://www.ucu.org.uk/media/6908/UCU-survey-of-work-related-stress-2014---summary-of-findings-Nov-14/pdf/ucu_stresssurvey14_summary.pdf

19 http://www.hse.gov.uk/statistics/causdis/stress/index.htm

20 https://www.ucu.org.uk/media/6908/UCU-survey-of-work-related-stress-2014---summary-of-findings-Nov-14/pdf/ucu_stresssurvey14_summary.pdf

21 http://workload.web.ucu.org.uk/joint-statement/

22 http://www.ed.ac.uk/news/students/2017/teaching-excellence-framework

23 https://www.ucu.org.uk/media/8196/Executive-summary---Workload-is-an-education-issue-UCU-workload-survey-report-2016/pdf/ucu_workloadsurvey_summary_jun16.pdf

24 http://www.hefce.ac.uk/news/newsarchive/2015/Name,104986,en.html

25 http://www.ecu.ac.uk/equality-charters/athena-swan/

26 http://www.ecu.ac.uk/wp-content/uploads/2015/10/AS_10th-Anniversary-Booklet-FINAL.pdf

27 http://www.ecu.ac.uk/wp-content/uploads/2015/10/AS_10th-Anniversary-Booklet-FINAL.pdf

28 https://www.imperial.ac.uk/media/imperial-college/staff/public/Institutional-culture-and-gender-equality.pdf

29 http://www.ecu.ac.uk/wp-content/uploads/2015/10/AS_10th-Anniversary-Booklet-FINAL.pdf

30 http://www.rcuk.ac.uk/media/news/120117/

The current landscape at the University of Edinburgh

Judy Robertson

The University of Edinburgh is situated in the capital city of Scotland, which is known variously as the Athens of the North, birthplace of the Enlightenment, British Entrepreneurial City of the Year [1], and Auld Reekie. The University, established in 1583, is a community of around 50,000 people. It has a wide global reach; it is ranked at 23rd in an international rating of world universities [2], and has alumni in 200 countries across the world. Nobel laureates from the University include Peter Higgs, Winston Churchill and Alexander Fleming. Charles Darwin, David Hume and James Hutton all studied here. It is the only (known) institution at which the Principal of the University hits graduates over the head with a medieval space bonnet [3], and even our Library Cat publishes books [4].

The alert reader may spot that the historical figures typically associated with the University (and even Library Cat) are male. To be fair, this is partly because of historical bias – we are more likely to have heard of male intellectuals of previous times because women were until recently denied opportunities in almost any sphere outside the home. Relatively speaking, the University of Edinburgh was forward thinking in admitting the first women undergraduates to any British University in 1869. The University (and the Scottish patriarchy) appears to have mucked this one up to my untrained historical eye – after the women were admitted, there was a riot, scholarship skulduggery, court battles, graduation denials and then the final insult of de-matriculations. The first women eventually graduated from the University in 1893 [5].

Happily, we have come a long way in our quest for gender equality. Now around 60% of our students are women, and 42% of our academic staff. Women alumni and honorary graduates are celebrated by the University [6,7] including Gabi Hegerl who was part of an international team of climate scientists which won a Nobel Peace Prize; the pioneering surgeon Gerturde Herzfield, the chemist Christina Cruikshank Miller, and honorary graduates: Malala Yousafzai (who then went on the become the youngest recipient of the Nobel Peace Prize), Anneila Sargant (NASA astronomer), and Julia Sebutinde (judge on the International Court of Justice). Dolly the sheep, the first cloned animal from an adult cell is also a famous University of Edinburgh female, although unlike Library Cat, she did not publish her memoirs. Progress has been made in appointing women to senior positions. In the 2016/17 academic year, the University Court is gender balanced and two out of three College heads are women. The Principal is male, one of the eight Vice Principals is a woman, as are twelve of twenty Assistant Principals.

In 2015, the University of Edinburgh received an Athena SWAN Silver award for gender equality [8]. It is one of only seven universities in the UK to hold this prestigious award, and the first in Scotland to achieve it. No university has been awarded a Gold institutional award to date.

Having read all the Athena submissions from the schools, and the University level award, I can tell you that gaining a Silver award is no mean feat. It requires sustained effort over a period of years – the Silver award came nine years after the institutional Bronze award – from extremely committed individuals and teams, the wholehearted support of senior managers, and painstaking data collection at an institutional level. In a national evaluation of the Athena SWAN scheme, one Athena team lead likened the effort required in co-ordinating an Athena submission to writing a PhD thesis (Fox, 2014). There is no question that this University, individuals and the institution as a whole, has seriously invested in advancing gender equality, and has made considerable progress in doing so.

In spite of this progress, if someone asked me: "Do we study and work in a university where men and women are equally likely to succeed?", hand on heart I would have to say, "No". At Edinburgh, women are less likely to be promoted to the highest grades, are employed on more precarious contract types and receive less money for equivalent work (UoE, 2015). Men are less likely to study here, and those who do are less likely to achieve the highest degree classifications than their female counterparts (UoE, 2015). There is some indication that male students may be less satisfied with their experience at University than women students. In short, there is still work to be done, as described in the following article. I consider progress with respect to women staff, students and teaching, and then describe how progress has been achieved with reference to the action plans of Athena SWAN teams across the University.

Staff

When Darwin studied at the University of Edinburgh in 1825, there were no women academic staff. By 2014, 1623 of the 3875 academic staff were women [9]. I fondly imagine that if Darwin had had the good fortune to be taught by our illustrious women colleagues in our medical faculty now, he would not be under the misapprehension that women are intellectually inferior to men (Saini, 2017).

The University of Edinburgh didn't get around to appointing its first woman professor until 1958 [10], but there are 180 of us now. Today, while 42% of UoE academic staff are female, only 22% of the highest grade (Grade 10, professor level) are women

(UoE, 2015). Perhaps this low figure is skewed by STEMM subjects (science, technology, engineering, medicine and mathematics) which we know have low proportions of women? In fact, the figures for STEMM subjects reflect those of the University as a whole: 40% of staff are female and 20% of grade 10 staff are female in our STEMM schools [11]. So while the humanities and social sciences may have better balanced gender profiles at entry level positions than the STEMM subjects, they too have significant gender barriers to address.

To put these figures in context, the proportion of women professors at Edinburgh is similar to the average across UK universities, although the proportion of female academic staff overall is slightly lower (the national average is 45% [12]).

Even if women do make it to professor level, they face a pay gap: they receive on average 91% of the salary of a male professor. This is worth the non-trivial sum of £6,609 a year. The gender pay gap across all staff grades is 4% at Edinburgh: the average woman member of staff earns £1,814 a year less than the average male member of staff [13].

Working conditions are also likely to be precarious for women, with more women in fixed term contracts or hourly contracts. Nationally, women are more likely to encounter job uncertainty, with a lower proportion of female academic staff on open ended/permanent contracts (5% difference) [14]. In line with the national average, at the University of Edinburgh there is also a 5% difference, with 45% of female academic staff on fixed term contracts. The highest proportion of fixed term contracts occur at the lower end of the grade scale, and more women are employed on these grades than men.

The University of Edinburgh no longer uses 'hours to be notified' (zero-hours) contracts (in which the employee is not guaranteed to be given a minimum number of working hours). In 2013, the University reviewed its use of these contract types and moved staff to guaranteed-hours (GH) contracts (in which the employer is obligated to offer at least a guaranteed minimum number of hours over a given period, usually for the academic year); 21% of staff now have these contract types. In 2015/16, the proportion of women amongst staff on guaranteed hours contracts was 51.6% overall, although there was wide variation across disciplines ranging from 32.4% in the College of Science and Engineering to 71.2% in the College of Medicine and Veterinary Medicine [15]. The impact of guaranteed-hours contracts depends on an individual's circumstances. It can be stressful and economically difficult for staff who are trying to patch together a full-time salary from multiple GH contracts. For others, such as PhD students, it is beneficial because it gives them the flexibility to turn down work if they are busy with their studies (most of the GH contracts in the College of Science and Engineering are for student lab demonstrators in this position). It also enables the University to bring expertise from working professionals onto teaching programmes – for example from lawyers, doctors or teachers. Indeed, many of the GH contracts in the College of Medicine and Veterinary Medicine are doctors with specialist expertise required for guest teaching spots.

The University and College Union forecasts, based on the rate of progress in addressing the gender pay gap in the last decade, it will take until 2050 to close the gap. That's a long time, especially when the average shortfall is £6,103 per woman per year across the sector. That's an average loss of £207,502 for each woman over that time period [16]. The UCU's strike action in 2015 was partially in response to this issue.

The University of Edinburgh is committed to closing the gender pay gap (and addressing inequalities for other protected characteristics). Like other large employers in the UK, it is obliged to publish an equal pay audit report [17]. I encourage you to keep an eye on these figures as they are published, and firmly lobby your employer if it has not lived up to your expectations.

In between reports, you can daydream about what you would do with £207,502.

Students

Let's consider student recruitment and attainment. Matters have improved since the University initially admitted seven women medical students 148 years ago. There are 37,861 students enrolled at the University at the time of writing [18]. Around 60% of undergraduate students at the University of Edinburgh are female, 54% of postgraduate taught students and 45% of postgraduate research students.

At the University of Edinburgh, women students are considerably more likely to graduate with a first class or upper second degree. This is similar to the national picture, where 56% of students are female, and women outperform men in every subject apart from social studies [19].

Student satisfaction with teaching

Teaching is one of the most important aspects of an academic's job, and as such, the University considers student evaluations of teaching (SET) carefully. However, there is research evidence to believe that in general students' evaluations of staff are gender-biased with female lecturers receiving harsher ratings (MacNell et al., 2014). Apparently some male students apply the same biases to their peers, as a recent study of biology students found that male students were inclined to overestimate the performance of their male peers while women did not exhibit this bias (Grunspan et al., 2016).

One source of data about student satisfaction is the National Student Survey (NSS) [20] – a feature of university life in the UK which is guaranteed to make staff groan. All final year undergraduate students are invited (fairly insistently) to complete an online survey commissioned by HEFCE (the Higher Education Funding Council for England) and its counterparts elsewhere in the United Kingdom. The numerical results are then made publicly available [21], and each

institution receives a confidential copy of the free-text comments. This information is aggregated by national newspapers, along with other public data sets, to assist applicants and their parents to make choices about where and what to study. NSS consequently has a high profile, and a lot of energy is consumed by university managers in trying to improve scores. Currently gender data is not published by HEFCE but institutions can request it, as University of Edinburgh did this year.

On the question about overall student satisfaction, 82% of women students across the University agreed or strongly agreed that they were satisfied with their course, whereas only 76% of men did. It is difficult to interpret this finding without further investigation. Are men being discriminated against in the way we teach? Does this feed into men's comparative under-performance and the attainment gap noted above? Is the effect real or an artefact of the survey e.g. could women have been socialised into responding more favourably about their teachers? What underlying theory can account for such differences? Are there different patterns between disciplines? The patterns of answers to individual questions are intriguing – for example there are gender gaps in the students' responses to whether staff make the subject interesting and whether they are good at explaining. Given that we don't have gender apartheid in classes, where does this difference come from? Are women more generous in describing how interesting their lecturers are, or do lecturers make a special effort to be interesting in individual tutorial sessions with women students? Or do women just intrinsically find their subjects more interesting to begin with? A team at the University of Edinburgh will pursue answers to some of these questions in the coming year.

I was also interested to see whether there might be gender bias in student's perceptions of staff at the University of Edinburgh, so I decided to check the data from the Teaching Awards scheme to see if it might shed some light on the matter. Every year, the Edinburgh University Students Association (EUSA) organises a Teaching Awards scheme in which students nominate teaching and support staff who have made a difference to their learning, in categories such as best overall teacher, best dissertation supervisor, and best personal tutor. It's useful to consider this because: a) it is student-led and therefore might be said to reflect the views of those being taught on their own terms; b) staff promotion criteria are now based on evidence of teaching excellence, and teaching award nominations are regarded as a fair source for that evidence; and c) the awards are high profile. Alarmingly giant photos of the winners are displayed on public billboards all round campus. If those photos were all of men, it could perpetuate the bias that men are the brilliant teachers.

Information about the nomination and awards is shown in Table 1. The data is drawn from a report published by EUSA with additional information on teaching staff gender from HR (Human Resources). First of all, it's encouraging that so many students took the trouble to nominate their lecturers, and wrote so much in praise of their work. Secondly, it would appear that in 2015/16 there was not a gender bias in nominations as the gender breakdown in nominations is very close to the gender proportions of teaching staff. Either University of Edinburgh students are not biased in their evaluation of staff, or it doesn't manifest itself in award nominations for some reason. Either way, it is an important outcome because roughly equal numbers of giant male and female

faces will beam down at us from billboards as beacons of teaching excellence.

Of course, the Teaching Awards data considers only evaluations relating to the excellent end of the spectrum. There may well be bias in the more routine evaluations of course lecturers – I invite lovers of data with time on their hands to take up the challenge to investigate this!

Summary of Athena initiatives at the University of Edinburgh

Athena SWAN is a charter of the Equality Challenge Unit which recognises higher education institutions which support "advancement of gender equality: representation, progression and success for all". The scheme started with a focus on the experiences of women students and academic staff in the STEMM disciplines, but since 2015 has been expanded to include arts, humanities, social sciences, business and law (AHSSBL) as well as professional services and support staff. The University of Edinburgh has been a founder member of Athena SWAN since its inception in 2005.

Currently 22 departments and schools within the University of Edinburgh hold Athena Awards at Silver or Bronze level. All Athena SWAN applications for the University can be found at [22]. After reading the Athena SWAN reports, and discussing more recent developments from the Athena SWAN teams by email and in meetings, I identified several common themes and approaches across submissions.

Teaching staff 2014 - 2016	Number of nominations by students of their female and male teaching staff			Shortlisted	Award winners
Female: 863 (40%) Male: 1301 (60%)	2015/2016	Female	790 (40%)	10 (40%)	6 (46%)
		Male	1162 (60%)	15 (52%)	7 (54%)
	2014/2015	Female	905 (36%)	12 (57%)	5 (45%)
		Male	1588 (64%)	9 (43%)	6 (55%)

Table 1. EUSA teaching award nominations by gender 2014/15 and 2015/16

Financial commitment

It is worth noting at the outset that some of the Silver award-holding departments have invested financially in their commitment to Athena SWAN. For example, the Roslin Institute, The Royal (Dick) School of Veterinary Studies and the Schools of Informatics and Economics have funds for childcare and conference travel to make it easier for those with young families to attend conferences and meetings. The Schools of Molecular, Genetic and Population Health Sciences, and Clinical Sciences offer funded fellowships for transition between career stages. For example, the Roslin Institute has invested in Career Track Fellowships (CTFs) which are time-limited training and career development positions designed to offer the opportunity to develop the skills and experience required to be eligible for appointment to Group Leader. They include funding for a research support position or PhD studentship, consumables budget and one internal and one external mentor. The Royal (Dick) School of Veterinary Studies has spent £8,000 in its Coaching for Success scheme.

Keeping everyone informed

The importance of keeping staff informed and up to date on equality and diversity news is a common theme. If the aim is to increase uptake of family-friendly flexible working policies, then staff need to know about it. As one of the Athena team leads told me, "The University can have some brilliant policies, but if no one knows about them or implements them, they are useless." Many of the schools with Athena awards maintain a Wiki with information relating to family-friendly policies and other related material, or distribute it via email or social media. The Royal (Dick) School of Veterinary Studies keeps a "You said, we did" document on the intranet to inform staff of progress towards achieving goals suggested by staff. The School of Engineering also distributes paper copies of the University's Dignity and Respect policy in staff and student induction packs.

Communication policies

Athena SWAN has become integrated with standard school business. For example, in the School of Health in Social Science, the Athena SWAN team produces an annual progress report, there is an Athena SWAN section in the school plan, and it is a standing agenda item for the management committee. In addition, there is benefit to including at least one member of senior management on an equality and diversity committee (as in Engineering) or have section heads sit in on Athena SWAN meetings (Schools of Molecular, Genetic and Population Health Sciences, and Clinical Sciences). In the Schools of Mathematics and Engineering, updates on Athena SWAN issues are given at staff meetings. The scheduling of staff meetings is also important to enable those with caring responsibilities to attend. For example, Institute meetings are held in teaching weeks and not in school holidays at the Institute for Sport, Physical Education & Health Sciences. It is also common to hold meetings in the middle of the day, and to rotate the day of the week on which events are held to avoid a situation in which people on flexible contracts can never attend.

In the schools and units with awards, great efforts have been made to keep Athena SWAN an ongoing topic of conversation. A team leader emphasised this as a key factor: "I think the central thing is communication. That is so important in raising awareness."

Leadership

Each Athena SWAN submission has an accompanying letter from the head of school (or unit). I have noticed that the content and tone of this letter really gives a clue as to what will follow in the report. Some letters reveal the strength of commitment from the head of school, their personal investment in making sure that change happens and their pride in what has already been achieved. For example, one head of school wrote a list of the initiatives which he personally had led or been part of and concluded:

In summary, the implementation of strategies as part of our Athena SWAN agenda has had, and continues to have, my strongest support and commitment. We take pride in providing an outstanding student experience and a supportive work environment for all of our staff. I am incredibly proud that these efforts have been recognised in both student and staff surveys alike.

Other letters inadvertently gave me the impression that the author was performing a duty in writing it, rather than embracing the change process from personal conviction. The Athena SWAN leads commented on the importance of leadership in acting on data collected during the benchmarking process: "One thing that really helped with that was feedback to heads of centres on the findings from the [staff satisfaction] survey, [which was] conveyed in confidence by the heads of schools."

Other teams mentioned the role of leaders at various levels in the organisation in making new initiatives work:

> ...really key is leadership – we had two hugely supportive heads of school who were ready to push through the things we suggested and who supported our initiatives, including visibly by attending meetings. We also had a head of college with an 'open door' who was receptive to our initiatives, whilst not directly being involved (though he did appoint the two female heads of school and has gone on to recruit several other women to key leadership roles).

Facilities

An effect of Athena SWAN nationally has been to put the provision of family-friendly facilities on universities' agendas. This is commonly in the provision of a breast feeding room and a fridge for storing expressed breast milk in order to support nursing mothers in their return to work. The Roslin Institute, for example, has dedicated facilities for baby changing,

feeding, storing and heating milk. While it may be easy to allocate a room for breast feeding on paper, it requires more thought to make it comfortable and usable. Details such as where to get the key, whether it is used for only this purpose, whether it is quiet and clean and who has access to it make a difference to how successful it will be. It would be beneficial to have a map of the breastfeeding facilities available in each building of the campuses.

The University of Edinburgh recently opened a new nursery in the King's Buildings Science and Engineering campus, and (partly as a result of the Athena SWAN initiative) will invest £2.3 million in a new nursery for the more geographically remote Easter Bush campus in 2018 [23]. Having access to high quality childcare on site makes a big difference to staff who are parents. It is worth noting that student parents also appreciate high quality childcare, and currently feel that their needs are not being adequately met [24]. In 2016, the Edinburgh University Students' Association passed a motion at Student Council to improve facilities for student parents, including calls for more co-ordinated support and advice for student parents, access to child-friendly facilities in all academic schools, affordable childcare and flexible provision in the University nursery, free transport for parents between all campuses and the nursery campus and a revision of the library policy which currently restricts access to the library to 30 minutes to those accompanied by children [25]. Personally I feel that the University libraries should make a point of actively welcoming children as part of its civic mission of sharing knowledge but then I am a professor of education, not a health and safety officer.

The Students' Association also passed a motion in 2015 pledging to offer at least one gender-neutral toilet in each building they manage which already offers toilet facilities (and the same for changing rooms) [26], and later in the year updated this with the target of two-thirds of existing toilet facilities to be made gender-neutral [27]. Perhaps where the Students' Association leads, the University will follow. Some schools already have plans for introducing gender-neutral toilet facilities (e.g. the School of History, Classics & Archaeology).

If you are interested in how buildings can be designed to promote a comfortable working environment for all, see *Asking for equitable buildings* by Derek Jones.

Annual review

As one of the main formal contact points between staff and their line managers, annual reviews (AR) have an important role in promoting and maintaining equality and improving work satisfaction. If you have worked as an academic, you may be inclined to roll your eyes at the words "annual review" or start muttering about "waste of time" – annual reviews sometimes do have a bad reputation among academics. Sometimes, I have noticed (at other institutions of course), older male academics might prefer not to have to bother with reviews because they believe they know what they're doing already. This may be why some schools, including Informatics, have been working on improving staff perceptions of annual review and training annual reviewers. The School of Biomedical Sciences runs reflective workshops for appraisers after the review cycle is complete.

Schools have also considered who conducts reviews – for example by introducing a choice of reviewer with at least one female on the review team (Economics), or ensuring that reviewers prioritise this task by mandating that an individual cannot be promoted if they have not completed their reviews of others (Chemistry). The topics for discussion at AR can also make a difference. The Schools of Molecular, Genetic and Population Health Sciences, and Clinical Sciences have cleverly changed the default position by rewording their AR forms: promotion and flexible working should both be routinely discussed at each review, and the reason for NOT doing this should be recorded if necessary. Across many schools, teaching and leadership and management are now routinely discussed

and recorded during AR to show that all duties are valued; previously research may have dominated such meetings. In Economics the review also includes work-life balance.

Promotions and career development

One of the University's goals is to increase the proportion of women at senior lecturer, reader and professor levels. Data from across the University suggests that although more promotion applications come from men, those which do come from women have a higher success rate. There are potentially two problems here: men apply before they are ready, and women delay for too long in applying. In either case systematic consideration of all staff as to whether they have a promotion case would benefit both staff and employer. The default should switch from expecting staff to present themselves for promotion, to the school actively supporting staff to achieve it. In the Roslin Institute, the HR manager and head of school systematically consider all eligible academics, and in the School of Biomedical Sciences a promotion committee considers all staff. In the School of Chemistry, line managers encourage people to apply for promotion, and in the School of GeoSciences each staff CV is reviewed annually for strengths and weaknesses with respect to promotions and additional salary increments. It is also important to consider part-time staff for career development opportunities, rather than assuming that they will be unable to take on a new role. For further perspectives on promotion, see *Proactive Promotion*.

In Psychology, the gender balance for sabbatical leave applications is also monitored and care is taken to ensure adequate cover is provided during sabbatical leave to avoid overloading other staff.

Schools are also thinking about how to support development for early career staff which is important given the precarious nature of postdoctoral work. For example, the University has a talent register [28] which is a first port of call for internal recruiters. Postdoctoral staff who are coming to the end of their contracts can sign up with the talent register to be considered for upcoming vacancies if they have the requisite skills. The School of Informatics has a portfolio manager to enable staff redeployment at the end of research contracts. The School of Chemistry is now focusing on postdoctoral career development. Postdoctoral staff can take the postgraduate certificate in academic practice course, get support in applying for fellowships, undergo appraisals, and are given opportunities to supervise students.

Staff development

The Athena submissions are very enthusiastic about mentoring, coaching and buddying. The University as a whole offers the Mentoring Connections scheme which matches staff who want some advice on work-life balance, career progression or promotion paths with volunteer mentors across the University [29]. The University also funds 20 women each year to attend the Aurora women's leadership development initiative which includes mentoring, and has successfully piloted a Returning Parents Coaching Scheme for those returning from maternity leave or shared parental leave to make an effective transition back to work [30].

In the School of Mathematics, new staff are assigned a mentor for five years (as well as having a reduced teaching and administrative load in the first year to help them establish a research career). The Schools of Economics and History, Classics & Archaeology, and The Royal (Dick) School of Veterinary Studies have a mentoring champion role for the purpose of matching staff with mentors and ensuring that mentors have adequate training. All junior academic staff in the School of History, Classics & Archaeology have a research mentor. There are mentoring groups for career issues in the Schools of Molecular, Genetic and Population Health Sciences,

and Clinical Sciences; in Biological Sciences there are mentors for all new principal investigators and mentoring for people going on maternity leave; the Roslin Institute and The Royal (Dick) School of Veterinary Studies have a parental leave mentoring scheme; and Divinity offers mentoring for PhD students.

Given all the effort which is devoted to mentoring programmes, it is worth bearing in mind Sheryl Sandberg's pithy comments on mentoring [31]. When reading most of her Lean In book, I was leaning back in incredulity about how very different her life is to mine, but she does have a point with the following suggestion: "Shift your thinking from 'If I get a mentor, I'll excel' to 'If I excel, I will get a mentor'". In my own role as research lead for my institute, I encourage staff to seek out flexible and fluid mentoring relationships to suit the area(s) of their career they wish to work on. I want staff to have a set of approachable people they can ask for advice when they need it, but I don't want them to feel unable to progress without outside help. I have also noticed that assigned formal mentor pairings can be problematic; sometimes taking advantage of more naturally occurring relationships can be effective.

> "Shift your thinking from 'If I get a mentor, I'll excel' to 'If I excel, I will get a mentor.'"
>
> Sheryl Sandberg

Coaching is similar to mentoring in that they are both confidential, developmental conversations. Mentors are often people a few years ahead on a similar career path and mentoring relationships can be informal and can last for a long time. Coaches tend to have formal training in a range of coaching models and techniques and, as they are often external to the department or subject area, they can be more neutral sounding boards. Their expertise lies not in the details of an individual's field, but in the process of exploring and untangling complex problems to provide clarity and new perspectives. They can also provide support and accountability for people seeking to achieve their goals. The Institute for Academic Development offers coaching for staff [32], as do various units including the Roslin Institute, the Business School and Informatics. You can read about a Roslin staff member's experiences in the recipe *Career coaching for individuals*. The Roslin Institute runs a coaching seminar for all line managers to assist them in conversations about promotion during annual reviews, while the head of school at The Royal (Dick) School of Veterinary Studies offers promotion coaching workshops for the heads of departments within the school. This head of school personally coaches women going through the promotion process. They also help all staff who have been unsuccessful in a promotion application to set objectives for the next two years. The Moray House School of Education has senior mentors who can provide support and guidance on the promotion process to junior colleagues which makes applying for promotion a more positive and enabling experience.

Schools have also focussed on specific training needs for staff in particular roles. For example, the Schools of Molecular, Genetic and Population Health Sciences, and Clinical Sciences have mandatory principal investigator training on managing research groups, and the School of Mathematics offers unconscious bias training for those involved in postgraduate recruitment.

Parental leave

In the United Kingdom, employees are entitled to shared parental leave and statutory shared parental pay after maternity leave for the first year of the baby's life. This means that the other parent, or the mother's spouse, civil partner or joint adopters can share in caring for the baby. The University of Edinburgh implements a more financially favourable version of this scheme [33], although uptake is currently low.

In addition, the schools with Athena SWAN awards have developed processes to help parents make the transition between work and parental care. The tenure process for Chancellor's Fellows (the University of Edinburgh's flagship scheme aimed at future research leaders) can be delayed due to parental leave. The Royal (Dick) School of Veterinary Studies has a checklist to help managers give the best support to women going on maternity leave and temporary staff are recruited for maternity leave cover (oddly this is not always the case in universities). Those at the Schools of Molecular, Genetic and Population Health Sciences, and Clinical Sciences can apply for technical support to enable them to generate key research data while on maternity leave. Staff returning to their posts after maternity leave have six months of release from teaching duties in the School of Biomedical Sciences, and in the School of GeoSciences care is taken to ensure that women return to teaching/admin duties with which they are already familiar to avoid a time-consuming learning curve. Here women are offered flexibility about whether they want to focus on their research when they return or prefer to ramp it up slowly.

Many staff members care for other family members (perhaps in addition to children). In recognition of this, the Schools of Molecular, Genetic and Population Health Sciences, and Clinical Sciences and The Royal (Dick) School of Veterinary Studies are piloting a Caring for Carers scheme.

Flexible working

Employees in the United Kingdom have a statutory right to request a flexible working arrangement, and the University of Edinburgh has many employees on flexible contracts. The University's flexible working policy is at [34]. I have had various flexible working arrangements (at two different universities) to help me with childcare arrangements – 100% compressed hours, 80% time and 90% time. I have had colleagues who work part-time to enable them to manage health conditions or wind down until retirement. The great benefit to the department is that it retains skills and expertise of individuals who otherwise may choose to leave. This is worth the inconvenience of scheduling meetings with a team of people on different flexible hours.

There can be a reality gap between a flexible contract on paper and the personal experience of trying to cope with an academic job on a flexible basis (see *Flexible working: being realistic*). The Athena SAWN award holder departments have worked on various ways to make flexible working more manageable. In Psychology, the Athena SWAN team is reviewing procedures for appropriately scaling down work for part-time staff. Various departments have a policy of scheduling meetings between 10am and 4pm to enable staff to do school drop-off and pick-up, or ensure that seminars are in the middle of the day. One problem with working part time is that routine admin tasks and meetings take up a higher proportion of your working time. So my personal favourite is the School of Health in Social Science's policy of having meeting-free periods each month to enable people to focus on teaching and research.

The good news is that these efforts appear to be working: in a major turn-around which helped the Royal (Dick) School of Veterinary Studies achieve their Silver award, staff now agree that they have a good work-life balance, which is partially attributable to a transparent workload model.

Recruitment

To move from an Athena Bronze to Silver award, a school or department must make progress in improving the proportion of women staff. This requires careful attention to recruitment practices.

Part of the difficulty is to attract women to apply for posts in the first place. Adverts often include a statement to welcome women applicants, and links to family-friendly working policies. The School of Health in Social Science routinely advertises posts with a part-time/flexible option, and is piloting an option for job sharing. The School of Informatics offers relocation assistance for new hires to make it more attractive for international candidates. When using third-party recruitment companies for executive searches, the University requires diversity in the long list of candidates.

A strategy to address gender inequality is to ensure that people involved in recruiting staff or students are aware of the effects of unconscious bias, particularly those who chair panels. It is University policy that all those on recruitment and promotion panels have undergone unconscious bias training. After a request from the Schools of Molecular, Genetic and Population Health Sciences, and Clinical Sciences, the head of college made it mandatory for anyone recruiting staff to first attend a day of training about managing a research group. In addition, schools attend to the gender balance in interview panels in various ways. The School of Molecular, Genetic and Population Health Sciences, and Clinical Sciences found that their appointment success rate for women rose from 56% to 67% since they introduced the policy that a woman must be present on all interview panels for permanent jobs. Some schools have a regulation that interview panels should have at least 25% female and 25% male members, while others insist on a gender balance. To counter the problem with senior women getting overloaded with serving on interview panels, there is some effort to pool interviewers across colleges.

See the three recipes on *Gender balancing staff recruitment* for further suggestions about recruiting equitably, and questions about some of these practices.

Committee work

Athena SWAN shines a light on the proportion of women who serve on influential committees. When departments preparing a Bronze submission put all the data together, they commonly realise that the committees with more decision-making power (the management group) or prestige (the research committee) are dominated by men. Clearly shifting this balance benefits individual women in terms of promotion possibilities and the departments themselves in terms of using the full range of talent available. However, the drive towards ensuring that women are represented on important University committees can have the unintended consequence that senior women become overloaded with committee work and blink out of existence in a silent yawn. The Athena SWAN submissions have a variety of approaches to this. In the School of Divinity, for example, the senior management team can co-opt members to redress a gender imbalance if necessary. The School of Chemistry ensures that committee membership is covered in the workload model so that service is explicitly factored into working life and other work is reduced accordingly. Committee meetings are always held between 10am and 3pm. The Schools of Molecular, Genetic and Population Health Sciences, and Clinical Sciences have staggered terms for Athena SWAN team members. They factored succession planning into the committee from the outset to ensure there are more opportunities to be in a leadership role, and to prevent any one person from being over-burdened over a long time period. The School of Health in Social Science is experimenting with opening up opportunities for committee membership which don't require seniority (such as marketing and communications) and the Roslin Institute has a system where more senior staff can have delegated deputies on committees to offer opportunities and avoid committee overload.

Students

Athena SWAN should not just be about staff – we have a responsibility to create a supportive learning environment for students too. The award-holding departments have made some progress in this direction. For example, several schools have requirements about the gender balance of thesis committees, PhD students in Chemistry may request a female thesis advisor and the School of Mathematics makes sure both genders are represented in staff student liaison committees. In the School of Informatics, there is a policy never to put just one female student in a group (see *Stereotype threat*), and unconscious bias training for male students is offered during Innovative Learning week. Gender bias is also included in a third-year course on professional issues. The School of

GeoSciences reminds tutors to call on women students for answers as part of a tutor training course in direct response to comments in a student survey. In response to survey data from students, the School of Divinity also addresses equality and diversity in tutor training, covering legal and policy commitments, how to teach inclusively, how to model good behaviour and how to challenge inappropriate remarks or behaviour. It has made diversity a key part of postgraduate induction, with a 45-minute compulsory session encouraging students to think about what it means to be collegial and professional, as well as spelling out the University's Dignity and Respect policy and obligations regarding the Equality Act.

Athena SWAN benchmarking focuses more on arrangements for maternity leave for staff, rather than students. At the University of Edinburgh, full-time undergraduate and taught postgraduate students may apply to the Scottish Government means-tested childcare fund [35, 36], and a limited number of bursaries for the University nursery are available. PhD students funded by the RCUK are entitled to up to 26 weeks of maternity leave on full stipend and a further 26 weeks of unpaid maternity leave. In addition, the Schools of Molecular, Genetic and Population Health Sciences, and Clinical Sciences have negotiated six months of stipend for maternity leave for PhD students from the College of Medicine and Veterinary Medicine, regardless of funding source.

Summary

The gender landscape at the University of Edinburgh has changed slowly, but dramatically, since the fathers of the Enlightenment studied here. In the last decade in particular, staff and students at the University of Edinburgh have tirelessly worked to improve gender equality, as demonstrated by Athena SWAN recognition.

One benefit of participating in the Athena SWAN process is the requirement to gather benchmark data. The University now has a history of data, much of which

is publicly available, which combined with the data it must publish to comply with equality legislation, makes it comparatively easy to find answers to questions about how the status quo has changed. As Bohnet notes, benchmarking is an essential part of behavioural design for equality (Bohnet, 2016).

It is clear that the University has improved opportunities for women staff and students over the years, but that it cannot rest yet. In my view, tackling the gender inequalities relating to pay and the precariousness of working conditions needs further attention. The success of Athena SWAN initiatives could be usefully applied to addressing other inequalities concerning BME (black and minority ethnic) people, trans people and intersectionalities including social class and age.

It appears to me that Athena SWAN currently focuses more on the experience of staff rather than students. Obviously we have to start somewhere; ensuring that the people employed by an institution are not subject to gender inequality is a good beginning. As this aspect improves, I believe that we should put effort into ensuring that student experience and attainment is not subject to gender inequalities – either to the detriment of men at undergraduate level or women in some postgraduate courses.

The University has an opportunity and responsibility to educate all of its graduates about inequality and inspire them to take action to tackle inequity wherever they encounter it. As our honorary graduate Malala Yousafzai and passionate campaigner for education has said: "We should learn everything and then choose which path to follow" (Yousafzai, 2013).

Online references

1 http://www.edinburgh.gov.uk/news/article/2204/edinburgh_is_british_entrepreneurial_city_of_the_year

2 https://www.topuniversities.com/university-rankings

3 http://www.scotsman.com/future-scotland/tech/one-small-step-for-john-knox-one-giant-leap-for-university-1-1413074

4 http://www.cityofliterature.com/meet-people-library-cat/

5 https://en.wikipedia.org/wiki/Edinburgh_Seven

6 http://www.ed.ac.uk/alumni/services/profiles

7 http://www.ed.ac.uk/equality-diversity/celebrating-diversity/inspiring-women

8 http://www.ecu.ac.uk/equality-charters/athena-SWAN/

9 http://www.docs.csg.ed.ac.uk/EqualityDiversity/Uni_Silver_2015.pdf

10 http://ourhistory.is.ed.ac.uk/index.php/First_Woman_Professor,_1958

11 http://www.ed.ac.uk/files/atoms/files/equal_pay_audit_2017.pdf

12 https://www.hesa.ac.uk/data-and-analysis/publications/staff-2014-15/introduction

13 https://www.ucu.org.uk/media/7959/Holding-down-womens-pay-Feb-16/pdf/ucu_IWDpayreport_mar16.pdf

14 http://www.ecu.ac.uk/wp-content/uploads/2015/11/Equality-in-HE-statistical-report-2015-part-1-staff.pdf

15 http://www.docs.csg.ed.ac.uk/EqualityDiversity/EDMARC_15_16/Staff_report.pdf

16 http://www.ucu.org.uk/media/7959/Holding-down-womens-pay-Feb-16/pdf/ucu_IWDpayreport_mar16.pdf

17 http://www.ed.ac.uk/equality-diversity/monitoring-statistics/equal-pay-reports

18 http://www.docs.sasg.ed.ac.uk/gasp/factsheet/StudentFactsheet310117.pdf

19 http://www.ecu.ac.uk/wp-content/uploads/2015/11/Equality-in-HE-statistical-report-2015-part-2-students.pdf

20 http://www.thestudentsurvey.com

21 https://unistats.ac.uk/

22 http://www.ed.ac.uk/equality-diversity/innovation-development/athena-SWAN

23 http://www.ed.ac.uk/easter-bush-campus/where-people-thrive/campus-development/campus-buildings/childcare-facilities

24 https://www.eusa.ed.ac.uk/eusapolicy/liberation/improveuniversitysupportforstudentparents/

25 http://www.ed.ac.uk/information-services/library-museum-gallery/using-library/join-the-library/policy-child-access

26 https://www.eusa.ed.ac.uk/eusapolicy/welfare/genderneutral/

27 https://www.eusa.ed.ac.uk/eusapolicy/liberation/stoptakingthepiss/

28 http://www.ed.ac.uk/human-resources/recruitment/talent-register

29 http://www.ed.ac.uk/human-resources/learning-development/mentoring-connections

30 http://www.ed.ac.uk/human-resources/learning-development/dev-opportunities/a-z-courses/courses-a-l/aurora

31 https://leanin.org/tips/mentorship]

32 http://www.ed.ac.uk/human-resources/learning-development/dev-opportunities/leadership-development/coach-mentor/coaching

33 http://www.docs.csg.ed.ac.uk/HumanResources/Policies/Shared_Parental_Leave_Policy_.pdf

34 http://www.docs.csg.ed.ac.uk/HumanResources/Policies/Flexible%20Working%20Policy.pdf

35 http://www.ed.ac.uk/student-funding/financial-support/students-children .

36 http://www.ed.ac.uk/files/atoms/files/studentmaternitypolicy.pdf

A model for change

Alison Williams & Judy Robertson

We are what we repeatedly do.
Excellence then is not an act but a habit.
(Aristotle)

If a university has decided to adopt gender equality as a goal, how should it go about achieving it? It is not easy; it is not a single problem to solve. Various factors interact to produce inequitable and inhospitable working environments including overt discrimination and harassment, societal stereotypes, unconscious bias, and promotion and hiring procedures which promote or fail to protect against bias. Gender inequalities affect different people in different ways. Some people may struggle as a result of working under stereotype threat – a well-researched psychological phenomenon where an individual's performance and confidence on a task is reduced by being a member of a minority group which has negative stereotypes associated with that task.

Others may be held back by anxiety stemming from imposter syndrome which is the result of feeling as if one does not belong in an academic environment. Even if a working environment is now welcoming and equal, some people may have a legacy of their previous negative experiences to counteract. There are interactions with other members of staff and students to contend with. Some colleagues may be overtly sexist or harassing; others may make so-called "joking" comments which still hurt to the bone. There are colleagues who are apathetic – they may feel this is a problem which does not concern them or believe that gender inequalities have already been "fixed". They might wonder what all the fuss is about, or even feel slightly hostile to the whole Athena SWAN agenda because they perceive it as special treatment for women at the expense of opportunities for men. A less obvious form of inequality results from benevolent sexism where the colleague is well-intentioned but still treats women differently by patronising them or attempting to protect them. Yet, among this mix of colleagues there are also committed people who have dedicated a huge amount of effort to reducing inequalities and improving the working lives of their colleagues. Such people are often, but not exclusively, to be found on Athena SWAN working groups.

For the many universities in the UK which have teams of colleagues committed to the Athena SWAN and other equality challenges, what is the most effective way for the initial committed few to make lasting changes? Lasting change requires a strong and public university commitment to fully support people who face harassment and a set of clear procedures which make it harder to inadvertently discriminate. A set of procedures by itself is not a complete solution; organisational change also requires changes to people's behaviour. Universities must find ways to guide, encourage and educate a critical mass of colleagues to routinely behave in a way which contributes to a fair and equal working environment. This is not easy to accomplish, given the range of existing attitudes and perspectives among staff and students. But recent research illustrates that it is possible.

In this article and other articles in the book, we describe our understanding of the approaches which universities can take to gender equality with reference to current theory and evidence in behavioural economics, behavioural change and psychology. We have prioritised findings from carefully designed studies of real work environments, and tracked down syntheses and meta-analyses which represent the best evidence available. Our aim has been to find useful, actionable advice which can make positive differences to the working lives of our colleagues, setting it within a theoretically informed framework for practice. Elsewhere in the book you can find contributions from authors, illustrators, and photographers which give a rich layer of personal experience and expertise from those who have disrupted gender inequalities when they found them.

Gender bias as a remediable habit

A useful way to consider the problem is to regard gender bias as a bad habit which a university is trying to break. Carnes and colleagues suggest that addressing structural issues alone, while necessary, is insufficient to achieve gender equity. They propose that it is also necessary for individuals to change their behaviour, based on an appreciation of their own biases (Carnes et al., 2015). They approach gender bias as a remediable habit, and between 2010 and 2012 conducted a cluster randomised controlled trial to gauge the effect of an intervention that sought to break the gender bias habit of faculty in a range of academic departments.

The study involved 2,290 staff members from 92 academic departments at the University of Wisconsin-Madison. Participants in the intervention group took part in a 2.5 hour interactive workshop about reducing gender bias. At a three-month follow up, in the departments in which 25% or more of staff attended workshops, there were significant increases in self-reported action to promote gender equity, and staff expressed significantly greater perception of fit within their departments, and greater comfort in raising social or personal issues at work.

The effects sizes ranged from 0.11 to 0.32, which are small but are in the expected range for behavioural research. This study is instructive in the modesty of the intervention. The fact that improvements took place when only 25% of staff members of a department attended is encouraging, as is the fact that the workshops did not require a large time commitment for individuals. Future research could unpick how increasing the workshop length or coaxing a larger proportion of staff to attend would change the size of the effects, but the wider point is that education for a relatively small proportion of staff appears to make a difference to individuals' experience of the working environment. Further, Carnes et al. note that the perceived improved climate created by their educational and behavioural intervention benefited both male and female faculty (Carnes et al., 2015).

Universities across the UK have already invested in equality and diversity training courses for staff. It is relatively common within Athena SWAN submissions to note that particular groups of staff are required to attend such sessions. Unfortunately, the evidence for the effectiveness of equality and diversity training is generally not compelling (Wilson, 2011; Bohnet, 2016) partly because they are often not evaluated robustly. The work of Carnes and colleagues is important because their evaluation uses rigorous research methods, and the content of the workshop is informed by theory and empirical research (Carnes et al., 2012). We should have a high threshold for the quality of workshops universities require their staff to attend!

The work of Carnes and colleagues is based on a four-stage conceptual model (see Figure 1) charting how faculty, as individuals, moved from being unaware that lack of women in leadership roles is a problem (specifically in departments of academic medicine, science and engineering where the study was focused), through awareness (Stage 1), external motivation (Stage 2), self-efficacy, and expectations of positive outcomes/internal motivation (Stage 3), to action (Stage 4).

Awareness	Motivation	Self-efficacy	Positive outcome expectations	Action
Is unaware that lack of women in leadership in academic medicine, science, and engineering is a problem	To move from motivation "I want to do it" to action requires both self-efficacy "I can do it" and positive outcomes expectations "I will benefit from doing it". To habitually change behaviour requires deliberate practice of the desired behaviour.			
	Acts without bias to avoid appearing prejudiced to others (external motivation) Is bias illiterate May be sincere in desire for equity but cognitive processes lead to biased behaviour	Acquires knowledge and skills, feels confident in applying them, and desires the outcomes of promoting gender equity in academic medicine, science, and engineering		Is internally motivated to habitually, unconsciously act without gender bias in academic settings Is bias literate Attends to cues for bias reduction strategies Automatically acts to prevent gender bias from emerging

Figure 1. Conceptual model underpinning multistep process for reducing gender bias (Carnes et al 2015; adapted with authors' permission)

They say:

> To move from motivation (I want to do it) to action requires both self-efficacy (I can do it) and positive outcome expectations (I will benefit from doing it). To habitually change behaviour requires deliberate practice of the desired behaviour. (Carnes et al., 2015, p. 222)

Approaching gender bias as a remediable habit rather than a 'bad thing which makes me a bad person' removes blame and defensiveness, opening up possibilities of behavioural change through changed practices. In Carnes et al's research intervention ('gender-bias-habit-changing' workshops) participants first identified their own biases, then replaced them with deliberate practice of non-biased behaviour, motivated externally (Stage 2) and then internally (Stage 3) until the new behaviours became habitual (Stage 4).

Stage 1: Awareness

 At the start of the first stage, staff may be unaware of the extent of the inequalities which women still face, and might (consciously or otherwise) assume that there are proportionately fewer women leaders because they lack leadership skills, or because they would prefer not to be leaders, or that being an academic is incompatible with being a mother or that it is a pipeline problem which will eventually resolve itself. Accurate information and education can raise an individual's awareness of a problem, but they may require an additional external motivator to accept the responsibility to take action to change their habits.

Recent publications in high-profile journals which have drawn attention to the extent of gender bias in academia are a great contribution to convincing people that action should be taken (Bedi et al., 2012; Eagly & Miller, 2016; Lerback,

2017). Athena SWAN has worked well to propel people within UK universities along the behavioural change stages. The requirement to benchmark data for an Athena award raises awareness of the scale of problems with inequality in the proportions of women staff or students.

Stage 2: External motivation

 Individuals at this stage in Carnes' model, may be sincere in their desire for equity, but be "bias illiterate" i.e. unfamiliar with the cognitive biases which are part and parcel of our human psychology, regardless of gender (see *Unconscious bias* for a further discussion of these). At this stage, motivation to reduce gender bias comes from external sources, including the desire to avoid appearing biased to others.

At the very least, senior management are under some pressure to commit their universities to Athena SWAN principles because they do not wish the institution to appear prejudiced. At the level of interpersonal interactions, people begin to realise that certain words and deeds are not acceptable to others and modify their behaviours. The pressure from Athena SWAN to shift towards more equal numbers of women, particularly in promoted posts, drives departments to change their recruitment and promotion procedures. Such human resource policies are also external signposts to routinely behave in a non-biased way.

Research from behavioural economics can inform us about effective ways to design procedures to act as external motivators for non-biased behaviour on the part of individuals. Iris Bohnet's book What Works: Gender Equality By Design (Bohnet, 2016) suggests easy, low cost but surprisingly effective changes to the work environment which might help to reduce gender inequalities. The goal of behavioural design is to nudge and shift processes used by organisations so that they are likely to yield fairer results. Bohnet (2016) is a carefully researched synthesis of meta-analyses and empirical work relating to a range of topics including staff recruitment, work-life interactions, working in groups and interactions between colleagues at different career stages. Bohnet introduces the mnemonic DESIGN – Design, Experiment, SIGN. That is, organisations should (re) design a fairer process, experiment to see if it is effective and then signpost that design to ensure people use it. The signposts should point us in a direction where we can easily make unbiased choices. Bohnet takes the view that one should not try to change minds, but rather use signposts – "the very purpose of signposts is to help us find the way without having to memorise or even think much about it".

An integral part of this approach is to gather benchmark data to make it possible to evaluate and refine designs. For example, the Athena SWAN Bronze award requires applicants to gather benchmark data sets on student applications and acceptances as well as staff at various grades. The accompanying action plan is a design for improving the benchmarks.

In the EqualBITE team, we are open to behavioural design strategies, but we also believe that we should try to change attitudes particularly in the University environment. As educators, we are in a powerful position to persuade our students of the moral importance of equality and encourage them to act to promote inclusion in their future lives. This brings us to the next stage of Carnes' model where external motivation to act becomes internalised.

Stage 3: Self-efficacy and positive outcome expectations

Those at stage 3 in the conceptual model have acquired the knowledge and skills to replace their previously biased habits with less-biased behaviours. They have the confidence to apply their knowledge, and desire the outcome of gender equality.

Carnes and colleagues provide five evidence-based strategies for workshop participants to practise, and two counter-productive strategies to avoid. Bias can be overcome by a) stereotype replacement where an individual notices that they have fallen into the trap of a stereotype and consciously replaces that stereotype with more accurate information; b) positive counter-stereotype imaging through which a person imagines an effective women leader in detail; c) perspective taking during which a person imagines what it would be like to be a member of a minority group; d) individuation where the person replaces assumptions about a student or a job applicant with specific factual information and e) routinely interacting with successful women who run counter to stereotype. They note that attempting to suppress stereotypes or holding a strong conviction that one is bias-free are not likely to be effective at kicking the gender bias habit. Workshop participants become confident at using these strategies over time with deliberate practice – which is often the key to successful behavioural change.

However, before an individual goes to the mental effort of applying these strategies, they have to believe doing so will have a positive outcome. The slogan we used to recruit people to our early recipe-writing workshops was "When it's better for women, it's better for everyone" by which we mean that warming up a chilly climate makes all staff members' lives easier.

Everyone benefits from courteous behaviour, transparent promotion procedures and flexible working arrangements. But clearly not everyone directly benefits from women-only initiatives such as women's networking groups or scholarships for women. Such opportunities can be resented by men (Fox, 2014) particularly if they view academic life as a zero-sum game in which wins for a female colleague necessitate losses for them. It is true that some areas of academic life – such as research funding – are fiercely competitive. Other areas are not – since the advent of online publishing it would appear there is no end to the journal articles which the world can absorb. At any rate, in our view, initiatives which target women or minority groups are a small step towards rebalancing the scales of opportunity.

Stage 4: Action

 People in stage 4 of the conceptual model habitually act in a way to reduce bias, are bias literate and notice when bias-reduction strategies are needed. Having reached this state of enlightenment, they are then ideally placed to assist other people on their own quests. Currently, it may be possible to find such people on Athena SWAN self-assessment teams, or in the Equality and Diversity section of Human Resources. However, the longer term goal is for everyone to gradually move towards this stage. The higher the proportion of individuals within a department at stage 4 in the conceptual model, the more likely it is that everyone in that department will find the working environment positive.

We aspire to a university where people in teaching roles such as lecturer, personal tutor or programme director have also reached stage 4 and make teaching decisions accordingly. If we want more women and members of minority groups to choose to study and thrive in disciplines traditionally dominated by white men, teaching staff need the skills, confidence and pedagogical knowledge to create supportive learning environments in every class. We know that being exposed to stereotype threat and having experiences of working or studying within a chilly climate can prevent individuals from reaching their potential. There is evidence that these psychological circumstances can impair people's performance and reduce their confidence and ambition (Steele, 2010).

If teaching staff were aware of the literature on 'wise psychological interventions' in educational settings (Walton, 2014) and routinely applied this knowledge with their students, classrooms would be warmer for all learners, and some of the consequences of stereotype threat which students may have previously experienced could be mitigated. Wise psychological interventions attempt to change the attitudes, narratives and mindsets within individuals. They are based on specific, precise well-founded psychological theories which have been validated in the lab and then developed to be applicable in real world settings. The reason that small interventions of this sort can have surprisingly long-lasting effects is that they operate recursively. A small adjustment to the way an individual perceives their situation (when applied early enough) can disrupt a self-reinforcing downward spiral, and begin a snowball of positive effects. See *Stereotype threat* for further explanation of how wise psychological interventions can be applied to teaching.

The role of senior leadership within the institution

Representation and inclusion

Lumby (2009) examines how an institution's approach to diversity is informed by senior leaders' different value sets. She uses two case studies (a community college and a sixth form college) to explore how leadership approaches and values relate to how the colleges tackled diversity issues (gender as well as ethnicity, age and dis/ability).

Through interviews and surveys, Lumby asked: a) how senior leaders understood diversity; b) what, if any, did they see as their goals; c) what the leaders believed to be pressure(s) for action or inhibitor(s) of action, and what degree of pressure they experienced; and d) what action, if any, resulted (Lumby, 2009, p. 428). From the data, she identified two main leadership approaches: leading for and leading with diversity in which:

Leading for diversity essentially targets the injection of more people from under-represented groups into leadership positions. Its goal is representation. [...] Leading with diversity aims to achieve structures and a culture which are equally supportive of all so that people, whatever their nature or background, can work productively while remaining true to themselves. (Lumby, 2009, pp. 441-442)

From Lumby's perspective, achieving equality in education is not just about achieving representative or equal proportions of people with particular protected characteristics in a department. It is about creating a working culture which thrives on diversity. Leaders should recognise the importance of welcoming new staff and students into the culture and building on their strengths, rather than asking them to work in the style of the dominant group.

Lumby posits a four-box model where high and low importance is given by leaders to representation (y axis) and inclusivity (x axis) (see Figure 2).

To some extent this can usefully be mapped onto Carnes et al's stages as part of systemic change drivers. Thus, as individuals and leaders develop their own bias awareness and make a shift in their espoused values, their departments can move from compliance with gender equality regulations, then to ensuring a more equal gender representation (working for diversity), next to creating a culture of inclusivity that in turn, finally becomes systemic (working with diversity) as part of what Mackay (2014) calls the 'institutional blueprint'.

High **For diversity** **Low**	**Entryist** The goal is representation Difference viewed as irrelevant Difference to be eradicated by homogenizing leaders' values and practice Little to no attention paid to effect of culture and discourse	**Systemic** The goal is inclusion with representation embedded as an objective Difference viewed as an attribute of everyone Difference celebrated as a fundamental source of strength Careful attention paid to effect of culture and discourse
	Indifferent The goal is minimum compliance with legislative requirements Difference viewed as irrelevant or negatively No public position on difference No attention paid to culture	**Multicultural** The goal is an inclusive culture Difference viewed positively as an attribute of some Difference celebrated as a potential source of strength Careful attention paid to effect of culture and disclosure
	With diversity	
	Low	High

Figure 2. A model of orientations to diversity (Lumby 2009) reproduced with author's permission

It is worth noting, however, that the Carnes model is focused on removing bias without necessarily promoting an inclusive culture. Thus a leader who has reached Stage 4 of the Carnes model may highly value working for diversity, and habitually act to do so without also promoting inclusivity and the celebration of difference. We agree with Lumby that it is important to value both representation and inclusion.

Sustaining change

Mackay (2014) sets out the difficulties encountered in embedding gender reforms:

> The central findings of empirical research highlight variable outcomes across cases and the coexistence of elements of continuity and change and caution that change in one institutional arena may be supported or confounded by the effects of other institutional arenas, illuminating the difficulties encountered in embedding gender reforms (see, for example, Chappell 2011; 2014; Goetz 2003; Kenny 2013; Majic 2014; Waylen 2007). (Mackay, 2014, p. 550)

As part of the EqualBITE project, we invited senior University leaders to reflect on the key issues about gender equality as they saw them (see *Leadership perspectives on gender equality*). They spoke of the

"significant structural barriers" to gender equality that could only be tackled through "a systems level change".

The senior leaders' conversations acknowledged the need to continue to "work within the institution" to support and maintain the "fragile new power structures" and the progress already made, and the particular "need to be careful we don't revert back". Mackay identifies "two mechanisms through which institutional innovation is actively resisted or passively neglected: 'remembering the old' and 'forgetting the new'" and argues that:

> The stickiness of old rules (formal and informal) about gender, the "nestedness" of new institutions within the wider environment, and the way newness functions as a gendered liability provides a powerful explanation for why it is so hard to make gender reforms – and wider institutional change conducive to the regendering of politics – stick. (Mackay, 2014, pp. 550-551).

A leader in Carnes et al's fourth stage, will habitually and automatically act to reduce bias when she encounters it; that is, she remembers the new. Old rules about gender are seen as a habitual way of thinking; habits embodied in the old rules can be systematically replaced by new non-biased rules. It may take some time before the old habit has completely gone, and the temptation to return to a newly broken habit may be strong at times of stress, or when surrounded by people who still enjoy the old habit. Despite these potential setbacks, it is entirely possible to change behaviour, and as the work of Carnes et al. demonstrates, useful results can be achieved when a relatively low proportion of staff commit a small amount of time to changing their habits of thought. A future study on the impact of remediating the gender bias habit in senior leaders would be instructive: to what extent do changes in the attitudes of

leaders impact the day-to-day experiences of staff? Do staff have higher work satisfaction when their leaders embrace inclusivity as well as representativeness?

Conclusions

We believe that achieving gender equality is such a challenging task that it needs to be tackled on several fronts. We need institutions to remove barriers and facilitate structural change; behavioural design of procedures and processes can assist with this. This will not be sufficient on its own – a productive working and learning environment requires people to treat each other equally and with respect. If we consider gender bias as a habit which can be broken, then carefully applied strategies for behavioural change will help. For those individuals who have already experienced the negative consequences of bias or stereotype threat, insights from wise psychological interventions may be useful. Leaders who habitually act to reduce bias, who celebrate inclusivity and see strength in differences will also help to achieve institutional change.

However, we believe that we should not stop with changes within the academy. At the heart of the EqualBITE project is the conviction that universities can – and should – be beacons of gender equality, acting as agents of change, building a society of gender equality, and enabling change in the attitudes and behaviours of the people who work, study and research within them. While change can begin within the walls of ivory towers, we would like our graduates to use their experiences of learning in an inclusive university to challenge the inequalities they meet in wider society.

Gender balancing your seminar speakers

Vicky MacRae & Helen Sang
(As told to Alison Williams.)

In October 2016, the journal Nature, focusing on women in science, published an article headed: "Women need to be seen and heard at conferences". The article talks of "the vicious circle of invisibility" where women aren't thought of "for a scientific opinion for the media, or to mentor aspiring young scientists". Nor, they continue, are women "apparently thought of when conference organizers put together lists of speakers to invite to meetings" (Nature, 2016).

This recipe sets out how the Roslin Institute at the University of Edinburgh, having identified this issue, is tackling it with surprising and interesting results. They agree with BiasWatchNeuro that:

> The progress of science benefits from diverse voices and ideas. Conference panels that are diverse with respect to gender, race, ethnicity and national origin help advance this goal. Homogenous conference programs are generally not representing their field, missing out on important scientific findings (https://biaswatchneuro.com/about).

The Roslin Institute holds a weekly seminar – compulsory attendance for all postgraduate students, and strongly recommended for all staff – inviting external speakers annually from across the range of scientific interests at the Institute within animal and biomedical/veterinary sciences. Prior to their successful 2014 Athena SWAN submission for Silver, the proportion of women external speakers was typically between 15 and 20%. The Institute's stated aim was to change the external speaker programme "to ensure gender balance in proportion to female staff, with the expectation that female speakers will now form at least 30% of the annual programme" aiming for this to increase over time. The 30% has been reached and overtaken. A mere 18 months later, between January and December 2016, 56% of the external seminar speakers and 44% of the hosts were women.

A gender balance of seminar speakers also supports Roslin Institute's strong mentoring programme. For example, after a recent EBRC (Easter Bush Research Consortium) Fellows Seminar the two seminar speakers – both BBSRC (Biotechnology & Biological Sciences Research Council) Future Leader Fellows –

stayed on to participate in and contribute to a career development workshop with the postdoc and PhD students. This more diverse set of seminar speakers is beneficial for Roslin's postgraduate students and for recently appointed group leaders because it introduces them to a wider range of potential role models.

Ingredients

- A departmental culture that is actively working for gender equality with supportive policies in place.
- An engaged Director.
- A wider University context where Athena SWAN is taken seriously.
- A financial context where funders, for example the Wellcome Foundation, and the Company of Biologists, expect "diversity in speakers in terms of geography, gender and age" (http://www.biologists.com/grants/).
- A proactive programme team with 'a good plan'.
- A proactive programme committee.
- Unconscious bias (UB) training:
  - Compulsory unconscious bias, and Equality and Diversity online training for the whole department.
  - Face-to-face unconscious bias training for senior positions and new fellows.

Method

Instructions for the programme team (1 woman, 1 man):

1. Convene the planning committee (gender balanced) and ask everyone to put forward their suggestions for speakers. Names are written on sticky notes and put up on the wall.

2. Shake your heads sorrowfully at the low percentage (usually only 20 – 25%) of women suggested.

3. Challenge the planning committee to think of another 10 – 30% of potential women speakers. This pushes them well beyond the usual suspects and they almost always come up with the names of women doing interesting and cutting-edge work. Each person then makes supporting arguments for the scientific research that their suggested speakers (men as well as women) are doing.

4. Create a shortlist from which you pick your external seminar speakers (and have a few left over to fill any gaps that might arise as the year progresses). Create a second list of prominent high-profile women speakers for national and international conferences you may be holding in the future.

5. Pick the women first. The men can wait until a slot becomes available the following year.

6. Be ready to challenge colleagues who are worried about "losing the quality" of their seminar series by inviting so many women.

    -   Remind them of the recurring bias that women are not as likely as men to be 'brilliant' particularly in fields where top-level success is believed to depend on 'innate intellectual giftedness' (Leslie et al., 2015).

    -   Remind your colleague(s) about the outstanding research work presented in the seminar programme by women that they would otherwise have missed.

    -   Refer to the context within which they are protesting: funder support, Athena SWAN submissions, the Director's focus.

    -   Send them links to the many websites (see Cook's tips below) in which senior men refuse to serve on all-male panels, the statistical work that sets out why the odds that a panel would randomly be all-men are astronomical, and sites such as biaswatchneuro. org that publish unequal gender representation in international conferences – do they really want the department to figure in this?

    -   If all else fails, show them the card Female Conference Speaker Bingo: Because making excuses is way easier than making progress (Caperton, 2012) that you have been marking as they talk.

7. Look after your seminar speakers and attendees:

    -   Day: Always hold your seminar on the same day of the week so that everyone can plan round it.

    -   Time: Hold it at lunchtime – this is within flexible working hours, and works well when invited speakers are local.

    -   Support: Offer your speakers (men as well as women) childcare or childcare expenses. Roslin allocates a budget of up to £200 for childcare costs per speaker.

8. The Institute has found that if a speaker has to cancel it is more likely to be a woman than a man, and is most likely to be due to family issues. If a gap appears, pick a woman first rather than a man to fill it.

Cook's tips

Things can easily slip back, so having an engaged Director is an essential ingredient. Despite the Institute's Athena SWAN goal of 30% women external speakers, at first the seminar programme continued with its previous 15 – 20% average. The 'Bingo' phrases crept in, from women as well as men. When the programme team became aware of this, they asked the Director to intervene. This shifted the whole approach from passive to active, with the excellent results described in this recipe.

Some senior men refuse to serve on all-male panels. See:

http://www.
womensmediacenter.com/
shesource/

http://speakerdiversity.
com/#about

http://www.embo.org/science-policy/women-in-science (Contains databases of female life scientists in Europe.)

https://biaswatchneuro.com/

http://www.feministe.us/blog/

http://www.academia-net.org/ (Contains a database of leading female scientists in Europe.)

Female Conference Speaker Bingo				
Women just aren't interested in this field	There aren't enough qualified female speakers	We need big-name speakers, and few of those are women	It's a male-dominated field	There aren't a lot of women in C-level positions
Both women we called were booked that weekend	Both women we booked bailed at the last minute	All the women were probably busy	Female speakers are always burnt out from speaking so much	Trying to get more female speakers is sexist
The organisers just wanted to get the best speakers they could find	You can't kick out a male speaker just to fit a woman in there	FREE	You can't shoehorn in a woman where she doesn't fit	Women never volunteer to present
You have to be bold; people aren't just going to invite you to present	Woman are shy	Women only ever want to talk about woman-stuff	Women need to act more like men	No one has complained about this before
Attendees want to hear from people like themselves	Well, there aren't that many female attendees either	We're only responding to demand	Fine, YOU tell me who they should have invited.	Who? I've never heard of her

Female Conference Speaker Bingo: Because making excuses is way easier than making progress. Source: Caperton (2012), http://www.feministe.us/blog/archives/2012/09/24/why-arent-there-more-women-at-stem-conferences-this-time-its-statistical/

Gender balancing Wikipedia entries

Melissa Highton

Less than 15% percent of people who regularly edit Wikipedia are women: this leads to skewed coverage of topics (https://en.wikipedia.org/wiki/Gender_bias_on_Wikipedia). The reasons for this are not simple, but may be similar to the structural and cultural attitudes present in other tech environments. Wikipedia editathons are a proven way of encouraging and supporting new editors by engaging them on a topic of interest, supporting skills development and building confidence.

The editathon is a reusable learning design which can be adapted and modified, supported by research evidence that this activity leads to a deep approach to learning (among others: Marton et al., 1997; Marton & Saljo, 1976; and Richardson, 2005). Learners who take a deep approach have the intention of understanding, engaging with, operating in and valuing the subject. Wikimedia UK offers advice on how to make a basic editathon. You can then flavour yours with topics and themes to taste (https://en.wikipedia.org/wiki/Wikipedia:How_to_run_an_edit-a-thon).

Editathons offer:

- opportunities for professional development and workplace learning of digital skills;
- opportunities to build networks of social capital among workplace teams;

- a scheduled time where people edit Wikipedia together typically focused on a specific topic, such as science or women's history;
- a way to give newcomers an insight into how Wikipedia works.

Editathons redress the skewed coverage of topics in Wikipedia, develop digital literacy skills, strengthen social ties and build social capital networks for women in the workplace. This recipe is based on the editathon for the Edinburgh Seven Wikipedia entry (https://en.wikipedia.org/wiki/Edinburgh_Seven) about the first group of matriculated undergraduate female students at any British university.

When interviewed after the event, the participants (university staff and students) described rich learning experiences, extending their range of skills and knowledge, for example:

- technical knowledge (how to create a Wikipedia page, how to edit, how to cite other sources etc);
- information literacy skills (an understanding of copyright in an open knowledge environment);
- factual knowledge around the topic (names, dates, locations of historical events);

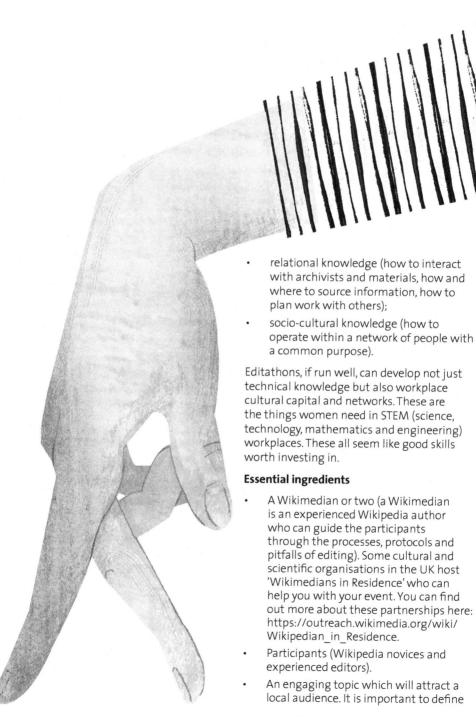

- relational knowledge (how to interact with archivists and materials, how and where to source information, how to plan work with others);
- socio-cultural knowledge (how to operate within a network of people with a common purpose).

Editathons, if run well, can develop not just technical knowledge but also workplace cultural capital and networks. These are the things women need in STEM (science, technology, mathematics and engineering) workplaces. These all seem like good skills worth investing in.

Essential ingredients

- A Wikimedian or two (a Wikimedian is an experienced Wikipedia author who can guide the participants through the processes, protocols and pitfalls of editing). Some cultural and scientific organisations in the UK host 'Wikimedians in Residence' who can help you with your event. You can find out more about these partnerships here: https://outreach.wikimedia.org/wiki/Wikipedian_in_Residence.
- Participants (Wikipedia novices and experienced editors).
- An engaging topic which will attract a local audience. It is important to define

an achievable set of goals for the event, so that participants have something to show, something to point to at the end of the day as a 'take home'.

- Some librarians.
- Some books.
- A computer lab or area with good internet connections and power sockets for those bringing their own devices.
- Baked goods for sustenance.
- Wiki-swag (Wikimedia merchandise to take away).

Method

1. Advertise the event on Wikipedia and social media. Depending on the size of your editathon, the activity can last one afternoon to one week.
2. Mix novice editors with experienced ones.
3. Add the specialist knowledge of an experienced Wikimedian.
4. Surround participants with books, articles and online databases.
5. Feed regularly.
6. Report on Wikipedia the outcomes of the event in terms of coverage and articles improved.
7. Use data in Wikipedia profiles, history and edit logs to see whether your participants have continued to edit. Have you created new editors who stay part of the community?
8. Run follow-up events.
9. Survey participants to discover what they have learned.

Warnings

If you try this without an experienced Wikimedian to help, you may not get the 'before and after' detail of the Wikimedia training and etiquette. This, however, is a knowledge base which can be developed locally if running repeated events.

As a result of the editathon's success, the University of Edinburgh has a Wikimedian in Residence during the academic year 2016/17. Our resident Wikimedian is available to help to deliver editathons across the University (https://en.wikipedia.org/wiki/Wikipedia:University_of_Edinburgh).

Gender balancing the curriculum

Simon Fokt

In disciplines where women and minorities are under-represented they are often increasingly under-represented with consecutive levels of education.

For example, in philosophy we may typically see a women:men split of 50:50 at undergraduate level, 40:60 at MSc, and 20:80 as faculty members (Beebee & Saul, 2011; Norlock, 2011). This dropout is likely caused by things happening during the yeas of secondary education, and at least some of it is caused by the fact that the great majority of texts students read were written by white guys (Paxton et al., 2012; Dougherty et al., 2015; Thompson et al., 2016). This grounds the stereotype: philosophers are white guys. This in turn feeds stereotype threat and implicit bias which makes female students underperform, or be graded lower, or just not encouraged.

Various departments try to address this issue by requiring lecturers to make sure a certain percentage of texts they use are written by under-represented authors. But given the current state of many disciplines, there simply aren't that many relevant texts to use, or those texts are less popular, harder to find, etc.

So, getting to the point, it would be useful to have something that would help finding appropriate texts easier – no matter what subject you are working in.

Ingredients

- A large number of existing reading lists on the subject, sourced from within your department and from free online repositories.
- Several committed people with at least some teaching experience.
- A decent website and someone to manage it.
- A Google doc or sheet.

Method

1. Use people to:

   - Find the existing reading lists.

   - Look through them and copy every text by a female author (with any comments from the author of the list).

   - Optionally, provide teaching comments on all selected texts, varying in complexity from long lists of suggested discussion topics or exercises, to a simple: 'This is a light read'.

   - Write it all down in a shared Google doc or sheet.

2. Create a website and upload the content to it.

3. Note: WordPress works well for this and making the site look good will make it more user-friendly and so more likely to be used.

   Check http://www.diversityreadinglist.org/ for an example.

4. Categorise the list entries – this will make finding them easier.

5. Serve to lecturers with a note: Need to find new texts to diversify your syllabus? Tired of spending hours you don't have on searching? Check out this resource! You can just visit the page, find the topic you're teaching using all the neat categories, et voila! You'll see a selection of texts on that topic that other people have used, and even some teaching notes on it.

Notes

Finding volunteers is hard. Grants might be available to pay people for the work.

Presentation is key. You probably don't want to force people to use the list, because they will resent it. Present it as a resource that's there to make life easier for them.

If time is short this recipe can be used as part of a strategic approach at the group level.

The University of Edinburgh School of Divinity reviewed the reading list for gender bias as part of their Gender Equality Mark action plan (Moore, 2013).

Creating a safe space for classroom discussions

Andy Hancock
(As told to Judy Robertson.
With thanks to Zach Murphy
for his comments.)

I have worked in initial teacher education (ITE) for fifteen years. In this time, I have learned that it is important for teachers to explore their own values, beliefs and assumptions about their learners as part of their journey towards creating inclusive classrooms. In our ITE programme, we direct students to the work of Bourdieu and his notion of habitus. Bourdieu explains this as a system of dispositions, and unconscious ways of thinking and behaving, that individuals internalise over time as a result of their location in particular environments and sets of social relationships (Bourdieu & Wacquant, 1992). We want our students to reflect on their view of the world and engage with socialised norms and dominant discourses. You can find some of the approaches that I and colleagues at Moray House School of Education use to discuss social justice with student teachers in our book *Social Justice Re-examined* (Arshad et al., 2012).

In other disciplines, e.g. STEM subjects (science, technology, engineering and mathematics), the content of classroom discussions will generally be on curricular areas unrelated to equality or other sensitive issues. However, on the occasions when it is appropriate to discuss equality in the classroom, it is important to establish an atmosphere of trust. For example, consider informatics students studying material relating to the low numbers of women in IT in their professional issues course. In

such a class, the few women students in the room will ideally take an active part in discussion, and will not feel uncomfortable or marginalised by the opinions of their male peers. This recipe contains some of my thoughts about how to create a safe space for discussion in the classroom.

Ingredients

- Time.
- Ground rules. You may choose to develop these with the students. Section 12 of the University regulations might be a good starting point: http://www.docs.sasg.ed.ac.uk/AcademicServices/Discipline/StudentCodeofConduct.pdf
- Recognition that your students have different world views and life experiences.
- Commitment to teach all students with respect.
- Desire to give all students a voice.
- Empowerment.

Method

1. **Choose the design of the lesson.** It will probably be most effective to enable the students to discuss their opinions in small groups, at least initially. In this way, members of the minority groups have a voice in a smaller, safer space. The "think, pair, share" approach might be helpful even if you're timetabled to be

in a large lecture theatre. Students think about their responses to a discussion question individually for a time, then pair up with the person sitting next to or behind them to exchange views, before the pairs join up to form small groups to share their thoughts. Lecture format is not ideal. The experience of listening to a single authoritative voice (of the lecturer) or the opinions of vocal classmates during question time might be uncomfortable or alienating for students in the minority groups under discussion. Being reminded of

negative stereotypes of a group to which we belong makes people anxious and concerned that we don't reinforce that stereotype by our behaviour (see *Stereotype threat*). A woman electrical engineering undergraduate, for example, might avoid joining in a large lecture discussion about acceptable professional conduct precisely because she doesn't want to confirm a societal stereotype about women "over-reacting" to sexist jokes. It may be productive to ask the students to privately reflect on why they find something funny.

2. **Plan how to include students who are in the minority.** There is a tension in valuing the knowledge of a minority student without turning them into a cultural artefact. We want to give the student an opportunity to share their insight as a member of the minority group under discussion, but we don't want to put them under the microscope because of it. For example, in my class where I discuss Islam with my student teachers, I try not to keep the spotlight on the few Muslim students in the class. If you're not sure how a student in the minority group would react to the class, have a quiet word beforehand about what they would like their involvement to be and what they might find uncomfortable – don't spend the class worrying about how they are feeling. It is also important not to make assumptions about students' faith or cultural heritage as there is diversity within diversity.

3. **Establish ground rules.** Spend some time establishing ground rules with the class (or reminding them). There needs to be a code of conduct for what is acceptable, starting from the basics of respectful listening and allowing others to be heard. Part of the lecturer's job is to be aware of inappropriate behaviour and call students out on it. "Banter" and mild jokes may seem borderline offensive, but can escalate so it is worth drawing attention to this. What one student finds funny might be offensive to another. Ideally, the students themselves will start to challenge unacceptable conduct – a recent study of "laddism" in sports courses reported that mature students, particularly women, were vocal critics and challengers of disruptive behaviour in the classroom (Jackson et al., 2015).

4. **Model and promote good listening.** As you interact with and observe groups of students, be a good listener and encourage the students to listen. This involves making sure everyone is listened to, being mindful of body language such as nodding and focussing entirely on what someone is saying rather than deciding what you will say next.

5. **Deal with challenging conversations.** In a situation where a student voices an opinion with which you disagree, take a moment to unpack where they're coming from. It's useful to think about why they might have these views. You want to encourage each student to have a voice, but it is necessary to challenge them at times. Acknowledge their contribution and summarise their view: "I hear what you're saying. You mean that..." If appropriate you can go on to say: "I disagree for these reasons" and then articulate them.

There may be students who have strong views but have chosen not to express them so far. In this case, you can offer them the chance to join in – "What do you think? Do you agree?" or "You have been very quiet during this discussion. How do you feel? How would you like to be included?"

6. **Challenge prejudice.** If you do encounter prejudice among students, then there are three levels of response. In the immediate term, you should make it clear that prejudice is not acceptable in class. This includes the nature of the context and any impact on a possible victim and students in general who are being exposed to it, and how you respond to all those involved. At the next level, consider whether the University's code of conduct is clear on this matter, and whether it needs to be updated, clarified or challenged. Lastly, in the longer term, there is both a responsibility and an opportunity to think about how you can change these attitudes and behaviours through your teaching. Teaching can be a powerful force for social justice.

Gender balancing your scholarly journal

Ros Attenborough

Scholarly journals are in a position of power when it comes to setting the agenda for an academic field. Journal editors can highlight knowledge trends that they want to encourage, and pass over those they see as less promising. A journal editorial board is typically populated by senior members of the academic community that the journal serves and influences. Because in most academic fields women are under-represented in senior positions, they are also under-represented on editorial boards. This has been documented, for example in medicine (Jagsi et al., 2008); management (Metz et al., 2015); mathematics (Topaz & Sen, 2016); and environmental studies (Cho et al., 2014). In all of these cases, women occupied less than 20% of board positions; in mathematics only 8.9% of editors were women.

These figures are improving, but more slowly than the representation of women in senior academic positions (Metz et al., 2015, p. 712). This is perhaps not surprising because editors themselves are usually responsible for new editor recruitment, drawing on their own extensive but nonetheless partial networks. Gender may not be explicitly considered in these decisions, allowing unconscious bias to flourish. As the journal Nature (2012) admitted in a stunning self-critique, when "thinking about who is doing interesting or relevant work...men most readily come to editorial minds".

However, precisely because editors have such power, there is a great opportunity for top-down change. If you are an editor, reviewer, author, or reader, you can begin steering your favourite academic journal towards a more inclusive future.

This recipe is based on my personal experience as a journal staff member working with editors to improve our board's gender balance. It can also be used for other types of academic board or panel and can be applied to increase representation of ethnic and other minorities, as women are not the only demographic systemically under-represented in expert boards and panels.

Ingredients

- Male-dominated academic editorial board.
- Membership of the board, a friend/colleague who is an editor, or a relationship with the journal via reviewing/authorship/readership.
- Humility and persistence.

Method

1. **Document the gender balance** on the board: produce some stats! Editorial board members are usually listed on the journal website.

2. **Think about your goal** for representation of women on the board. 50% would be ideal and may be realistic in the

medium term if the existing editorial leadership fully embrace the project. However, short term incremental goals are also valid: to lead from the top down, find out the approximate percentage of women occupying senior positions in your field, and aim for a higher percentage on your board.

3. **If you are an editor with power to influence the hiring of board members:**

   - Talk. Talk about gender balance on the board with your colleagues. If you are a man, seek out female colleagues with whom to discuss this issue. Use the board gender statistics to convince them that this is an important issue. Point out that gender imbalance is a growing concern inside and outside academic communities, and it could affect both the quality and reputation of the journal (see http://allmalepanels.tumblr.com/).

   - When hiring a new board member, come up with a list. Think hard about the candidates who come to mind. If they are all men, are there any equally qualified women? Don't just rely on your personal

connections; if you don't know of an equally qualified woman, ask your colleagues of all genders, and do some research. Nature (2012) recommends this mental exercise: "Who are the five women I could ask?" Consider hiring a woman over a man if she is equally qualified: this is how you will incrementally redress the imbalance.

   - Eventually, establish best-practice guidelines for hiring new editors, so that considering gender equality becomes journal policy rather than your own personal quirk. Be careful here as you do not want to put other editors offside: establishing a policy too quickly or without consultation could make other editors feel like (and thus, be) part of the problem instead of part of the solution.

4. **If you know an editor with power to influence hiring:**

   - Again, talk. If you regularly review, publish in, or read the journal, mention that this gender imbalance affects the journal's reputation in your eyes.

- Ask about their process for hiring new board members. If they do not consider gender in their decision-making, share this recipe with them, or just the key message: consciously nominate equally qualified female candidates for any board vacancy. They may also find the article Nature's sexism (Nature, 2012) convincing.

- If things go well, offer your services as an advisor on this issue. Depending on your expertise, you may be able to suggest new female board members of whom the editors were not previously aware.

5. **If you don't know an editor,** but are a reviewer, author, or reader of the journal then try to find an editor contact on the journal website and follow the steps above.

6. **Persist.** Gender-balancing your scholarly journal will take some time. You may be discouraged if you encounter resistance, or if nothing seems to be changing. Try to stay with this project by producing new board gender statistics at regular intervals: track any changes and add them to your evidence base. If at first you don't succeed in changing minds with the actions above, try again. Sometimes when nothing seems to be happening, attitudes will slowly be changing.

Cook's tips
You may encounter difficulties recruiting female editors, even if you are trying. As Arnold (2015) points out, you may find that women decline invitations at a higher rate than men. There are many recipes in the rest of this book that highlight some of the reasons for this and what you can do about it.

Raising your profile on a grant application

Judy Robertson & Barry Lovern
(With thanks to Catherine Burns
for her comments.)

Research Councils UK says that female principal investigators are disproportionately unsuccessful in grant applications (RCUK, 2016). Assuming that the imbalance is for reasons other than the quality of the research, we should look to redress this. One way to approach this is to ensure that the application and review process itself is not biased (see *How to become a better scientific evaluator*).

This is a companion recipe, written for any individual who is applying for grants, and would like to know what they can do to increase the likelihood of success.

Ingredients

- Confidence in your capabilities and the value of your achievements to date.
- Assertiveness: if you have done great work which implies the potential to do further great work, say so.
- Recipe *Dealing with imposter syndrome*.

Method

1. **Carefully read the call and check that your idea fits the terms.** Take the time to properly understand what is required and the remit of the funder. Manage your expectations: funding schemes are very competitive and the chances are high that you will not succeed first time. This is not a reason to despair, though. Before you begin writing, think of Plan B and Plan C with other funding schemes just in case this one is not awarded.

2. **Review successful grant applications for the funding scheme you are applying to (your research support office should be able to provide you with these).** Analyse how the applicant has described their previous experience and achievements, and how they have described the importance of the research idea. Read the guidelines for each section carefully so you know what the funder is expecting.

3. **Go for your full research vision.** Funders are looking for confidence and ambition so don't compromise for the sake of the budget. Consider how much to apply for. In an analysis of the monetary value of grants awarded to male and female researchers by the UK funder Wellcome Trust, it was found that women were awarded on average £44,735 less than men (Bedi et al., 2012). As the authors point out, because the funder normally awards the amount which was requested for successful proposals, this suggests that women are less ambitious about the amount for which they apply. If you're a woman, consider whether you have applied for enough; if you're a man, weigh up whether the funders would consider the amount economical!

4. **Write your application.** Bear in mind that you are writing a business case rather than a journal article. Assume it will be read by an intelligent person who may not have disciplinary expertise. You will need to make it clear for them.

5. **Pay particular attention to sections which describe the researcher.** In a study of applications to the Netherlands Organization for Scientific Research, women received slightly (but statistically significantly) lower numerical ratings of the applicant's research profile, but not for the content of the proposal itself (van der Lee & Ellemers, 2015). Review your application and highlight any sections which could seem to minimise or downplay the importance of the research idea or your experience. Be careful about your choice of words, particularly in the adjectives in your track record. Language that is often used to describe women includes 'grind' adjectives like 'conscientious', 'trustworthy', 'reliable', as opposed to those used about men, 'stand-out' adjectives like 'brilliant', 'excellent', first-rate' (Dutt et al., 2016). It's a grant proposal – you're expected to claim brilliance. Similarly, if you have to include a letter of recommendation with your application, tactfully make sure your referee knows to avoid 'grind' adjectives. Experiment with writing track record sections in a confident way. Play with phrasing and language even if it feels as if you are 'talking yourself up'. Before investing in your project, the funders need to know you will deliver what you plan. You can edit systematically to make every statement more assertive once you have completed the main draft.

6. **You may find it helpful to list the achievements which are relevant for the application and note the objective evidence for these.** Do not cross the line to sounding aggressive. Similarly, on the first draft, do not be afraid of sounding arrogant – this can be toned down later. Any seemingly arrogant statement that can be backed up with objective evidence is fair game.

7. **Reshape your CV for every application to tailor it to the funding call.** Show that you have the experience in people management and budgetary skills from your previous work.

8. **Get feedback from a 'critical friend' or a more senior mentor who has experience in writing successful research grants.** Do they think it sounds over the top or inaccurate? Or is it pitched at the right level? Are there relevant achievements you've missed or not drawn enough attention to? Leave time to make any changes they suggest to the proposal before the deadline.

9. **Leave it in a drawer for a week and then re-read it, pretending it is a colleague's application.** What can sound over the top when you are talking about yourself can seem perfectly acceptable if someone else writes it. Are there any further adjustments to be made?

10. **Complete your final proofs and edits as you normally would and submit.**

11. **Be a critical friend to other colleagues who may be finding this aspect of writing applications challenging.**

12. **If you have an opportunity to respond to reviewers.** Everyone feels upset at reviewer criticism, but don't be defensive in your response. If you find yourself typing "Reviewer X missed the point", delete it and think about how you could make the point clearer. Run your reply past an experienced colleague before you submit it. Ask them to be neutral or critical.

13. **If you get rejected, curse and howl, but don't give up!** Resubmit the proposal if the funder allows, or put Plan B into action by reworking the application for a different funder. In the Netherlands study, although there was a gender gap in applications submitted for the first time, this difference had evened out for proposals which were resubmissions (van der Lee & Ellemers, 2015).

For University of Edinburgh staff, Edinburgh Research and Innovation hold a dossier of successful grant applications and funding guides: http://www.ed.ac.uk/research-support-office/toolkit-for-applicants. Staff in the College of Arts, Humanities and Social Sciences could consider applying for a mid-career research fellowship to get mentoring and feedback on grant writing – talk to your director of research.

How to become a better scientific evaluator

Meriem El Karoui & Judy Robertson

Recently some data was published about the success rate of women in the UK driving test (DVSA, 2015). It is significantly lower than the success rate of men. Yet, data from insurance companies show that women are by far safer drivers and in particular are involved in fewer accidents and accidents with less serious outcomes (Hartley, 2015). This suggests that the "success criteria" used for the driving test are possibly biased against women and more importantly are not measuring accurately who is a safe driver which is, after all, the main purpose of the driving test.

We wondered whether similar problems could happen in science when we evaluate a scientific proposal or article. There is widespread evidence of the existence of "implicit bias" in science (McNutt, 2016) and at least in some disciplines the proportion of women who are principal investigators on grants is considerably smaller than that of men (Kaatz, 2014).

RCUK (Research Councils UK) is the umbrella body for all UK government-funded research councils. The proportions of women applicants are much smaller than those of men for research grants from the Biotechnology and Biological Sciences Research Council (BBSRC), Engineering and Physical Sciences Research Council (EPSRC), Medical Research Council (MRC), Natural Environment Research Council (NERC), and the Science and Technology Facilities Council (STFC). Of course, there are fewer

women who work in these areas to start with but even then, proportions of female applicants are lower than estimates of the proportions of women researchers in eligible institutions for almost all the research councils, apart from the STFC. So women do not apply for funding as often as men.

Are women successful when they do apply? In the last published data set (2014-2015), women had lower success rates as principal investigators for BBSRC, EPSRC, MRC and NERC. Women had a higher success rate in AHRC and ESRC. The gaps in success rates are mostly in the region of 3 – 5% and these have closed to 1% over the years in NERC. An exception is STFC where the success rate for women was 52% in comparison to 72% in 2014-15 (RCUK, 2016). This is consistent with the gender success gap in a study of funding in the Netherlands (van der Lee & Ellemers, 2015), and with the European Research Council (ERC WGGB).

It is entirely possible that this is because the women's grant applications are not as good as the men's, but one wonders what exactly do we mean by "good" here. Is the women's science not as good? Or are the applications themselves not as good because they do not conform to the set criteria? Or is it simply our perception of the applications? Is there bias (implicit or otherwise) in the reviewer pool? RCUK aim to have at least 30% of the minority gender represented on all peer review panels during

2017 – this is a tall order given that the most recent data set from 2013 shows that five of the major funding councils had not yet achieved this. EPSRC was farthest from the target at 17% female panel membership. There is a large body of literature around this problem and I am not sure we can really answer these questions definitively. However, based on substantial experience of evaluating grant proposals and articles regularly, we feel that it is useful to think about how to become a less biased evaluator.

Ingredients

Evaluation of grant applications is often performed in two steps: pre-evaluation remotely, followed by discussion of the proposals and ranking at an evaluation panel.

For the pre-evaluation:

- A quiet/peaceful room to perform the pre-evaluation.
- A reasonable amount of time to perform the evaluation (usually twice as much as what you would think).
- A healthy dose of self-awareness and humility, taking time to reflect briefly on your own gender, age or subject biases can help overcome them. Also you may form an initial opinion that is not the most informed one: it's OK to change your mind.

At the panel:

- A chair of the evaluation panel committed to gender equality and ready to remind all the panel members of this commitment.
- A well-organised workflow with sufficient time to discuss proposals.

Method

1. Remind yourself of potential biases (such as gender, age, etc, remembering that gender is not the only cause of bias) from yourself and/or from the external referees if you have external reviews. These include: anchoring bias, where the reviewer over-relies on one piece of information and it colours their subsequent judgements; halo effect where the candidate's competence in one area causes the reviewer to assume they are competent in other areas; and shifting standards of reference in which cultural stereotypes about particular groups cause different standards to be used for judging individuals e.g. women in maths might have to be "twice as good to get ahead" because of cultural stereotypes about women's poorer maths aptitude. You can find a full list of how cognitive biases might influence peer review decisions in Table 1 of Kaatz et al. (2014).

2. When you're reviewing applications
    before the meeting: make sure you set
    aside enough time for each evaluation.
    Perform a first-level evaluation and let
    a few days pass so that you can come
    back to the grant with a fresh mind. Be
    ready to change your initial opinion.

3. Prepare a file with a "template" of
    all the criteria that you are asked
    to evaluate and make sure you can
    back up each of the criteria with
    actual facts (e.g.: the proposal is
    groundbreaking because of such and
    such; there is enough preliminary
    data as shown in figure 1; the value for
    money is not so good because they
    are asking for two postdocs but it is
    not clear that they need so many).

4. At the evaluation panel, don't be afraid
    to speak up if you recognise a bias at
    work. This is often more apparent during
    discussions of track record and career
    breaks. If you are chairing a panel, you
    could use the "consider the opposite"
    approach to challenging bias in which
    you systematically encourage panel
    members to play devil's advocate
    and come up with reasons why their
    thinking might be wrong (Bohnet, 2016).

For funders: make an effort to reduce
the conditions under which implicit bias
might fester in your peer reviewers.

- Be careful about the language you
  used in the assessment criteria.
  Certain words are associated with
  masculine stereotypes and are likely
  to increase the chances of male
  applicants – such as "risk-taking" or
  "technological breakthrough" (Kaatz,
  2014; van der Lee & Ellemers, 2015).
  Make sure commitment to a fair
  assessment devoid of bias is clearly
  communicated to the external referees.

- It is still unclear whether anonymizing
  the applicant pool will impact
  women's success rates (Ledin et al.,
  2007) and many funders – such as
  RCUK – do not do this. Such funders
  would no doubt argue that the
  track record of the applicant needs
  to be assessed and it is not possible
  to do so anonymously. It is also
  important to be aware how the same
  credential can be valued differently
  depending on who has it (Uhlmann
  & Cohen, 2005). It would, however, be
  possible to anonymously review the
  proposed research itself and combine
  these scores with the track records
  afterwards, and then re-anonymise.

- Try to reduce time pressure at panel
  meetings or review periods. Cognitive
  biases flourish when decisions have to
  be made quickly (Kaatz et al., 2014).

- When people believe in their own objectivity, they are more vulnerable to acting on their biases. Remind your panel members that everybody has implicit biases, even so-called objective reviewers (Kaatz et al., 2014). Emphasise the equality policy of your funding body, and make it clear that the "gender problem" is not yet solved so reviewers must remain vigilant (van der Lee & Ellemers, 2015). Brief discussions of how to practically deal with bias among panel members may also be very useful. Consider setting a little bit of time at the beginning of the meeting for such discussions.

Gender and the Research Excellence Framework

Emily Yarrow

Outcomes of research evaluation are arguably playing an ongoing and increasingly important role in academic careers and success, but there are several factors that hold the potential to militate against fairness, gender equality and equality of opportunity (Yarrow, 2016). This article discusses my recent PhD research into women's lived experiences of research evaluation in a UK Russell Group university and explores some of the factors that may affect submissions to the Research Excellence Framework (REF). The last run of the REF occurred in 2014 with results being published in December 2015; 154 UK institutions submitted to the exercise. Currently there is a national requirement at the institutional level for a combination of research outputs (65%), the impact of research (20%), and the institutional research environment (15%), though at the individual level, each university currently decides which academics' work will be included or excluded. However, the inclusion criteria are under review for the 2020 REF after the publication of the Stern Review (Stern, 2016).

The Stern Review is also significant in that currently recommendations for the next REF are being made, as well as the Stern Review strategically informing not only how the REF should be adapted, but also implemented at the national and institutional level in the future. However, I argue that the recommendations made in terms of equality and diversity issues, are not clear or tangible and that there is a clear need for further investigation into the equality and diversity issues surrounding research evaluation. Conversely, it is noteworthy to consider the potentially very significant game-changer which is proposed (Stern, 2016), to include all research-active staff in future exercises and allocate them to a UOA (unit of assessment). Although this may appear to remedy career issues associated with non-inclusion, it is currently not clear whether this recommendation will be recognised and subsequently implemented, and so there is an ongoing need to better understand the current method of selective inclusion.

It is important to demonstrate that whilst the exercise is designed to evaluate research outputs and not individual academics per se, based on my findings I argue that the two are inextricably linked. It is further of note that I found high levels of anxiety surrounding individual submissions that have ramifications not only for individual academics' identities, but also stress and academic well-being (Yarrow, 2016).

My study focused on female academics' lived experiences and career aspirations in the context of the 2014 REF, as well as the views of research directors and heads of school in the study entitled National Research Evaluation and its effects on female academics' careers in the UK – A Case Study (Yarrow, 2016). The sample in the case study drew on 80 semi-structured, life-history inspired interviews with academics across humanities and social sciences in an anonymous UK university, made up of 65 female academics and 15 key respondents. The sample covered a broad age range, as well as a range of female academics spanning ECRs (early career researchers) to professors, as well as career academics and individuals who had been in practice prior to pursuing an academic career. It is important to make clear that my research was not conducted at the University of Edinburgh, but another Russell Group University, though a number of the findings may be generalised across UK higher education institutions that submit to the REF.

This article will cast light on why women are not only less likely to be submitted to research evaluation exercises in the UK, but also the role that informal networks and unconscious bias may play in some academic careers.

Why are women still less likely to be submitted to the REF?

It is clear that there is a stark disconnect between women's ongoing under-representation in leadership positions, for example, and the increasing representation of female students (Grove, 2012). Women in the UK continue to be under-represented not only in leadership positions in industry and academia, but in the upper echelons of academia (HESA, 2015; Fletcher, 2007), particularly in the professoriate, where only around 23% of professors are female (HESA, 2015). Conversely, women are over-represented in temporary, or part-time academic positions (ECU, 2015).

It is of note that women at the national level are still less likely to be submitted to REF than their male colleagues (HEFCE, 2015), despite gender equality initiatives such as Athena SWAN, and the Equality Challenge Unit's equality charter mark scheme. In the last REF in 2014, nationally around 67% of men were entered compared to around 51% of women. However, the HEFCE report also found UOA differences in that:

> In Education, 62 per cent of the eligible staff were female and the average percentage of staff selected was 21 per cent; whereas in Electrical and Electronic Engineering, Metallurgy and Materials, where only 12 per cent of the eligible staff were female, the average proportion of staff selected was 65 per cent. (HEFCE, 2015, p. 9, point 51)

This therefore demonstrated that there are indeed differences between disciplines, but that these tend to be in areas where women are proportionately well represented, however that overall women are still less likely to be submitted to the REF.

More male scholars are included in programmes of national research evaluation than their female counterparts in the UK, but for what reasons?

It is clear that women who reach full professorship are in the minority compared to their male counterparts; it is argued here that outcomes of research evaluation play an increasingly important role in this. Contemporary female careers in the academy are argued by Van den Brink & Benschop to be still to an extent marred and constrained by practices of inequality that have no relation to merit (2011, p. 518), it is clear from the study that there are gendered perceptions of merit which appear to affect women's lived experiences not only of research evaluation, but of academic careers more broadly (Yarrow, 2016).

Findings from my research suggest that outcomes of research evaluation, and whether an individual is included in the REF or not, may play a role in continuing vertical gender segregation in humanities and social sciences, because of the increasing importance of REF inclusion, also often referred to colloquially as 'REF-ability' and the associated career leverage gains in an increasingly 'marketised' academy, characterised by ever-increasing competition and corporatisation (Rogers et al., 2014; Deem, 1998; Willmott, 1995; 2003).

The long-term impact of maternity leave and time taken out on academic careers, particularly during an REF cycle, is an ongoing issue. This appears to be a factor that is damaging to women's career development, primarily because the REF is a time-oriented mechanism (Yarrow, 2016). Whilst periods of maternity leave are accounted for in terms of a reduction of one paper per period of maternity leave, the longer-term caring responsibilities still hold the potential to detract from women's longer-term career development, which becomes further problematic and typified when it is also considered that women are still engaged disproportionately in domestic labour in the home. Furthermore, women in academia take shorter periods of maternity leave than many other professions, which may be indicative of an awareness of the potential implications of taking maternity leave, and the associated anxiety (Bawden, 2014).

The importance of informal networks

Informal networks play an integral, yet somewhat indirect, role in submissions to, and management of the REF. The importance of informal networks was clear throughout the study, often expressed in terms of learning 'the rules of the game' as well as finding out about opportunities for promotion or development and having access to decision-makers, and having them 'on-side' which also plays a role in women's submissions to the REF, particularly as it is often the head of school or research director who make the final decisions on inclusion or exclusion (Yarrow, 2016). It is also noteworthy that the head of school role is often disproportionately occupied by male academics, and this was so in the anonymous university in my case study.

Informal networks have also been found to play an integral role in the recruitment and selection of REF panel members who evaluated submissions, a finding that echoes earlier findings in the REF analysis of panel membership (REF, 2011). It is of note that the 2014 REF panels were disproportionately male, and that this in itself may import issues of gender bias, particularly when the reliance on informal networks for the recruitment and selection of panel members is considered. Informality is the invisible hand that holds the potential to affect equality and diversity, and particularly women's experiences of research evaluation in the UK today, yet it is a factor largely ignored by the recent Stern Review (Stern, 2016).

The pervasive role of unconscious bias

A growing body of literature surrounds the notion of unconscious bias specifically in higher education. Unconscious bias may be defined as "the associations that we hold which, despite being outside our conscious awareness, can have a significant influence on our attitudes and behaviour" (ECU, 2013, p. 1). Implicit bias may be defined as "when we have attitudes towards people or associate stereotypes with them without our conscious knowledge. A fairly commonplace example of this is seen in studies that show that white people will frequently associate criminality with black people without even realising they're doing it" (Perception Institute, 2016).

The tensions between unconscious and implicit bias are being increasingly questioned in academia, though this is still an area which requires further awareness and training in order to better understand its potential implications. The main differences and tensions between unconscious bias and implicit bias, though the terms are often used interchangeably in the current discourse, centre on the notion that individuals are unaware of their biases (unconscious), but that increasingly, bodies such as the Equality Challenge Unit argue that the notion of implicit bias must be questioned as to how unconscious it may actually be, as individuals are being made more actively aware of biases and stereotypes for example through equality and diversity training and that: "Once we know that biases are not always explicit, we are responsible for them" (ECU, 2013, p. 1).

The importance of the potential role of unconscious bias in higher education has been made clear by the Equality Challenge Unit in that they acknowledge that "bias is likely to be relevant to many areas of an institution's work, for example appraisals and grievances, Research Excellence Framework submissions, student admissions and course evaluations" (ECU, 2013, p. 4), thereby demonstrating the wide range of aspects of academic life that unconscious bias may affect.

Moreover, it is important to note that there appears to be a disparity between institutional promises and policies surrounding equality and diversity in general, with the ECU highlighting that institutional strategies and promises are simply not equal to an institution actively practising its commitment to equality and diversity (ECU, 2013, p. 4). It is argued that in the gaps between organisational practice, the equality and diversity discourse and some universities' policies, opportunities for inequalities persist through the presence of unconscious bias, as well as informal subversion of policy and practice. It is these grey areas or lacunae, which appear to actively contribute to gender inequality in academia. The policies and processes are indeed in place, partly due to compliance with legislation such as the Equality Act, 2010, but in some instances these serve to be merely tick-box exercises, and in reality decisions are made quickly and informally, but may still be portrayed to be in line with organisational protocol.

The notion of unconscious or implicit bias is currently being increasingly explored theoretically, and the recent research of Milkman et al. whilst focusing on doctoral students applying to universities in the US, demonstrates that multiple decisions are made before formal entry into organisations (Milkman et al., 2015). This also contributes to the notion that unconscious bias is notoriously difficult to identify, measure, and correct.

However, unconscious bias is an issue which appears to be encompassed in several aspects of the processes, contributing to REF submissions, peer review processes in journals and the readers of materials for REF submissions in some institutions. This becomes increasingly problematic when the issue of the lack of clarity surrounding the recruitment and selection of REF panel members is deliberated, and that journal editorial boards are still dominated by (often well-networked) men (Özbilgin, 2009). Additionally, the recruitment and selection of panel members, as well as a lack of female and BME (black and minority ethnic) panel members, has again been identified. Although there is an acknowledgement from REF that there are issues with REF panels (REF, 2011), there is little indication as to what the concrete actions may be to remedy this in order to improve the current situation.

Van den Brink & Benschop further find that:

> Academic excellence cannot be treated as an objective and measurable attribute, but that it is a social construction that is always embedded within a social context and is thus subject to multiple cultural and political influences. (Van den Brink & Benschop, 2011, p. 50)

With specific regard to unconscious bias in higher education, the main research focuses on its role in recruitment and selection, and decision-making. However, Roos (2008) argues that workplace interactions are permeated with gendered and institutionalised status beliefs, as well as organisational policies and decision-making processes that are also marred by institutional gender stereotypes (2008, p. 186), thus demonstrating the linkages between institutional policies, decision-making and how this may interact with gender inequality.

Of further note is the work of Easterly & Ricard (2011) who reviewed women's departure from academia, and although based on a US STEM context, valuable insight can be drawn regarding the role that unconscious bias plays in women leaving academia. One of their main assertions is that:

> Not only do these lenses shape how people perceive, conceive, and discuss social reality, but because they are embedded in social institutions, they also shape the more material things – like unequal pay and inadequate day care – that constitute social reality itself. (Easterly & Ricard, 2011, p. 62)

This demonstrates again the role that not only unconscious bias, but gender assumptions can play in the construction of social reality for women in higher education organisations. Whilst the effects are evident through the under-representation of women in the upper echelons of the academy, but how change can be sought

and implemented, and unconscious bias tackled, remain to an extent theoretical. However, the following section outlines some of the recommendations from participants in the study, which may be helpful or insightful for others, as well as providing some insight into what may be anecdotal, but constructive advice to departments to avoid potential unfairness.

An integral aspect where the role of unconscious bias was pertinent was with regard to the recruitment and selection of REF panel members, internal university readers of outputs for submission, and peer review. There is a body of literature which suggests that unconscious gendered bias plays a role in the conceptualisation of excellence and suitability for certain types of work. See, for example, Leslie et al. (2015).

Whilst focusing on the gender biases of faculty favouring male students in the sciences in the US, Moss-Racusin et al. (2012) found that female students were less likely to be hired because they were perceived (notably by both male and female faculty members) to be less competent, and that ultimately this may well undermine academic meritocracy. Budden et al. (2008), found that even in processes of double-blind peer review, this is often not adhered to in practice; when double-blind review is used, where neither the author's nor the reviewer's identity is known, the number of women who are subsequently published increases. This has linkages to my PhD research upon which this article draws, in that it may be argued that where panels are disproportionately male with an under-representation of female academics, the scope for the impact of unconscious as well as implicit bias may potentially be increased (Yarrow, 2016). This holds the potential to further contribute to gender bias in research evaluation processes, thereby being further potentially damaging to the careers of female academics. Although these linkages may appear tenuous on the surface, my empirical findings suggest the contrary – women's lived experiences in the academy still appear to be shaped, in some instances, by the permeation of unconscious bias into university practices, such as recruitment and selection, and inclusion in research evaluation, both of which play an important role in academic careers.

Helpful pointers from participants

- The following section outlines some of the pointers from the PhD study findings that participants gave as to what has helped them in their careers, and might be useful for others:

- Building up a positive relationship with the head of school.

- Learning to say 'no'.

- Building up your own network and alliances within your university and further afield.

- Not letting others take credit for your work such as by being first author on a paper.

- Having a senior mentor who is also willing to introduce you to their contacts.

Department-level advice to help avoid unfairness

My findings indicated that departmental culture and leadership within a department plays an important role in women's experiences of REF. The following points are some of the strategies that some key respondents in my study outlined as being useful to help avoid unfairness:

- Have open meetings to discuss the workload model if there is one in place, and hold the meeting in hours when people with children and caring responsibilities can attend.

- Actively engage with and know about research from the Equality Challenge Unit and the University and College Union; there may be issues at play that you're simply not aware of.

- Reassure academics who are not included that this will not affect their internal promotions.

- Discuss the myths around REF and REF submissions that may be present in the department and actively involve everyone in better understanding and then dispelling them.

- Ongoing emotional support, reassurance and kindness.

Summary

Women are still significantly under-represented in the upper echelons of the academy nationally and research evaluation evidently plays a role in this. The REF may hold the potential to provide positive opportunity for change, as well as equality of opportunity through a more transparent framework that makes use of gender-balanced panels, for example, though currently it appears that women are still at a disadvantage, particularly in the context of increasing individualisation of academic work and in an academy where gentlemen's agreements still hold weight and networks play an extremely important role in many aspects of academic life.

Be sceptical when researchers claim sex differences

Judy Robertson

It's hard to avoid news stories about differences between men and women. As I write this, for example, there is a hot debate about an ill-judged memo written by a Google employee in which he claimed that women are under-represented in technology jobs because men and women have different traits. In his view, women have more of an interest in people and aesthetics, while men tend to be attracted to coding and systematizing.

Today there are also various media reports of a neuroimaging study which claims that women are better at empathising because they have increased prefrontal cortex blood flow in comparison to men, and the Daily Mail tells me that viruses target men because they (the viruses, not the Daily Mail) see men as weaker.

In the last two decades, the number of journal articles about sex differences has doubled, and the number of articles in news media has increased five-fold (Maney, 2016). In 2013, the National Institutes of Health in the US introduced a policy which mandated the inclusion of both sexes in preclinical research with animals, tissues and cells, as well as a requirement to disaggregate the data by sex and compare the sexes where possible (Clayton & Collins, 2014). This will no doubt have increased the number of headlines about the inability of lady mice to read maps, and the sexual prowess of male adrenal gland cells.

If you join the dots between an increase in studies about sex differences and the criticisms about the major flaws in commonly used statistical methods across the sciences and social sciences (Ziliak & McCloskey, 2008; Wasserstein & Lazar, 2016), it gets rather worrying. Ioannidis's classic paper revealed that most published research findings are false (Ioannidis, 2005). There is a set of prevalent but poor research design and analytical practices which contribute to the publication of misleading results – Simmons et al. have demonstrated that if you're over-flexible with your data collection you can get significant results for just about anything, including support for the hypothesis that listening to the song "When I'm 64" literally does make you younger (Simmons et al., 2011).

Another problem is that once a study with misleading claims is published, it's not very likely to be checked through replication. The Open Science Collaboration rocked psychology by repeating 100 landmark studies and finding that only 36% of the replications confirmed statistically significant results (Open Science Collaboration, 2015). If you prefer a Bayesian perspective on this project, see Etz & Vandekerckhove (2016). It is also known that lab-based gender studies have particularly low validity, mostly because of their small effect sizes (Mitchell, 2012). It's not just psychologists who have these problems. For example, in a review of published studies of claims of sex differences for genetic effects, Ioannidis and colleagues discovered that it was uncommon for the studies to document good internal and external validity. Of over 432 claims of sex differences, only 60 had internal validity, and only one of these claims had been consistently replicated in two other studies.

So, we know that the scientific literature is riddled with false results due to statistical flaws and publication bias. That's enough of a reason in itself to be sceptical of sex differences reported in journal articles, never mind news articles which have been garbled by journalists who don't have specific training in science reporting. In addition to this general background error rate, there has been a historical bias towards looking for scientific results which confirm stereotypical beliefs about men and women, as described by Angela Saini in her book Inferior (Saini, 2017). Cordelia Fine's books Delusions of Gender (Fine, 2010) and Testosterone Rex (Fine, 2017) are witty and coruscating well-argued explanations of the biases and flawed reasoning which lead to "men are from Mars, women are from Venus" type arguments and dubious "Just so!" stories about how our modern day behaviour can be explained (or excused) through deep biological urges shaped by evolutionary pressures. (Fine, 2010, 2017).

...of over 432 claims of sex differences, only 60 had internal validity, and only one of these claims had been consistently replicated in two other studies...

Such arguments often share a flawed line of reasoning, as elucidated by Donna Maney:

> Assertions are based on the following logic: (i) a structure (or hormone) we'll call 'X' differs between men and women; (ii) X is related to a behaviour we'll call 'Y'; (iii) men and women differ in Y; therefore, the sex difference in X causes the sex difference in Y. This argument is invalid because it invokes the false cause fallacy – a sex difference in Y cannot be deduced to depend on X. In addition to being invalid, the argument is also often unsound in that rarely are all three premises supported. (Maney, 2016, p. 3)

In a recent article in Frontiers in Human Neuroscience, Rippon and colleagues point out that scientists often have a layperson's understanding of gender scholarship, writing:

Sex/gender NI [neuroimaging] research currently often appears to proceed as if a simple essentialist view of the sexes were correct: that is, as if sexes clustered distinctively and consistently at opposite ends of a single gender continuum, due to distinctive female vs. male brain circuitry, largely fixed by a sexually-differentiated genetic blueprint. (Rippon et al., 2014, p. 1)

There is not such a simple dichotomy. As Fine argues, there are not natural "essences" of men and women, naturally occurring characteristics which are determined by biological factors and invariant to history and culture.

> The genetic and hormonal components of sex certainly influence brain development and function ... – sex is just one of many interacting factors. We are an adapted species of course, but also unusually adaptable. Beyond the genitals, sex is surprisingly dynamic, and not just open to influence from gender constructions, but reliant on them. Nor does sex inscribe us with male brains or female brains, or with male natures and female natures. There are no essential male or female characteristics. (Fine, 2017)

Indeed, meta-analyses indicate that considerable support for the gender similarity hypothesis that males and females are similar on most, but not all, psychological variables (Hyde, 2005; Hyde, 2014): in a review of 46 meta-analyses, Hyde found that 78% of the gender differences reported in previous studies were small or very close to zero (Hyde, 2005). Men and women are more alike than stereotypes – and news reports – would have us believe.

It could be that in focusing the analysis on the binary of whether a difference exists or not, we are falling prey to what Maney terms the "methodological fallacy", the belief that "with respect to any trait the sexes are either fundamentally different or they are the same" (Maney, 2016, p.

2). Perhaps "Is there a difference?" is a misleading question, and both "yes" and "no" are wrong answers. Better questions are: "How much do they differ?", "How much are they alike?", and, finally, "What (if anything) should be done as a result of understanding this?"

Practical steps to being sceptical

If you're a research student, it is well worth reading recommendations about non-biased experimental design and analysis practices in full (Simmons et al., 2011; Rippon et al., 2014). Geoff Cumming's book about new statistical methods is also well worth reading for a general understanding of why p-values should not be trusted, regardless of your area of study (Cumming, 2012). I hope that these recommendations will be a good starting point for students and non-specialist readers who want a quick guide to being sceptical about reading and researching sex/gender differences. The tips are drawn from recent articles about gender bias in research, and my previous book on modern statistical methods in Human-Computer Interaction (Robertson & Kaptein, 2016b).

It's important to note that although this article is critical of empirical research and the misuse of statistical methods, I am absolutely not arguing that science is doomed and that we should resort to anecdotal understanding. I'm arguing that if we're going to use science to investigate sex/gender similarities or differences (if we must), we should use the most robust methods we have.

Next time you read a news report about gender or sex differences, take it with a pinch of salt. Look out for these red flags: the phrases "hardwired", or other suggestions that sex differences are genetically predetermined or unchanging (Maney, 2016); leaps from animal models or preclinical research to speculation about human behaviour; evolutionary hand-waving explanations; and studies of only small samples of people.

If you spot any of these red flags, adjust your internal scales of belief downwards.

Certainly check it out a bit more before you choose to man- or lady-splain it to your colleagues.

If you have read an article which seems to be well reported, and you are considering using it to inform a gender policy you are working on or including it in an argument for your own research, track down the original paper to visualise the effect sizes using the tool at https://sexdifference.org/. Enter the sample size, mean and standard deviation for the experimental groups (e.g. men and women), and the software generates a graph which shows the overlap between the distributions on the independent variable. This gives you an intuitive grasp of how large or small the differences between men and women are in a way that p-values do not. Then ask yourself whether the difference in the independent variable between the groups is enough to make an actionable real world difference. For example, if the independent variable is a reaction time, and an effect size of one millisecond difference is observed, would that millisecond be perceptible (or dangerous) in everyday situations? If the independent variable is an attitude survey, what does it mean if one group tends to answer "strongly agree" rather than "agree" on two questions in a larger set?

If you're a researcher, and you are planning to look for sex/gender differences, consider: is this important, and why? Are there other issues which might be more important (Hyde, 2014)? Is sex/gender a proxy for other factors such as body mass or levels of particular hormones which might be more informative? Do you have a well-formed theory for why there would be differences? The Gendered Innovation project (https://genderedinnovations.stanford.edu/researchers.html) offers useful checklists which can help you to decide which considerations of gender may be important for your area of study (Klinge, 2013).

Assuming that you've decided to go ahead with a study of gender differences, bear in mind that doing subgroup analysis will reduce your ability to detect an effect, and so you will need a large sample size. If you're at the stage of sketching out ideas, glance at Cohen's power primer table which shows roughly how many participants are required to detect small, medium or large effects with different numbers of comparison groups in the behavioural sciences (Cohen, 1992). You'll be astonished. For example, consider a study which compares two groups in a between-subjects design. For analysis using a two-tailed independent samples t-test with alpha set at .05, with a power of .80 and attempting to detect a medium-sized effect (Cohen's d = .30), the researcher should recruit 177 participants in each group.

Research Report Bingo		
Hardwired	Mars	Intuitive
Evolution	Add your own	Testosterone
Mice	Venus	Predetermined

Do a power calculation (you can use R or a free online tool) before proceeding with the experimental design. Statistical power is a function of sample size, population effect size and the significance criteria (known as the alpha value, which is set by convention in behavioural sciences at .05).

Decide on your hypotheses, inclusion criteria and when you will stop collecting data in advance. This will help to prevent "fishing trips" or "p-hacking" later – these are pejorative terms for the practice of running various unplanned analyses until you find the result you wanted, or a significant result you think a journal will publish. You could also consider whether you want to use Null Hypothesis Significance Testing at all. A Bayesian approach might be more constructive because it enables you to estimate the strength of new evidence for different hypotheses based on prior evidence (Kruschke, 2010).

Don't torture your data to make it confess. Look at graphs of your data first. Avoid running squillions of tests without correcting for multiple comparisons. Use tests appropriate to finding interaction effects (such as ANOVA). Check your effect sizes before you start claiming substantial differences (Robertson & Kaptein, 2016a). Remember: "How much of a difference" is usually more interesting than "Does a difference exist?"

When you write up your study, pay attention to fair statistical communication (Dragicevic, 2016). Avoid the temptation to over-interpret your results, or to over-emphasise small differences. Talk your university press officer down from writing a cute press-baiting story about why woman and men are from different planets. Insist that what really matters is how your results can help the world, not further divide it by reinforcing stereotypes.

Unconscious bias

Derek Jones

What is bias?

We are not aware of most of our cognition and thinking (Mlodinow, 2012; Norman, 2005). Each and every day we respond subliminally to a huge range of events and conditions. Most of the time we do not question or challenge these cognitive processes since the whole point of them being subliminal is for them to process things efficiently in the background.

We use a number of different techniques to enable this effectiveness and many of these lead to biases in our enacted thinking. Bias is essentially pre-existing or primed knowledge and beliefs brought to bear on immediate situations and contexts. Without such shortcuts, we would be far less able to operate effectively in the world.

But there are times when these shortcuts can have negative effects – the snap judgements we make for unknown reasons; the immediate reactions we have that result in other consequences; or simply the benefits we take for granted as we go about what we think of as a normal life (seen from our own perspective).

When these individual decisions add up we start to then see larger scale biases. The gender pay gap is still there (https://www.gov.uk/government/consultations/closing-the-gender-pay-gap), even in academia. But the gap itself is a symptom of deeper structural, social and political issues. In Moss-Racusin et al. (2012), both male and female science professors rated female applicants as less competent than male applicants and they offered female students a lower starting salary. And students of both genders tend to rate female academics lower than male (MacNell et al., 2014).

There tends to be no 'consciously' executed rationale to bias, although when bias is identified, we are more than able to create such rationales (Ariely, 2012). On top of that, the bias against bias is difficult to research and address (Moss-Racusin et al., 2015). We don't like to believe that we are not entirely in control of our own thinking. Being reminded that our decisions, ideas, attitudes, or actions may have resulted from some other source than 'me' can be a difficult situation to accept.

But accepting and using it can be a very valuable, albeit challenging, process.

It works both ways

Gender bias can work positively and negatively for and against both genders mainly because stereotyping is one of the primary underlying mechanisms (Mlodinow, 2012). For example, we readily (and subliminally) make use of appearance when we ascribe, accentuate or confirm attributes to people, such as lower reporting of shoplifting if a person has a tidy appearance (Steffensmeier & Terry, 2016). This simple social appearance stereotyping is a reasonably trivial and obvious example.

For example, in Brescoll et al. (2010), women working in roles associated as male were judged far more harshly when compared to men working in those roles.

> When they made mistakes, people in gender-incongruent jobs – female police chiefs and male women's college presidents – were ascribed a lower status and seen as less competent than their gender-congruent counterparts. (Brescoll et al., 2010)

A similar result is reported in Brescoll et al. (2012), where a negative impact on male subordinates was observed.

The lesson here is perhaps that tackling bias wherever it is found or can arise is simply a healthy thing to do for any community. The unfair unevenness and asymmetries observed in social groupings have to be continually appraised and challenged. But it is perhaps also true that, as with the title of the study by Brescoll et al. "Hard won and easily lost: the fragile status of leaders in gender-stereotype-incongruent occupations" (Brescoll et al., 2010), it can be so easy to assume that a problem has been sorted and forget that the problem is far deeper than the symptoms.

The other lesson is that when working to resolve an existing imbalance, the really hard work perhaps only starts when a new balance is being tried. Implicit biases do not stop operating and can arise in particular ways when a shift in normative positions is realised.

For example, women being perceived as 'coldly ambitious' instead of 'assertive' (Okimoto & Brescoll, 2010). Moving to a more even gender balance may bring to the surface a number of other symptoms of deeper issues.

The effort required to identify, challenge and then keep working on implicit biases can be significant. But there are practical things that can be done to affect bias, and we review them below.

Balance your work

When creating anything (when creating materials for a general audience) get into the habit of balancing it wherever possible.

- Imagine a wider audience than just yourself. There is strong evidence to suggest that gender gaps in educational attainment, especially in STEM subjects (science, technology, engineering and mathematics), are socially constructed (Good et al., 2010). We tend to write for ourselves and that's OK but once you have that first draft, imagine reading it to a varied audience. This is healthy for your own ideas and thinking as well as your readers'.

- Use gender-neutral language; use all the tricks in the writing book to avoid any gender preferences. Studies show that gender neutral language alienates far less than gender-specific ('he' or 'she' only) or gender-balanced ('he and she') text (Stout & Dasgupta, 2011).

- Use examples of a range of different people and role models: using relevant examples of people that students can identify with (in terms of in-group) is a well-known effect in maintaining educational attainment. In terms of gender, the study by Good et al. (2010) shows that mixed examples of gender in images in science textbooks lead to comparable attainment results in students (when compared to single gender or counter-stereotypical images). Similarly, simply having female role models in maths can improve female student attainment (Marx & Roman, 2002), although the wider effects are not as simple as a single result (see below).

Increase positive exposure to imbalances

This is perhaps one of the simplest and most obvious changes that can be made – if you have staff that are representative of students, attainment will be affected positively. We all identify with a certain amount of self-similarity and this personal bias is very often projected.

Having female lecturers and professors can reduce the attainment gap observed between female and male students in STEM subjects by improving female attainment (Carrel et al., 2010). Importantly, this research also showed that as the level of study increased, so too did the importance of gender representation on attainment – that gender representation at all levels of study is essential to achieve equipotential achievement.

Having said that, recent findings show that students perceive female professors to be generally less capable than male professors. Prior bias in terms of role assignment or gender capability assessment is something that can take time to change when it is acculturated socially. Similarly, the counter-intuitive result shown in Hoyt & Simon (2011) suggests that simply having role models is not enough to engender an immediately positive effect.

But there is evidence to show that exposure can work on short and long-term bias structures and that such longer-term benefits are the real reward. For example, Beaman et al. (2008) show that existing and prior biases remain in terms of preferring male leaders in local politics but that stereotypes of gender roles are weakened with repeated exposure to female leaders or politicians. Most significantly, this seems to have a cumulative effect over time and exposure, leading to longer-term changes in gender balance as demonstrated through local election results.

Reduce the opportunities for bias to be expressed or realised

In studies on employment and pay negotiation:

> Reducing the degree of situational ambiguity constrains the influence of gender on negotiation. (Bowles et al., 2005)

It seems that, with ambiguity, comes the opportunity to allow implicit bias to emerge. In certain economic negotiations, this emerging bias affects women negatively in terms of outcomes – lower salaries or increased payments.

But this also allows a fantastic opportunity for simple, good practice: being explicit and very clear about standards and conditions of employment can reduce gender pay gaps:

> In job negotiations with clear industry standards, there were no differences in salaries negotiated by men and

women. When industry standards were unclear, female MBAs accepted wages that were, on average, $10,000 lower than those accepted by male MBAs. (Bowles et al., 2005)

Similarly, having rigorous, transparent and accessible processes for decision-making can also help reduce the ambiguous 'spaces' within which bias can emerge. For example, removing gender bias through anonymising hiring processes was demonstrated in the famous blind audition research in Golding & Rouse (2000).

Another technique reported in Bohnet et al. (2012) demonstrates reduced bias when joint evaluations were carried out when compared to single evaluations. Again, the behavioural 'nudge' that Bohnet et al. refer to may result in reducing the opportunities for unchecked biases to fully emerge.

Beware of priming

Being told you are good at something can have different effects on different individuals and different groups of individuals. A specific gender grouping study is provided by Shih et al. (1999), where Asian-American women were primed to consider themselves as either Asian or women and then immediately tested in maths. In the former group, they performed better than in the latter.

The hypothesis here is that being reminded that you are in one group affects your own view of yourself and even your ability to do certain things. Of course, this also relies on the prior bias that 'Asians have superior quantitative skills'. More disappointingly it also relies on the corollary too – that women have lower quantitative skills and self-identify with that group and group stereotype.

When adjusted, neither of these stereotypes is true in and of itself – but the threat or promise of it is more than enough to have an effect.

So this priming effect took a prior bias and seemed to leverage it positively to enhance student attainment. But great care has to be taken when priming of any kind is utilised – not least in terms of the ethical issues involved in deliberately (and secretly) affecting other people's cognitive states.

In addition to the ethics, the actual responses will vary depending on the individuals being primed. For example, reinforcing positive reactions in some might lead to stereotype threat in others (see *Stereotype threat*).

In fact, research shows that all you need to trigger an in-group perception is simply to be told that you are in that group (Mlodinow, 2012). So, think before you prime...

Don't rely on meritocracy

One of the basic arguments against positive discrimination is that of pure meritocracy – that it should only be talent, skills or ability that ensures an individual's success. Unfortunately there aren't too many absolutely neutral methods to measure such merit that do not also call into question other basic skills and abilities. We rarely employ or make decisions based on single metrics and very rarely are we sufficiently objective to do this properly.

For example, Castilla & Benard (2010) found that explicitly applying meritocratic methods tended to increase gender imbalance in favour of men.

Participants in the meritocratic condition showed greater preference for the male employee over an equally qualified female employee.

Interestingly, when participants were instructed to apply a values-based method and use 'managerial discretion', the imbalance moved significantly in the opposite direction (towards women).

This was thought to be due to priming that suggested an imbalance did need to be addressed in favour of women.

But perhaps most significantly, when participants were instructed to take a values-based approach without using discretion, then the imbalances largely disappeared! This may tie in with findings in Bowles et al. (2005) that by removing space for bias, gaps can be reduced.

To put it simply – if we are left to not only measure but to create the method of measurement, we might be getting it very wrong (see *Defining excellence*). But if we are given good methods by which we can measure (even using subjective criteria) and clear space within which such measurement should take pace, then most people are actually pretty good at being fair.

Likeability and the double bind

Alison Williams

Be good, sweet maid,
and let who will be clever.

Charles Kingsley, Poems of Home:
IV. Youth A Farewell (1904).

Within academia, men are over-represented at professorial level. Although the focus of enquiry has, thankfully, moved beyond the argument: "Such a big book for such a little head" (Edna St Vincent Millais, 1941) and past Virginia Woolf's angry professors (1929), nevertheless, the ratio of women to men at senior levels remains stubbornly out of balance.

One barrier to equality is stereotypical views of women. This article draws on recipes and articles in this book and looks at the impact, prejudices and expectations that stereotypes create, particularly around likeability, and the behaviours that can result. It then suggests ways forward.

The idea that there is a 'right' way to be a woman, to perform one's gender, is ongoing and pervasive. Good women are modest, charming, polite and unobtrusive, content to earn, on average in the UK, 16.4% less than their male counterparts (see *Salary negotiation*), and to pick up the double load of career and house/child/elderly parent care. 'Good' women are liked. 'Bad' women are those who don't adhere to these standards (Gay, 2014, pp. 303-304), and by performing their gender 'wrong' initiate a set of punishments both obvious and indirect (Butler, 1988). 'Bad' women are disliked.

Stereotypes – fixed, oversimplified and widely held ideas about particular groups – have their origins in cognitive mechanisms, developed at a very young age, of early and primitive generalisations which deeply influence our judgements about members of a kind (Leslie, 2017). Fiske et al. (2002) shed light on the social and cultural complexity of stereotypes, proposing that they can be delineated on two axes: competence and warmth. Competence is aligned strongly with perceptions of another's status or power and hence their competitiveness for available resources; warmth is the extent to which the group is seen as warm, trustworthy and friendly.

Fiske et al. examine the emotions people hold in relation to the stereotypes, and the prejudices that ensue (Figure 1). In quadrant 1 (top right), with high competence and high warmth, all the group members have status and power, and at the same time do not perceive each other as competing for resources. In the context of this study they are part of the institutional in-group or close allies: 'one of us', as opposed to the meaning in psychology of 'my group, whatever it is' (Fiske, in correspondence with the author in 2017). Fiske's study

participants (reflecting their US university student demographic) identified quadrant 1 members, among others, as 'whites', 'middle-class', 'Christians' and 'students'.

In quadrant 2 (top left), with low competence and high warmth, people are perceived as "subordinate and non-competitive" (p. 878) and therefore warm, friendly and trustworthy – i.e. 'good'. The study participants identified and included 'housewives', 'the disabled' and 'the elderly' in this cluster.

People placed in quadrant 3 (bottom right), with high competence and low warmth, are perceived as high competence, high status and powerful, competitive, exploitative and self-serving, therefore threatening. Study participants identified and included 'black professionals', 'feminists' and 'the rich' in this cluster.

In quadrant 4 (bottom left), group members are perceived as exploitative, low-status

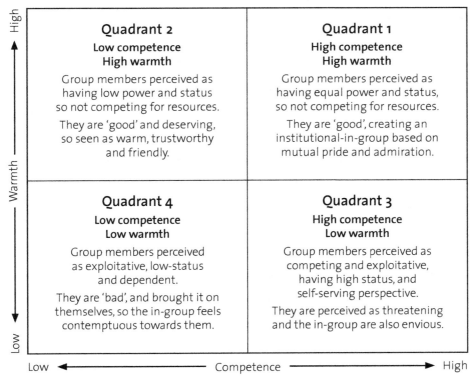

Figure 1: A model of stereotype content and prejudice (adapted with permission from Fiske et al 2002)

and dependent. Study participants identified and included 'the homeless' and 'welfare recipients' in this quadrant.

The researchers then describe what they call prejudiced emotions arising in the four different quadrants.

Paternalistic prejudice is directed towards people placed in quadrant 2 (top left) eliciting sympathy and pity. Paternalistic power relations can show up as benevolent sexism, with traditional 'good' women – home-makers – serving as the 'women are wonderful' default (Haddock & Zanna, 1994). "This form of response is paternalistic when directed at out-groups, because it combines assumed superiority with potential care taking" (Fiske et al., 2002, p. 896).

Envious prejudice is elicited in response to people placed in quadrant 3 (bottom right) where "high status represents a positive outcome, and competence implies control over it, so these groups are seen as responsible for their position. The lack of warmth imputed to these groups corresponds to perceived competition and hostile intent. When people's own controllable, positive outcomes deprive others, those others feel envy" (Fiske et al., 2002, p. 896). Mixed into envious prejudice is a grudging admiration for their perceived skills.

Contemptuous prejudice is shown in quadrant 4 (bottom left) towards "low-status, free-loading groups that are perceived as neither competent nor warm [...] encompassing anger, contempt, disgust, hate and resentment" (Fiske et al., 2002, p. 896).

Admiration and pride are central to quadrant 1) where "some groups elicit unmixed positive regard: pride, admiration, and respect. [...] Admiration is directed towards those with positive outcomes when that does not detract from the self" (Fiske et al., 2002, p. 896).

To belong to the institutional in-group, therefore, is to be admired and valued, supported and appreciated by one's colleagues – to be liked.

Fiske et al. use the term 'warm'; however the terms 'like' and 'dislike' arise when they are referencing descriptions of:

> ...perceived subgroups of women (Deaux et al., 1985; Eckes, 1994; Noseworthy & Lott, 1984; Six & Eckes, 1991): disliked, dominant, competent, non-traditional women (eg career women, feminists, lesbians, athletes) versus likable, dependent, incompetent, traditional women (eg housewives, sometimes 'chicks'). (Fiske et al, 2002, p. 879)

To be perceived by others as belonging in any of the out-group quadrants can be uncomfortable:

> Humans are not biologically or psychologically prepared for being unloved and unwanted. [...] it feels good to feel valued by and validated in a group. Just as important, not having these things feels bad, or worse than bad: incomplete. (Dissanayake, 2000, p. 51)

Things get difficult when the necessary criteria for belonging are mutually in conflict, so if one set of criteria are met, the other set of criteria cannot be met. But they must, somehow and impossibly, be met for membership of the in-group. This is known as the double bind (Bateson et al., 1956; Gibney, 2006). The central tenet of the double bind, in this context, is the tension between being in Fiske's quadrant 2 and likeable, but eliciting paternalistic prejudice and pity, and being in quadrant 3 and disliked and eliciting envious prejudice and grudging admiration. Likeability is weighed against success, but to be included in the institutional in-group a person has to be both successful and liked: two mutually exclusive conditions when applied stereotypically to women.

There are consistent experimental findings of how people assess women in stereotypically male roles (Bohnet, 2016) which indicate that when they have information about performance, people rate successful women as less likeable than men; if no performance information is available, successful women are rated as less competent than men. "Women, thus, are in a double bind that men are not. They are perceived as either likeable or competent but not both." Men in counter-stereotypical roles are also perceived as less competent but their likeability is not affected.

The double bind is experienced by both women and men in differing ways at all levels of seniority; however, the emphasis in this exploration is gendered. This is not in any way to deny or seek to minimise the incidence of the double bind across the genders in higher education and elsewhere. There is evidence of the double bind in *Educated Pass* and in *Allies in the classroom* where young men run the risk of performing their gender wrong by stepping outside what van der Gaag calls the architecture of masculinity (2014).

For a woman to be liked can mean performing one's gender 'correctly' and being nice; however this carries the danger of maintaining and reinforcing paternalistic prejudice and benevolent sexism.

Dardenne et al. (2007) propose that benevolent sexism, in suggesting women's inferiority, can cause women to doubt their abilities. In the recipe *Damning with faint praise*, an unwilling (ungrateful!) recipient of benevolent sexism says:

> [When I was] taking on a new role with considerable responsibility, a senior colleague (already on the management team) welcomed me with the phrase "I'm sure you will do a good job, you are very conscientious". Does he think I am not up to the job?

The recipe goes on to set out how the writer dealt with the faint praise, but for some women:

> ...by focusing on positive stereotypical characteristics of women [in this case conscientiousness], benevolent sexism thus implicitly conveys the idea of their incompetence and that idea coloured women's thoughts and affected their autobiographical memory. (Dumont et al., 2010, p. 551)

One of the senior women leaders in the University referred to the:

> ...drip, drip, drip of undermining comments you face as a female academic. It just becomes normal. (From: *Leadership perspectives on gender equality*)

The issue of competence, perceived as well as internalised, has serious implications within higher education.

> Whilst focusing on the gender biases of faculty favouring male students in the sciences in the US, Moss-Racusin et al. (2012) found that female students were less likely to be hired because they were perceived (notably by both male and female faculty members) to be less competent. (From: *Gender and the Research Excellence Framework*)

And in *The current landscape at the University of Edinburgh*, Judy Robertson writes:

> Teaching is one of the most important aspects of an academic's job, and as such, the University considers student evaluations of teaching (SET) carefully. However, there is research evidence to believe that in general students' evaluations of staff are gender biased with female lecturers receiving harsher ratings (MacNell et al., 2014). Apparently some male students apply the same biases to their peers, as a recent study of biology students found that male students were inclined to overestimate the performance of their male peers (women did not exhibit this bias).

Likeability is also important, not just for the sake of personal and work relationships, but because it has an impact on an individual's career. Unlikeable colleagues do worse in performance evaluations and are deemed less worthy of salary increases and promotions. Bohnet (2016) observes that our biases lead us to react similarly to successful women as to dishonest men, with dislike and a desire to avoid working with them. The result can be that capable individuals are dissuaded – and even prevented – from going for promotion, or move out of academia altogether, unwilling or unable to deal with the issues of likeability.

This University of Edinburgh student expresses clearly the double bind she finds herself in:

> Yet it troubles me that for women, being serious so often is treated as being aggressive, and being cheerful is treated as naivety. I've wasted too much time moulding myself to avoid this, forced into an unfair dichotomy where being taken seriously comes at the expense of being approachable and friendly. (From: *Perspectives from students*)

Many of the authors in this book explore what it means to be liked or disliked, the causes, and the effects. How do women move beyond the need to be liked when a respected academic can write:

> I work hard, I volunteer for things, I try to deliver when I say I will do something. I try to do my job well. I extend myself, then overextend myself. I work at work and I work at home. [...] I sit with my colleagues and think, Please like me. Please like me. Please respect me. At the very least, don't hate me. (Gay, 2014, p. 12)

Some of the EqualBITE authors describe the impossible choices they see as open to them:

Option 1: Be one of the boys

For many years I tried to fit in. Every time a colleague unthinkingly made a sexist comment I awkwardly laughed and brushed it off. I was telling them that it was OK, that I was cool and one of the guys – not like those other women. In the end this just filled me with repressed rage and self-loathing. I had become part of the very thing I despised. (From: *Say something*)

Option 2: Be nice

Women are often expected or forced to provide emotional labour in the form of smiling. How many times have you been asked to smile? At work, at school, in arguments, on the street, in a bar? It's a way to make us provide comfort and aesthetic pleasure even to those we may owe nothing, and a way to ensure women appear unthreatening. (From: *Perspectives from students*)

Option 3: Be a pain

There is a risk when you do call out bad behaviour – there is a backlash. I wouldn't be able to call out bad behaviour until I got to this level of seniority. And now I am at this level I feel I have a responsibility to. (From: *Leadership perspectives on gender equality*)

Being a pain takes its toll:

It can be hard to challenge behaviours that are so embedded that you stop noticing. Small everyday injustices. (From: *Leadership perspectives on gender equality*)

The double bind can make these choices seem as if they are the only ones available, and make it appear so difficult to open up more positive and constructive options. When issues of stereotyping, prejudice and likeability overlap, many women at all levels of academia can be caught in a double bind where they are, apparently, presented with a stark choice, you can be successful, or be liked. In Kingsley's words you can be good or clever, but you cannot be both.

What next?

Unpicking the double bind is possible through what Bateson calls a process of demystifying, where the previously hidden process is made visible. Once something is seen, it cannot be unseen. In both *Gender balancing your seminar speakers* and *Leadership perspectives on gender equality*, for example, women talk about continuing to put only male names forward for speakers and panels until this is pointed out to them (often by male colleagues). At which point their attitudes and behaviours shift.

In the senior leaders' conversation one of the first people to speak said: "The first step is to recognise that you have a problem." So, having recognised that the problem exists, the demystification process starts, and it becomes possible to work towards everyone being an accepted and valued member of a team irrespective of gender.

Awareness is the first part of Carnes et al's model (see *A model for change*) and Athena SWAN has already started this process. The award brings to the surface and challenges practices that have hitherto been simply part of "that's how things are". The section in this book on career development, for example, reviews approaches to gender balancing recruitment; the gender and language section suggests what individuals can do to uncover their own double binds, challenge and demystify them.

With awareness comes external motivation to make changes, and a wish not to appear biased to one's colleagues. As people practise this, they discover there are benefits to tackling their biases, and the motivation becomes internalised. As the leadership balance shifts from an over-representation of men to a more even gender mix, attitudes also shift. Increased levels of women leaders and exposure to a different style of leadership can shift attitudes. For example, in rural India attitudes to women leaders changed significantly once a quota system was introduced for women village leaders (Bohnet, 2016).

Many of the recipe authors in this book give practical advice, based on personal experience, and grounded in the research, to others who are feeling stuck in the double bind of the first three options – to be one of the boys, to be nice or to be a pain. They raise awareness of the unhealthy dynamics of these choices, and open the possibility of moving to a fourth option: to bring the best of oneself to work, and in the process to ask how everyone might be an accepted and valued member of a team, irrespective of gender.

Option 4: Be the best of oneself – good and clever

In *Leadership styles and approaches in GeoSciences* a preferred leadership style is pace-setting.

> Pace-setting leadership occurred in the majority of [the] female leadership. [..] I often observe senior female academics setting themselves very high standards.

It is worth noting that these leaders were aware of the dangers of burnout and the need to avoid it:

All interviewees who do implement pace-setting leadership had an awareness that these high expectations needed careful monitoring so that the team is not overwhelmed by the pace setter's demands. (From: *Leadership styles and approaches in GeoSciences*)

The senior leaders in the University championing the conversation are under no illusions themselves about what is involved. Creating an inclusive culture takes effort and courage.

> [Where] there is a disparity of gender and power, if it is not called out it sets the culture where that imbalance is OK.

and

> Gender inequality is pervasive [in our society] – in my view it's not really changing. The least we can do is work within the institution. But new power structures are fragile: you need to keep your foot on the pedal. (From: *Leadership perspectives on gender equality*)

Reflection is a continuous part of the process for individuals and for teams and departments, as is recognising one's own unconscious biases (see *Challenging bias*) and adapting one's style to better work with colleagues. One EqualBITE author noted:

> The democratic style of leadership was identified as particularly useful when dealing with senior male colleagues. The challenge of leading older male colleagues was raised by a few of the interviewees who were all extremely comfortable with leading students, postgraduates and peers, but felt less confident with older or dominating (and not always senior) male colleagues. (From: *Leadership styles and approaches in GeoSciences*)

A final word from *Leadership perspectives on gender equality*:

> Once people are openly talking, senior managers set the tone, culture, everyone speaks out.
>
> It is about being human.

Intersectionality

Amy Burge

Who are you? How do you know who you are? What are the elements that make up your identity?

When we talk about equality or about protected characteristics, we often talk about one characteristic at a time. So we think about gender, about the pay gap between women and men, sexism, or the glass ceiling. We think about race, about the lack of people of colour in senior positions, about educational attainment gaps for young BME (black and minority ethnic) young people, and about the Black Lives Matter movement. We might think about class and wealth, for example, the fact that working class boys are least likely to attend university (see *Educated Pass*) or that four million children are still living in poverty in the UK (DWP, 2017).

But we know inequality doesn't happen one characteristic at a time. Different aspects of our identity overlap and entwine to make up who we are – we are gendered AND classed AND raced. Intersectionality, at its simplest, is a way of understanding how these different characteristics 'intersect' and how this contributes to inequality.

Defining intersectionality

Intersectionality was coined by lawyer and academic Kimberlé Crenshaw in 1989. While not exactly new – feminists and activists had been writing about overlapping markers of identity for many years (McCall, 2005) – intersectionality was not formally named as such until Crenshaw's paper (Crenshaw, 1989).

Crenshaw argues that a focus on "subordination as disadvantage occurring along a single categorical axis" (i.e. gender OR race OR class) "marginalizes those who are multiply-burdened" (Crenshaw, 1989, p. 140). Currently a professor of law at UCLA and Columbia University,

Crenshaw based her definition on several legal cases, including DeGraffenreid v General Motors (1976), a case in which five black women (including the lead plaintiff Emma DeGraffenreid) alleged that General Motors was discriminating against black women.

In a 2016 TED talk, Crenshaw explained how this case influenced her thinking on intersectionality. She said:

> Now, the judge in question dismissed Emma's suit, and the argument for dismissing the suit was that the employer did hire African-Americans and the employer hired women. [...] [W]hat Emma was actually trying to say, [was] that the African-Americans that were hired, usually for industrial jobs, maintenance jobs, were all men. And the women that were hired, usually for secretarial or front-office work, were all white. Only if the court was able to see how these policies came together would he be able to see the double discrimination that Emma DeGraffenreid was facing. (Crenshaw, 2016)

Crenshaw ultimately points out "that Black women can experience discrimination in ways that are both similar to and different from those experienced by white women and Black men" (Crenshaw 1989, p. 149).

Crenshaw went on to propose a metaphor for understanding Emma's experience.

> So it occurred to me, maybe a simple analogy to an intersection might allow judges to better see Emma's dilemma. So if we think about this intersection, the roads to the intersection would be the way that the workforce was structured by race and by gender. And then the traffic in those roads would be the hiring policies and the other practices that ran through those roads. Now, because Emma was both black and female, she was positioned precisely where

those roads overlapped, experiencing the simultaneous impact of the company's gender and race traffic. The law [...] is like that ambulance that shows up and is ready to treat Emma only if it can be shown that she was harmed on the race road or on the gender road but not where those roads intersected. (Crenshaw 2016)

Thus, the term intersectional was born.

Applications and uses of intersectionality

Intersectionality is simultaneously simple and difficult to define. While Crenshaw's explanation makes sense, the widespread use of the term in different disciplines over the past 25 years has resulted in ambiguity. Patricia Hill Collins and Valerie Chepp summarise the various definitions of intersectionality as theory (including as a theory of identity, theoretical contribution and paradigm), as perspective, concept, or type of analysis, as a methodological approach or analytical perspective, and as something people 'experience' (Collins & Chepp, 2013, p. 2). They conclude that "while this ambiguity and inconsistency likely result from a well-intentioned effort on the part of scholars to advance the promise of intersectionality, the slippage in terminology can feel imprecise and foster uneven outcomes" (Collins & Chepp, 2013, p. 2).

In an essay, Crenshaw (1991) set out three categories or arenas for intersectionality:

1. structural intersectionality – the way race and gender intersect and mean women of colour experience inequality (rape, domestic violence) fundamentally differently than white women.

2. political intersectionality – how women of colour have been marginalised from liberation politics.

3. representational intersectionality – that women of colour are either invisible or problematically represented in popular culture.

These are the key areas on which intersectional thinking has focused in the past 25 years. In a 2008 article exploring the usefulness of intersectionality, Kathy Davis indicates that intersectionality has been useful in a wide range of feminist areas, including postcolonial theory, diaspora studies, and queer theory (Davis, 2008, p. 71). Leslie McCall, in a 2005 article 'The Complexity of Intersectionality', writes that "one could even say that intersectionality is the most important theoretical contribution that women's studies [...] has made so far" (p. 1771). Certainly, it is almost unimaginable in 2017 that any examination of lived experience would not take into account intersecting categories of identity.

The broad understanding of intersectionality has led to much debate about the application of intersectional theory and its usefulness for studying society. Some have criticised the way intersectional approaches that begin with Women of Colour (WOC), like Crenshaw's, are in danger of reproducing black women as the Other, and reifying sex/gender as the foundational identifier: "that is to say, sexual and gender difference is understood as the constant from which there are variants" (Puar, 2011). Furthermore, Puar argues that "the centrality of the subject positioning of white women has been re-secured through the way in which intersectionality has been deployed" (Puar, 2011). Puar defines intersectionality and then offers an overview of critiques of intersectional theory, drawing on Donna Haraway's cyborg/goddess distinction.

However, Davis ultimately concludes that it is "precisely the vagueness and open-endedness of 'intersectionality' [which] may be the very secret to its success" – its wide applicability and the ease with which it can be incorporated into any analytical approach.

Intersectional thinking is certainly evident at the University of Edinburgh. In Philosophy, teaching staff created a Diversity Reading List to help lecturers diversify an overwhelmingly white male curriculum to include people of colour and women (read more about the project on Teaching Matters: http://edin.ac/2hRkYP6). In History, a postgraduate student created an online tool to help others teach more inclusively (find out more via Teaching Matters: http://edin.ac/2iaQ1oU). The University's LGBT+ staff network (University of Edinburgh Staff Pride Network) works proactively to improve the experiences of LGBT+ staff at the intersection of other identities.

There is certainly a need for a measured and careful approach when thinking about how different aspects of identity overlap and intersect, but it's clear that the fundamental need to think intersectionally about people's experiences is not going away. On the contrary, it is becoming increasingly important: and there is plenty we can do.

Find out more about intersectionality

Videos, talks, blog posts

Crenshaw TED talk.
https://www.ted.com/talks/kimberle_crenshaw_
the_urgency_of_intersectionality

A recording of a 2014 Lecture by Crenshaw, 'Justice
Rising: moving intersectionally in the age of post-
everything'.
http://www.lse.ac.uk/website-archive/
newsAndMedia/videoAndAudio/channels/
publicLecturesAndEvents/player.aspx?id=2360

Intersectionality Matters – a series of short videos
by MenStoppingViolence.
https://www.youtube.com/
watch?v=eBb5TgOXgNY
&list=PL809F7D5DF51ED9CE

Buzzfeed. (2015). What is Privilege?
https://www.youtube.com/
watch?v=hD5f8GuNuGQ&feature=youtu.be

An Intersectional Gaze at Nationalist Projects: Prof
Nira Yuval-Davis.
https://www.youtube.com/
watch?v=OiOAdou8B90

Thinking Gender 2010: Race-ing Resistance in
Queer and Trans Politics.
https://www.youtube.com/
watch?v=SF3n7bOeUUA

Everybody Belongs: A Toolkit for Applying
Intersectionality.
http://criaw-icref.ca/sites/criaw/files/Everyone_
Belongs_e.pdf

http://tigerbeatdown.com/2011/10/10/my-
feminism-will-be-intersectional-or-it-will-be-
bullshit/

http://www.newstatesman.com/
lifestyle/2014/04/kimberl-crenshaw-
intersectionality-i-wanted-come-everyday-
metaphor-anyone-could

Additional reading

Bowleg, L. (2008). When black + lesbian + woman
[not equal to] black lesbian woman:
the methodological challenges of qualitative and
quantitative intersectionality research.
Sex Roles, 59, pp. 312-325.

Brah, Avtar and Phoenix, Ann (2004). Ain't I a
woman? Revisiting intersectionality. Journal of
International Women's Studies, 5(3), 75-86. http://
vc.bridgew.edu/jiws/vol5/iss3/8
[A historical approach examining class,
imperialism, and postcoloniality in nineteenth-
century feminist anti-slavery discourse.]

Collins, P. H. (2008). Black feminist thought.

Erevelles, Nirmala; Minear, Andrea (2010).
Unspeakable offenses: untangling race and
disability in discourses of intersectionality. In
Journal of Literary & Cultural Disability Studies,
4(2), pp. 127-145. DOI: 10.1353/jlc.2010.0004
[Looks at the experiences of those at the
intersections of race, class, gender, and disability.]

Ilmonen, K. (2017). Identity politics revisited: on
Audre Lorde, intersectionality, and mobilizing
writing styles. European Journal of Women's
Studies, 1–16.
http://doi.org/10.1177/1350506817702410

Educated Pass: engaging young males from low socio-economic status backgrounds with learning

Neil M Speirs

The underachievement of males, and their lack of engagement with academic work and formal achievement are well documented (Harris et al., 1993; Rudduck et al., 1996; Kessels & Steinmayr, 2013). However, the lengths that males will go to in order to conceal any interest in or involvement with classwork are incredibly sophisticated. For example, Jackson et al. (2015) suggests that for some secondary school boys, the construct of 'laddishness' acts as a self-worth protection strategy. These extenuated efforts are made in order to preserve the individual's status within their peer group (Younger et al., 1996; Warrington et al., 1999). Males, in order to avoid social exclusion, act in line with peer-group norms which are very often in direct conflict with the ethos of participating constructively in the classroom environment (Skelton, 2001; Martino & Pallotta-Chiarolli, 2003; Tinklin, 2003). Educational achievement does not make adolescents more popular with peers (Coleman, 1961; Sebald, 1981; Landsheer et al., 1998).

Boys are often seen as 'troublesome' (Jones & Myhill, 2004). Such stereotypes affect the perceptions and expectations that teachers have of pupils (Heyder & Kessels, 2015). However, Bleach (1998, p. XV), pointed out that boys do not form a strict homogeneous grouping that are all "victims of the education system in terms of pedagogy and practice". Indeed, a more sophisticated analysis (Collins et al., 2000) generates a "which boys, which girls" approach to under-achievement. Poverty is the primary indicator for attainment for both males and females (Burnhill et al., 1990; Paterson, 1991; Sammons, 1995; Goodman & Gregg, 2010), with the inequality of education attainment between the social classes growing since the late 1980s (Gillborn & Mirza, 2000). As Lucey & Walkerdine (2000, p. 37) underline: "mainly working-class boys continue to fail, while other, mainly middle-class boys, maintain their educational success". Connolly reminds us that:

> It is not all young boys who are underachieving but rather certain groups of boys – particularly working class boys [...] and the problems they face are actually much more about social class and ethnicity than about gender per se. (Connolly, 2004, p. 232)

In order to promote participation and engagement with learning, I employ an approach that is credible to working-class boys (Allen et al., 2015). My project, Educated Pass, draws on early notions of Olympism (Olympic Charter 2016). 'Blending sport with culture and education', this sophisticated approach is delivered through 'the educational value of good example'. Educated Pass works with under-achieving young males, from lower socio-economic status backgrounds, that play for local football clubs. The strong relationships that are built provide opportunities for the

boys to develop bridging and linking social capital (Woolcock, 2001). The project has worked with some 1000 young males over the past ten years, in small wooden huts, old community centres and University of Edinburgh sporting facilities – normally under showers of rain and a gusty breeze. Spirits are never dampened though. Various partners have helped us to deliver the project, including the Scottish Youth Football Association, West Lothian College, Edinburgh College and the Centre for Sport and Exercise at the University of Edinburgh.

Educated Pass has a very close relationship with the University of Edinburgh football team. Team members and coaching staff act as positive role models, assisting the project delivery through 'the educational value of good example'.

You see, Educated Pass is about promoting taking part in life, making positive life choices. It's about spending time with communities as development takes place, not simply giving them new footballs and some gym kit. Sport is an enabler in all this; United Nations (2005) notes that "by its very nature sport is about participation. It is about inclusion and citizenship."

This all converges on the four capacities of the Curriculum for Excellence in Scotland: being successful, effective, responsible and confident learners. Capacities which the young boys that Educated Pass works with exhibit freely outside of the classroom. The challenge is to transfer this application and effort to the classroom – to give their best on and off the pitch.

We are aiming to open up a world of possibilities in order to challenge the situation in which "agents shape their aspirations according to concrete indices of the accessible and the inaccessible, of what is and is not 'for us'" (Bourdieu, 1990, p. 64).

We do not believe that it is reasonable or acceptable to allow the boys and their families to be wedded to life outcomes that are predicted by socio-economic status, or as Bourdieu continues, "inclining agents to 'cut their coats according to their cloth', and so to become the accomplices of the processes that tend to make the probable a reality" (Bourdieu, 1990, p. 65).

Research into those boys that have completed Educated Pass and subsequently left school shows a 98% positive destination (Educated Pass, 2015) compared with national figures in Scotland of 89% for males and 92% for females. The same report showed that participants in Educated Pass were almost 10 times more likely to study at degree level than to become a professional footballer. So, the message of positive life choices is starting to make its way through, highlighted by a parent of one of the boys who said:

> If Educated Pass inspires just one child every year to think differently about their future, then it will have been worth it. Without it, horizons are narrower and aspirations less ambitious, and our society less diverse and more restricted.

We can probably summarise all of this with words from former French international footballer Eric Cantona when he said: "It is better to be a good man than a champion".

The ideas in this recipe will be useful for other groups within universities and communities who want to open up educational possibilities for young men from low socio-economic status backgrounds.

Ingredients

- A member of staff with a true love, appreciation and respect for education and sport, particularly football.
- Staff that hold an encyclopaedic knowledge of football.
- Experience playing in any team sport – at any level.
- A personalised pedagogical practice that fully understands the boys and their families.
- Access to quality university sporting facilities.
- The co-operation of student performance-level sportsmen and sportswomen and their managers.
- Community football teams for young males led by inspirational mums, dads and grandparents.
- Support from local colleges, local pro-teams and national sporting governing bodies.

- A desire to positively influence the lives of young people and their families.

Method

1. It's vital to establish a sense of credibility with the boys and their families. This is achieved through the shared social interest of football and sport in general. According to FIFA (the governing body of association football), 1 in 25 people play football in some shape or form globally (FIFA, 2006). The message of participation in class will be lost, as it can be if delivered in the classroom, unless this credibility is established. Knowledge and understanding of the game is vital to form an initial rapport of trust. After all, football can unite people across generations as well as across class and race. We all love the game – regardless of where we come from or who we are. The message of taking part in class is delivered in the new classroom – the club house, under the approval of the new teacher – the head coach.

It's not a good idea to base interventions on assumptive gender stereotypes. However, if the individual, group or community that you are working with clearly express that they are indeed interested in an activity that just so happens to conform to such stereotypes – then it is OK to use this as the hook to engage them with their learning. In this case the boys and their families are part of local youth football teams – giving large amounts of their time and energy to what is their passion.

> The program had a very positive impact on the team and boys. I was a coach, as well as a parent, and I noticed that this program provided more opportunities for the boys. Particularly, it enhanced their creativity in new ways they couldn't have imagined. (Coach/Parent)

2. It's important to bring relevancy to the curriculum; this involves linking any part of the curriculum to football and sport in general. A great way to do this is through inter-disciplinary learning – which also helps the boys to understand how what they do now is linked to what they might do in the future. So, for example, this might involve a class based on human rights. Discussing this with 13-year-old boys and their families at 9pm at night isn't as tricky as you might think. The Pinochet regime, conflict in the former Yugoslavia or the civil war in Côte d'Ivoire may seem to be non-starters – but you couldn't be more wrong. You see Didier Drogba, the captain of Côte d'Ivoire stood against the conflict, Bosnian Pedrag Pasic opened a multi-ethnic football school in the heart of war-torn Sarajevo and

Carlos Caszely said 'no to dictatorship' in Pinochet-ruled Chile. Before you know it, a critical appraisal of three devastating world events has taken place.

A second example would be the application and context of language learning. What if the boys had to be able to speak French because their favourite team were playing in Paris? They would need to get from the airport to the stadium, find out how to get to their seat. Buy a match programme, a drink and some food. After the match? Well they might meet some of the home fans and have a short discussion with them about the match. All of a sudden learning French is relevant. And if you want to work for UEFA, Europe's footballing governing body, well you'll need to be able to speak French or German as well as English. The fact you can do 100 keepy-uppies is irrelevant. (Keepy-uppy is a game where the aim is to juggle a football with any part of one's body, except the hands and arms, for as long as is possible. Each successful touch is numbered as one keepy-uppy.)

> Educated Pass was extremely worthwhile and provided a perspective which was very interesting and relevant to all, as it linked sports and the importance of education as well as highlighting some important social issues. (Parent)

3. Next, we make sure that the experience is immersive and that it involves families and communities as well as the boys. This really follows the footballing idea of the home and away fixture. So we will visit the community where a particular club is based and deliver content. They will also visit us and experience the academic and sporting infrastructure that they will be unfamiliar with. But this goes on – local college partners will also welcome the boys and their families to campus so that all further and higher education is represented. And of course the final way to make the experience immersive is to have the support of a local pro-team that will allow their high-level facilities to be used.

This selection of experiences in new and unfamiliar environments is facilitated by key partners. This could be role model student athletes, such as semi-professional student footballers or student athletes that have taken part in Olympic, world or Commonwealth competition. As well as university and college teaching staff, the coaching teams and sports scientists work with our students. Overall, the case for participating in class is richly illustrated by a number of places, people and facilities. The key is that the parents and families of the boys are also present and are able to witness the case for participating and to see that achievement and attainment in an educational setting have value and pay-off that may have thus far gone unnoticed, but also that it is relevant to their son, family and indeed wider community. Having support at home is vital for progression through school and beyond for the boys.

> Educated Pass gave my son the confidence to get out and socialise more and to understand more about the working world. It also provided him with an idea of potential career paths, something to aim for and see what he could achieve. (Parent)

4. Our fourth step involves linking engaging and staying on at school with positive post-school destinations. We are clear in our presentation of the myriad of professions in sport that require the application of a vast selection of subject areas. For example, the marketing executive, the nutritionist, the physio, the lawyer, the administrator, the sports scientist or the business manager to name a few. But it is also important to illustrate opportunities outside of the world of sport, many of which could come from this list but used in a non-sporting environment. Ultimately we are looking for the boys to make positive life choices related to their education and training as well as their physical and mental health.

> Educated Pass helped me to think that I want to go on and study health and science at uni or college when I leave school. Nobody in my family has done that before. (Player, holding midfielder)

Student recruitment: planning visit days

Judy Robertson

There is a good deal of hand wringing about how to encourage girls to study STEM subjects (science, technology, engineering and mathematics) at university. The WISE Campaign for women in science and engineering laments (with admirable candour): "Nothing has worked! Despite more than 30 years of focus on 'enthusing, fascinating or encouraging' girls into STEM, there has been NO CHANGE in the proportion of girls choosing physics A-level" (WISE PLM).

They recommend a fresh approach which doesn't try to change girls to fit with the world of science, but rather presents STEM subjects as stepping stones into careers for "people like me". They note that one-off interventions which are meant to excite people about science don't generally work to change minds about careers and make some rather scathing remarks about "untrained and narrowly prepared speakers" whose visits to schools might do more harm than good. They disapprove of science competitions too, on the grounds that competition isn't necessarily appealing to girls who might prefer more co-operative activities.

Given that girls outperform boys at school generally, including in STEM subjects, the problem is persuading girls to apply for STEM courses when they have the qualifications to study any number of courses which could lead to careers that they might consider more alluring or rewarding. This recipe focuses on a later stage of

the "leaky pipeline" – how to make sure that women (or applicants from minority groups) choose your course rather than other courses at different universities. How to get women to apply in the first place is a mystery we will leave to another time.

I organised applicant visit days for school students to a computer science department at a Scottish university for many years. These events are for people who have applied to a university course and have been accepted (conditionally upon their exam results), but are still trying to decide which university to choose. I used to love this role, but I was very fussy about doing it in a particular way. For me, the main aim is to give applicants the sense that "this is a place for people like me". Your job is to help them to see your department as somewhere that they would fit in.

And if you believe your department is not really a place where women do fit in then make it so! You have a whole book of recipes here to help you.

Ingredients

- Ability to remember what it is like to choose a university course.

- Ability to see your department with fresh eyes.

- Willingness to ignore academic pride and prestige.

Method

1. **Match up your applicants with a compatible student ambassador.** Have a range of ambassadors such as those who are familiar with local school systems as pupils or parents, or international students, mature students, or those who have studied at FE (further education) colleges to match the spectrum of applicants.

2. **Make your applicants feel comfortable.** It's a good idea to involve first or second year students in planning applicant visit days, because they remember what it was like to visit for the first time – what they were worried about and what they enjoyed. Select staff and student helpers for their warmth, friendliness and ability to relate to applicants' backgrounds (this isn't an opportunity to impress with your most brilliant peacock researchers). If your department has a policy by which everyone must help at open days to spread the workload (an excellent way for the department to shoot itself in the foot as not everyone is suited to this task) your head of department can no doubt be creative in assigning alternative tasks to people who are more at ease lurking in their offices.

3. **Make the environment comfortable too.** Pay attention to the physical space you bring applicants to. I remember being dragged around grey, windowless basements known as the machine halls to look at Sun Microsystems servers when I was applying for a computer science degree place. It may have impressed the geekier applicants but it literally left me cold because the air conditioning was on full blast. It wasn't a place I wanted to spend time (and although in fact I did study on that course I spent as little time as possible in those labs throughout my degree).

Seemingly little details such as the posters on the wall, or the T-shirts worn by helpers cue people about whether they would fit in within an environment. While the (mostly male) applicants around me might have enjoyed discussing their Red Dwarf T-shirts with the host PhD students, I felt like an outsider as I had never watched the show. It turns out it's not just me – my experience on the open day relates to a of sense ambient belonging, which "includes fit with the material (e.g. physical objects) and structural (e.g. layout) components of an environment along with a sense of fit with the people who are imagined to occupy that environment" (Cheryan et al., 2009). Women typically feel less comfortable in environments which broadcast masculinity.

4. **Choose your open day speakers carefully.** Make sure you have seen them speak before so you know that they are capable of being simultaneously inspiring and comprehensible. Vet them first so you can predict whether they will suddenly go off on an alarming elitist rant about accepting only the highest calibre of student. Regardless of your actual selection policy, the point is that you're trying to persuade the audience members to choose your department and invoking brilliance often evokes stereotype threat for those who don't match the stereotype profile (Cheryan et al., 2009). Also, just to make your task of finding staff to help extra hard, the WISE report cautions against relying too much on role models who are too perfect, because young people may feel: "I could never be that good". Why not choose some of your less eccentric undergraduate students to speak? The applicants are probably more interested in finding out the sorts of things they will learn in their first year than what they might eventually do if they ever become a research student. They may find it easier to relate to a student who is closer to them in age or career stage.

5. **Focus on how great your subject is, and the opportunities it will bring.** The WISE report notes that girls are less inclined to study a subject because they enjoy it or they are good at it – they would prefer to know how they can use it in their future. So make sure that girls know what career opportunities studying a STEM subject might bring, and also that it is important to keep their options open.

6. **Reach out to families too.** Parents are very influential in career choices. In particular, WISE suggests that it would be effective to discuss the range of career opportunities relating to a subject with mothers so that they in turn influence their daughters. After all, why would a parent want their daughter to work in a world where she feels she does not belong?

At the University of Edinburgh, Informatics, Engineering and Maths all match their applicants with ambassadors who welcome them and their questions via email.

Cook's tip

One of the reasons I feel so passionate about this is my own applicant visit experience (see Method step 3), and that in some respects I felt an outsider for the four years of my course. But I did spend a lot of time teasing members of the in-group who I made friends with about their nerdery!

Warning

It is not a good idea to make a big issue out of gender – don't mention it unless someone brings it up as a concern. There is no point in worrying applicants about issues which they may not have yet encountered. And at the same time, if it is raised, have an honest and constructive reply ready.

Gender balancing staff recruitment: attracting the right candidates

Lara Isbel & Judy Robertson

The University of Edinburgh established the Chancellor's Fellowship scheme in 2012 to recruit 100 people with the potential to be future research leaders in their fields. Two-thirds of the first intake of Chancellor's Fellows were men. However, two-thirds of the people who applied to the scheme were also men: it is very challenging to address gender imbalances internally if the starting point is a very unbalanced pool. The same is true for recruitment to our Information Services division where the University faces many of the same challenges as other tech employers in Edinburgh.

In fields where there is a significant gender imbalance, such as computer science or nursing, getting a more diverse pool of qualified people to apply isn't easy.

This recipe provides some practical steps which may help you to promote job vacancies to reach a wider pool of people with relevant experience and qualifications.

Ingredients

- Critical perspective.
- Openness to ideas.
- An awareness of your own bias.
- Willingness to experiment with and evaluate different approaches.

Method

1. **Write an inclusive job advert.** Job seekers interpret subtle linguistic clues to decide whether they would "belong" within a particular working environment. Women are less likely to find it appealing to apply for jobs based on adverts which are full of words with masculine associations, regardless of whether they think they could do the job. If you're wondering what masculine words are, consult the appendix of Gaucher et al. (2011) for a handy list from the literature. As a small sample, "decisive", "ambitious", "intellectual" and "adventurous" are all words more associated with men. Yes, men get the good words, and they get Lego. There really is no justice.

    So-called feminine words include "loyal", "co-operative" and "responsible" and a whole lot of other words which might be better associated with dogs like "affectionate" and "submissive". Also be aware that within academic fields (such as philosophy, maths and physics) where women are under-represented, success is associated with innate talent rather than hard work, (Leslie et al., 2015). Advertising for a "brilliant" professor is unlikely to improve gender balance in these domains.

2. **Pay attention to how the salary is described.** Women are more inclined to negotiate salary if the advert gives them "permission" to do so by stating "salary

negotiable" or including a range on a salary scale (see *Salary negotiation*). This detail is important to avoid perpetuating the gender pay gap. Adverts which frame a salary in competitive terms are off-putting to both men and women, but will deter women more.

For example, if the salary scheme links the applicant's pay to performance in comparison to colleagues, women will be less likely to apply, although this effect can be mitigated by making the language in the advert more gender neutral (Gaucher et al., 2011).

3. Include in the job information links to the University's family-friendly policies, flexible working opportunities, facilities, support for LGBTQ+ (lesbian, gay, bisexual, trans, queer/questioning and other) staff and other information which might make the job more attractive to

a wider range of candidates. To attract a diversity of talent, the University needs to make itself attractive to candidates who have a life outside academia. These include people with family responsibilities such as caring for young children or ageing parents.

4. **Have visible role models.** For a large recruitment campaign, you could include short profiles or mini-interviews with people from a broad range of backgrounds who are in similar roles to the post advertised.

5. **Ask for advice from HR (Human Resources) on where to advertise the vacancy** and ask candidates how they heard about the job to check which channels are most effective. Experiment with different routes and social media to see if that has an impact on the balance of applications.

6. **Ask current staff members to share the vacancy with their networks and to encourage talented contacts (of both genders) to apply.** If someone feels like a role is 'not for them', encouragement or support from a third party who is aware of their professional expertise may increase the likelihood of them applying.

7. **Check that the evidence you ask for matches the qualities and experience you require.** Make sure that the essential criteria are well thought through (see *Defining excellence*).

8. **Check that your recruitment process once applications are received follows best practice.** This involves shortlisting (see *Gender balancing staff recruitment: shortlisting*) and selection (see *Gender balancing staff recruitment: interviewing*). Consider which aspects of the role you can check at the application stage and what to look for in an interview. Structured interview questions will help you decide whether each candidate meets your criteria. For example, if the ability to perform the duties of a personal tutor is required, ask for examples of prior experience at interview because it is unlikely to be included in the standard academic CV.

In the Schools of Molecular, Genetic and Population Health Sciences, and Clinical Sciences, all job adverts include a statement which welcomes applications from women. In the School of Health in Social Science at Edinburgh University, it is routine to advertise that posts can be part-time or flexible.

Gender balancing staff recruitment: shortlisting

Stewart Anderson

It can, sometimes without fault, be all too easy to have an unconscious bias when selecting candidates for interview. Have you ever heard someone say things like: "Her application is OK although I feel I could get on better with this one as it's a man" (or of course "...a woman") or maybe even the poisonous "good application but she might want kids, so not sure"?

Shame on those individuals! They need to take time out and think about what they have done. If you're on a selection panel when this happens, make sure someone also points out what they have said and why it's wrong.

Selection of a good candidate should rarely, if ever, be based on the sex of the individual, instead we should focus on what each candidate is bringing to the table. It is their skills and previous knowledge which are relevant to the job. This is a great thought, but how can we reduce or even eradicate bias during the selection process?

Ingredients

- Selection panel, mixed, (optionally one or more members from outside of the team).
- Pack of Post-it notes, all the same colour, size and shape.
- Room with a table of suitable size.
- Enough pens for the panel members.

- Selection of tasty treats and beverages (non-alcoholic).
- Job description.

Method

1. Prepare a checklist by breaking down the job description into the key skills/ knowledge that you are looking for candidates to have and the level you would expect as a minimum for the position. Check that the selection panel members are familiar with the checklist (see *Gender balancing staff recruitment: attracting the right candidates*).

2. Anonymise the applications by covering over name, gender and other identifying demographic information. Prepare the Post-it notes by separating each on a table and then having each panel member write out "Candidate" and then the next letter in the sequence (A through to Z). If there are more than 26 candidates, add numbers 1-99 for each letter thereafter (e.g. A1, B1, C1... etc). Cover the names and other information with the Post-it notes.

3. Ask each member of the selection panel to review all of the applications, referencing the checklist as they go and taking notes of the reasons why they have picked each candidate and ensuring that each candidate is referred to by the relevant Post-it note on the application, e.g. "Candidate A".

4. When reading recommendation letters, be aware that studies have shown that women get short-changed by their referees. A study of reference letters about medical faculty found that letters written for women medics were shorter, missed out basic features, and used language which raised doubt in the mind of the reader (Krawczyk & Smyk, 2016). They were also inclined to associate women with their teaching and men with their research. Watch out for letters which use gendered language or weasel words or phrases like: "It appears that her health and personal life are stable" or "She has worked hard on the projects she has accepted". These are actual examples from the corpus gathered in Krawczyk & Smyk (2016)!

5. When looking at the candidates' publications, take into account career breaks which might explain publication gaps to avoid penalising people who have taken time out to care for children and other family members.

6. Remember to feed the panel members! Being tired and hungry doesn't help with decision-making. For example, a study of judge's meal breaks found that their decisions reflected status quo just before they took a break, but were more deliberative (and lenient) after a meal break (Danziger et al., 2011).

7. Have the panel pick six candidates each and then come together as a group and agree across the panel on a final six candidates to take forward to interview. As discussed in *Gender balancing staff recruitment: interviewing*, it is a good idea to recruit for several posts at once.

Gender balancing staff recruitment: interviewing

Judy Robertson

I was so nervous before the interview for my present job that I was tempted to run away. I was to be interviewed by a panel of nine including the Principal, the Head of College, two heads of school and a motley collection of professors, one of whom had examined my PhD fifteen years previously. It was like a scene from The Lord of the Rings! I didn't run away, of course, and managed to forget the experience until I was researching this book. While such intimidating interview panels are unusual even at Edinburgh, a panel-based interview following a presentation is fairly standard for academic posts. Put it this way: all the academic jobs I have ever applied for or recruited for have involved panel-based interviews. This is very expensive in terms of staff time so it is important that it pays off in terms of hiring people who will perform well in their jobs.

As I read the research on the topic, it became clear to me that the current interviewing practices at universities in the UK could do with a rethink.

Evidence from other industries suggests that current university procedures are likely not effective in selecting the best people for the job, irrespective of how intimidating they are to candidates. Here's what Bohnet's review of the research evidence recommends we should be doing instead (Bohnet, 2016).

Ingredients

- Knowledge of the literature on bias in recruitment.
- Willingness to challenge tradition.

Method

1. **Beware of a false sense of security: equality and diversity training.** I have read a lot of Athena SWAN applications, and it is common to mention that interview panel members have all undertaken equality and diversity training as if this might be a magic bullet. Unfortunately, there is no evidence that equality and diversity training in general actually works (Wilson, 2011; Bohnet, 2016). We know from lab-based studies that there is a small positive effect for training interventions to reduce implicit prejudice overall (Lenton et al., 2009), but that it is by no means straightforward to get the training right (Lai et al., 2013). For example, someone who is aware they could be biased may try to suppress automatic stereotypes, which does not always help; in some cases it can make the stereotypes more salient and lead to an increase in bias (Bohnet, 2016). Receiving feedback that you are progressing towards the goal of being more egalitarian can increase your implicit bias and make you act in a more discriminatory way (Kim, 2003). Although there is a large literature on implicit bias, there is still a lack of evidence that reducing implicit bias reduces discriminatory behaviour in the short term, never mind in the longer term (Lai et al., 2013). Given that a lot of the evidence to date is from lab-based studies, we still don't know how these effects will play out in the real world. In short, don't make equality and diversity training for interview panel members your only way of ensuring equality when making hiring decisions.

2. **Beware of a false sense of security: a woman on the panel.** Another common feature of Athena SWAN applications is a statement of a departmental policy in which at least one member of each gender is represented on an interview panel (usually to guarantee one woman on a panel of men). Presumably this is on the reasonable assumption that the presence of a woman on the panel will reduce bias. In the slippery world of unconscious bias, though, it pays to question common sense. There is some evidence that having women on a panel can prevent male panel members from making biased decisions

(Zinovyeva & Bagues, 2011), but the female panel members themselves may act on their own biases. In a study of a large professional services firm, being interviewed by a woman hurt the success rates for the more competent women (who might turn into competitors) (Bohnet, 2016). A study of gender quotas on academic hiring committees in Spain indicated that junior women panel members operated as if they were in competition with applicants and were less likely than men to hire women at the same career stage (Zinovyeva & Bagues, 2011). Female professors did not do this, perhaps because they no longer feared same-sex competition and were looking for allies (Bohnet, 2016).

3. **Define "good fit".** The idea of recruiting someone who is a "good fit" for the department is seductive, but can be problematic if this shorthand phrase is ill-defined. For sure, hire someone who is collegiate or possesses other explicit qualities which are necessary for the job, but make sure that "good fit" doesn't mean "someone like me" or "someone like everyone else who already works here". Where there is ambiguity, biases thrive.

4. **Interview candidates in batches.** If possible, recruit for multiple positions at the same time. Use comparative evaluation between candidates against explicit planned criteria because this focuses attention on the individual's performance rather than on stereotypes about their group. Making multiple hiring decisions at once has the additional benefit of encouraging recruiters to embrace variety (Bohnet, 2016).

5. **Use structured interviews based on a checklist so that every candidate is asked the same questions in order to reduce potentially biased subjective criteria.** Create a scoring system for the questions in advance and decide how each question should be weighted. Put this into a structured interview form to assist with note-taking. Resist the temptation to deviate from the interview schedule. As Bohnet notes, "the data showing that unstructured interviews do not work is overwhelming" (Bohnet, 2016). Meta-analysis indicates that combinations of tests of general mental ability, work sample tests and structured interviews are the best predictors of future job performance (Schmidt & Hunter, 1998).

6. **Choose skilled interviewers to be on the panel.** Check that the panel members have experience in interviewing, or have had some training. Subject expertise will not be sufficient.

7. **Don't interview as a panel.** Panel members should interview each candidate separately, with each

interviewer focusing on the same set of competences each time. Compared to the standard procedure, this requires a similar time commitment from each interviewer, but ensures that they get a longer period of quality time with each candidate to ask relevant questions and form an opinion. This procedure results in more independent data points about the candidate which helps to make an informed choice later. It requires a longer time commitment from the candidate to attend a series of interviews on different topics, but people are usually willing to do a lot for that dream job!

The panel member should assign scores for each candidate straight away to avoid bias creeping in when trying to recall characteristics of the interviewee. The notes and scores should not be shared with other panel members until just before the review meeting when everyone has written their notes.

8. **Consider other forms of assessment.** You could ask candidates to perform a job-related task to demonstrate their competence more authentically. For example, a software developer might solve a programming problem, or a lecturer might teach a short "class" as if to first-year students. Ask another colleague, not on the panel, to anonymise the test results. The panel reviews them, sorts them and then compares those results with the interview ratings. This procedure has been used within the Institute for Academic Development at the University of Edinburgh, where it made a big and positive difference. On at least three occasions, the task results meant that the person who performed best at interview didn't get the job – another candidate did. This has helped the Institute for Academic Development to make much better recruitment decisions.

9. **Review candidates together.** Once the interviews are complete, the panel convenes as a group to review scores and make hiring decisions. It is good practice to compare responses horizontally across the structured questions as you would when marking exam scripts so that the halo of one good answer doesn't influence the evaluation of an individual's performance on other questions.

10. **Don't settle for an "OK" candidate.** It can be helpful to have a group member with the role of "bar raiser" to ensure that the group doesn't settle for a comfortable consensus and hire someone who is unsuitable, to avoid widening the candidate search again. Academics on open-ended contracts will be around for a long time – don't spend the next twenty years managing someone who was never right for the job!

Advertise all opportunities large and small

Jane Norman

In every organisation there are lots of "additional tasks" to be done over and above the "day job" that people carry out. Some additional tasks are more high profile, require more specialised skills, are more desirable and are better rewarded than others. Many have a specific title, with a set of associated responsibilities. Almost all provide opportunities for staff to develop their skill set, experience and curriculum vitae. And carrying out small roles successfully gives individuals the confidence and track record to move on to bigger roles.

Universities are good about equality of opportunity when appointing to a new post. There is a job description and person specification, an advert, and equality of opportunity of application (see *Defining excellence* and *Gender balancing staff recruitment: attracting the right candidates*). Such strategies should also be employed (even internally) for titular roles within institutions such as Programme Director or Accessibility Officer. Several Schools in the University already follow this process.

This recipe is for whoever is charged with assigning the roles.

Ingredients

- A role that needs to be performed.
- All the people who could undertake the role.

- A means of communication with all the people who could undertake the role.
- Time to think through what the role requires, and to consider all the applications.

Method

1. **Decide what task needs to be done.** This is usually obvious – e.g. course organiser. It might be useful to group tasks together. If the role is vacant, it is worth considering whether the task still needs to be done, and whether it needs to be done in the same way.

2. **Decide what skills and experience are required for the role.** The lion tamer probably needs to have some experience with big cats, but having been to Africa may not be essential, even if the previous incumbents have been.

3. **Write the job role, and the essential and the desirable person specification, down.** This takes a bit of time, and is often missed, but "I will recognise it when I see it" is not the best approach, and if the task is important, it's just lazy. (If the task is not important, why are you trying to find someone to do it? See step 1 above.) Factoring in the extra time to write out the job role and person specification is well worth it.

4. **Advertise the role.** You may know just the person who would be great at this, but there may be others who would be even greater. Appointing without advertising (and considering all the applications) is a shortcut to implicit bias. The School of Divinity has taken the approach of emailing all academic staff to invite them to apply for internal roles. This may work well in other areas too.

5. **Encourage those who you think would be good at the role to apply.** Sometimes people need a bit of a push. Even if they don't put themselves forward this time, they might next time. It is also worth highlighting upcoming opportunities to line managers to reach a wider pool of potential applicants. (See *Raising your profile within your organisation*.)

6. **Consider all the applications.** Have a predefined process for reviewing the applications. It doesn't need to be too heavyweight for smaller internal roles, but it does need to be systematic, fair, and involve more than just your own opinion. (See *Unconscious bias*.)

7. **Be aware of workloads.** If someone is taking on a significant additional task or role, you will need to review their overall workload to avoid placing staff under too much pressure.

8. **Use this as a development opportunity for the near misses.** Good talent management involves encouraging people to develop, and helping them to address gaps in their training or experience. Give feedback to the applicants who didn't make it this time, so that they can work with their line manager or PDR (Performance Development Review) reviewer to develop the skills they were missing.

Women, competition and beliefs

Noémi Berlin

Women are under-represented in highly competitive top positions in corporations, in governments, and in academia such that they make up between 15% and 30% of these positions in most of the developed countries (see as an example figure 1 that shows women's share of employment in senior and middle managements). This share has increased since 1996, but very slowly. Moreover, the gender wage gap, despite some progress since 2006 still exists, such that in developed countries, for the same job, a man is likely to earn about 20% more than a woman.

For many years now, researchers have tried to come up with explanations for these gaps. Through different theories and observations, men and women are found to exhibit differences such as in the value given to the time spent with their children, a different perception of holding high-level positions (Gino et al., 2015), bargaining ability (Bowles et al., 2007; Mazei et al., 2015), or discrimination. Indeed, researchers have raised the question of role incongruity (Koenig et al., 2011), an inconsistency arising because women's expected characteristics (kindness, compassion, warmth) differ from the expected characteristics of a manager or a negotiator (assertive, competitive, demanding) which are usually considered as more masculine. Hence, women are not considered for these types of positions or are less likely to negotiate their wage, and end up with a lower position and salary. Those stereotypes impact the decisions of employers and make it harder for women to obtain leadership jobs.

As opposed to employers who decide to hire according to potential stereotypes, the way women behave or make their own education and career decisions can also explain those gender differences. Schuh et al. (2014) raise the issue of power motivation that they define as "an interpersonal difference in the desire to influence others (McClelland, 1985; Miner, 1975)". According to the authors, men have higher power motivation which would affect their aspiration level and consequently their leadership occupancy achievement, compared to women.

Recent work in behavioural economics has addressed other explanations for the lack of women in promoted posts. This paper focuses on one of them, which is that women avoid competition. If that is the case, women would choose to enter less-competitive tracks, hence missing the chance of succeeding in competitions that lead to higher positions on the labour market where they are then under-represented.

With a laboratory experiment methodology, and by using a simple task (adding five two-digit numbers) Niederle & Vesterlund (2007) show that when women and men are asked to enter a tournament or not, in which pay-offs would be earned conditional on winning the tournament, a significant gender gap appears. Men do enter the competition, while women self-select themselves out of entering it. It becomes even more surprising that this gender gap persists even when comparing the decisions of men and women of the same performance level. This non-optimal decision hence implies a loss in global welfare. The gender gap in competitive entry is robust and has been found in various later papers (for example: Datta Gupta et al., 2013; Booth & Nolen, 2012; Kamas & Preston, 2009; Vandegrift & Yavas, 2009; Ertac, 2011; Dohmen & Falk, 2011) which consider other types of tasks, look at different age groups and identify other circumstances such as the gender of the opponent. One interesting result from Gneezy et al. (2009)

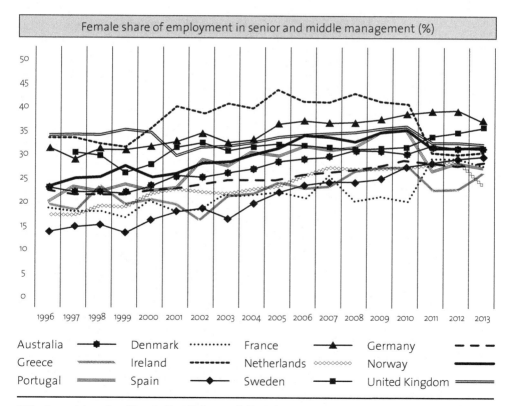

Table 1. Source: International Organisation of Labour, available statistics.

is that the gender gap in competition is reversed in a matriarchal society compared to a patriarchal one, showing that cultural differences and the way women are considered in society impact the competitive behaviours of both men and women.

In societies where gender differences are less in favour of women, the women seem to not enjoy competition even when they have the ability to benefit more from this "scheme". Different reasons for their competition avoidance have been studied in the literature such as risk attitudes or beliefs. Here we are interested in the latter.

Let's place ourselves into a general economics framework where one considers the decision to engage oneself in any kind of competition. That means one faces opponents and one has to perform better than them in order to win the competition. When analysing the decisions to compete or not, economists will consider self-confidence as the belief, which is a subjective probability, of succeeding in the task involved. Those beliefs will play an important role in the process of decision-making. The person making the decision will take into account all the available information in her environment: the opponents, the difficulty they think of the task, the setting (number of opponents, of rounds, etc), and how likely they think it is that they can win (self-confidence). If one has very low confidence in one's success, then one will avoid the tournament thinking that one will lose, even though it is objectively not true. We call this under-confidence. Over-confidence can of course also arise, implying an increase in the motivation in performing the task, with sometimes a higher risk of failing. And in a sense, failure might also be perceived differently by men and women.

When looking at the self-confidence of men and of women, a robust result is found such that men are usually more confident than women. Many psychologists found these results before the economists (Lichtenstein et al., 1982; Beyer, 1990; Beyer & Bowden, 1997; Pulford & Colman, 1997). Previous research shows that people are generally overconfident in diverse areas such as car-driving, investment decisions, entrepreneurial behaviour, running, stock market forecasts

(for example: Beckmann & Menkhoff, 2008; Bohnet, 2016; Croson & Gneezy, 2009; Deaves, 2010; Koellinger et al., 2007; Svenson, 1981). Even when both men and women are over-confident, men are even more over-confident than women. So it might be the case that this lack of self-confidence does not push women enough to choose competition.

One solution to increase confidence in this type of situation is to create competition in teams. A study by Healy & Pate (2011) shows that competing in two-person teams reduces the gender competition gap by two-thirds. Moreover, women prefer to compete in teams whatever the sex of their partner whereas men prefer to compete as individuals. Another study, Dargnies (2012), finds that high-ability men are reluctant to enter the competition in a team because they fear being the victim of a teammate's free-riding behaviour.

If we consider a real-life example such as choosing an educational track, it might be very well the case that in very selective tracks we observe fewer women not because they are discriminated against, nor because they have no taste for the track, but because they self-select themselves from not going into this track. They may choose one that they would think easier or in which they are more confident (Ayalon, 2003; Bettinger & Long, 2005). But everything is related, and the confidence they build may also be related to a stereotype threat that women (and men) integrate at very young ages (Spencer et al., 1999). For instance, if people believe that mathematics or sciences are for men and humanities are for women, then it is very likely you will find more men in the science tracks and women in the humanities tracks. If people believe that competition is for men rather than for women, men will be more likely to be found in competitive situations. The hard task is to be able to disentangle the actual taste for the discipline or the competition, from stereotype effects or competition avoidance based on wrong beliefs. A solution to this misallocation could be to provide people with better information. For instance, relative feedback on their performance should decrease the uncertainty, soften existing stereotypes, and might facilitate decision-making in a competitive environment and reduce the gender gap (see Bohnet, 2016). However, the psychology literature suggests that women incorporate negative information more than men, with the opposite occurring for positive information (for example, Roberts & Nolen-Hoeksema, 1989). In economics, Berlin & Dargnies (2012) tend to confirm this result such that women seem to respond more strongly to the information they receive and especially to negative information. Hence, non-optimal self-selection because of negative information is found more for women than men, which means that providing information also has some drawbacks. It could very well be the case that women and men seek and value information differently. It seems that women exhibit a demand for information when they already know about the level of their ability whereas men will ask for information if they are uncertain of their abilities.

Why do we observe this discrepancy in beliefs and in demand for information? Are there any other ways to encourage women to choose to compete in the workplace when it is actually more beneficial than not to compete? It is a very complex issue. On the one hand, we do observe that men and women would react in different ways according to the same information they receive which has an impact on decisions they might make. Because we observe this difference, it does not mean, on the other hand, that women need to be treated differently. Because men and women do not differ in their ability level, one has to improve the information process made by women so they can make more optimal decisions for their career and manage to reach the same status as men, if that is what they wish for.

Maybe it is the case that women take too much account of what others think of them, which is not the case for men. To our knowledge, even though results on the analysis of beliefs tend to point in that direction, there are no clear results. Moreover, evolving in an environment mainly dominated by men is not easy. Women can be judged for not meeting role stereotypes, and both men and women can expect a specific behaviour from women

that they would not expect from men (likeability, ability in some fields) which makes the stereotype threat a real issue (see role incongruity discussed earlier). You may even hear that women either have to become a "shark" and more aggressive, scaring their female and male counterparts to achieve higher positions, or that they are not affirmative enough and can be eaten by the "sharks", whatever their gender.

Particular attention should be paid to situations where incorrect self-selection can arise. Every time an individual self-selects herself from continuing to the most difficult track and chooses an easier option, authorities and policies should make sure this choice is not based on biased beliefs (underestimation). Not all women and men have the ability or aspiration to reach top positions, but because we know that men are no better than women, tools for women should be developed so they can overcome their fear of competition. Equality in that case is not a question of saying that men or women are the same but that, when the same objective measures between a man and a woman are observed (such as abilities), the same behaviour should also be observed. However, as Gino et al. say about existing data:

> We cannot make value judgments about whether men's and women's differing views of professional advancement are good or bad, rational or irrational, at any level of analysis (e.g., for individuals, for organizations, or for societies). It is possible that men and women are correctly predicting the unique experiences that they are poised to encounter upon professional advancement and are making sound decisions accordingly. (Gino et al., 2015)

What maybe matters is that women manage to do what men do, if that is what they want.

The understanding of these different mechanisms will hopefully provide insights for policymaking to drive men's and women's behaviours towards situations in which each are satisfied, and leading eventually, in a few years, to a significant decrease in the gender gap.

Proactive promotion

Jon Turner, John Ravenscroft
& Lara Isbel

In 1991 the number of female professors of physics in the UK doubled: it went from one to two! By 2009/10, it had risen to 36 – clearly a huge improvement. But that is still 36 out of a total of 650 professors of physics. (Tapping all our Talents, 2012)

The above report was published by the Royal Society of Edinburgh in 2012 but there continues to be a much lower proportion of women in senior academic roles such as senior lecturer, reader and professor compared to the proportion of women in lecturer and postdoctoral researcher posts in most academic disciplines.

One factor which may be influencing the relatively low proportion of women at senior grades is the promotion process. Fewer women than men apply for promotions. Similar to recruitment, when you start with a gender imbalance in the applicant pool it is very difficult to change this without unfairly discriminating against the majority group.

Several schools in the University have made changes to their promotion processes to reduce the pressure on individuals to nominate themselves for promotion. This is not positive discrimination. The aim is to ensure that all those who should be considered for promotion are considered.

There are benefits to organisations in addressing this issue. Taking a more proactive approach to recognising the qualities and skills that individuals could bring to leadership roles can demonstrate that there are many different ways to be a successful leader. This may increase the appeal of senior roles to a wider pool of people (women and men) held back by narrow perceptions or experiences of how senior staff 'should' act or the level of performance required to be promoted to those roles. It can also mean organisations are more likely to reward and recognise talented people who feel uncomfortable or boastful talking about their successes.

Putting systems in place to support people to apply for promotion can turn the experience from something which causes anxiety and frustration into one that is supportive and enabling: this is better for everyone.

Ingredients

- Annual cycle of academic promotions, and annual reviews and performance development reviews.
- Job descriptions and information on achievement and contribution for all staff.
- Process by which manager and/or head of school or service can identify potential cases for promotion without depending on self-nomination.
- Senior colleagues who can mentor and support people through the promotion process.

Method

1. **Clearly communicate the level of performance or achievements required for promotion** to different grades so staff know what to work towards and prioritise. Academic grade profiles can be a helpful starting point. For academic posts, it is likely people will need evidence of achievement in research, in teaching and in academic citizenship and engagement. Where possible, provide examples of achievements relevant to your discipline. This can provide a useful benchmark and help people to judge their progress. The University's 'Exemplars of Excellence in Student Education' (UoE Exemplars, 2015) and the Teaching Matters website (http://www.ed.ac.uk/staff/teaching-matters) are useful resources to explore.

2. **Discuss promotion and career development as part of everyone's annual review/performance development review.** The School of Engineering and the School of Biomedical Sciences introduced this as part of their Athena SWAN action plan. Most university HR (human resource) departments provide guidance and training sessions for reviewers on how to have effective development conversations.

3. **Take time to discuss and recognise achievement**s. Some people are very confident in talking about their achievements; others would rather have their teeth pulled out. As a reviewer, look at the evidence for achievements – and tell people when they are down-playing their experience compared to their peers.

4. **Identify senior staff members who can advise on the process**. The Moray House School of Education have senior mentors who help and support colleagues to prepare their promotion applications, particularly the job matching forms. Feedback on how to build a narrative around your experience and achievements, and the level of evidence to provide, can be particularly useful.

5. **Systematically consider all eligible candidates for promotion in each round**. The Roslin Institute and the School of Biomedical Sciences now do this as standard. This reduces the need for people to self-nominate and ensures that all potential candidates are considered to see which meet the criteria for promotion. In these departments, if the case for promotion is confirmed it is submitted through the normal process to college/support group committees.

6. **Fair promotion process**. Transparency is important. Do you have clear guidelines on what to submit for

promotion, the criteria used to assess application, how decisions are made and who makes the decision? Is there also guidance on how to appeal a decision or resubmit an application? Providing briefing sessions to staff and nominating experienced people who can answer promotion-related queries can make the process less daunting.

7. **Give constructive feedback**. If someone has been unsuccessful in the promotion round, providing guidance on specific reasons why with advice on how to address this in future applications is helpful. Being knocked back from promotion can be difficult news. It is harder to move on from with limited feedback.

8. **Track who you are promoting**. Does the gender balance of the people receiving promotions and additional increments generally reflect the gender balance of your department? How long does it take people to be promoted to different grades? If there are any unexpected trends, these may be worth exploring further.

9. **Be mindful of the salary gap**. Does your school have a significant disparity in pay for men and women on the same grade with equivalent levels of experience? What steps can you take to rectify this?

Cooks tips

Not everyone wants to be promoted. This is fine. It is important that there is an equal opportunity to apply and that the process is fair and transparent, but individuals shouldn't feel pressured into progressing to more senior roles. We fully acknowledge that you can have a successful and rewarding career at any grade.

Defining excellence

Lara Isbel

A friend was unexpectedly asked to judge the best cow competition at a highland show. A city girl with very little in the way of cow judging expertise, she was understandably apprehensive. The organiser reassured her: "It's really straightforward. Here is the checklist of what to look for". Sure enough: the length of the back, height and so on were all neatly described. She managed to pick out the most outstanding cow, prizes were awarded and celebrations commenced.

Sadly, she used the same checklist in the best pig competition and all ended in disaster.

On a more serious point, who defines excellence in institutions? How do YOU define it and what criteria do you use? How often do you stop to question the factors that are influencing your decisions? As an institution, words like 'excellence' and 'outstanding' and 'world-leading' crop up all over the place: strategic plans, job adverts, promotion applications. Institutions can seem to demand excellence in everything, all at the same time. This puts people under pressure, but also in the dark about what to focus on and what to prioritise.

Ingredients

- Honesty.
- Consistency.
- Critical perspective.
- Open-mindedness.
- An awareness of your own bias.

Method

1. **What are you talking about when you talk about excellence?** Be specific. On a practical level, how would someone provide evidence of excellence? Are the best indicators being selected, or the ones that are easy to quantify? How will you give weight to things that are important rather than easy to measure? Are the measures you use current and fresh? Jobs change – have your criteria?

2. **Be aware of historical biases in your department.** Attitude is crucial, but research shows that we unconsciously recruit in our own image (Bohnet, 2016). If you explore the kind of characteristics that would 'fit' best in your department or in a leadership role, or would be worthy of promotion, are there any that are stereotypically associated with particular groups? How do you talk about the attitudes and qualities you value? Whose successes do you tend to notice or be more aware of?

3. **Check with colleagues.** How would they define excellence or fit? Does it match your view? Getting different perspectives could help you to pick out any blind spots and focus on what's most important for the role and for the department and to develop criteria which are fair.

4. **Notice and share examples of 'excellent performance' – particularly where it is harder to quantify.** Grade profiles, explicit definitions and concrete examples of the level of performance required for certain roles or promotions can give people tangible things to work towards and more confidence in their own abilities.

5. **Be realistic.** Staff are being asked to do more and more tasks, often requiring a broader range of skills. Excellence across every domain may not be feasible, especially as roles get broader. The vast majority of our staff are driven, have high standards and aspire to be excellent. This is no bad thing, but if expectations are unrealistic this can leave people feeling under enormous pressure and at risk of burnout. Where is 'excellence' important, and where is 'good enough' perfectly acceptable? Is the workload manageable in reality?

6. **Be clear about the priorities and the benchmarks.** Being brilliant at everything at all times is unattainable. The crucial thing is knowing what to focus on when. This can depend on career stage and experience. Careers are long, requiring different strategies – sometimes building and consolidating expertise, sometimes actively seeking new responsibilities. Support people to plan their career development in a sustainable and manageable way – don't expect or ask for the moon! Use annual reviews to reflect and re-evaluate, particularly when someone is preparing for promotion.

7. **Give people time and space to develop expertise and confidence.** Learn how to give encouraging feedback as well as constructive criticism. Academic careers can be full of knock-backs and rejections. If you notice people are doing things well and making progress, tell them. 'Excellence' is often a work in progress: are you giving people a boost or dragging them down?

8. **Actively support a great working environment.** A productive and inspiring culture where people feel supported, valued and able to do their best work can reap massive rewards in terms of job satisfaction, well-being and productivity. But this takes time, attention and a surprisingly large amount of tedious

and often invisible admin. Is 'community building' work split equally? Does everyone pitch in supporting colleagues, running seminar series and events, welcoming new staff? Are you noticing, thanking and acknowledging people who contribute? Don't underestimate the cumulative effect of small actions: they shape the culture.

9. **Put your money where your mouth is.** Are the tasks staff are told to prioritise to develop their careers aligned with reward and selection processes? If not, your workplace may end up with two sets of guidelines: the 'official' priorities versus the 'unofficial' things you should really focus on to have any hope of getting promoted. This can leave people feeling understandably cynical. Be upfront and transparent about what is required so people know where they stand.

10. **Reflect on your decisions, particularly when you are assessing another person's performance.** If there are several ways to define excellence in an area, are the criteria flexible enough to accommodate this? What are the criteria for being a great judge? Are you reaching it?

Cooks tips

This recipe is particularly useful for new leaders, or when assessing applications for a new role or promotion.

University of Edinburgh grade profiles, and useful resources like the 'Exemplars of Excellence in Student Education' and guidance related to excellence in interdisciplinary work can be found here:

http://www.ed.ac.uk/ human-resources/ pay-reward/ promotions-grading/ academic-staff/ procedures-criteria

Career progression on a shoestring

Anonymous

Returning to work after one or more periods of maternity/paternity leave brings with it a host of considerations related to how that work will take shape or form now that life has changed so much. There can suddenly feel like a lot more work and a lot less time to do it in. Plus there are now additional 'constraints' (beautiful, grubby, lovely, and demanding constraints) on previously 'free' time which could have been dedicated to work.

Career progression can seem particularly problematic, especially as progression typically involves taking on extra roles or responsibilities (which require more time) and delivering on these (which also requires significant time and dedication) at a time when there have never been more demands and stress placed on your seemingly measly 24 hours a day (e.g. O'Laughlin & Bischoff, 2005; Bianchi & Milkie, 2010; Aiston & Jung, 2015).

So how can a new mum or dad (perhaps for the second or third time) still make some headway with career progression on such a tight time budget?

Ingredients

- Pen and paper or laptop.
- Your University strategy document.
- A good pinch of reflection.
- Some quality coaching and mentoring.

Method

1. Consider your professional work values – what are the ultimate ways in which you desire to behave in your working environment? It can help to undertake a values clarification activity to do this. A coach or mentor can help you focus on these.

2. Consider how these values underpin your overall vision and mission as a professional (i.e. what is it you are working towards or trying to make a difference to?)

3. Identify the main objectives of your working role (e.g. research; external engagement; learning and teaching; leadership and management).

4. Identify the goals and action plans which will allow your role to grow in the direction you want to. Ask yourself what you find most enjoyable about your job.

5. As long as your goals and actions are broadly in line with the overall strategy of your employer, you can be sure that you are progressing your career, while developing in an organic way that matches and you don't have to compromise on your core values.

You can find the University of Edinburgh mission statement at http://www.ed.ac.uk/about/mission-governance/mission

Different schools within the University offer a range of mentoring (see Mentoring Connections website: http://www.ed.ac.uk/human-resources/learning-development/mentoring-connections) and coaching opportunities (see *Career coaching for individuals*). In fact, R(D)SVS (the Royal (Dick) School of Veterinary Studies) and the Roslin Institute offer specific mentoring for those returning from parental leave. The Schools of Molecular, Genetic and Population Health Sciences, and Clinical Sciences have a "buddying" system for those returning from parental leave to get support from peers.

Cook's tip

It can be helpful to think of your career progression as a 'tree' with your values as the nutrients in the soil, your vision and mission forming the trunk, your objectives as the main branches and your goals and action plans as the smaller branches and leaves. You can even have more than one tree and grow your own orchard!

Warning

Beware of the trend for employment negotiations to favour men compared to women (Bowles et al., 2005; Castilla & Benard, 2010) and note that this does not have to be the 'norm' (Golding & Rouse, 2000; Bohnet et al., 2012; Bowles et al., 2005).

Research isn't the only route

Anonymous
(As told to Judy Robertson.)

This recipe is about the experiences of one of our colleagues (let's call her Juliet) who works in academic development, supporting all disciplines throughout the university.

The recipe starts with a pivotal moment in Juliet's life when she decided to change her career track from research in molecular biology to a teaching and learning support role within the University. Her decision was made for positive reasons and she is now thriving personally and professionally. This story highlights the important point that talented and well-qualified women have agency in their own careers and that therefore the onus is on universities to make the working environment attractive enough to entice them to work there.

We know from a recent study of attitudes to professional advancement that women tend to have more life goals, and a wider spectrum of goal types than men (Gino et al., 2015). The female participants in that study felt equally capable of achieving professional advancement and assuming powerful roles – it's just that they found this less desirable. They had other things to do with their lives. The STEM (science, technology, engineering and mathematics) leaky pipeline is a problem for universities: year on year they are losing much of their talent pool. It isn't necessarily a problem for the women themselves.

When I was writing up my PhD at home, I spent hours at the computer, with my daughter pestering me so much that I wondered: "Why is she acting so needy?" and then I realised. She had been missing me.

During all that time when I was doing my research – working early, working late, working weekends – she was being ignored. Due to the nature of my research in molecular biology, experiments are very intensive. If you want a 24-hour growth curve, you need to get yourself a camp bed in the lab and wake yourself up every 30 minutes. While I was looking after my cells, my husband was looking after my daughter. In a way, she had done both degrees with me.

Now I was pregnant again and I suddenly thought I couldn't do this for another child. I asked myself whether I would be able to regulate my working hours to 9 – 5, and my answer was "no", not even if I had the self-awareness to try. I had only ever known two part-time researchers in my field: it wasn't the norm. You wouldn't be able to get the results doing part-time. I also realised I wouldn't be able to control my need/desire to get the results. I had seen a lot of people in the lab become obsessed by it. They were so interested in finding out, and refining their ideas that they forgot everything else as I had done.

What could I do? I had to find another job which I would love too. I had some experience of teaching in the department. I enjoyed this, and was progressing fast, getting roles which other PhD students didn't get.

That might be a solution, but I then realised there were very few teaching-only roles available. It is hard to compete with someone who has a full research profile even if you are a fantastic teacher. What seems to matter is whether you can bring the research funding in.

I needed to think sideways – what other jobs could I do with my skills? I looked around and realised that there were roles within study skills and academic development which were a good fit. I got a job in a department that works in academic development. I love my new occupation and have had several roles around skills and

academic development in the department since joining. I have had a huge number of experiences and developed skills that I would never have had if I had I stayed in research.

I am constantly learning new things, and responding to new challenges. In fact, when a possible teaching job within my old department came up, I didn't apply. I realised I would be bored by it. Working within a department that is about development has had a huge impact on me personally and professionally.

I have become much more self-aware and reflective; importantly, I implement change based on reflection, so I find myself constantly developing both in work and at home. Hopefully, the benefits are not just for me, but have knock-on effects for those around me, family, friends and colleagues.

Ingredients

- Honesty.
- Self-awareness.
- An open mind.

Method

1. **Acknowledge when there is a problem.** Now I am more reflective and take stock of life. I try to have an ongoing awareness of balancing all aspects of my life. When I was doing my PhD, I didn't think: "Does this fit with me and my family?" It is useful to reflect from time to time, and to identify when you are feeling unhappy with your situation.

2. **Consider the impact your choices have on those around you.** Focusing purely on work is to the detriment of everything else. Taking time to move your focus away and notice "life" happening around you can enhance your life or at least let you make a start at it – and life is for living!

3. **Consider what your wider skills are and look further than what the seemingly obvious career path is.** Maybe your

"dream job" isn't really so dreamy after all. Your PhD has given you a valuable set of skills: I know my PhD has enabled me to quickly pick up an issue, analyse it and decide what to do. Look carefully at job ads and think about how they relate to your research experience. For example, your experience in overseeing and ordering lab equipment is an example of budget management. Attend a careers service course on career management to help you consider what you want in your next job – don't be blinkered. The careers service also holds records of graduate destinations which can give you new ideas of what you could do. Alumni networks can also be helpful.

4. **Consider: are you suffering from martyr syndrome?** Academics put up with too much. It is sometimes a badge of honour to work too much and it can give you a chip on your shoulder. Is the work really necessary? Could you be suffering from imposter syndrome where you feel you always have to work harder so you don't get "found out"? Imposter syndrome, which refers to the usually unfounded anxiety that you are an incompetent fraud, is not uncommon among highly capable academics, particularly women (Hutchins & Rainbolt, 2016). See also: *Dealing with imposter syndrome.*

5. **For principal investigators: don't imply students who follow other careers have failed.** When I decided to give up research, I wondered how to tell my principal investigator. He loved science too. He seemed distraught if his students didn't want to do research. It would be helpful if supervisors could instead encourage their students to consider a range of careers from the outset and help them to build their skills accordingly, for example by valuing inquisitiveness and skills such as logical analysis of situations, and the development of processes. If everyone could do that, we'd be in Star Trek.

6. **For universities: consider different funding models.** To encourage more people to stay in academia as researchers, change the funding model. Departments could have a fund which every researcher is entitled to, as has been piloted in some universities. This would take the pressure off getting results and enable longer term research. It's not just that women leave academia. Talented researchers, men and women, move to industry where they have open-ended contracts, 9 – 5 jobs, good equipment and funding, more staff and no worries that the lab will collapse without the next grant.

Since Juliet received her PhD, various schools at Edinburgh University have been working on trying to improve the career routes for new researchers to make working in academia a more attractive proposition. For example, the Roslin Institute has invested in Career Track fellowships which fund a research assistant, budget and one internal and one external mentor. This is intended to support an academic to get started, and reduce the burden of lab work so that he or she can have more flexibility in how they spend their time.

Raising your profile within your organisation

Lara Isbel & Sara Shinton

Academic disciplines are international communities. At early stages in your career it is important to raise your profile in your chosen field and there are often many opportunities to do so. The benefits of raising your profile within your organisation, particularly outside your discipline can be overlooked.

Universities tend to have a lot of working groups, task groups, committees and a whole range of other events where academics can present or contribute. There is an expectation that academic staff will contribute at some point to university committees etc. If you see it as a chance to develop your wider career, this can be a positive opportunity rather than a chore. It can also potentially open up new career options and be a chance to meet interesting colleagues you may never have come across otherwise.

However, it can be hard to find the right people to invite to participate in these opportunities, particularly as everyone already has far too many emails. This can result in the 'usual suspects' being asked repeatedly, some people agreeing to get involved with things because they feel they have to and others feeling annoyed that they weren't asked.

Academic roles are increasingly varied. Taking time to identify how the different aspects of your role could align can make it easier to manage workloads – and expectations.

Ingredients

- Time to think.
- A friend or mentor (optional).
- Confidence to ask for things, and to say no.

Method

1. **Define your priorities.** Take a sheet of paper and draw five columns, one for research, one for learning and teaching, one for external engagement, one for the University and one for your personal vision and values. Write down your top areas of interest in each one. The 'general University-related' column can cover whatever most interests you, e.g. widening participation for undergraduate students, research training for postdocs, sustainability, gender equality, international partnerships, assessment and feedback etc.

2. **Adapt and flex your interests.** How could your interest in a topic be adapted to fit the different domains of academic roles? For example, if you are very interested in public engagement, are there any crossovers with teaching? Or opportunities to join committees or working groups to raise the profile of public engagement in your school? Or apply for public engagement funding?

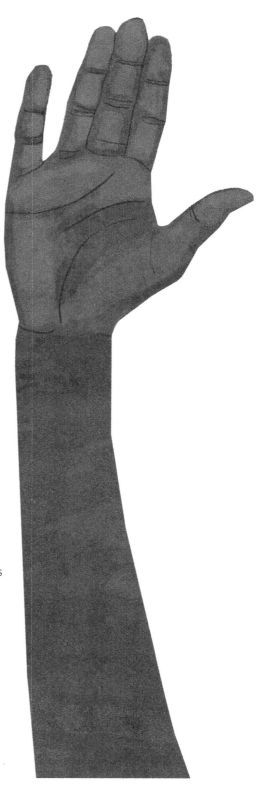

Explore all the angles you can see to working on this area of interest. Do the same with other areas you have identified. Are there any new opportunities which could be worth exploring? Look for overlaps.

3. **Consider your options.** Write down the most promising opportunities to develop your areas of interest. This might be responding to a call from a funder, teaching or developing a new course or module, doing consultancy or getting involved in a festival event, arranging a meeting with someone with expertise in that area, etc.

4. **Prepare, then review an initial plan.** Of the options you have identified, which ones are most appealing? Are they things you can implement now or do you need to do a bit of work to develop them further? Do you have a sense of how you would like the different aspects of your role to link together? How far are you from that? What is a realistic timescale for getting there? Then check this with a critical friend. What have you missed? Are you being realistic?

5. **Who can help?** Review your network and think about who you know in each area. Are there any gaps? Make an effort to find out more about the University by asking people for their insights and to share their networks.

6. **Look for starting points.** Could you present or chair at some internal meetings to build confidence? Do you know any people currently working on projects that you are interested in? You could meet them for a coffee and find out more about what's involved. Could you apply for a small grant to run a pilot workshop or activity? Ask people for ideas about how you could get started.

7. **Articulate your ambitions.** If there aren't current opportunities, what three things do you want people to know about you? For researchers in your field, those three things might be entirely based on your research priorities. For colleagues in a more general university role, it could be a much broader summary. Once you have your summary, then tell people! This is a simple but incredibly effective strategy. You don't even need to be very good at networking – just find people who are super networkers or have a coordinator role and get on their radar. In a huge university, people who are on the lookout for staff to involve in working groups etc often ask colleagues, particularly those in coordinator-type roles, if they can suggest anyone. If people know you are interested in a particular topic, particularly in the 'general University-related' space, they will usually try to connect you to relevant opportunities. Make it easy for people to help you.

8. **Say no to things which don't fit your interests (where possible).** Getting involved in wider University projects is usually fairly inevitable. If you are proactive about it and choose projects which align with your interests this has a double benefit: the projects may well support other areas of your work and be more interesting, and it also means you can say no to other committees or roles with no guilt as you are already making a contribution.

9. **Plan your exit strategy.** If you do something a few times, it can be a great learning experience. If you are volunteering for the same thing twenty times, it might be worth reconsidering if something else might be a better learning opportunity or a little more interesting.

Career coaching for individuals

Helen Sang

The engine of research in biological studies is the PhD student/postdoctoral scientist body. It is very challenging for an individual to move from being a postdoc to becoming a principal investigator (PI), and, once a lecturer, to progress up the academic career ladder. The opportunity to step outside day-to-day work and line management to reflect on goals and progress with a coach can make a huge difference.

This recipe explains the steps used at the Roslin Institute to get the career coaching scheme up and running. Be aware that it can be expensive when done with external providers – the cost can be as much as £300 per person.

Ingredients

- Money (so that the department can pay for the coaching).

- An individual who wants to develop themselves.

- A clear-headed experienced independent person to make the selection.

- A supportive environment – including a supportive line manager – to facilitate the outcomes of the coaching experience.

- A qualified coach.

Method

1. Find the people who will put most into coaching, and benefit most from it. Advertise the opportunity for coaching. In their applications, individuals must describe their reasons for wanting coaching. Have the selection done by an independent person, based on the applicants' reasons.

2. Set up the beginning and end parameters of the coaching process.

3. Coachees must be allowed time set aside for coaching. Line managers should be aware of the coaching process and encourage coachees to implement their plans.

4. Individual coaches work with coachees to identify their personal challenges in career aims and ambitions.

5. Individuals develop action plans, seek additional training opportunities, and in turn give better support to workplace colleagues.

6. Close the organisational learning loop. Coaches can give feedback to the organisation on how in-house career development support could be improved. Remember that individuals' experiences must be kept confidential.

Additional notes

This recipe focuses on working with external coaches and this is always a potential option for departments and line managers to consider. There are also a number of trained internal coaches in the University, most of whom are based in the Institute for Academic Development, the Business School and University Human Resources (HR) Services.

Working with an internal coach can be more cost-effective (this is usually part of someone's role and is not normally a service with an additional fee). Having a coach who is familiar with the University culture can be a benefit for some clients.

A research fellow in the Roslin Institute participated in a coaching programme from the Institute for Academic Development. Here are some of her reflections on the experience:

I started coaching without having a clue what coaching was about. Now, some years later, I know that this was one of the best presents the University of Edinburgh has given me. I am really grateful to my coach who helped me to understand initially what I wanted work-wise and then how to get there. In a very short time I became more effective, efficient and confident.

With coaching I managed to deal in a productive way with all the obstacles I came across. With reflection and good guiding I overcame the confusion and stress I had regarding my workplace and I became more motivated.

My coach provided the voice of logic when I could not see things clearly, and helped me understand the culture – not always straightforward since I come from a different background. She supported me through difficult personal times of loss, and helped me to create a good work-life balance during and after my pregnancy.

I met almost all my coaching targets, and I highly recommend the process to anyone who wants to advance their career and have a balanced life.

Talking about your achievements

Lara Isbel

It is not enough to do great work: to progress in your career – you also need to be able to talk about it. Writing CVs, and applying for promotion, funding or other opportunities often require you to describe your achievements and experience. This process can be cringe-worthy (a very Scottish emotion – often referred to as "the Celtic Cringe") and uncomfortable for some people (see *Dealing with imposter syndrome*). There can be an inner aversion to anything which seems boastful or shameless self-promotion, and also a justifiable nervousness about the 'double bind' (Bateson, 1972) that women in academia often face (see *Likeability and the double bind*) where likeability and competence are seen as incompatible (Fiske et al., 2002).

While humility certainly goes a long way in a lot of areas in life, there are times when it helps to be able to shine. Describing your accomplishments accurately and positively is important. It is not about selling yourself (or your principles) but demonstrating the impact you have had.

Ingredients

- Time to reflect.
- Paper or a laptop to make notes.
- Trusted people who can give you constructive feedback.
- Willingness to feel a bit uncomfortable.

Methods

1. **List your achievements.** Think back to the roles you have held in the past, or aspects of your current job. What are you most proud of? Write as long a list as you can.

2. **Write a short summary of each one.** The CAR acronym (Context, Action, Result) is useful for this. Focus on the result section. It's not what you did – it's the difference you made. Think about who benefited from this piece of work, or the wider impact it had. Include that in your summary. Write some keywords for the skills or experience each achievement relates to make it easier to pick out relevant examples.

3. **Use positive language.** Be bold (while still truthful): 'led', 'delivered', 'achieved' can have more impact than 'helped to', 'tried', 'contributed to', depending on the context. For inspiration, look at how colleagues describe their expertise on their CVs, profile pages or LinkedIn summaries. Don't feel intimated by other people's successes though: behind every glittering super-amazing CV there will be failures too. Jobs or grants that a person didn't get, projects that didn't go according to plan. All you are seeing is a carefully curated snapshot. What phrases or statements stand out or make a strong impression?

Experiment with the language you use to describe your achievements.

4. **Select relevant examples**. Pay close attention to what you need to demonstrate to be successful for the job or funding opportunity etc. and choose the most important, relevant examples. Less is often more; you don't need to list everything you've ever achieved in your whole career.

5. **Get feedback from trusted people**. Peers and mentors can be useful for this. It is often much easier to see someone else's strengths than your own. If you can, try to get feedback from people who have a lot of experience in recruitment or sit on promotion panels or grant funding schemes. They could help you by reviewing applications you have written or giving you a mock interview. If you feel your application or interview response is accurate but peers, mentors or colleagues tell you that you are downplaying your experience, trust them. Experiment some more with the language. Don't be discouraged if it feels a bit uncomfortable – it's a new approach so it is likely to be unfamiliar.

6. **Practise saying it out loud.** As well as writing short concise statements, preparing short pitches about your expertise can stand you in good stead. This could be for a job interview, but also networking at events. If there is an area you are keen to get more experience in, having a good, brief story about your interests can open doors. Saying it out loud over and over again, (this could be when driving the car or washing the dishes), helps embed it until it sounds easy and natural.

7. **Celebrate success.** Recognising the difference you made after the time and effort you put in can make your job more rewarding, and also make things feel more like 'real' accomplishments. Championing others, particularly junior colleagues and noticing their achievements can support a positive working environment. When accomplishments are celebrated as a matter of course, writing or talking about them becomes less cringe-worthy and more of a natural reflection of the progress you've made because of the time, energy, care and effort you put into your work.

Salary negotiation

Judy Robertson & Alison Williams

We should make sure that, when they leave university, all of our women graduates know and understand salary negotiation skills. And because we firmly believe that institutions shouldn't exploit people, let's make sure that anyone in charge of a hiring process understands how gender relates to salary negotiation.

According to the University and College Union (UCU), there is a 16.4% gender pay gap in the UK despite equal pay legislation being in force for forty years (UCU, 2016). The gap is slightly less in higher education at 12.3%, and it tends to increase at higher grades. At Edinburgh, the gender pay gap across all staff grades is 4%: the average woman member of staff earns £1,814 a year less than the average male member of staff (UCU, 2016). Over a career of forty years, this is worth over £70,000. What would you spend the back pay on?

Of course, it's not just an issue in academia – there are eye-watering salary differentials in many industries. For example, in technology jobs, women earn around £17K a year less than men (Mediaworks). And in case you're not already completely in despair, try this: there is a motherhood pay penalty (Budig, 2015). Yes, that is as depressing as it sounds – women who are mothers earn less than women who are not mothers. Sadly, there is also a fatherhood pay premium.

A report by AAUW (American Association of University Women) found that it takes mothers an extra five months to earn what fathers earn in a year (AAUW, 2016).

There are many complex societal reasons for this inequity which we will not go into here. But you're not powerless to change your own circumstances, and the first step is to ask for more. It is vitally important for a woman to negotiate her salary in her first job because if she doesn't, she will start her career earning less than her male counterparts, and the gap will be compounded over the years. Half of the readers may be thinking: "Well of course you negotiate a salary – duh!" Other readers might be thinking: "Oh, but I couldn't possibly do that. I should just be grateful to get a job".

When Judy started working, she was in the latter group. It simply didn't occur to her to do anything except to accept the employer's first offer. In general, women tend to negotiate salary less frequently, and ask for less money when they do (Bohnet, 2016). This is because there are societal expectations about how women are "meant" to behave. Studies show that managers are less likely to want to work with female employees who had asked for a pay increase, but this was not the case for such a request from a male employee (Bohnet, 2016). It is the price for being seen to violate gender norms. This recipe is about how to negotiate a salary, and also how to create an environment where women don't pay a social price for doing so.

Ingredients

- A spark of indignation or burning sense of injustice (adjust to taste).
- Facts about salaries in your sector.
- Steely resolve to ignore any childhood socialisation about how "ladies don't mention money".

Method

1. **Find out what the average salary is in your sector.** This external legitimacy can give you confidence in asking for your starting salary. You can use the average to anchor your request in a reasonable range. In academia, you could use the UCU Rate for the Job website (https://www.ucu.org. uk/ratefortjejob) for information on expected salaries at various stages.

2. **If you're recruiting staff, advertise the expected salary range in the job particulars.** Add the phrase "salary negotiable" to the advert. Transparency is required because gender bias thrives with ambiguity. If women are given information about the range of wages for the position, they are as good at negotiation as men (Bohnet, 2016).

3. **Ask for a salary increase when you switch jobs.** When Judy last moved job, she spent a sleepless night trying to work out what salary increase she should ask for after receiving the initial offer. To save you the effort, 15% seems to be about right (Miller & Miller, 2011). In fact, this is what the University did offer her, so she could have enjoyed her sleep instead.

4. **These three qualities for successful negotiation cropped up in Judy's desperate nocturnal reading: be confident, be prepared and be willing to walk away** (Miller & Miller, 2011, p. 16). You need confidence to reach an agreement, and to convince the other party that your request is based on an accurate understanding of the facts, it is fair and it will benefit you both. Part of being confident is not being apologetic about your position, or weakening your argument by saying: "I may be wrong but...". You can prepare by thinking through your priorities and

goals – perhaps what really matters to you is flexible working or a good holiday allowance – but know your bottom line and be prepared to reject an offer which does not meet it. "You do need to understand the value of what you bring to the table and refuse to accept less" (Miller & Miller, 2011, p. 16).

5. **Be persistent – don't give up at the first attempt.** When Alison was invited to take over running an undergraduate seminar programme at a university which shall remain nameless, the assumption was that she would work on the basis of pre-existing expenses and a small honorarium. Running the entire programme, however, involved a lot of work: planning, facilitating, formative and summative marking, and student guidance. The university didn't seem minded to be generous – or even fair – and was trading on her love of the work, and her desire to keep the programme running.

   Complaining to a woman friend that "they want to pay me peanuts" there was a pause, and then the reply: "I've always thought of you as more of a pistachio person, myself". Alison went back to the university with a fair, not extravagant, pistachio proposal. The thought "I'm a pistachio person" (confident of the value she was bringing

– see point 4 above) carried her through two attempts to knock her back: and the pistachio proposal was accepted.

6. **Review your salary against the sector average and compare your work to promotion criteria regularly to avoid stagnation.** You can frame it in terms of someone else's suggestion if you prefer: "My team leader suggested I talk to you about a pay rise" (Bohnet, 2016). You could request someone to negotiate on your behalf if the whole thing gives you the horrors.

7. **If you're a senior manager, make sure there are routine procedures through which all staff can apply for a pay increase with transparent guidance about what is required.** At the University of Edinburgh, there is an annual timetable for regrading, promotion and one-off contribution payments (Reward Processes Timetable, 2016). Consider all applications systematically, and if you're really serious about closing the gender pay gap, consider all staff for grade increases whether they have applied for them or not. Evidence across the University of Edinburgh Athena SWAN applications and the senior mangers' focus groups shows that women are less likely to apply for promotion or compensation than men: they may need encouragement to apply.

If you really want to put your money where your mouth is, do what the University of Essex did and increase women professors' grades by three points to raise their average salaries to those of male professors (Times HE, 2016).

Get an international audience for your research without leaving your office

Martyn Pickersgill

International invitations to visit other universities and speak at conferences are a key way of disseminating your research and showing international impact – and hence represent a major criterion for promotion to senior (reader/professor) university positions. Yet, international travel can be challenging for those with caring responsibilities, and we know that women disproportionately bear this load (Gaio Santos & Cabral-Cardoso, 2008). Further, monies for international travel are often part of the discretionary funds made available to principal investigators through grants. However, these monies can relate to salaries, and we also know that there is a gender gap in pay especially at mid/senior career levels, with men faring better (UCU, 2016).

These organisational and cultural factors place limits on the extent to which women, especially, are able to disseminate their work and evidence international impact – and hence progress into leadership positions. Social media – specifically, Twitter – can provide a means a generating an international 'presence' without leaving your office. New ways of measuring journal impact – such as altmetrics – can quantify the amount of attention your research is getting online, for example by measuring tweets and retweets about your work. Hence, the attention generated by your work on Twitter can be quantified for the purposes of promotion and related applications

(Botting et al., 2017). For example, the University of Edinburgh's promotion guidance relating to excellence in knowledge exchange rewards engagement with media including "significant social media outlets" in which researchers contribute "significantly to public debate and enlightenment" (Exemplars of Excellence, 2015).

Finally, Twitter can be a good means of getting to know other research and academics – especially early-career scholars – that are of relevance to your field. Indeed, a study of academics' use of social media for scholarly purposes suggested that the overwhelming motivation for women/female researchers was reported as: "To be part of a professional community".

Ingredients

- A working Internet connection.
- A Twitter account.
- A willingness to speak out about your research.

Method

1. Open a Twitter account, and chose a username that will make you easy to find – for example, your name.

2. Start following your colleagues, and key people in your field. Over time, you'll also get a sense for other academics who regularly tweet with authority about issues of relevance to your work (e.g. science policy, equality and diversity), but who are not necessarily in your discipline.

3. Start tweeting! You can retweet things you think are relevant and/or important. Experiment with your own original tweets.

4. Your tweets might be about a paper you're reading at the moment that you find particularly interesting, or details of a conference you think would be relevant to people who follow you (and people who you'd like to be followed by).

5. If you're a mid-career or senior academic, make sure you use your account to promote the work and achievements of early-career researchers (ECRs) – and try to follow ECRs back if they follow you.

6. Every so often, tweet about your own work. When you've got a paper accepted, tweet about it and tag the journal.

When it's in press, let people know when it's online. When it's out, tweet the title, and later on some of the questions it addresses. There's no harm in tweeting about the paper a few times over the course of a week once it's out (but probably no more than twice a day, maximum). Being blunt about your work and achievements can feel uncomfortable, but it's far better than the 'humblebrag' ("My new Nature paper probably won't be of interest to anyone..."). Just say that you're pleased about the paper/invitation/prize and give the link, or just list the article title and a link.

7. If people tweet nice things about your work, or those of your colleagues (again, especially ECRs), retweet them and thank them.

8. If there's a key issue igniting the passions of the twitterati at a particular time (regarding your discipline specifically, or in society more generally), don't be afraid to tweet past work if it relates to wider current concerns or debate.

Cook's tips

Make sure to use hashtags, which will make your tweet more discoverable (e.g. #ClimateChange, #SocialScience, #WomenInScience, etc). If mentioning other people, make sure to use their Twitter handle rather than their name.

Remember that people are likely to be following you because they are interested in your work, not because you post exactly the same newspaper article that all the other people they follow are also tweeting about.

Warning

Don't overdo it! Twitter can be a great way to find out about new work and researchers, about trends and concerns in your discipline, and to get the message out about your own and colleagues' scholarship. But it can also be incredibly distracting! Also, while Twitter is a great way to promote your research, you won't win many people over if that's the only thing you use it for.

Approaches to planning your career

Lara Isbel

There are a lot of hills in Scotland. Some people climb them for fun. Others get dragged up them by their outdoorsy friends. I've generally been a bit sceptical about the joys of walking up hills for hours just to walk back down again, but I'm slowly being won over.

Time outdoors can provide a useful opportunity for reflection and some of the principles of planning a successful day in the hills can also be applied to managing your career.

Method

1. **Have a plan.** How big the plan needs to be depends on your timescales. You might be mapping out a whole PhD, or just trying to figure out how to get something useful done this afternoon. But without a sense of direction, it's just an aimless wander. Aimless wanders are all well and good, provided they are an active choice. Otherwise they are a luxury you may not be able to afford.

2. **Be aware of the wider environment.** If you go walking in Scotland, your plans are heavily influenced by the weather. Work is only one aspect of your life. If other parts of your life are particularly challenging – caring for young children or elderly parents, or going through a divorce or bereavement, or working with horrendous colleagues or any number of things that leave you reeling, don't hold yourself to the same expectations of

progress when life is carefree. Climbing a hill in sunshine and good weather can be straightforward; the same hill in a blizzard can be perilous. Careers are long and life inevitably has storms at certain points. Look after yourself and accept that there will be times for pausing or sustaining your career as well as times for growing and developing it. Your health is more important than your job.

3. **One step at a time.** It is possible to climb many enormous mountains, just not in a single step. Multitasking is rarely productive. The more you can focus on one thing and then another, the less time you will waste trying to tune back into fragmented tasks. This may be easier to say than do with the volume of work and varied commitments you are trying to balance, but it is more important in these circumstances to find focus. Notice which times of day you have most energy and protect this time (as much as possible) for your most challenging work.

4. **Ask for help if you need it.** The duties people can cover in a single role can be very wide. If you are trying something new, be realistic about how long it will take to build up your expertise. Start with smaller projects, looking for mentors or experienced colleagues and relevant training courses. Focus on what to improve, figure out your strategy and give yourself time.

5. **Celebrate small wins.** Complex projects can take ages to complete. Take time to identify and celebrate the milestones along the way. This doesn't need to be anything major, just a small thing that will bring you a little bit of joy. This can counterbalance the inevitable setbacks.

6. **Change the route.** Things don't always go according to plan. If you keep getting stuck with a project, sometimes you need to have a break from it and then approach it from a whole new angle. A detour is still moving. If it's still not working, cut your losses and move on to something else.

7. **Save positive feedback.** If you get a nice email or other boost to your confidence, keep a note of it. Later, when you are in the depths of despair or feeling stuck, rereading these can help you to rediscover some confidence. On a related note, if you appreciate the contribution someone has made to your project or if they have produced a great bit of work: tell them.

8. **Reflect on your progress.** An advantage of going uphill as it is easier to look back and see how far you have travelled. Tackle the dread of a never-ending to-do list by keeping a 'have- done' list. Spend 10 minutes at the end of your week scanning through the list of all the things you did manage to get done. This makes the list to tackle next week less daunting.

It is also helpful to schedule time for a broader review every six months of what you have accomplished and to check you are still on the right track.

9. **Savour your success.** A highlight of climbing mountains is taking a bit of time to enjoy the view at the top, a reward for some strenuous effort. If you have a project on at work that has been incredibly tough to complete – celebrate it. The things that most mattered to you at 16 or 26 might be a distant memory now. If you don't celebrate the real highs of your career, you'll have forgotten what they were by the time you retire or forgotten how momentous they seemed at the time. If you've achieved something you are proud of, acknowledge it, preferably in the company of people you care about. And celebrate their successes too.

10. **Reassess the plan.** Big successes and big setbacks are useful points to re-evaluate the overall plan. Do you still want to climb the mountains you thought you did? Are your goals things you want to achieve or things you 'ought to' or 'should' achieve? Our career aspirations and priorities shift. The more your work priorities are aligned to your career aspirations, the more job satisfaction you will have and it will be easier to stay motivated. This is your career. Only you can decide what is most important, what brings you the most energy and what inspires you the most.

Dealing with imposter syndrome

Judy Robertson

Do you feel like a fraud?

Do you secretly think that you know less than your colleagues and that it is only a matter of time before you get found out? If so, you may have fallen prey to imposter syndrome. And you're not alone. Imposter syndrome, characterised by "persistent thoughts of intellectual phoniness" (Hutchins & Rainbolt, 2016), is common in high performers across a range of careers. Graduate students, early career researchers, women, and minority groups suffer from it. But you know what? So do professors and so do men (Hutchins & Rainbolt, 2016; Woolston, 2016). When you think about it, it's not that surprising that so many academics are wracked with self-doubt.

Academia is a high-pressure environment with too many people competing for limited resources and where performance is measured against ridiculously high standards. To be an academic – even a successful one – is to live with regular rejection from reviewers, journal editors, promotion committees and grant funding panels. The continual cycle of trying one's best, being rejected in highly competitive circumstances and then mustering the strength to try once more is draining.

Imposter syndrome provokes anxiety and stress, and can lead people to give up their academic careers because they feel they are not good enough (Woolston, 2016). This is unfortunate because people in this position are often highly talented when considered objectively: they are their own worst critics.

However, imposter syndrome can cause people to underperform despite their talent, for example by micromanaging their team, by delaying making decisions, by procrastinating, or by insisting that all tasks must be done perfectly rather than prioritising (Mount & Tardanico, 2016).

It is important for managers to recognise that different groups may experience imposter syndrome differently. It is likely to be more common among staff vulnerable to stereotype threat, often women and minority groups, (Dasgupta, 2011). Women and men may employ different coping mechanisms. In particular, men may be more prone to maladaptive coping strategies which could lead to health problems (Hutchins & Rainbolt, 2016). Here are some ways we can overcome imposter syndrome by taking care of ourselves and our colleagues.

Ingredients

- Empathy (as a manager) and appreciation.
- Self-awareness and introspection.
- Accurate feedback on your performance.
- A mentor or peer with whom you identify.
- Understanding of imposter syndrome.

Method

1. **Look out for what triggers imposter syndrome for you so that you can avoid or prepare for such situations in the future.** In a qualitative critical-incident analysis of how academics are affected by imposter syndrome, Hutchins & Rainbolt (2016) identify a series of events which trigger or revive persistent feelings of inadequacy:

    -   Questioning expertise. "Do I know enough? Do I belong here?" and questions triggered by conversations with colleagues who appear to be much more knowledgeable, or who are rude enough to tell you that you are wrong. In my experience there will also generally be a few top-of-the-class students who are perfectly happy to comment on how wrong you are, in public or in earnest after-class conversations. It's not surprising that you can start questioning yourself, particularly in situations of stereotype threat.

    -   Comparisons among colleagues. "Why is everyone doing so much better than I am? I'll never measure up." In my view, the Research Excellence Framework (REF) really stirs this up. During the week I wrote this recipe, our college conducted an "REF readiness" exercise. This required staff to enter all their publications and evidence of other scholarly super-powers onto a database so the outputs could be counted. This database feeds public facing web pages so it is very easy to see your colleagues' achievements and equally easy to worry that your performance is being evaluated negatively against others'. In fact, new proposals for restructuring the REF are intended to have a more collegiate setup where everyone contributes to the pool of papers for the entire department. Logically, the success of others should be no threat to you. But imposter syndrome is not logical.

    -   Scholarly productivity. "Will I ever get this paper finished? What will the reviewers say? Aaargh, look what the reviewers said." The pressure to produce high quality work can lead to performance anxiety and writer's block. Expectations (in research, teaching and admin) have to be fulfilled, particularly for those on probation like the Chancellor's Fellows at Edinburgh or new lecturers, and much effort can be expended on high stakes grant applications and papers. Many tears can be shed over the brutal rejections of those applications and papers. If you want more proof of this, have a look at the Tumblr site "Shit my reviewers say" (https://shitmyreviewerssay. tumblr.com/) and marvel.

• Experiencing successes. As if all these triggers were not enough, by some perverse twist of psychology, some people find that experiencing success triggers imposter syndrome. Some people squirm when introduced as an expert, others worry that they will not be up to the challenge of managing a grant or assuming a more senior role.

Among this woeful catalogue of triggers, the women in Hutchins & Rainbolt's study were more prone to worries resulting from peer comparison and harsh reviews. The men spoke about it in more general terms, although they did mention being labelled an expert in the media as a trigger. I am sure this problem would crop up for women too, if there were more opportunities to appear in the media as experts in their field rather than wearers of pretty dresses.

2. **Own your successes.** People with imposter syndrome are often reluctant to attribute success to their own abilities, preferring to say that they were just lucky, or they just worked hard. While modesty is a virtue, failure to acknowledge your own success is self-defeating. It can be very valuable to learn to take the time to acknowledge your success and consider what skills led to it so that you can build on this for the future. Mount & Tardanico (2016) suggest setting a timer for five minutes and writing down ten things you do well. If you find this difficult, ask a trusted friend or colleague to help you. Reflect on these skills to see if you can identify a common factor and then consider which future roles would benefit from such a skill set.

3. **Remind yourself of the facts.** Imposter syndrome thrives on half-conscious misperceptions about your lack of success and what it takes to succeed. It is worth taking some time to challenge these beliefs next time you notice them surface. For example, if you find yourself thinking: "I could never be a professor because professors all speak perfect BBC English" challenge yourself to collect examples of professors with regional accents. If you think: "I'll never be able to do this", remind yourself of the last time you achieved something similar. It is possible to use the offensively superlative descriptions in the REF to your favour here. If you know what your papers were rated at through internal

peer review then you can use this as a way to describe your work to yourself. According to the REF 2014 assessment criteria (http://www.ref.ac.uk/panels/assessmentcriteriaandleveldefinitions/), papers which are rated as one-star are considered to be of "Quality that is recognised nationally in terms of originality, significance and rigour". Two-star is "recognised internationally", three-star is "internationally excellent" and four-star is "world-leading". It amuses me that internationally recognised papers only get two stars in this ranking scheme. Outside academia, international recognition would be something to aspire to, not to give half marks to! At any rate, try telling yourself: "According to a panel of subject experts, my work is nationally/internationally recognised/excellent/universe beating". Changing to this way of thinking gave me confidence to apply for my current post.

4. **Talk to yourself kindly.** Get in the habit of positive self-talk rather than mentally running yourself down. The women academics in the Hutchins & Rainbolt (2016) study found that they had to remind themselves over and over again of achievements which made them proud. Think of the range of things you have achieved and why they matter. I like to save emails and cards from students to remember that when I am a teacher or a mentor I make a difference to people's lives. Some of the women in the study liked to remind themselves of their successes in other areas of their lives when they feel their confidence drain. Last week when I had a paper rejected, my family were surprised to witness me stop brooding in order to blurt out "Well, at least I can grow lemons!". I understand that not everyone takes comfort from citrus fruit farming, but there is robust empirical evidence that even short exercises in self-affirmation such as writing about the values which are most important to you can protect you from stereotype threat over a surprisingly long period (Cohen et al., 2009).

5. **Find social support.** Talking to a trusted colleague, mentor or coach may help. You may be surprised to learn that some of your peers have similar difficulties and would appreciate reciprocal support. Ask the person you confide in to help you acknowledge your strengths and objectively evaluate whether your limitations are as crippling as you think they are (Mount & Tardanico, 2016). You could arrange to meet each other at potential trigger points, such as helping each other to read grant reviews or prepare keynote talks.

6. **What to avoid.** Some academics develop maladaptive coping strategies which are counter-productive in the long run. A common and understandable response to imposter syndrome is to work harder and longer. But there is longer term risk of workaholism which is associated with a range of health problems such as burnout, stress, insomnia, work-life conflict and poor job satisfaction (Hogan et al., 2016).

7. **If you're a manager, be aware of and address the potential impact of imposter syndrome among your staff.** Imposter syndrome can lead to anxiety and stress, and in some cases reduced work performance and burnout through workaholism (Mount & Tardanico, 2016). You could well have members of staff in your team who suffer from imposter syndrome, but who are unwilling to admit it to you. This underlies the importance of making sure that all your staff know that you value their work across the spectrum of different academic activities, nourishing them "when you reward or recognise

their good work, encourage them or offer emotional support" (Amabile & Kramer, 2012, p. 33). I also believe that as the university places strain on staff to fulfil REF obligations, managers have a responsibility to help their staff through it by reducing anxiety and offering support. Minimising circumstances where staff feel they are under obvious pressure from social comparison could help. Another useful avenue for this is social support with colleagues. Mentors and peers who belong to the same ingroup can "socially vaccinate" against negative self-perceptions if the staff member identifies with them (Dasgupta, 2011). For example, a new female lecturer would benefit from mentoring from a senior female academic particularly in disciplines where women are in the minority. This can be hard to achieve without over-burdening the few existing female staff with additional mentoring roles, but it may be possible to trade across discipline boundaries where the gender mix is the opposite (e.g. engineering with education). Mentoring and positive role models are particularly beneficial for those entering academia, and those at transition points in their career (Dasgupta, 2011).

As Amabile & Kramer observe: "Although nourishers may matter more to some people than others, none of us can truly thrive without them" (2012, p. 33).

If you are finding it hard to cope, the University of Edinburgh provides a free and confidential counselling service to staff members on issues such as: debilitating stress; anxiety; depression; and alcohol and drug abuse. You can get help at http://www.ed.ac.uk/counselling-services/staff.

Rose surprise: when your period comes early

Hope Bretscher

You have just got to the lab on a Monday morning, and are planning on working there until your afternoon lecture. As soon as you sit at the data analysis computer, you feel a tightening in your abdomen, and realise that soon, you'll receive a rosy surprise down yonder. Surprise! Your period came unexpectedly, and you failed to prepare. Here's a nice recipe on how to use up that unwanted ingredient spilling from your cupboard.

Ingredients

- A labful of men.
- No women (other than you).
- One period.
- One backpack (and its contents).

Method

1. Search your backpack frantically, making sure to sufficiently mix its entire contents. You do not find a tampon.

2. Go to the bathroom and confirm that you have the third ingredient (as this is essential and cannot be substituted).

3. Search your backpack again, thoroughly stirring its contents. You can be slow and methodical or mix rapidly, by pulling everything out and stuffing it back in. Use whatever suits your personal taste.

4. Check your phone and remember that you work in the laboratory sub-basement where there is no cell reception or wifi to prevent interference with the experiments.

5. Wait for a few minutes, until your postdoc mentor leaves the room, and then mix your backpack for the third time. Vigorous searching creates the best taste.

6. Go to Facebook and GMail on the desktop computer and send a plea to your girl friends to see if they are near your lab building.

7. Sigh when they are not.

8. Whoops! Your postdoc has returned, so close social communication and return the screen to MATLAB work mode.

9. Type angrily in frustration.

10. Your frustration has simmered enough. Take a breath, and remind yourself that it's fine to leave the lab to go to the shop for some tampons and painkillers. Don't let the pain stew and simmer any longer.

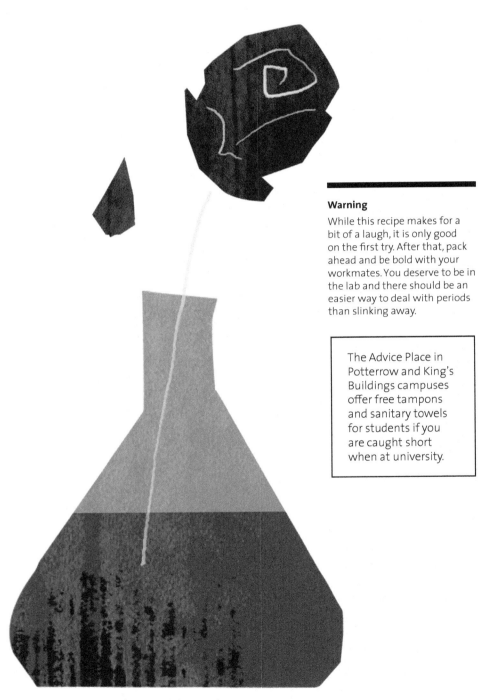

While this recipe makes for a bit of a laugh, it is only good on the first try. After that, pack ahead and be bold with your workmates. You deserve to be in the lab and there should be an easier way to deal with periods than slinking away.

The Advice Place in Potterrow and King's Buildings campuses offer free tampons and sanitary towels for students if you are caught short when at university.

Flexible working: being realistic

Anonymous

When returning to work after a period of maternity/paternity leave, your attention may inevitably turn to flexible working and the policies that outline this seemingly attractive option. The answer to all your worries and woes about childcare, drop-offs, and pick-ups, while still getting your teaching prepared, your research grant appications written, and all those high-impact papers accepted for publication.

A range of 'voices' may emerge from the mist as you swither about the 'number' of days, which days, condensed hours, compressed hours, after hours, and weekends. "Don't do it – you will still find yourself working full-time" to "Go for it – I wish I had done that – the kids are only wee for such a short time". If discussions with your line manager go well, you may be encouraged to take your time, and have a proper think about it and then submit your application when you are ready.

After much deliberation you submit your flexible working application, and joy of all joys, it is accepted! Just like that – it was easy really after all that worrying, angst, and uncertainty – it has all paid off... Your beautifully balanced and flexible working life has just begun... And then the unforeseen and formidable reality gap emerges right in front of you...

Your letter of confirmation arrives, and there it is in writing: a reduction in hours to a 0.6 contract. Perfect – just what you had asked for! But just a minute, what about the associated reduction to your workload? Ah, then a different set of 'voices' emerge: "Well, everyone is over-worked..." Yes, but you've just taken a huge reduction in your wage to work fewer hours... "Well, no-one is paying me extra to work over my full-time workload, so why should it be any different for you?" Hang on – this wasn't part of the deal (or so you had thought)! All of a sudden the reality of flexibly working a 0.9 workload in a 0.6 contact does not seem quite so attractive. In fact, it is downright stressful! Before you know it you are working just as much as you were before at even more unsociable hours (around pick-ups and drop offs), and being paid just over half of what you had previously earned! The so-called "motherhood penalty" relating to the gender pay gap is well documented, but that is small comfort when you are living with it (Budig & England, 2001).

Ingredients

- Flexible working policy.
- Flexible administrator.
- Flexible & supportive line manager.
- Cognitive flexibility – the human ability to adapt cognitive processing strategies to face new and unexpected conditions.

Method

1. Speak to as many trusted sources as you can about the flexible working

culture at your institution. Do many people have this arrangement and what is their experience of it?

2. If there is not a precedent for this type of working, despite the institution having a flexible working policy, why is this? What are the experiences of those who tried this type of arrangement? Why did it not work? What are the challenges to offering a reduced contract to a member of your staff team?

3. It can be useful to know the likely tensions and sources of conflict prior to making a new agreement about working hours. For example, who will cover the 'extra' hours that will become available?

The University of Edinburgh flexible working policy can be found here: http://www.docs.csg.ed.ac.uk/HumanResources/Policies/Flexible_Working_Policy.pdf

4. Give some thought as to how the new arrangement would look in terms of workload. How would this take shape? What would you or your staff member lose or gain, and how will this be managed?

5. Assess whether you have buy-in from your line manager. Everyone is all too willing to implement a flexible working policy, but will they back and protect a reduced workload or are their hands tied? For example, will there be someone else brought in to pick up the extra work? If not, the chances are you (or they) will still be doing it! Ask about what is not listed (e.g. likelihood of a reduced workload following reduction in hours and practices, policies, and people in place to ensure this).

6. Once you have the warts and all details, and if you still wish to proceed, it can make a lot of sense to push for a temporary reduction in hours for a time-limited period (e.g. until junior goes to school). This way the contract can be adjusted again, more or less, at a later period.

7. It can be extremely difficult in all the chaos and madness of returning to work and flexible working to know what you want, and what might work out best, so a temporary adjustment to your contract leaves your options open for later.

Cook's tip

Cognitive flexibility can be trained through meditation and mindfulness practice, and good for stress reduction too! See Moore & Malinowski (2009).

Warnings

If you find yourself in a situation similar to the one described above, then get in touch with your HR (human resources) department, or your union, and ask for some support. Flexible working policies sound good, but do not solve all problems. Speak up if the new arrangement is not working out or is not what you expected.

Flexible administrators and line managers are readily available (to agree adjustments to contracts). Supportive line managers who are prepared to reduce your workload in accordance may be more difficult to find.

Deadlines and diapers: being an academic dad

Graham Baker

Fatherhood represents the most emotionally stirring and challenging but ultimately satisfying experience most men will undergo. Once you have exhausted (pun intended) the brief paternity leave typically available, a demanding situation quickly arises where the dual roles of 'academic' and 'father' require to be balanced.

As an academic dad with a newborn baby in the house, you may have concerns over the potential detrimental impact on your career. Clearly, there will be less time available in the evenings and at weekends for lecture preparation, manuscript writing or to pursue the ever-elusive research grant funding. What will this mean for your status at work, how colleagues perceive you or your chances of promotion?

And as a father with a workload equal to that 'pre-child', you will undoubtedly be anxious about ensuring you play an active role in raising your child within the limited time available outside of work. How will you be able to best support your child and your partner? Perhaps as a single father you are concerned with who will support you? Will you be able to cope with the different daily tasks of feeding, changing nappies and settling the child through the night, while conscious of the fact you have a deadline for the next day?

However, this chef has learned in the process that priorities in life change. Having

that first-author paper published, or that grant application submitted, suddenly becomes less significant and satisfying than being able to make it home for bath time or seeing your new son or daughter smile for the first time. Your family is the priority, so keep that in your mind as you continue to work hard as an academic dad.

Ingredients

- One newborn baby (adorable, but potentially cranky and unsettled). In recipe terms, this ingredient is the equivalent of chilli peppers – more than one can be added, but proceed with caution!

- One line manager or head of institute – an essential ingredient, but one where the quality may be variable.

- Supportive colleagues.

- University policy documents related to family leave.

Method

1. Get prepared! Review your institute's family leave-related working policies and discuss with a member of Human Resources. The recent introduction of policies for shared parental leave, flexible working and time-off for dependants provide greater opportunities for fathers to spend time with, and give support to, their families at home.

2. Discuss your pending new arrival with your line manager. Statistics would suggest that although the number of hours worked by fathers has decreased in recent years (Aldrich et al., 2016), many still work far in excess of their contracted hours. Consider your workload model, reduce where (if) possible, and agree your strategic priorities for the next 12 months. Take a reality check. You will be combating tiredness and may have several unplanned interruptions from work for hospital visits or trips home. Recognise that it will take longer to get to tasks and then to complete them, as this chef can testify to from drafting this recipe! Learn to say NO to those additional jobs that always seem to emerge and expand your To Do list.

3. Then, discuss with colleagues, many of whom will have children of their own and will be understanding of your situation. Within your teaching team, and research collaborations, identify where and when your input is required and plan accordingly. You will need to implement strict time management but things will invariably slip! Make sure you keep colleagues updated when this happens.

4. A change of attitude will be required. You may need to remove any pride of being perceived as 'a hard worker' within your department. Arriving early for work,

Warning

It is likely, even after following this recipe, that becoming a father will have a significant impact on every other aspect of your life. Not just on your academic work, but also on your social life, activities and hobbies. You might not be able to see friends at the pub every weekend or train for that marathon. Be under no illusions, having children is hard; balancing fatherhood and academic life can be demanding to say the least. If you are part of an 'academic pair' then this can be even more challenging (O'Laughlin & Bischoff, 2005).

According to the University of Edinburgh's shared parental leave policy, you and your partner can share up to 50 weeks' leave and up to 37 weeks' statutory pay. http://www. docs.csg.ed.ac.uk/ HumanResources/ Policies/SPL_Key_Facts_ Father_Partner.pdf

staying late and taking marking home, all of which may once have been aspects of a typical working day, may no longer be possible. Instead, your academic work ethic will need to be shared with your new role in the home as a father.

5. In comparison with other professions, academia offers dads a degree of flexibility in regard to their working schedules. Take advantage of this and find a pattern of working that best suits your family. For this chef it was to start work early, ensuring a substantial period in the evening was available for family time and sharing household duties.

6. The seemingly all-consuming roles of father and academic often take precedence over our other role as husband/partner. Thus, an often-neglected part of this recipe is to ensure quality time is spent with your wife or partner. If possible, arrange a babysitter, rope in the relatives for help and enjoy some time as a couple doing things you did before you became a family.

Cook's tip
Despite this being a difficult recipe to master, always be aware that others may be working on a much more demanding recipe. For example, research shows that the impact on academic mums is far greater than on academic dads (Gaio Santos & Cabral-Cardoso, 2008; O'Laughlin & Bischoff, 2005). Also, marking first-year undergraduate assignments is a breeze in comparison to your partner dealing with a newborn 24/7!

Some schools, such as the Schools of Molecular, Genetic and Population Health Sciences, and Clinical Sciences, delay the Chancellor's Fellow review to take account of parental leave, so you could discuss this or similar arrangements in advance with your line manager.

The kids
are alright

Gale Macleod & Jonathan Hearn

We're an academic couple. Gale is a senior lecturer and dean in the College of Arts, Humanities and Social Science. Jonathan is a professor of political and historical sociology, and about to take on the role of head of subject. We have been together for 18 years, and have a 14-year-old daughter and an 11-year-old son. The children were both born during Gale's PhD, when, towards the end, she was also working as a research assistant. Over the years we have managed to find a balance for our work and home lives. Although we joke that the University of Edinburgh is the family business, our kids have turned out normal, kind and caring people. Here are some of the ways to look at parenting which work for us as an academic family.

Method

1. **Both:** Relax about your children's academic achievements: focus on bringing up good and kind people. Gale is from an academic family of high achievers, but has become more mellow about the children's progress because of Jonathan's experiences of having spent his non-traditional school days catching snakes and looking for arrowheads. Both our children attend the local state school. We know that middle-class kids with well-educated parents do well wherever they go; it's complicated, but see for example Crozier (2011), and we feel it is important to be part of the local community. Gale does try not to let her teacher educator background show when talking to the teachers though.

2. **Jonathan:** Decide how you're going to tackle after work-hours events. I rule out evening seminars, whereas Gale often works on building a sense of academic community...in the pub, and I deliberately tell my colleagues "I can't go because I need to pick up my kids" to show that family life is important. Gale does not make such a point of talking about picking up kids unless she knows the colleague well. She thinks it is harder for women to say it in case people think she is a 'part-timer'. It is important to her to be seen to do her fair share.

3. **Both:** We co-ordinate so that only one of us has a major admin role at a time. Although we both believe that we have a responsibility to our colleagues to take our turn at administrative duties, it can be very frustrating and emotionally challenging. We don't want for both of us to bring that frustration home every night. So, for example, Jonathan deferred assuming the role of head of subject until Gale's term as dean comes to an end.

4. **Jonathan:** For the sake of marital harmony, acknowledge your spouse in any books you write.

5. **Jonathan:** Nip guilt in the bud.
Bringing up children is making a huge
contribution to society, so don't feel
guilty about spending time on your
kids. Jonathan: Don't feel guilty about
working either. Make others responsible
for telling you if they don't get what
they need. Kids are good at telling you if
they don't get enough attention – don't
imagine stuff in your head. Establish
a clear norm where the children know
they can ask for attention and their
request will be listened to. Gale: There
are lots of myths about the working
mum not doing either thing very well.
But a "good enough" parent is as good
as anyone will ever be. Children are
very resilient – they will survive if you
don't have time to play with them

tonight. Their lives are their own – they
benefit from a mix of activities.

6. **Gale:** Don't stress about having
work conversations at the dinner
table. It is good for the children to
see that people enjoy their working
lives, and to hear about how adults
get frustrated too, and to learn how
adults deal with difficult situations.

7. **Gale:** if you need to decide whether
a sick child can go to school or not,
ask them if a chocolate button would
help. If so, send them to school (note:
they get wise to this after a while).

8. **Both:** Don't worry about your
children, just get to know them.

Show your daughters the joys of science

Danai Korre

I still remember how excited I was the first time I 'fixed' my first digital pet, with the most basic electric circuit and when I made an LED flicker by using code and a single-board microcontroller. I believe that watching my dad in his workshop got me interested in electronics and many more technical things after that. I used to sneak into the workshop and play around when he wasn't looking. These early experiences paid off as I am now a PhD student in informatics, and I have a masters degree in Design and Digital Media.

I think academia and research are predominantly diverse working environments, or at least that is how it seems to me, compared with my working experience outside academia. Gender equality in STEM (science, technology, engineering and mathematics) is a different issue that could be traced to systemic sexism imprinted in women's minds through society and media. There is a stereotype which says that women are not as good as their male counterparts on technical issues or roles. A male acquaintance once proposed that women are unfit for such positions, because their brains "work differently and men are better in math and technical issues". Tell that to Ada Lovelace and Grace Hopper and the long list of successful women who thrived in such positions. If our brains work differently – and the evidence for this isn't good (see Fine, 2010; Rippon et al., 2014) – wouldn't having more women in STEM lead to even more amazing accomplishments for the whole of humanity?

Maybe if we want more women in STEM we should treat them equally and inform them about this from the first days of their lives. We prepare our girls to be princesses and we prepare our boys to become leaders while we should prepare them both to be great.

Women need to grow up knowing that they should not be objectified, they are not the 'damsel in distress' type of princesses waiting for a strong male figure to save them, but more like Amazon princesses, strong, confident and ready to take on the world. We need to educate women about other strong women that made a change in this world. We also need more male feminists to get more females into STEM. We need men who will not be threatened by a strong woman or think less of her, and men that will help raise that strong woman. Parents play an important role in technology career choices, so it is important that they are well informed (van Tuijl & van der Molen, 2016).

Ingredients

- A working Internet connection.
- An open mind.

Method

1. If you have a little girl, tell her about the marvellous women that came before

her and made this world a bit better. If you can't think of any beyond Marie Curie, this will get you started: http://www.smithsonianmag.com/science-nature/ten-historic-female-scientists-you-should-know-84028788/?no-ist. You could read the book "Women in Science: 50 Fearless Pioneers Who Changed the World" with her (Ignotofsky, 2017).

2. If you have a boy, do the same.

3. Let them both get their hands dirty and play around with tools. My dad had a small workshop with a soldering station where I made my first solder rings (sounds dangerous I know) and braided bracelets out of colourful telecommunication cables.

4. Take them to a museum or observatory with a hands-on approach. The Edinburgh International Science Festival (https://www.sciencefestival.co.uk/) and the Royal Observatory Edinburgh (http://

www.roe.ac.uk/) are great for this.

5. Make it a game to build something together, like programming a single-board microcontroller or a (safe) chemical experiment. Try https://code.org/ for computer programming activities, or try http://makezine.com/ for electronics and making activities.

6. Be aware of how toys are marketed to children. Why should toys or books in shops be labelled 'for boys' or 'for girls'? It's a problem if girls see science and engineering toys labelled for other people but not for them. For that matter, it is a problem that boys should be led to believe that toys related to cooking and caring are not for them. Draw your children's attention to this unfair marketing and discuss it with them: provoke their sense of unfairness. For further information, see http://www.lettoysbetoys.org.uk/why-it-matters/

The annual Edinburgh International Science Festival has a great children's programme full of hands-on science and technology activities. In 2016, 200 university staff and students contributed to a range of events on topics including space, genetics and robotics (http://www.ed.ac.uk/events/festivals/highlights/all-events/2016/science-festival-interview-with-dr-janet-paterson).

How to convince your family to let you study

Theresia H. Mina

I come from a family who used to believe that the very purpose of being a woman is simply to get married and raise children. The view was that a young woman needs to attend university so that she is more eligible in the marriage market. I was once taught that women do not need to be too knowledgeable, let alone think of pursuing doctoral study. After all, doctoral study is for men as it requires a lot of brainpower, it is very expensive (and it's not worth investing in sending women for postgraduate study), and most importantly if I were to further my studies I might not find a man who

would like to marry me because men are scared of smart women, or so it was said.

At first, I could only see one scenario: get a secretarial job, marry, raise kids. But now I have furthered my studies on my own accord, obtained an MSc and a PhD, and now I work in an ever bigger role in clinical research. I am still doing some secretarial tasks as part of my admin duties, but this is only one out of so many responsibilities.

And yes, I am still going to marry and I plan to raise kids, out of my own freewill.

Ingredients

- Patience.
- Perseverance.
- An excellent track record of what you are passionate about. If you like dancing, you might want to include a dancing competition trophy. If you like basketball, it could be a medal for winning an important match or being the best player. If science is your thing, you might want to gather together your certificates from winning science competitions.
- A bunch of friends sharing similar passions.
- A mentor, teacher, lecturer, professor who believes in your potential and is willing to write you a reference letter.
- A variety of scholarship schemes for which you are eligible to apply.
- A female role model, your favourite dancer, the female basketball player of the year or the top female professor/ minister in your country (or it could simply be your own mentor).

Method

1. Do your homework: plan in advance to apply for a scholarship, and always have an up-to-date track record.

2. Invite your family elders to a formal dinner or gathering and declare your intention to further your studies at least a year in advance of your study plan, the earlier the better. I informed my family regarding my intention to further my studies abroad about three years in advance of my actual plan.

3. Demonstrate your plan. This may include the list of universities you would like to apply to and a list of courses you would like to attend.

4. Showcase your excellent track record.

5. Mention the female role model and how you aspire to be like that. In my case it was helpful to mention that another female student in my class was also thinking of pursuing a similar course so at least my family could see that I was not going to be alone.

6. Show a reference letter from your mentor.

7. Demonstrate how you plan to support yourself financially, such as a list of scholarship applications, and whether you have a plan B if this does not work.

8. Repeat step 1-7 until the concept starts to get ingrained.

Guidance on how to apply for postgraduate funding at the University of Edinburgh can be found here: http://www.ed.ac.uk/student-funding/postgraduate/international.

Cook's tip

You could also write a diary about how you feel, have tissue boxes to absorb those tears, and read inspirational books to keep your spirits up. You may need to channel your frustration somewhere.

Warnings

If you receive offensive comments, don't start swearing and being rude to your elders no matter how much you are offended, but do stand your ground firmly.

Be realistic about your family's financial circumstance so that you don't get too disappointed. In the meantime, keep an eye on those competitive scholarships.

There is always a risk that your first plan doesn't work, so have plan B ready. For instance, what type of work would you apply for should your study plan be rejected completely by your parents, family or scholarship bodies? If you receive an offer but not the scholarship, devise plan C on how to fund your study.

Stereotype threat

Judy Robertson

Stereotypes are everywhere. We are so used to them that if we don't happen to be at the sharp end of a stereotype, we might not realise the harm that they can cause. It's important for teachers in higher education to understand the damaging consequences of stereotypes on the academic performance of minority groups.

Claude Steel's account of several decades of psychological research into academic under-performance of African-American students in US universities gives a fascinating insight into the difficulties our students face and how we can assist them (Steele, 2010). Steel explores the concept of stereotype threat which affects the performance of people who belong to a group which is negatively stereotyped as being poor at a particular task. Stereotype threat has been demonstrated in studies of a variety of groups including white sports people, French working class undergraduates in language tests, women in maths tests, men in situations which require empathy, older adults in memory tests and so on. It is possible to evoke stereotype threat in a lab situation even for activities and groups who might not normally experience it.

> Whenever we're in a situation where a bad stereotype about one of our identities could be applied to us – such as those about being old, poor, rich or female – we know it. We know what 'people could think'. We know that anything that we do to fit that stereotype could be taken as confirming it, and we know that, for that reason, we could be judged and treated accordingly. (Steele, 2010)

The consequences of stereotype threat are powerful. It affects highly motivated, highly skilled individuals who are deeply committed to an outcome, causing them to under-perform. Even without encountering direct prejudice or discrimination, an individual can labour under the ghost of stereotype threat to the detriment of their performance and well-being. In a situation where a person identifies with a group which has a related negative stereotype, the stereotype will be evoked.

For example, imagine a high-ability female maths student sitting a difficult exam who has just noticed a cue that reminds her of the stereotype that women are no good at maths. The student then becomes anxious and the anxiety has associated physiological symptoms which detract from performance (curiously, the participant might not be aware of this anxiety even if their heart rate and blood pressure tell a different story). The student's mind starts to race: considering the stereotype and how she doesn't want to confirm it by failing the test, denying that the stereotype will apply to her, suppressing unwanted thoughts, giving herself a pep-talk and monitoring her performance. The problem is that if this happens in a situation where the person needs all her cognitive resources to solve a challenging problem at the cusp of her abilities, the mind-racing slurps up some of the raw thinking power which is needed to solve the problem. She then self-monitors, finds that her distraction has impacted her performance and the cycle goes on during that test, and at the next test and in other learning situations.

There is strong experimental evidence for this from a range of sources, with effect sizes large enough to substantially suppress a student's grades over the years of a degree course. It's not that people under stereotype threat aren't clever, or don't have the prerequisite learning, are unmotivated or don't work hard. It's that the environment that they learn and are assessed in interacts with their identity in a negative way. It is actually less of a problem for lower ability students, or those who don't care about the outcomes of the test. Unfortunately, it can be counterproductive for a student

to increase effort to combat the effects of stereotype threat. For example, a series of studies of black students found that they redoubled their efforts in the face of failure and stereotype threat, but that those efforts did not use particularly effective strategies. For example, the black students in the study were more likely to spend long hours studying in their rooms and getting stuck, whereas white and Asian students were more likely to benefit from shared cognitive resources by studying in groups.

Stereotype threat can be triggered by environmental cues, such as a low proportion of other women in the room, a low proportion of women in positions of power, or the environment reflecting the cultural interests of the more dominant group. For me as a female computer science undergraduate, this meant noticing that I was the only woman in the tutorial group, that the lecturers were almost always male and that the labs were covered in posters about Red Dwarf. Such environmental cues do make a difference to behaviour and performance under lab conditions: women taking maths tests under stereotype threat in the company of men performed worse. Women scientists looked more frequently around the room and were better able to recall who was present when they watched a video about a science conference which depicted a low proportion of women; the cue of stereotype threat made them more vigilant regarding their surroundings (Murphy et al., 2007).

Dealing with stereotype threat day after day is tiring and can lead to a vicious cycle of under-performance, then possibly withdrawal from education. Evidence suggests that it has a longer term negative impact on health outcomes. In this light, it is not surprising that there are low proportions of women opting for advanced scientific and maths departments in universities. Even without encountering direct prejudice, the threat in the air caused by stereotypes is seriously damaging.

Is there anything we as educators can do

about this? Happily, yes. Several seemingly small educational interventions have recently been shown to be surprisingly effective, even in the long term. In an article in Current Directions in Psychological Science, Walton refers to interventions of this type as "wise psychological interventions" (Walton, 2014). They are based on specific, precise, well-founded psychological theories which have been validated in the lab and then developed to be applicable in a real-world setting. The reason that small interventions of this sort can have surprisingly long lasting effects is that they operate recursively.

A small adjustment to the way an individual perceives their situation (when applied early enough) can disrupt a self-reinforcing downward spiral, and begin a snowball of positive effects. Some wise psychological interventions are based on the story-editing approach in which individuals are encouraged to change the narratives they tell themselves in order to address a wide range of social and personal issues (Wilson, 2011). This approach is based on the assumptions that changing behaviour requires changes in the way individuals interpret themselves in their social worlds, that these interpretations can be fruitfully and wisely redirected, and that these redirections can be self-sustaining, which leads to long-term behavioural change.

Here are some examples of successful 'wise psychological interventions' which have important lessons for how we can reduce stereotype threat in our teaching environments.

Belonging

A successful intervention which aimed to help participants edit their stories about themselves focused on developing a sense of belonging to the student community (Walton & Cohen, 2007). If you're a first year black student at college where most of your classmates are white, or a woman student on an engineering course which is male-dominated, you may question whether you belong (this is referred to as belonging uncertainty). This may well provoke stereotype threat and its dampening effect on performance. If you find classes hard, or have trouble making friends you may attribute these difficulties as being related to your sense that you don't 'fit in'.

In Walton and Cohen's study (Walton & Cohen, 2007), first-year college students were presented with the results of a survey which showed that all first-year students (regardless of ethnicity) had initial worries about fitting in, but that over time they settled in, made friends and felt part of the community. This encouraged the students watching the presentation to construct a positive story in which their feelings of belonging uncertainty were attributed to the stage in their academic career rather than their social identity. This gave them hope for the future. Black students who took part in this hour-long intervention got on average one-third of a letter grade higher the following semester than those in the control group. This study has implications for possible successful interventions to assist women studying subjects where they are a minority and which are associated with negative gender stereotypes.

> ...this encouraged the students watching the presentation to construct a positive story in which their feelings of belonging uncertainty were attributed to the stage in their academic career rather than their social identity...

Mindset

Dweck's work on mindset (Dweck, 2007) has far reaching consequences for education in general, and has implications for productively intervening to reduce the impact of stereotype threat. Mindset refers to people's theories about how ability relates to challenge. Those with 'fixed mindsets' believe that ability and intelligence is fixed and can't be expanded: you're either good at maths or you're not. Those with 'growth mindsets' believe that it is possible to meet challenges by learning new abilities – you can get better at maths if you practise. If you have a fixed mindset, and are under stereotype threat then you are not in a hopeful situation because it seems as though it is not worthwhile to take on new challenges in case you fail, thus confirming the negative stereotype. If you have a growth mindset, then you have the more optimistic view that you should take on challenges because there is always room for improvement. The stereotype threat is removed because someone with a growth mindset doesn't see failure as confirmation of innate intelligence of themselves or their group, but as a step in a journey to improving performance.

Luckily, quite short interventions can change people from fixed to growth mindsets. Indeed, in a study of women maths students, Good et al. demonstrated that "the message that math ability could be acquired protected women from negative stereotypes, allowing them to maintain a high sense of belonging in math and the intention to pursue math in the future" (Good et al., 2012, p. 1). As educators, then, we need to support all our students to learn growth mindsets in order to help them to overcome the difficulties which they will encounter during their studies. Yeager and Dweck: "We have found that what students need the most is not self-esteem boosting or trait labeling; instead, they need mindsets that represent challenges as things that they can take on and overcome over time with effort, new strategies, learning, help from others, and patience" (Yeager & Dweck, 2012, p. 312, emphasis added).

Values affirmation

Self-affirmation theory gives us another clue about how to interrupt the downward spiral caused by stereotype threat. This is based on the idea that it's basic human nature to see oneself as good and competent, and that if that perception is threatened we try to repair that self-image. Repairing one's self-image may involve rationalising and re-explaining events to fit with the view of self-competence. However, it is productive to encourage people to 'self-affirm' their wider valued sense of self so that this minor threat to self-image seems smaller and there is less need to rationalise it away. Stereotype threat causes regular damage to one's self-image of competence, so one possible intervention to reduce it is to give students an opportunity to develop a self-affirming narrative. It turns out this is an astonishingly effective intervention. In an experiment with 7th grade children, researchers asked a random sample of children to write a paragraph for 15 minutes on their three most important values (e.g. family, friends, being good at music) and why they were important to them (Cohen, 2006). There were a few similar follow-up writing exercises in later school terms. The affirmation-writing exercise improved the grades of all but the strongest performing black students, with those with the poorest initial performance improving the most. It closed the racial achievement gap between black and white students by 40%, and this lasted for two years. More recently, Miyake et al. found that a similar writing exercise for female college students studying physics boosted students' modal grades from a C to a B (Miyake et al., 2010).

These results are extremely promising. They suggest that refocusing students' attention on the values that are important to them helps them not to dwell on poor early performances and so frees up cognitive resources which might otherwise get consumed worrying about stereotype threat. This enables a better performance next time around and interrupts the negative snowballing.

Feedback

Much has been made of poor feedback practices in higher education in recent years, particularly because in the UK, national student survey results are scathing about feedback on undergraduate degrees. Negative feedback has a detrimental effect for those studying under stereotype threat (Mangels et al., 2012). In a study of women tackling a challenging maths test, Mangels and colleagues found that negative feedback was a predictor of disengagement from learning and interference with learning attempts. That is, stereotype threat when combined with negative feedback drags down not only assessment performance but learning itself.

Steele describes studies (Cohen et al., 1999) which found that black students interpret critical feedback on their writing in different ways from white students; they are less likely to trust it and less likely to find it motivating. The studies found that it didn't work to try to be neutral in the feedback, or begin the feedback with a positive general comment. What did work for both black and white students was for the marker to explain that she had high standards, and that she believed the students could meet these standards by acting on the following specific advice.

This strategy is successful because stereotype threat is reduced. The learner knows that the clearly stated high intellectual standards are for everyone (not just their identity group) and that the marker believes that they personally are capable of meeting those standards by improving various features of the work. They have hope, and they have a plan for the next steps in their learning. As a related note, publishing clear and transparent assessment criteria along with an assignment helps with the first part of this equation. No one has to second guess what the marker might be 'looking for'.

The learning and teaching environment

Lastly, but not necessarily related to 'wise psychological interventions', paying attention to the environment for teaching and learning can reduce stereotype threat. "If enough cues in a setting can lead members of a group to feel 'identify safe', it might neutralise the impact of other cues in the setting which might otherwise threaten them" (Steele, 2010). A useful concept here is critical mass, which refers to the point where there are enough members of a minority group in the setting so that individuals no longer feel uncomfortable or vulnerable to identity threat. It's hard to quantify what critical mass means in proportional terms.

However, Steele reports studies of the gender balance in orchestras in which orchestras with 20% female members experienced problems, in contrast to 40% female member orchestras in which all members reported more satisfying experiences. This converts into a practical teaching suggestion about allocating groups in classes with minority groups. Bohnet suggests that teachers should make sure that every subgroup of students is represented by at least three people or makes up about a third of the total (Bohnet, 2016). In a maths class with a small number of women for example, if you prioritise critical mass, then you could have some groups with at least three out of seven female members and many groups with no women. This would enable the women to be closer to critical mass, and would work better for them rather than putting one woman in as many groups as possible. (I did a six-week long group project in which I was the only women as an undergraduate and it was not fun.)

Other environmental cues of stereotype threat which we can address in teaching environments is the proportion of women staff members, and the proportion of women in positions of power. This is something which one would hope would be addressed by other initiatives such as Athena SWAN; my point here is that women staff members should be highly visible to the students.

My point is not, however, that women should bear the responsibility of 'fixing' gender balance on our degree programmes. It's everyone's responsibility and so if women staff are asked to teach high profile courses as part of a gender equality commitment, then it should be factored into their workload rather than being an added extra.

Summary

There is a convincing pool of research which indicates that women under-perform in challenging intellectual situations where they encounter stereotype threat. This is not a unique characteristic of women, but a general psychological effect which it is possible to trigger in members of any group by negatively comparing their group to another. Fortunately, it is possible to reduce stereotype threat by paying attention to cues that might trigger it in our teaching environments, and by using small but extremely effective wise psychological interventions including promoting a sense of belonging, using values-affirmation writing exercises, encouraging growth mindsets, and structuring feedback in a way that encourages students to strive for high standards.

A reflection on EUSA sexual harassment campaigns

Chris Belous

I am a fourth-year German and Linguistics student who was elected as Women's Liberation Convenor for Edinburgh University Students' Association (EUSA) for the academic year 2016/17. My work involves representing women and non-binary students on issues affecting them as students who experience gender-based discrimination at the University and in wider society. This includes everything from organising demonstrations against street-based sexual harassment and sexual violence, running workshops and film screenings, and consulting on policy which impacts women and non-binary students – for instance, policy around issues of gender-based violence such as sexual violence and abuse.

Sometimes you can forget that things have come a long way in the space of a few years. Changes can be small, and they can take so much energy and time to make, that you forget that any change was actually made, and that the positive effects were actually felt. Within an old and well-established academic institution like the University of Edinburgh (UoE), it can sometimes feel like change is impossible – but in some aspects we've come a long way since 2013, when Edinburgh University Students' Association conducted a survey which found that a third of respondents had experienced some form of sexual harassment during their time at Edinburgh.

The past few years have seen sexual violence at universities in the UK become a much more visible issue, one which many people – women, survivors of sexual harassment and abuse, students, academics, union staff – have been working to combat all over the country. At Edinburgh this has been no different, although we still have work to do.

Since 2014, there have been several campaigns run at UoE and through the Students' Association to tackle the high amount of sexual harassment and sexual violence on our campuses and that people face during their university lives. The core three are the 2014 Students' Association Monsters campaign, the 2015 Students' Association Consent campaign jointly run with Sexpression Edinburgh, and the 2016 No One Asks For It (NOAFI) campaign jointly run by UoE, the Students' Association and Edinburgh University Sports Union (EUSU).

In this piece, I want to discuss my views of the merits of these campaigns, where we are at now, and the challenges we faced and continue to face in fighting sexual harassment and sexual violence in the context of academia.

The first campaign, coming out of the Students' Association's sexual harassment survey, was mostly a marketing one, centred around a set of cartoon monsters with the slogan, "Have you seen this monster?" It was designed to call attention to less obvious harassment, like unwanted grinding in clubs, and stalking, and it encouraged students to report incidents. Anecdotal evidence would suggest that it was effective in highlighting issues, raising awareness and encouraging people to come forward about any problems.

This is positive – considering that lack of awareness about what counts as problematic behaviour has been part of the issue for as long as rape culture has existed, it's important to have marketing campaigns which try to reverse this. "Consent", for example, just hasn't been talked about in UK schools until very recently. The year this campaign was launched was also a particularly key year for fighting rape culture and lad culture at Edinburgh. Eve Livingston,

the then-Vice President Societies and Activities, was also running a series of talks and workshops on these topics in the light of veterinary school students making rape jokes at women students and the news which came to light of the extremely disgusting misogyny, transphobia and threats of violence against women propagated by the now long-gone Edinburgh chapter of the DKE (Delta Kappa Epsilon) fraternity.

The Monsters campaign and other coinciding work also attempted to highlight reporting procedures and other sources of support you could turn to, like Edinburgh Rape Crisis Centre. However, changing attitudes and behaviours regarding sexual violence is a slow process – undoing patriarchy is a lifelong task, after all, and while the Monsters campaign had its successes, more work was unfortunately needed to reach more students.

In 2014 we saw the resurgence of the Edinburgh branch of student-led sex and relationships education (SRE) charity Sexpression on campus and their work both in schools around Edinburgh and among UoE students on raising awareness about consent and prevention of sexual harassment and abuse. The group was asked by the Students' Association to help out with another campaign, starting in 2015, which involved some marketing and also the presence of a fortnightly stall at Big Cheese, Potterrow's big Saturday student club night, where Sexpression volunteers would chat to students about consent and related issues, as well as giving out freebies (including free condoms, temporary tattoos and badges) with one of three slogans on them – "The way I dress is not a yes," "You can't always get what you want," or "It's not me. It's you". The stalls have been hugely successful so far and are in their second year of existence as of 2016.

This campaign had less of a focus on reporting forms of harassment and more on education, especially at grassroots level. Rather than being a poster campaign alone, it also involved direct face-to-face

Free condoms with slogans
from the Sexpression and
Students' Association consent
campaign. Photo: Chris Belous.

outreach with a group of people who might not otherwise engage much with Students' Association campaigns as well as those who do. Week after week, the stalls are extremely popular and a majority of students have now heard of Sexpression and know the campaign and the stall.

Very early on in the campaign, there was one story told to Sexpression about how a person was being harassed on the dance floor but remembered the anti-harassment temporary tattoo they were wearing which they had got from the Sexpression stall, and this made them feel empowered enough to report the harasser. This and the fact the stall is reaching hundreds of students twice a month, especially freshers, in a fun setting but in a setting where harassment and abuse is arguably especially frequent, is incredibly powerful.

Both the Monsters and the Consent campaign had their fun elements – the cute cartoons, the sassy slogans, the freebies. They were also both Students' Association-driven – but what about the University? Cue an attempt by the University during the 2015/2016 academic year to launch a campaign around "dignity and respect" – a campaign which the then-sabbatical officers chose not to take part in and

promote. Why? Because, in my view and that of many students, staff and sabbatical officers, it failed to address the problems of violence, harassment and assault and instead skirted around the issue by focusing on more nebulous concepts of "respect".

While this is in line with the UoE's Dignity and Respect Policy, it is too vague to have much impact, and also isn't particularly radical. It's not an anti-violence campaign if you don't say the word. Nothing will change if you don't confront a problem head on. For the University to frame the campaign in the way they did was, arguably, a method of hiding a problem and of escaping responsibility. And that was an issue.

The University came back later on having changed direction, this time acknowledging that something more specific was needed: this is where the No One Asks For It campaign has come from. This UoE-driven campaign was interesting in two ways – it brought together the University, the Students' Association and the Sports Union, and it was also designed by an external marketing team. What resulted was a microsite with information about the principles behind the campaign and what it was aiming to combat and raise awareness of, a page where you could sign a pledge to fight sexual harassment and sexual violence and be an "active bystander", pages with information on consent and where to go for support, and information about UoE's reporting mechanisms and what the Students' Association offers.

There was also a very slick-looking marketing campaign, centred around some quite provocative slogans ("Grope me," proclaims one poster, with the slogan "No one asks for it" written underneath) all accompanied by some brightly-coloured lips. The video made for the campaign sees a voice-over with such slogans as these being spoken over quickly-changing lips and then "No one asks for it" flashing up at the end with some quite spiky music.

The campaign is designed to shock people into thinking about the issue, and while the content in its presentation and bluntness is potentially quite triggering for survivors of sexual

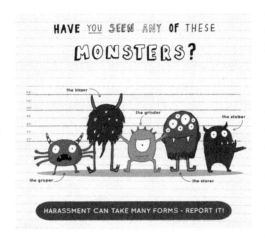

Images courtesy of Edinburgh University Students' Association

violence, it was received mostly quite well at the consultation stage. The campaign was also meant to lead to training being provided for staff and students around issues of sexual violence and support, which as of writing has been rolled out to students who are in positions of leadership and is being developed in some form for staff.

Students will have been exposed to this campaign in two ways – through the marketing being put up around campus and in Students' Association buildings, as well as

on social media and in student emails, and through the face-to-face outreach conducted by various students and staff from the three partner organisations in buildings around all the different UoE campuses. The face-to-face outreach was designed to raise awareness of the campaign and encourage staff and students to sign the online pledge – the aim was to get 4,000 signatures. But what happens, students would ask (and so do I), when you sign? What happens when you reach the goal? Nothing, really.

This is where a well-intentioned campaign unfortunately falls short, partly also because substantive change on these kinds of issues has always been difficult to achieve – it is at best slow-moving and at worst stagnant, and there are bureaucratic obstacles to contend with too.

The pledge is a pleasant gesture, but arguably it also means very little. The fact this is happening alongside UoE reforming its Dignity and Respect Policy (a set of guidelines, not very specific ones at the moment, which function as a kind of code of conduct for staff and students; it provides guidelines along which people might be disciplined) and finally adding a clear section with guidelines on reporting and support for those affected by sexual violence on the UoE website means there is some progress, but it's all very surface level.

Survivors of sexual violence still may not feel comfortable using the University or Students' Association's systems to report incidents due to issues around confidentiality, stigma and safety. It may be difficult to trust the outcome of an investigation into harassment, assault or rape when you are never allowed to find out how the perpetrator has been disciplined (if they have been at all).

It is worth pointing out here that none of these campaigns are without their flaws. The Monsters campaign, with its cutesy cartoons supposed to represent some quite heinous acts, seems quite jarringly gentle compared to the subject matter. The Sexpression Consent campaign has been brilliant for education and awareness, but does not challenge structural issues. And No One Asks For It has been rolled out only to a muted reception, with training for staff not yet fully in existence, and employs potentially quite problematic imagery and techniques to get its message across. There is the argument that these campaigns were all suitable in their purpose and audience, and that they have all been important steps in raising awareness and reducing sexual violence in the University setting. And they have all been relatively effective in raising awareness and at least challenging attitudes and trying to change them. But what's next if sexual violence is still happening and survivors don't feel safe enough to come forward?

In some ways, it's OK that none of these campaigns have really effected structural change within the University, because that wasn't their goal. Changing attitudes is just as important as changing structures, since the two go hand in hand. But we have now had three campaigns in the past three years which have focused on attitudes and awareness – so what's needed now is to make sure changing attitudes are reflected in improved reporting and support structures, and that survivors of sexual violence are safe alongside sexual violence being prevented.

As Women's Convenor, some of the work I have been doing this year alongside our sabbatical officers and Students' Association staff has centred around priorities in terms of reporting and support mechanisms, based on best practice advice and work from campaigns like #StandByMe from the NUS (National Union of Students). Some priorities involve transparency and accountability on the side of the University in terms of publishing reporting statistics and making the disciplinary outcome known to the person who reported an issue, as appropriate. Other priorities aim to ensure that survivors have their needs met in terms of special circumstances and reasonable adjustments, and more. This work is in its early stages and some priorities may be harder to achieve than others, especially in an academic institution where changes take time due to bureaucracy, never mind anything else.

Work is also being done within the Students' Association on the specific issues surrounding staff-student cases of sexual violence and harassment, and I am hoping to focus more on other forms of support for survivors in the coming months (for instance, guidance on how peers and staff can support survivors on a more day-to-day basis, and the possibility of an informal survivor support network). It's clear that a lot of work has been done in the last three years on prevention and reporting, but not so much on other forms of support for people who have been affected – so not only is there work to be done at the structural level, but also on the interpersonal level.

All of this is, ultimately, promising. And I do think it is fair to say that we have come very far in the past few years with regard to awareness of sexual violence and consent. People are becoming more and more willing to confront their own and other people's behaviours, and people take sexual violence, violence against women and marginalised genders in particular, more seriously now than in the past. What is curious though is that the University, even with the advent of No One Asks For It, has tried to take a back seat, and it seems there has not been a lot of willingness to confront problems head on. The original video campaign on "dignity and respect" completely missed the point, and while No One Asks For It discusses sexual violence more explicitly, it basically boils down to yet another marketing campaign with some training.

It is not clear what actual change will come from the pledge which some have seen as meaningless. No One Asks For It is useful – it is the University trying to take a step in the right direction, and a pressure point students and staff can use to make them enact structural change (as in, we can say: "Now that you have done this, students support it and also support further change building on this"). But why did it take some parts of the University so long to even begin to confront sexual violence openly? And why is it that the University, with all its power and all its desire to show off its reputation for being a progressive and innovative institution, has only produced a marketing campaign so far and updated their website a bit, but nothing more?

The potential reasons could be reputation and the neoliberalisation of education, as some academics have argued (Whitley & Page, 2015). The thinking could be that if the University of Edinburgh or other universities admit that they are institutions with a hidden problem with sexual violence, then they would lose reputation and trust. Therefore fewer people would "buy into" the University, as students, academics and indeed investors, and the University would lose out. But the reality is that the opposite is true: if the University were to be explicit in their admission that we have an issue to solve, and if the University were explicit in its attempts to improve its own accountability, then more people, especially and most importantly survivors of sexual violence, would trust the institution they are supposedly "buying into".

The very notion of "buying into" an educational institution is of course problematic. The commoditisation of education in recent years and the growing treatment of students as "customers" is incredibly dangerous for education and academia, and generally signifies a move towards academia being about capitalist worth rather than the well-being and development of students, and indeed staff, who walk a university's corridors. This means initiatives which don't directly benefit a university (i.e. don't bring it money or better reputation) might fall to the bottom of the pile. Which is why change can be slow, and universities can be reluctant to tackle problems openly and head-on.

It doesn't have to be like this, and this is why I and my fellow Liberation Convenors are working so hard on structural change within the University this year in all kinds of ways relating to gender, race, disability and sexuality, alongside staff from both the Students' Association and UoE. Progress is slow. It can indeed feel like not much has changed. But three years of anti-sexual violence campaigns definitely have not amounted to nothing.

What needs to happen now is that the University of Edinburgh as a whole comes to understand what role the institution has to play alongside work on increasing awareness and changing attitudes, because they have a duty of care and responsibility to their students which extends beyond the realm of money.

This is already the case among many staff members – there are of course many who do take their duty of care towards students very seriously and argue that academia must remain about the education and not the finance. But this culture needs to be something the University of Edinburgh stays true to and takes on as a whole. And it needs to make sure it is open, that it listens to its students – who want safety as well as a foot on the graduate career ladder – when we say, "You need to do more than this".

I hope they do listen.

A reflection on the University of Edinburgh's policy on sexual harassment

Gavin Douglas, Deputy Secretary of the University (Student Experience)

I very much enjoyed Chris' article which makes a number of powerful and important points.

The No One Asks For It campaign has very much been a joint initiative between the University, the Student's Association and the Sports Union – not "driven" by the University but conceived and delivered in partnership between all three groups. The campaign visuals are certainly and deliberately provocative, possibly shocking – but we tested them carefully pre-launch with current students and with the chair of a local women's support organisation and took on board their feedback and suggestions. We were really pleased that the campaign attracted the support of senior leaders including the University Principal, the President of EUSU (Edinburgh University Sports Union) and Chris herself.

Do campaigns like No One Asks For It actually "work"? We can of course use marketing techniques to track campaign success by clicks, likes, shares, page views and sign-ups. But these do not really tell us anything very important about whether attitudes have changed one jot, or whether survivors of sexual violence feel better supported. We do know that the number of students coming forward to disclose incidents of sexual violence has gone up significantly this year. We can't say whether this is because of the campaign and the new guidelines or not, but we think this increase is a good thing – though we recognise that we are still only dealing with the tip of the iceberg.

We also know that the campaign has not led to structural change in the University or to cultural change in the groups of people that make up the University community. A single campaign was never going to do that. But change in universities, which are complex organisations, is itself a complex thing.

Fullan & Scott (2009), senior academics who have written extensively on the leadership of change in higher education, approvingly quote Francis Bacon: "We rise to great heights by a winding staircase". A year on, you stop, look back and think – what have we achieved? What have we learned? What do we need to do to get to the next level? Chris' article is really helpful in this context.

We argue that we have come some way this year with the campaign and the new guidelines; we are seeing more students disclosing and we collectively – the University and student groups – are supporting more students who are survivors of sexual violence. All this is good in terms of progress with tackling sexual violence on campus.

But that doesn't mean, as Chris suggests, that anyone – including the University – is now ready to take a back seat. In fact we think we need to step up the focus in this area and do more to a) change the culture and b) do a better job of supporting survivors. We think this will require a greater, more co-ordinated and strategic response from the University – senior leaders, students, academic staff, professional services staff, working alongside other partners such as Rape Crisis Scotland and Police Scotland. We are very confident that this work will continue and grow in 2017/18 – and beyond.

Tackling difficult situations: supporting your staff and students

Anonymous

In my first month as a staff member at the University and brand-new lab head, I hired my first postdoc. She is an amazing scientist, but I soon realized that she had a problem with the working environment. She had been working in the same department during her PhD, and warned me when I started that a member of staff in the building was "creepy". As a line manager, I was not sure what I should do (if anything) about someone being "creepy" and asked her if there was anything I could do to help the situation. She said no, that it was fine. This was a big mistake – I should have tried harder to find out what was going on.

It was only several months later that she was brave enough to tell me what exactly "creepy" meant. In this case, it meant a member of staff making incredibly inappropriate, explicit jokes and references to several young women's anatomy and sex lives. I was absolutely shocked when I heard details of what had been said. With more prompting, I found out that she had mentioned it to her (older, male) PhD supervisor in the department. I think it took a lot of courage for her to bring it up, and her supervisor's reply: "Well, that's just him; we can't piss him off, he's really good at his job". This is wrong on so many levels! I slept on it and the next day went straight to HR (Human Resources).

When I started to tell the story, it turned out that multiple people had previously complained and HR was aware of the situation, but as a complaint had been withdrawn they could take it no further. I found it frustrating that HR had been unable to do anything, but there were confidentiality issues which meant they couldn't fully discuss the history with me. I offered to speak to the "creepy" person and make it clear that this harassment was completely unacceptable and making people uncomfortable. HR advised that his line manager would handle it. I was absolutely livid with the entire situation, but to their credit, HR and the line manager did handle it and all is much smoother now in the department (at least to my knowledge). And I avoided the confrontation with the offending member of staff that I was very anxious about. I also learned a lot about managing people, and now every time I have a new student or member of staff, and at everyone's annual review or before their thesis committee meeting, I let each person know that if they are uncomfortable at work for any reason, I would really like to hear about it and can help take care of the situation.

Ingredients

- Resolve to tackle uncomfortable situations.
- Phone number for HR representative.
- Note to self to remind all students and staff to tell someone if they are uncomfortable.

Method

1. Inform students and staff that they should never be made to feel uncomfortable at work. They should be briefed about this both when they arrive and at annual reviews or before thesis committee meetings.

2. Listen out for people who are uncomfortable at work – they may use subtle hints!

3. Work up the courage to tackle an uncomfortable situation with colleagues.

4. Work with HR or with the people involved, making it clear that any kind of harassment is not acceptable, even if they think it is a joke.

The University of Edinburgh has recently launched the *No One Asks For It* campaign (http://no-oneasksforit.com/support) which makes it very clear that sexual harassment is unacceptable:

"We're challenging sexual harassment and violence on our campuses. We want our University to be a place where students and staff feel respected, supported, and safe.

The term 'sexual harassment' is used to describe any unwelcome behaviour of a sexual nature, from what is often thought of as 'harmless banter' through to sexualised jokes, wolf-whistling, and unwanted physical contact including groping and even sexual assault. Sometimes sexual behaviour can be consensual but if someone else is making you feel uncomfortable, intimidated, or humiliated then it is harassment.

Edinburgh University Students' Association, Edinburgh University Sports Union and the University of Edinburgh are clear that sexual harassment, in any form, is never acceptable."

Support for students who report sexual harassment or assault

**Arianna Andreangeli,
Daphne Loads & Lindsay Jack**

In a recent survey by the National Union of Students (NUS), although 17 per cent of respondents stated they had been victims of some form of sexual harassment during their first week of term, 61 per cent of freshers were unaware of procedures for reporting sexual harassment (NUS, 2015). This recipe is to assist personal tutors and other staff members to whom students disclose sexual harassment.

Ingredients

- A broad definition of sexual abuse, to include: rape, sexual assault, sexual harassment, name-calling, insults, threats and intimidation.
- An understanding that anyone can experience sexual abuse, regardless of sexuality, age, gender, race, religion or disability.
- Time to listen.
- Empathy.
- Clear guidelines.

Method

1. Make sure the student is safe. If they are in physical danger or in need of immediate medical attention, call 999.

2. Advise the student reporting sexual abuse that they can, if they wish, be accompanied by a friend or supporter.

3. Explain to the student the limits of confidentiality. Say that you may be required to speak to someone else about the conversation. See 10 below.

4. Give space to the student: use welcoming body language (e.g. sit together at an appropriate distance, and avoid crossed arms); listen non-judgementally and carefully, preferably in a space that is reasonably private, yet accessible to other individuals who may be able to help.

5. Let the student know that the University is committed to supporting them and to taking appropriate action: mention the existence of policies/guidelines and possible remedies for the student, and answer any questions on these issues.

6. Suggest that another member of staff be present during the discussion, if the student is comfortable with that.

7. Encourage the student to make contact with the Advice Place or equivalent student support service.

8. Suggest alternative or additional sources of support, for example: Rape Crisis Scotland; the student's GP (general practitioner) or local hospital for injuries or infections; or the University's counselling service.

The University of Edinburgh guidelines for supporting students who experience sexual harassment can be found here: http://www.ed.ac.uk/staff/student-support/sexual-harassment and http://www.ed.ac.uk/students/health/things-not-going-well/sexual-harassment-assault

Students at University of Edinburgh can get help and support from the Advice Place. https://www.eusa.ed.ac.uk/support_and_advice/the_advice_place/

Information about the University's student counselling service can be found here: http://www.ed.ac.uk/student-counselling. For staff, see http://www.ed.ac.uk/counselling-services/staff

9. Following the meeting, send an email to the student's University email only, reminding them what was discussed, any instructions or support given and any decisions taken or follow-up required. Keep a copy of the email in case you need to refer to it in the future; make sure that this is marked as "confidential" in your email folders. You may also wish to make a copy of this email and hand it in hard copy to your school's student support office, with a request that it be kept confidential, according to the school's confidentiality protocol.

10. In your email, remind the student about the limits of confidentiality, as you had explained to him or her during your face-to-face meeting. Spell out clearly in writing that:

    • you may be required to give evidence about the conversation if there is a criminal case;

    • you are required to raise serious concern under the University's Dignity and Respect Policy;

    • in the case of rape or serious sexual assault you should report the details to the University Secretary's Office;

    • if the alleged perpetrator is still at large it may be necessary for the University to inform the police.

Cook's tip

Make sure you take good care of yourself. You are not required to offer specialist support to the student: your role is to listen to them, reassure them of the University's commitment to support and appropriate action, and to let them know about sources of support. However, listening to a disclosure of sexual abuse can be stressful or upsetting. The Staff Counselling Service provides support and counselling if you need it. You may also wish to speak to a senior colleague. In any event, it is highly advisable that the report is conveyed to your head of school and/or the senior tutor, in confidence – preferably via a face-to-face meeting if possible.

Warning

This recipe is based on University of Edinburgh procedures. If you work elsewhere, check your own institution's policies.

Perspectives from students

Lara Isbel & Judy Robertson

We wanted EqualBITE to have contributions from people across the University. Our recipe-writing workshops, held on each of the campuses, tended to attract staff members (usually women) but seldom students. This article describes some false starts in involving students in EqualBITE, and explains how the student photographs and illustrations contained in the volume were gathered.

Our aim in gathering content for the book was different from the aims of an academic research project. Where a research project might focus on the representativeness of the views, or whether the sampling strategy was effective, our goal was to give students the opportunity to contribute to the book if they wanted to, and in a way which they found appealing.

We felt it was important to represent the experiences and views of students on the topics which mattered to them, as often gender equality efforts in universities (such as Athena SWAN) have focused on the proportions of female students at various levels, without taking into account what the culture is like. Although Athena SWAN submissions now often contain survey data on staff work-life satisfaction, the analogous data for students has not been required. Our goal was to give the reader some insight into what it is like to be a women student at the University of Edinburgh.

An open survey

When we realised we needed to look for alternative opportunities to encourage students to contribute to the project, we asked the Edinburgh University Students'

Association for their help in reaching the student body. They believed that the recipe format was likely off-putting to students, and suggested that they get in touch with students on our behalf with a more concise way to gather views, such as a short online survey question. The editorial team spent various frustrating meetings trying to phrase a question.

The Students' Association staff kindly forwarded our questions to relevant student societies, but on receiving no response at all, they circulated a very brief survey to all the students in the University (around 38,000 people). We asked the students how stereotypes about gender affected their university experience, what might minimise this effect, and asked if there was anything else they would like to say about gender equality in the University.

We got a grand total of four responses. While the very small number of people taking part is far too small to be a representative sample, we wanted to include their opinions, particularly as the variety of experiences ranged quite broadly.

Our first response was from a male undergraduate in the Medical School who said gender stereotypes had 'not at all' affected his University experience. He added:

> Increasing pressure from the professionally offended make me worried that being a straight white male in itself is beginning to become risky. I study medicine. We have a gender inequality in med school group of females who like to complain about certain things. 60% of med school is female. If I started a male gender inequality in med school committee for that reason (and others) I would be vilified. The current level of hypocrisy is ridiculous.

An undergraduate student in the School of Chemistry who described their gender as binary also felt that gender stereotypes had minimal impact:

They don't. I ignore them [gender stereotypes] and get on with my life. It's pretty equal, but we don't need parity for the sake of it.

A non-binary (female), undergraduate student, School of Philosophy, Psychology and Language Sciences had a different experience.

> The boys/men in the class take up a lot of time asking questions to the lecturer, and are not suggested to wait until another time or to continue the talk elsewhere. Girls/women are often suggested to stop talking or simply don't get the chance to talk because the boys dominate the discussions.

> I also feel that, because I am non-binary, less people will talk with me in classes, I don't feel that I am as included as other people are. I think teachers should be aware of the time they are giving up in the classes for discussion, and how they may distribute it unfairly based on gender.

> I think it [the University] is generally good and progressive. It would be good to start having non-binary bathrooms, as I know this is something that many people would like.

Our last survey response was from a female undergraduate student in the School of Literatures, Languages and Cultures who reported a similar classroom experience:

> In tutorials and seminars, even though women outnumber men in my classes, male students often manage to take over the conversation, or limit the input of female students who might not want to have to raise their voice to be heard.

To tackle this, she suggested:

> Greater management by staff of conversation, focusing on inclusivity.

This student also reported having to deal with challenging behaviour outside of class:

> I have had various unpleasant experiences with male students outside of university time and off-campus in which I have been bullied, intimidated, or otherwise subjected to unwanted advances, physical contact and attention. The internal mechanisms for reporting this are inadequate. There is a culture on non-inclusivity among University of Edinburgh students, on class, gender, sexuality and ethnicity lines, and the University does not do enough to combat this. Students are ambassadors for the University and the University should take such inappropriate behaviour more seriously.

The issue of sexual harassment is considered in the articles that follow. For staff members who would like to improve their practice in these areas, the recipes on *Creating a safe space for classroom discussions and Support for students who report sexual harassment or assault* may be helpful. The *Educated Pass* recipe documents one of the University's projects which aims to give men educational opportunities.

Discussions with gender and primary education students

As the students did not have the time or inclination to reply to an online survey – and let's face it everyone's inbox is overflowing with online surveys – we decided to start discussions with students within academic classes.

One of the editors, Judy Robertson, visited the fourth-year Gender and Primary Education course at the Moray House School of Education (with the kind permission of the lecturer, Dr Ann MacDonald). It was particularly interesting to talk to student teachers about their view on gender equality, both because it is a female-dominated profession, and because primary school teachers have a powerful role in shaping children's attitudes which will in turn influence society in the future. It was the last class of the course, and the students were displaying posters of their ideas to help them draft an essay.

She started the session explaining about the book, and asked for the students' opinions about their experiences of gender equality at the University. When she asked the students "if you could change one thing at the University of Edinburgh relating to gender equality what would it be?" the students had nothing they wanted to share at that point although they agreed to write down their thoughts and return them later.

When the editor walked around the posters, and chatted to small groups of students, she found that they had plenty to say. They spoke about everyday sexism which they encountered on campus, in sports, in bars and in their workplaces. One student was frustrated because she felt her sport – cheerleading – is not recognised in the same way other sports are:

> We go to the competitions, making history in the UK cheerleading scene, but the university don't really care about that. How often do you hear about what we've done? We're the most trophied sport/club in the University but how often do you hear that? Never... We win nationals every year and no one knows about that... It's so annoying when we go down there and we achieve so much and I come back up and I am so scared to tell someone. Also I am not allowed to get time off [from studying] to go to competitions because it is not a registered sport.

The status of cheerleading as a sport is in flux. Cheerleading has recently been given provisional recognition as a sport by the International Olympic Committee. The student above is referring to recognition by Sports Scotland and the University.

Two of the written comments followed up on the theme of sports societies:

> While there are policies in place, lad culture is still very prevalent in sports societies.

> [the one thing I would change is] tackling "lad" banter within sports societies. There continues to be pervasive attitudes of male superiority and female objectification within some of the University's male sports clubs/teams.

Two of the students wrote that they thought it was important for the University to tackle the "lad"/"rape" culture, one emphasising that "girls should feel safe at uni".

The students mentioned how they felt comfortable on the School of Education campus (where a high proportion of the students are women) but that they felt less comfortable on the main campus because of what they described as the "lad culture".

They associated the problem with particular groups of students:

> There's a lot of white upper class boys. Not solely. But that's quite a lot of what Edinburgh Uni is made up of.

One student said that:

> If you go to [the student union] or the main library you can see it and like hear it [the lad culture] and if I go to the main library I feel like I should wear something nice and put on make-up. More so than if I came here because it is all girls here.

Another agreed, commenting that:

> It's the whole male gaze thing. If you go to the main library, you feel very looked at.

They also discussed campaigns organised by the Students' Association relating to sexual harassment and assault, consent and alcohol. The students mentioned a rape in the park near the main university campus a few years ago, which to their minds had brought a lot of attention to the issue of sexual assault, and whether women should be advised to change their routes and behaviour in order to stay safe.

One student said that: "That campaign, No One Asks for It, it is fantastic" (see *A reflection on the University of Edinburgh's policy on sexual harassment*) although the students were not convinced that the campaign had the necessary reach. They thought that students would benefit from education about sexual consent, particularly when alcohol is involved, but they were unsure what the student union was doing about this, or what approach would be effective in reaching the right student groups.

They thought that student unions in general should behave responsibly by refraining from selling alcohol at very low prices, one noting that: "I think our union is quite responsible about that".

The students spoke of double binds and contradictions they encountered in their social lives at the University and beyond. A male student brought up the contradiction between EUSA's active campaigning on equality issues (such as the campaign to provide gender-neutral toilet facilities, an issue which the students supported) and an event run on Students' Association premises in which:

> It was interesting that at the Saturday night club they were choosing to have shot girls who go around selling shots [of alcohol]. They wear high heels and are very very feminine – emphasised femininity. It was interesting that with the student union being seen as progressive that still on a club night they had people doing that.

When asked whether he would be more likely or less likely to buy alcohol when it was sold in such a way, he replied that it didn't make a difference. The Edinburgh University Students' Association stated that: "We have acted swiftly to make sure that this will not happen in Students' Association venues in the future, in line with our mission and values" when the editorial team brought this incident to their attention, further noting that the issue has been directly brought by their members previously.

There was a double bind related to their perception of men's inconsistent attitudes to women and alcohol:

> [when I am] around other sports teams (predominantly male), ... I get called "boring" because I am not out, smashed, all the time. Especially on social nights even if I still go to the club, have a fab night, the fact that I am not drunk – they don't like it.

Another student agreed:

> If a girl gets really drunk, then boys will say she can't handle it. Or she is a ladette, a binge-drinking girl. You can't win.

Expectation about women students' appearance caused them stress. This manifested in generalised expectations from one's peer group:

> We were talking about getting dressed up for a night out and how you can't go out on a night out wearing leggings and a jumper. As much as you'd love to, but it is so frowned upon. Even if you can't be bothered you are wearing the highest heels in the world and your feet are killing you, you have to do it.

But as well as social pressure, some of the students had experienced pressures about their appearance from their employers. The women had been asked to provide full body and face photographs with their job applications forms, had been required to wear extra tight T-shirts and shorts, and had been requested to change aspects of their appearance at work,

including removing their spectacles. One student explained about the exacting and contradictory instructions of her boss:

> You have to wear your hair down and wear heels. But then he was like "you're really tall, don't look too tall".

Another student was sent home from work for not wearing make-up in her role as a hostess at a bar. As she phrased it:

> I apparently wasn't pretty enough so I got sent home.

She chose not to return to her job because:

> I am not going to portray myself as someone different. You hired me for me! I wasn't any more made-up when you hired me.

The students finished this section of the conversation by saying:

> There is so much pressure, I would say. It's awful.

> Girls have the short straw don't they?

On a more positive note, the students' posters about gender and teaching in primary schools demonstrated that this sample of student teachers were thoughtfully aware of their responsibilities in teaching the next generation about redressing gender inequalities and reducing discrimination relating to sexual orientation and gender identity.

In summary, while none of the School of Education students had experienced gender inequality or discrimination during their studies, they described how they routinely contended with gendered expectations about their behaviour or appearance in social settings, and felt uncomfortable in some parts of the campus because of this.

The cases where the students had been told to dress in a particular way by their male employers are troubling; it would be useful to consider whether a joint campaign between the University careers service and the Students' Association could alleviate this. It is often necessary for students to work to financially support their studies; they should not be subject to male whims about their appearance while they do so.

The power of visual art

Visiting the School of Education students was very valuable to help the team to understand what it is like to be a woman student at the University of Edinburgh today. We were still no further forward in collecting student-generated content for the book. As the written word did not appear to be appealing for students, we decided to be more flexible about content type: what about visual art? This would enable students to be creative and expressive, and could help us to gather evocative experiences to give the reader insight into aspects of the students' lives. We took two approaches to this: one was to visit another class to ask our art students to draw their experiences, and the other was to respond to the serendipitous opportunity presented by a photographic exhibition organised by Edinburgh University Students' Association.

Illustrations by the Edinburgh College of Art students

Following the suggestion of Chris Belous, the Women's Officer for Edinburgh University Students' Association, we decided to include some illustrations drawn by students at the Edinburgh College of Art (ECA). We got in touch with Dr Harvey Dingwall, a lecturer in Illustration, to ask if we might visit his class to work with the students, to which he kindly agreed. We spent two hours working with his third-year class, discussing the students' experiences of gender inequality, at the University and in their lives more widely. In common with the students in the School of Education, at the start of the discussion, many of the students did not identify that they had experienced gender inequality. They spoke very positively of their safe and supportive learning environment within the ECA, and indeed the mutually respectful atmosphere during the discussion was a testament to the rapport between the class and the lecturer. However, after further discussion in small groups and through initial sketching, the students began to talk of their wider experiences with the University facilities (such as the need for gender-neutral toilets), University gym, clubs and the city in general. A story which we found particularly striking about the culture in a University bar is illustrated below. We learned, to our perplexity, that it is the habit of some (mostly male) students to throw their nearly, but not quite, empty beer bottles on to the heads of fellow (mostly female) patrons, soaking them.

The students then had the opportunity to work on their drawings further in their own time, and could choose whether to submit them to the editors for potential inclusion in this book. All of the drawings were of a high standard, and the editorial team selected those which were relevant to academic or social life at the University. All those who submitted a drawing received a token to spend at a local art shop.

You can see these wonderful images below.

I was taught in school that if I didn't live up to the standards of my male classmates, then I wasn't owed any respect.

I learned that people would turn a blind eye to abuse when it was at the hands of a boy.

But what's new there?

Alice McCall

I learned that people would turn a blind eye to abuse when it was at the hands of a boy. But what's new there?

Han Deacon

Open your eyes

Harry Whitelock

Special Ape: Masculinity in the night club culture

Madeline Pinkerton

Runners: "But I see and hear about it all the time"

Kathy Allnutt

Potterrow bar "It's just a joke - don't get all serious on us"
Throw the bottle, soak the girls (but blame them too...)

I mean, yeah...

they are 'just' microaggressions

but you'll have to forgive me

if my annoyance

ISN'T SO

Rosie Hawtin

Microaggressions

'just look down'   'don't attract attention'   'and you'll be ok'

Kathy Allnutt
Street sexism

Cael O'Sullivan
Bubble of safety

Christine Meyer

Elephant on guard

IF I GET PREGNANT WHILE STUDYING MY FUTURE EMPLOYER WILL BE MORE LIKELY TO HIRE ME BECAUSE THEN THEY DON'T HAVE TO PAY MY MATERNITY LEAVE

Amalie Hjelm

Pregnancy: a Scandinavian perspective

'Unapologetically Me' exhibition by University of Edinburgh students

The editors were kindly invited to the Unapologetically Me photography exhibition at EUSA's Potterrow building, and spoke to Jenna Kelly the EUSA Vice President Services who co-organised it and explained how it came about.

In autumn 2016, Edinburgh University Students' Association and the Women's Liberation Group invited women and non-binary people on campus to participate in Unapologetically Me.

The project was a:

> photography campaign designed to create an environment where we, and no one else, make the deliberate choices about how we present ourselves.

An organiser said:

> All too often images of women and non-binary folk are subject to unrealistic sexist beauty standards, as well as racist and fat-phobic ideals. Our bodies are objectified and sexualised without our permission, and it feels like everyone gets a choice about how we are portrayed except us.

The group organised a series of photography workshops to teach people how to use cameras and editing software. Workshop participants produced a broad range of thought-provoking and inspiring self-portraits. The photographs were displayed at the Unapologetically Me exhibition in the Students' Association building in November, 2016.

> We taught women and non-binary folk about the ins and outs of photography, and how to use a camera to make them look exactly the way THEY (and no one else) wanted themselves to look in a photo.

Several of the portraits and stories presented at this exhibition resonated with other issues that had emerged during the EqualBITE writing workshops. With kind permission of the organisers, we have included some of the student stories and portraits from the Unapologetically Me exhibition.

The focus of the campaign was about creating your own image. Several of the young women responded to the pressures created by mixed messages of beauty standards and how this affected their body image and self-esteem:

Stephanie

Have I got it? More or less? Should I show more? Should I cover up?

Should I be comfortable? Should I be practical? What do you want? We can't do them all at once.

Julia shared her frustration:

I have always felt torn between the admiration of women boldly embracing their own bodies and imperfections (YES!) and trying to live up to what society (including me) has labelled as a perfect body. This makes me feel stuck in a vacuum between two ideals, failing on both fronts: not having the 'right' body as well as giving (more than) a damn that I don't. Being unapologetically me means accepting the balancing between two ideals and trying to move to simply taking care of myself.

Julia

In this photo I'm putting on body lotion, something I have been doing on a daily basis for as long as I can remember. I realised this is one of the few ways I take care of my body for the sake of taking care of it. Not wanting to change it, not neglecting it, not judging it.

The focus on external appearance was particularly difficult for non-binary students.

Ester shared the dilemmas of bathroom choice:

Ester

Being myself often involves looking at the mirror in the morning and thinking whether I look feminine or masculine that day. I need to answer that question for myself because of bathrooms – whether I look feminine enough to go to the women's bathroom or masculine enough to get kicked out?

There were celebratory stories too, focusing on accepting yourself for who you are or ignoring the rules on what an 'acceptable' appearance should be.

Rumana said:

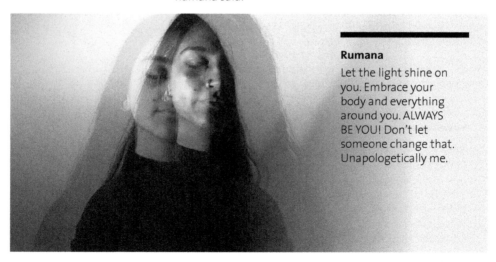

Rumana

Let the light shine on you. Embrace your body and everything around you. ALWAYS BE YOU! Don't let someone change that. Unapologetically me.

Amy described the importance of being free
to express yourself as you want to.

Amy

It's odd that if I change
one small aspect
about my body that it
suddenly encapsulates
my mind and makes me
feel isolated in simple
situations. However, I
find that when I break
away from social norms
of my body it helps me
realise who I am on the
inside.

Lola said:

In my photo I wanted to be completely covered in make up
because that's how I like it; I like to have giant eyeliner flicks
and OTT spidery eyelashes pretty much every day regardless
of what I'm doing. Lots of people say it's too much, that they
prefer natural girls, or ask me why I'm trying so hard when
I'm just at school or work. But for me it's not trying anything
or even effort; I love my make-up routine as part of my day.
At the last minute I decided to throw on lipstick too, because
it struck me that women's magazines would probably
strictly outlaw both at once and advise you only wear one
or the other, to go with the concrete 'cleavage OR legs' rule.

Lola

When I really think about
it, if I constructed my face
for anyone other than
myself I'm pretty sure
I'd take the extensive
feedback I've been given
and tone it down, but I
definitely prefer the idea
that when I'm 78 I'll still
be walking about with a
super-exaggerated cat-eye
and a matte-lip look.

Students also shared their thoughts on the pressures to behave in a stereotypically feminine way – to be pleasant, smiling and approachable. This was also mentioned by older women taking part in the writing workshops for the book.

Eli said:

Women are often expected or forced to provide emotional labour in the form of smiling. How many times have you been asked to smile? At work, at school, in arguments, on the street, in a bar? It's a way to make us provide comfort and aesthetic pleasure even to those we may owe nothing, and a way to ensure women appear unthreatening. I suppose many of us would be better off if we tried being a bit more gentle. Yet it troubles me that for women, being serious so often is treated as being aggressive, and being cheerful is treated as naivety.

Eli

I've wasted too much time moulding myself to avoid this, forced into an unfair dichotomy where being taken seriously comes at the expense of being approachable and friendly. If we aren't smiling, we have a good reason to do so.

Bella shared her dream of a less stereotypical approach to defining people.

I like the idea that our traits – intellect, mental faculties, affection etc – rather than our gender, race and class could define us. And I adore the idea that a woman could be defined by her brain, and her brain alone.

Bella

I am unapologetically nerdy. In the 19th century, scientists believed in phrenology – the concept that the skull represented character and mental abilities. So, being a neuroscience undergraduate, I plastered a phrenological map over my forehead (handily covering my unapologetically spotty skin).

Conclusions

Academic colleagues may be familiar with the difficulties in coaxing students to participate in activities. "They just won't engage", our colleagues say, in tones ranging from sorrow to frustration. In this case, we had no expectation that students should engage: writing an article – even a short format recipe – is a big investment of time. We are very thankful to Chris, Danai, Zach and Hope and our other student authors for their valuable writing time. Even with the more concise format of writing a response to an online survey, we did not believe that students had any obligation to participate. What we decided to look for – and what we found in the end – were more flexible and creative options to record students' views.

We make no claims about how generalisable these views are. The views are fascinating because of the insights which they share and the questions which they raise. We hope that they are of interest to the reader, and that other teams of researchers will take up the challenge of extending the work.

A common theme running through the students' views is that of safety – in the sense of safety from harassment and assault, but also in the sense of safety to be oneself without criticism or resentment from others. Both senses of safety are necessary to thrive and flourish in university life.

You can't be what you can't see: visible celebration of notable women

Jo Spiller & Sarah Moffat

Architecture articulates the experience of our being-in-the-world, [it] mediates and projects meanings. (Pallasmaa, 2013, p. 12-13)

Meanings are projected not just by the buildings themselves, but by how they are furnished and decorated (Williams, 2013). And where almost every image – portrait, photograph, statue – of academic achievement and leadership is masculine (and nearly always white middle-aged), the meaning is clear: to be a successful leader, gender and ethnicity matter.

Portraits of women of achievement are sparse across institutions such as the University of Edinburgh, apart from on exceptional occasions such as International Women's Day when images of successful academic women are made prominent (but not permanent). There is, however, a movement to change this.

Women are challenging the paucity of female portraits, empowered by research showing that: a) women are more confident, and speak with more authority and for equal amounts of time as men when surrounded by images of women of achievement (for men it makes no difference as they are used to being surrounded by images of men of achievement) (Latu et al., 2013); and b) that stereotype threat can be provoked "simply through visual reminders of [a] group's underrepresentation" (Steele, 2011).

This recipe is based on a current Edinburgh University Students' Association (EUSA) project to replace the all-male portraits outside the Debating Hall, Teviot Row House, with a more diverse collection of images. This idea emerged from a debated proposal: "You can't be what you can't see: implementing diversity in student spaces". The proposers referenced the negative impact such an overwhelming and unrepresentative gallery could have on students' confidence and sense of belonging at the University and the proposal's success gave EUSA the mandate to make the changes.

This recipe is also informed by a parallel project in Hertford College, Oxford, where to celebrate 40 years of women in the college, the all-male portraits in the Great Hall have been replaced by specially commissioned photograph portraits of women graduates, staff and students (http://www.theguardian.com/education/2014/sep/21/oxford-hertford-college-portraits-women-co-ed).

And finally, the recipe is also proposing the idea that other rooms in the University hung only with portraits of men could be diversified. A clear statement of intent for gender equality would be made by starting with the Raeburn Room (one of the most famous rooms in the University of Edinburgh Old College) and its celebrated portraits.

Ingredients

- Over 100 years of women graduates.
- Confidence to challenge the status quo, backed up by research.
- An imaginative curator.
- Estates storage (large, secure, temperature-controlled unit).
- Access to as many of the following as possible: personal and national portrait archives, photographer, royalty-free images.
- Imagination.
- Budget for frames, high quality print service, picture hooks and wire.

Method

1. Challenge the status quo – examine the academic research; hold a debate as EUSA did; find a champion, like Emma Smith in Hertford College, Oxford; invoke the Athena SWAN movement in the UK.

2. Identify first projects such as landmark rooms in the student union or central university meeting rooms. The University of Edinburgh project identified Teviot Row House and the Raeburn Room initially.

3. Appoint an imaginative curator/
curatorial team to:
   - design and implement innovative
   strategies (e.g. send the existing
   Raeburn portraits on tour to
   build cultural bridges);
   - make choices, and liaise with
   Estates and other specialists.

4. Where the removal of portraits
leaves a visible gap, capitalise on
the space. See the Wikipedia article
on Trafalgar Square's 4th Plinth:
https://en.wikipedia.org/wiki/
Fourth_plinth,_Trafalgar_Square

5. Recognise and respect: the artistic and
historical value of existing portraits.
For example, the Raeburn portraits are
extraordinary works of art and part
of Scotland's aesthetic legacy. EUSA
recognises the significant historical
value of the existing portraits, and
have decided to catalogue them and
offer them to the University archives.

6. Identify women graduates of note.
The University of Edinburgh project
browsed records of 100 years of women
graduates including the many women
graduates of Edinburgh College of
Art such as those in the 2015-2016
exhibition of Modern Scottish Women
Painters and Sculptors 1885-1965 in the
Scottish National Gallery of Modern Art.

7. Source images of women graduates
– if possible via personal and national
archives. If the women are alive,
commission a photographer, or if there
are prints available, aim to get relevant
permission to use them. Mount and
frame as your budget will allow.

8. Implement the curatorial strategy;
for example, send the existing
Raeburn portraits on tour to build
cultural bridges, 'resting' any others
by moving to a temperature-
controlled storage unit.

9. Replace with fresh portraits of
women of achievement.

10. If you encounter resistance, make
the points that that rooms can have
name changes, changes are never
permanent, the pictures aren't being
burned in a heap, they are being
circulated for the greater good of the
University, or 'rested' for a decade.
They can be reinstated as required.

At the time of going to press the EUSA
project, though delayed, is still happening.

The University has put up life-size
photographs on billboards across the
central campus celebrating academic
staff winners of Teaching Awards, and
there is a clear gender balance.

Allies
in the
classroom

Zach Murphy

Being a 'real man' in the traditional western sense very often means conforming to a stereotypical architecture of manliness (van der Gaag, 2014, p. 123) and demonstrating qualities such as independence, being intimidating, in control, muscular, tough, strong, respected and hard (Katz, 2006, quoted by van der Gaag, 2014, pp. 59-60). It can be difficult for young men, in particular, to cut across these stereotypes of gender performance. "A man questioning traditional masculinities is somehow less of a man rather than more of one" (van der Gaag, 2014, p. 31). This recipe, written by a male postgraduate student, reflects on some of these issues.

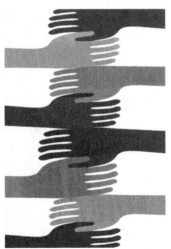

Years ago, as an 18-year-old, I had an amazing opportunity to travel with a cultural education programme for six months. Each week we addressed a different topic. I will never forget the week that we spoke about feminism. I was excited to learn how people in my own age range approached the topic. I had not grown up thinking one gender was better than the other; they were just not the same.

We had a few hours of education related to feminism. It was student-led, and it had attracted a few of the more passionate women in our group to speak on the topic. The open-minded young man that I was, I waited patiently for some revelation of how I could model healthy respectful and empowering behaviour. I was only to be disappointed and saddened at the way the topic traversed from women's rights to what felt to my young, untrained ears and mind like man-hating.

I have spent many years since then struggling with the idea that in order for one group to gain equal ground they will either need to lower the status of another group, raise their own or a combination of both. Now I believe that the question is: How can we find ways for gender, and all other aspects of equality, to be a win-win situation?

How do we talk about this? The challenge I face, and I see others around me facing, is that I don't want to lose my manliness or who I am as a man in order to help people feel better about who they are.

As a young male in academia, I have often found myself in a position of not taking a stance. Not because I didn't want one, but because I truly didn't know how to have one in a healthy way. This is not the place I wanted to stand, I wanted to be able to talk about racism, feminism, sexuality, and the other topics that relate to gender.

This recipe is my stance on being an ally – an agent for change and equality in the classroom. Since the original draft of this recipe I have been blessed to be surrounded by inspirational friends, partners in bravery, and role models who live their values each and every day.

Seeing positive behaviour modelled around gender, sex, orientation, race and age, has helped me realise caring about people means putting relationships first. People are people. I challenge myself and I challenge others to approach every day with courage, and above all else to be kind.

Ingredients

- Patience with yourself and others.
- Allies who have experienced the challenge and faced it.
- Compassion and empathy.

Method

1. Use 'different' instead of 'weird'. The words we use matter. If something is different that is a fact, not a judgement.

2. Stand up for yourself and for what you believe in, without being rude or disrespectful. Ask the hard questions (see *Unravelling rhetoric* for ways of dealing with rhetorical traps).

3. If you dig yourself into a hole, dig yourself out. We have all done this at one point or another: do not simply let the damage stand. Use open conversation, powerful questions and forgiveness.

4. Reflect. If you have a difficult conversation, take some time to write down the points that bothered you or that you didn't totally understand. This may help the next time you are in a similar situation or when you see this person again (see *Challenging bias*).

5. Find a kindred spirit. If you believe that people are people are people... find someone else who believes it just as strongly. Formidable change comes when like-minded people come together. Just make sure you get some outside perspectives as well and don't slide into groupthink (Janis 1972/1982). Seek a mentor specifically in this area, someone with experience who can help you see what you can't totally grasp.

6. Never hide your light. Do not shy away from the opportunity to lead by example. Practice everyday leadership by showing respect and care beyond your own point of view.

Grow and succeed with fellow students

Hope Bretscher

When you look around the lecture hall of a hard physics class and see a lot of men, with just a sprinkling of women, it is easy to feel like you are in a competition with the other women. It can feel like only one female flavour will be viewed positively and as successful, while all the other women will be regarded as inferior. But each woman has a special spice! She can stand alone and deserves to study and succeed in physics, and can also add a flavour to the class that helps everyone to grow and succeed. Mixed into the pudding with all the other ingredients, each ingredient enhancing the others makes the strongest delicious pudding!

Ingredients

- A lot of men.
- A few women.
- Guts, bravery and boldness.

Method

1. Remind yourself that you are sufficient as a person as you are, and do not need to be "the best" to make it.

2. Remind yourself that multiple women can succeed.

3. In class, go sit by another woman; introduce yourself and find out what they are interested in.

4. Study with the women – you'll do better if you work together and build on each other's strengths.

5. Study with the men. Note that they too may be struggling in some things and succeeding in others – you'll do better if you work together and build on each other's strengths.

6. Study in a group with both men and women. You will become less isolated and illustrate how each of you is valuable, debunking the stereotypes which can divide and weaken.

7. Go for a drink or a coffee with the men and women after a hard week. Remind each other that you are all people, interested in a subject, good at different things. Humanise each other.

8. Keep repeating steps 1-7 until all the flavours have mixed to create a tasty pudding, but one that you can still taste each distinctly and realise what an important ingredient it is.

Cook's tips

You may need to add a lot of guts and courage to get this right. Don't worry if at first there is a flavour of discomfort – it will transform with the other ingredients into something better!

The power of language: moving beyond past harms and present hurts

Alison Williams

> Language matters [because] it contains and conveys the categories through which we understand ourselves and others, and through which we become who and what we are.
>
> Lynne Tirrell (2000, p. 139)

Much of this book concerns language: what is said, who says it, how it is said and in what context, what meaning we attach to it, and how we react to it. Fifty-seven of the recipes and papers refer directly or indirectly to language: its use, its misuse, and its power. Authors describe times when language has been alien or absent, when they have – or have not – been able to access the words they needed in the moment, and they talk about the impact – positive and negative – that language (their own and others') has on their ability to work well, collaboratively, creatively and productively.

Language conveys layers of meaning. The structure of linguistic categories reinforces social categories, which in turn reinforce (and can create) patterns of behaviour, which are then reflected in the original linguistic categories (Tirrell, 2000). As Braidotti observes of how androcentric concepts are embedded historically, "the thinker needs some humility before the multilayered and complex structure of language" (Braidotti, 2000, p. 300). An in-depth analysis of feminist philosophical approaches to language is beyond the scope of this book. We point the interested reader to The Companion to Feminist Philosophy, and in particular to the essays by Tirrell and Braidotti.

The dictionary records cultural meanings, which we take to be descriptive, no matter who is speaking. It is, for example, only in the present century that it has been fully accepted that the title of Chairman is not (only) a description of a role, but a reinforcement of social norms and stereotypes. The change to the title of Chair was initially strongly opposed; on taking over the role, one academic colleague found herself having to protest that while she did not object to being called a chair, she did object to being called a man.

Exorcising the ghosts of past harms

Like the Chair/Chairman shift, many of the ways in which language has harmed women by erasing them from the discourse – past harms – have been challenged, and are now officially gone. However, as recipes such as *Damning with faint praise* and *Unravelling rhetoric* attest, some still arise and continue to have to be challenged. Recipes *Challenging bias* and *Allies in the classroom* point up the need to cultivate personal awareness to notice these harms in the first place, so normalised as they are, as well as the vocabulary to challenge them.

One of the most pervasive is the false generic. We all have pet hates: mine is guys – it is not inclusive, and at a recent undergraduate seminar the raising of this sparked a very difficult debate. (For suggestions about managing these kinds of discussions see *Creating a safe space for classroom discussions*.) Although 'mankind' is rarely used now in academic work, androcentric language and its consequent thinking are still present in different guises. An editorial headline in The Lancet (2016)

described a clinical trial as "First-in-man", as did the research paper itself (Kalladka et al., 2016). A leading piece in The Economist on climate change (2017) started: "For millennia mankind has moaned about the weather" and ends: "One thing is certain, mankind is forever cursed to moan about the weather" (http://worldif.economist.com/article/13542/changing-climate-opinion). It is tempting to ask if human beings are forever cursed to use the false generic?

Tirrell's (2000) call "Stop it, now!" and Gay's exhortation to men to:

> Make the effort and make the effort and make the effort until you no longer need to, until we don't need to keep having this conversation. Change requires intent and effort. It really is that simple. (Gay, 2014, p. 173)

are echoed, and practical ideas put forward in response, in *Be vigilant with your vocabulary*; *Say something*; and *Gender balancing your seminar speakers* (among many others).

> Address the issue: Make a decision to draw your colleague's attention to it immediately or wait until later when you can have a proper discussion. Humour is often useful in navigating potentially difficult situations as it de-escalates the threat of any confrontation while at the same time allowing you to navigate a potentially difficult situation with more ease. (From *Be vigilant with your vocabulary*).

Present hurts

Thirty-two of the recipes and papers explore how people in the University deal with language which contributes directly to gender inequalities, and 25 more contributions look at language's indirect impact. With raised awareness diminishing the more obvious harms, more subtle hurts come to the fore, many based on how language reinforces stereotype norms without our being aware of it, immersed as we are in the culture (see *Recognise your privilege*). For example, in his 2007 book The

Stuff of Thought, Steven Pinker notes in parentheses, and apparently without irony,

> (By the way, in this chapter I will refer to the generic speaker as a "he" and the generic hearer as a "she", just to help you keep track of who's who; this is a common convention in the linguistics literature). (Pinker, 2007, pp. 376-377)

Every time it is used, this 'common convention' reinforces the normalisation of men as worth listening to, and women as the receivers of their wisdom. Rebecca Solnit, in her essay Men explain things to me, describes the phenomenon of 'mansplaining' (although she does not use this term) when a man has explained to a woman, most often wrongly, things that they know little or nothing about, and in which the woman is an expert. Solnit is, however, clear that although this is in her experience usually a gendered activity it is not exclusively so; just "the intersection between overconfidence and cluelessness where some portion of [the male] gender gets stuck" (Solnit, 2012).

Tirrell points out that by producing and reproducing social and cultural norms in content, form and usage, language is normative. Much of what we think of as descriptive is in fact normative; it only appears descriptive if one has already accepted a rather large set of norms (Butler, 1993). For example, research into effective leadership qualities in research environments has identified the desirability of positive attitude, empathy, generosity, humour, open-mindedness and reliability (Robertson, 2014; Glaser & Smalley, 1995). These leadership traits are often stereotyped as feminine and contrasted with leadership traits such as assertiveness, dominance, and competitive agentic behaviour that are stereotypically described as masculine (as in Schein's 1993 think manager – think male paradigm). Koenig et al. point out:

> Even women who possess outstanding qualifications for leadership may have the burden of overcoming preconceptions that they are not well equipped to lead. Not only do the descriptive aspects of stereotyping make it difficult for women to gain access to leader roles, but the prescriptive aspects of stereotyping could produce conflicting expectations concerning how female leaders should behave. (Koenig et al., 2011, p. 637)

As well as creating barriers for women, this also makes it difficult for men to exhibit leadership qualities that are 'described' as feminine, without being thought of as soft or a pushover: "Gender norms are reinforced by everyone in the community" (Greene & Levack, 2010). This is explored with honesty and clarity by senior University leaders in Leadership perspectives on gender equality and in Leadership styles and approaches in GeoSciences.

Other present hurts include:

- The words we use in praising women differ from those used in praising men. Damning with faint praise and Raising your profile on a grant application look at the use of adjectives: 'grind' for women, 'stand-out' for men.

- Paper-cut comments (those little remarks that sting) and subtly sexist jokes contribute to the "drip, drip" effect (see Reflections on exercise and sport and Leadership perspectives on gender equality) that goes to create a "chilly climate" (see the illustration Microaggressions).

- Language that trivialises: for example calling an underpaid employee a girl implies that she does not have real financial responsibilities, and so justifies the below-minimum pay level (Merriam, 1974). More than one female professor has been called "love" and one of the editors of this book and a fellow-professor have been addressed as "girls" by the servitor.

- Girl is a term of abuse when used by boys to other boys, as is sissy (Van der Gaag, 2014).

How language is used in a wider societal context impacts everyone who works and studies in higher education. For example, Chimamanda Ngozi Adichie points out that "when we say fathers are 'helping', we are suggesting that child care is a mother's territory, into which fathers valiantly venture. It is not" (Adichie, 2017, pp. 13-14). Recipes *The kids are alright* and *Deadlines and diapers: being an academic dad* demonstrate how far beyond this position many people have moved; while *How to convince your family to let you study* suggests strategies to try with people who are still limited by social and cultural stereotypes.

The use of gendered pronouns (she, he) to maintain stereotypes and cultural norms is an area of growing importance as the trans and non-binary LGBTQ+ community is more widely recognised and their status beyond a simple binary gender framework is appreciated. In a 2017 talk at the University of Edinburgh, Chad Gowler made an impassioned plea to be referred to as 'they' and 'them'. Although some may assume that, because of physical characteristics, Chad is female, Chad describes themself as non-binary, and without a definitive gender, so to be referred to as 'she' is both inaccurate and offensive.

It is interesting that my spell check underlines 'themself' in red, and autocorrects it to 'themselves'; the algorithmic reinforcement of gender norms is an area for future research. There is an entry in the Glossary about alternative gendered pronouns and their use, such as 'ze' or 'hir' (pronounced here) and where to access more detailed information. You may also find https://minus18.org.au/pronouns-app/ interesting.

Healing: moving beyond

> By understanding how language really works, we might just understand how the rabbit of normativity gets pulled from the hat of articulation. (Tirrell, 2000, pp. 139-140)

Tirrell asserts that: "Those who seek to change the social order must not ignore the language that embodies it" (2000, p. 141). Language, we suggest, is a powerful tool to use when change in institutions is, as Mackay says, "actively resisted or passively neglected" going on to argue that old rules and mores around gender are 'sticky' (Mackay, 2014, p. 551).

Many of the recipes tell the story of how their writers have become aware of the power of language to shape their own and others' perceptions and behaviours (see *Raising your profile within your organisation* and *Talking about your achievements*). The recipes share how individuals have found their voice, the words and phrases needed to express themselves and their ideas and feelings, the power to respond calmly and with authority rather than to react without thinking (see *Finding my voice* and *Being visible in meetings*).

A recurring theme is the authors' conscious awareness in the moment of language used, and their developing practice in both attention and response (see *Pause*). The recipes also chart how the ground has shifted over the past two years of the project, and how previously unconsciously biased colleagues (of both genders) are now using the language of equality (see *Damning with faint praise* and *Leadership perspectives on gender equality*). Over the course of this project we have developed, like Tirrell, "a dual consciousness which is aware of injustices in past and present social practices, and yet is marked by an apprehension of possible futures in which women can flourish" (Tirrell, 2000, p. 140).

> Most women fight wars on two fronts, one for whatever the putative topic is and one simply for the right to speak, to have ideas, to be acknowledged to be in possession of facts and truths, to have value, to be a human being. (Solnit 2012).

Catalyst

Zach Murphy

Catalyst (noun) – A person or thing that precipitates an event or change. (http://www.dictionary.com/browse/catalyst)

Some journeys begin with a very obvious start. Vacations, for example, usually start when you walk out the door, passport in hand, locking the door with a deliberate turn as if to say: "I'm leaving and I'm going to be gone for a bit". Other journeys start well before we actually know we begin them, even if we fail to realise it in the moment.

My journey through the EqualBITE experience aligns closely to this second type. Maybe I began this great adventure when I was a kid, my mother teaching me about judgement and how people are simply people. Maybe it began as my siblings came into the world, two boys and two girls, creating, as I see it, a perfect balance. Maybe it was none of those, or a combination of those and many many more. Regardless where this journey began, I am on it now, and I am fully and completely committed.

I went to a workshop on gender equality. My wandering search for the room where the workshop was being held was uncomfortable, but not nearly as uncomfortable as walking into the room. Despite the topic of equality, I felt incredibly out of place. I was the only student in the room, the youngest, and one of only two men, the other being a member of staff. All of these factors combined to trigger my self-limiting beliefs about gender, age and status. To calm my nerves and discomfort, I methodically pulled out a notebook, my computer and a pen. Slowly I made more work out of opening a blank document and writing a few titles across the top of the page, avoiding eye contact and conversation. I was uncomfortable. I did not belong. As the workshop started, I did my best to listen, quieting my inner voice, which was telling me to get up and walk away. Despite this challenge, I relied on my most powerful coping mechanisms: responsibility and hard work. I was in that room because of my sense of responsibility for creating gender equality in the classroom and beyond. When the writing started I was able to immerse myself in the work and even managed to swallow the lump in my throat in order to share my experience and narrative.

The writing was powerful for me. I realised that I did have experience relating to gender equality, and that I wanted to be an agent for positive change. My original recipe highlighted the feeling that I had no voice because other people were just too loud with theirs.

A year and a recipe later (see *Allies in the classroom*), I have realised that the EqualBITE workshop was my catalyst. The journey that started years before moved into full realisation: I have a voice. Despite many people in the community standing on a mountain top and beating their drum, I have a voice.

Following on from the workshop I have been gifted with incredible feedback, powerful conversation, and most importantly belief that what I do matters. EqualBITE has been a catalyst in my life and for the people I am able to influence in a positive way. I believe that the only way we can find equality is if everyone wins, no matter their age, ethnicity, gender, sex or orientation.

I challenge you to find your catalyst, enlist the help of others, have courage and be kind. With kindness and courage your voice will be heard.

Finding my voice

Alison Williams

In 2015, shortly after starting work on the EqualBITE project, I attended a Cabaret of Dangerous Ideas (CODI) session at the Edinburgh Fringe entitled Women! Science is still not for you! [1]. We were discussing the real issue of what a female postgraduate student might do when her male supervisor or professor spends most of his time addressing her breasts rather than her face (the presenter's very effective response to her professor had been: "Could you please talk to the bit of me that thinks?") when from the audience a young male voice said: "What are you going on about? It's a perfectly natural human response." I was dumbfounded. My (faulty) memory was that no one challenged him directly. Nor did I. I felt deeply uncomfortable, but couldn't find my voice; I just didn't have the words I needed to deal with it.

Looking up 'dumbfounded' in the Collins English Dictionary [2], I found the following synonyms:

> Amazed, stunned, astonished, confused, overcome, overwhelmed, staggered, thrown, startled, at sea, dumb, bewildered, astounded, breathless, confounded, taken aback, speechless, bowled over (informal), nonplussed, lost for words, flummoxed, thunderstruck, knocked sideways (informal), knocked for six (informal).

I was all of those, and angry and frustrated too. This recipe chronicles how, over the time of being involved with the EqualBITE project I have learned about myself as well as about the many aspects of gender, feminism and outstanding women I have been studying. Intersubjectivity, what Reinharz calls "a circular process: the woman doing the study learns about herself as well as about the woman she is studying" (1992, p. 127), has enabled me to change – and continue to do so – through reflecting on myself and my own standpoint as an engaged researcher, and as a continually learning and growing person. And the recipe ends with how I finally found my voice.

Ingredients

- Provocation (something entirely unexpected/jarring/wrong-footing).
- Rage and embarrassment.
- Good friends and colleagues.

Method

I found the three A's approach to behaviour change a useful one:

> Awareness
>
> Acceptance
>
> Action

Until I became aware of my situation and response to it, and accepted the reality, I couldn't act or make any significant or lasting changes to either the situation or my response.

1. **Awareness of the provocation, and my rage and embarrassment.** I realised that I was doing the classic goldfish manoeuvre of opening and closing my mouth repeatedly, looking around the room to see if anyone else would pick up and respond to the comment, dumbfounded (lost for words, dumb, speechless) when no one did.

2. **Acceptance that I don't know what to do or say.** On the way home I asked myself what I should have said – l'esprit d'escalier (see *Unravelling rhetoric*) – and realised that I didn't have a clue. What should I do? Where might I find the vocabulary?

3. **Action: Asking other people for advice and possible phrases.** I asked my partner when I got home, still fizzing; I asked my colleagues and friends, female and male. Responses ranged from people who didn't know what to say, to people who knew only too well what they might say, stopping (just) short of violence.

   Suggestions included:

   - The metaphorical: "Hunger is a perfectly natural human response but you don't go about snatching sandwiches from other people's plates."

   - The stereotypical: "Typical male comment – that's all men ever think about. Every seven seconds, isn't it?"

- The confrontational: "Don't you go bringing that kind of sexist thinking into this situation."

But none of the suggestions felt right – the possible responses, I felt, drew me into the same space of polarisation and disagreement as the original speaker. I wanted something that would challenge and reframe the comment in my own mind, and potentially in his (or her) mind too.

Then a friend and colleague suggested a response that does both by putting the initial statement into context:

> Yes, it may be a biological response. It is neither appropriate nor respectful in a professional, or any other, context.

Setting the statement in its professional and public context challenges the speaker to rethink their own assumptions and perspective. As the philosopher Lynne Tirrell observes: "Feminist philosophy of language takes seriously the interplay between content and context" (Tirrell, 2000, p. 144).

Initially I thought that what I needed was a battery of responses to use in any situation, and to practice them out loud until they became natural (usually in the car, rehearsing the phrase over and over until it became automatic).

The first draft of this recipe concluded:

> Now I'm looking for someone to
> say something sexist in my hearing,
> so that I can practise my new
> vocabulary. Volunteers anyone?

Since then there have been four times – all
in social rather than professional situations
– when a man has said something to me
that was outrageously sexist (misogynist
and/or homophobic). Once again, the
shocking nature of the comments has left
me dumbfounded (speechless, bowled
over (informal), nonplussed, lost for words,
flummoxed) in the same mixture of rage
and embarrassment as before, and my
responses have been patchy. Again I went
back to asking friends and colleagues,
and found another approach which I
have used successfully – speak from "I".

When you... I feel... In future...

Savigny (2014) describes how "feminism
as praxis enables women to 'speak out',
have their voices heard, and in so doing,
question existing structures of power. This
in turn provides a mechanism through
which change and agency are possible"
(2014, p. 24). Learning to 'speak out' is a long
hard journey for men as well as women
(see *Allies in the classroom*) who have been
brought up to accept the status quo and
not to make waves (see *The double bind*).

As Solnit (2012) says: "Having the right to
show up and speak are basic to survival,

to dignity, and to liberty. I'm grateful
that, after an early life of being silenced,
sometimes violently, I grew up to have
a voice, circumstances that will always
bind me to the rights of the voiceless.".

In 2017, at an event given by a venerable
academic institution (not this one), my
neighbour during dinner moved – in equal
measure with the red wine – from a pleasant
conversation about my work on this book,
to the embarrassingly personal. This time,
eighteen months after the first incident, I
found the words I needed: "When you make
remarks like that, I feel very uncomfortable,
and please stop it now." But was met
by the standard defence: "It's a joke".

The after-dinner speeches thankfully
intervened and afterwards I moved seats
with the coffee, only to be pursued, a
handshake forced on me, and then –
appallingly – his finger run down the back of
my trapped hand. This time I was able to tell
him clearly that he had crossed a line; he left
smartly. I wrote, setting out briefly how I felt
he had broken the institution's guidelines,
and had a letter of apology within the week.

> But the experiences we have are
> not just of being worn down; these
> experiences also give us resources.
> What we learn from these experiences
> might be how we survive these
> experiences. (Ahmed, 2017, p. 235)

Finally, things are changing. People change. Cultures change: "Coffee-room conversations can be dangerous ground. Now, discriminatory talk is called out and challenged by colleagues. You wouldn't have seen this 10 years ago" (*Leadership perspectives on gender equality*), the author of the recipe *Damning with faint praise* observes that her experience has not been repeated, and the women students in Edinburgh College of Art talk of the safety they feel within the studios to express themselves and their ideas (*Perspectives from students*).

Finding and building my voice is a work in progress, and I continue to work at it, and to move beyond dumbfounded.

Online references

1 http://codi.beltanenetwork. org/event/codi-2015-women- science-is-still-not-for-you-2/

2 https://www.collinsdictionary. com/dictionary/english- thesaurus/dumbfounded

I recently met Pam Cameron, one of the 2015 CODI presenters, and asked how she remembered responding to the heckler. Her reply: "It is human nature to notice an attractive person. However, whilst it's "being human" to notice (and I certainly notice an attractive man), it's neither acceptable nor professional to stare at breasts, bottoms or crotches! It's inappropriate behaviour for any workplace and it's intimidating coming from someone in a more senior position.

I would expect anyone to be able to separate out their appreciation of an attractive person, put that to one side, and engage with them as simply another human being, without leering!"

She continued: "I'm reasonably sure I didn't say the last piece, in italics, from the stage but it's how I subsequently deal with the "human nature" defence of lecherous behaviour."

Say something

Marissa Warner-Wu

In any group which is primarily homogeneous, a culture starts to develop around the dominant culture. To participate in the culture, you need to engage in it. Everyone wants to fit in and be accepted by their peers. If you're surrounded by men who speak dismissively of women, for example, then you also feel the need to do this.

For many years, I tried to fit in. Every time a colleague unthinkingly made a sexist comment, I awkwardly laughed and brushed it off. I was telling them that it was OK, that I was cool and "one of the guys" – not like those other women. In the end, this just filled me with repressed rage and self-loathing. I had become part of the very thing I despised.

Recently I made a commitment to myself: every time this happened, I would say something out loud to the person who had made me angry. This was a lot harder than I originally thought. There is a kind of unspoken social rule which prevents you from saying something which might make someone else uncomfortable. It's easier to sweep something under the carpet and pretend it never happened.

The goal here is not to get the other person to apologise. If that is what you want, you will probably be disappointed. Instead, you will hopefully achieve two things. First, you will remove your own sense of burning resentment and allow yourself to sleep peacefully at night. Second, usually the other person is not speaking out of malicious intent or any real conviction. Calling them out is often all that's needed to make them aware of their language.

Ingredients

- A person who has just said something you find sexist or otherwise discriminatory or dismissive.
- Repressed anger.
- A desire to make change.

Method

1. Think about what has just been said. What about it made you angry? Why did you feel this way? Sometimes it's hard to move from thinking: "This person is a jerk!" into something more constructive, but this step is key to getting to the root of why you are mad. It's also important for helping you prepare for the next step.

2. Carefully frame what you want to say in a constructive manner. A good method is to use the non-violent communication framework (https://www.cnvc.org/learn/nvc-foundations). Observe... Feel...Need...Request. You do not have to make it complicated. Often simply observing what has been said is enough.

3. If you feel too choked up with rage to think properly, saying something like: "That sounds a bit sexist to me" is fine.

Remember that the goal is not to attack the other person or make it personal. Do not call them a jerk, even if you are thinking it. Say something to the other person in a neutral voice. You do not need to sound angry (you're not trying to start a fight), or upset (you're not a victim). This step is very difficult and can feel quite socially awkward. That's OK! Remember that even the tiniest thing can make a difference or change someone's mind. Even doing something small is still doing something.

4. If the other person replies to your comment or challenges you, be prepared to have a conversation about it. Try to remain neutral and non-confrontational. Explain simply why you had a problem with what they said. You don't need to belabour the point or make them feel badly.

5. Sometimes you will get no response, and that's fine. Don't expect the other person to reply – they might feel too embarrassed to say anything. Finally, remember that if the conversation continues to be difficult you do not have to continue – see U*nravelling rhetoric* for examples of how to leave this type of conversation.

Speaking to someone privately can help boost your own confidence about approaching them and also avoid turning it into a public shaming exercise.

Warning

It's not unusual for the other party to become angry or ashamed when confronted. They may even blame you for making them feel badly. Your relationship with the other person may become strained for a while, but hopefully you will both benefit in the long run from your honesty.

Grumpy

Daphne Loads

Recently I discovered the value of grumpiness. Prickly and dyspeptic with tiredness, I dropped my bag of papers and books all over the floor in the University Main Library. As I bent, grumbling, to pick them up, I caught sight of a portion of text. It was part of a display commemorating female scholars, leaders and pioneers at the University of Edinburgh. Beside the photograph of Brenda Moon, one of the first women chief librarians, was the following unattributed citation:

> A slightly built and softly spoken woman who cared about others and was always gentle and supportive. However, beneath this deceptive exterior there was a clarity of thought and purpose and a persistence which moved mountains.

I had read this many times before but now I saw it with fresh eyes. I was struck by the bewildering oppositions it seemed to set up. What, exactly, was deceptive about Brenda Moon's appearance? Why should we be surprised that a short person was clear thinking? Or that a woman with a quiet voice was persistent?

I imagined a parallel universe in which Bill Moon was remembered as:

> A big tall man with a loud voice who was uncaring, harsh and unsupportive to others. This exterior was perfectly in keeping with his clarity of thought and purpose and a persistence which moved mountains.

By turning it inside out in this way, the assumptions were revealed in all their absurdity. I pointed them out to a female colleague. "This is manspeak", she declared, and immediately set about finding the source of the silly quotation.

Now, if I had been what I like to think of as my normal self, I would have taken the memorial at face value, appreciating the generosity of the sentiments and thinking the best of the speaker. It was only because I was in a grumpy mood that I saw through the words to the mountain of silly assumptions that Brenda Moon had to tackle in order to get on with her work. And although I believe strongly that it's possible to be both purposeful and caring, kind and determined, nevertheless in this case it was actually quite helpful to be unkind for a moment, in order to grasp an important idea.

Ingredients

- A dash of grumpiness.
- A flash of insight.
- A big pile of leftover assumptions, well past their sell-by date.

Method

1. Take a load of old assumptions (available in all good universities: find them in publicity materials, learning resources and course descriptors).

2.   Incorporate a fresh perspective.
     The key to success is the perfect
     amount of grumpiness: too little and
     you don't notice it; too much and
     you don't notice anything else.

3.   Share with a friend, or in my case a
     complete stranger, who heard me
     harrumphing and came to find out
     why. Her support encouraged me to
     pass on what I had noticed to others.

4.   Enjoy.

Cook's tip

For recipes on what the
words we use reveal, see *Be
vigilant with your vocabulary*
and *Damning with faint
praise*. For a quick example in
politics, particular differences
in language around gender
are still prevalent resulting
in female politicians
being described as 'coldly
ambitious' instead of the
male adjective 'assertive'.

A forerunner of this recipe
originally appeared here:
https://iad4learnteach.
wordpress.com/

Pause

Derek Jones, Anonymous
& Alison Williams

Rollo May wrote:

> Human freedom involves our capacity to pause between the stimulus and response and, in that pause, to choose the one response toward which we wish to throw our weight. The capacity to create ourselves, based upon this freedom, is inseparable from consciousness or self-awareness (May, 1975/1994, p. 100).

This is a recipe on The Pause – that moment after you have heard or read something that triggers a reaction without you fully thinking it through. This can lead to the situation becoming (often unintentionally) worse, when a different response might have been far more effective. Making such judgements about the best way and time to react is not easy and we are all very human – so this recipe presents a few pointers on making use of that ... pause.

It can be hard to separate thought and action. We very often speak in order to think, as E.M. Forster put it: "How can I tell what I think until I see what I say?" (1927), and recent evidence suggests that the area of our brain that deals with 'word production' actually reduces in cognitive activity when we speak (Flinker et al., 2015). Like many other cognitive processes, we are largely unaware of it happening (e.g. Wilson, 2002; Mlodinow, 2012; Lakoff & Johnson, 1999): our 'conscious' selves are often left to deal with something our 'subconscious' has already started (Kunda, 1990). We are also pretty terrible at being objective when it comes to explaining such thoughts (e.g. Hastorf & Cantril, 1954).

It is perhaps hardly surprising that we (over) react when other people speak without thinking first – we are all human – but even if you are reacting to something that is obviously inappropriate, it is useful to consider The Pause. That extra split second not only can make all the difference to the effectiveness of your response, it can stop the situation escalating out of control.

Ingredients

- Some ideas (see Method step 1) to help develop the pause habit.
- Some good friends.
- A bit of self-reflective honesty.
- Self-respect.

Method

In the first few seconds:

1. Give your brain a chance to catch up with your mouth (or your email fingers). It's rarely a good idea to respond immediately to anything – especially if it's online!

   Possibilities include a physical reminder object (I have a "Keep-your-mouth-shut-Alison" pebble) or brightly-coloured PAUSE Post-it note on your desk.

   A deep breath is also effective in counteracting the "took my breath away" reaction.

2. While mentally, physically and emotionally pausing, ask yourself if you are reacting to a point or a tone? Is he/she reacting to what I said or how I said it?

3. Repeat back what you think you just heard and observe the reaction.

   • Ask a question rather than state an opinion

4. If you realise that you have said something that could be considered offensive (we presume here you didn't intend it) then apologise immediately. It clears the air and builds trust.

In the next moments:

5. How can I help adjust the tone of the meeting, or resolve things positively? So much depends on context and judgement

    •   If it's something that is clearly not OK then it's relatively straightforward – bystanding is no longer an option in the University. Have a look at *Be vigilant with your vocabulary* or *Say something* for circumstances where we should not remain silent. Some situations may be serious enough to require a more formal process and in such cases you certainly do not have to respond (see guidance notes).

•   If you are uncertain about whether it's OK, repeat back to yourself what you think you heard and try to imagine other ways of interpreting it. Ask for clarification of anything you think might be ambiguous.

•   If it remains ambiguous then it is OK to say so and see if two opinions on the matter can be discussed or created respectfully.

•   Sanity check: check it out later with someone else and ask their opinion on what was said.

Too late:

6. If it's too late then that's fine – it's rarely useful to restart a particular discussion but for your own peace of mind it is good to resolve it in some way. Have a look at the *Unravelling rhetoric* recipe and work on your timing for the next occasion.

Finally:

7. Online you should still be acting in a way you are happy with. The trick is to find your own set of personal 'rules' and stick to them. The authors' rules include NEVER responding immediately; ALWAYS write the response offline; ALWAYS run it past a neutral third party before transferring it to email; REMEMBER that the emotional bank account (http://www.stephencovey. com/blog/?tag=emotional-bank-account) which you have built up with colleagues over months, if not years, can empty in a split second.

8. Reflection at the time and afterwards is crucial; as G.K. Chesterton observed: "Merely having an open mind is nothing. The object of opening the mind, as of opening the mouth, is to shut it again on something solid" (Chesterton 1936).

Be vigilant with your vocabulary

Bróna Murphy

As a linguist, I am always aware of moments in my day when I notice language playing a role in constructing and maintaining unequal relations between genders. The words we use delineate boundaries and can cast shade on how women, for instance, are represented and portrayed (Sigley & Holmes, 2002; Baker, 2014). In a quick search of an online multi-million word database, I found that the most common words to appear alongside 'woman' include 'pregnant', 'dumpy', 'hysterical', 'old', 'married' and 'beautiful' whereas 'man' featured alongside 'right-hand', 'macho', 'sexiest', 'wise', 'good', 'great' and 'powerful'. Looking more closely at the word 'pregnant', it occurred in the following clusters: 'alone and pregnant', 'low and pregnant', 'large and pregnant', 'sick and pregnant', and 'single and pregnant'. Another search showed that while a 'bachelor' was 'eligible', a 'spinster' was 'elderly', and another search illustrated that while the word 'abrasive' can be used in 'abrasive coating', 'abrasive electronics', and 'abrasive blasting', it is also used to describe a female ('abrasive female') who has an irritating personality or is prone to causing friction or annoyance especially in the workplace. The adjective 'abrasive' does not occur with 'male'. For other examples, see Baker (2008) and Okimoto & Brescoll (2010).

These patterns, which include a commentary on personal appearance and the negative portrayal of personality traits, show the kind of social asymmetry that can be found in language patterns, and how revealing language use is when gender is brought into the mix. My recipe is informed by inappropriate language use by a male colleague to describe my personal appearance when I was pregnant. This happened just as our pre-meeting chat was coming to an end and my colleague felt the need to comment on my increasing size by stating: "You're getting bigger by the day". This led to a somewhat awkward interaction where I, firmly but humorously, made him aware of the inappropriateness of his comment.

This recipe details how to raise awareness of inappropriate gender-related comments, in the workplace, in a non-confrontational way, while still getting your point across.

Ingredients

- An inappropriate gender-related comment from a colleague.

Method

1. **Identify the gender bias:** Take a moment to note the effect of the comment on you. How do you feel? Label your emotions: embarrassment, anger, self-consciousness, etc. Do you feel like retreating from the situation? Do you think you've misheard? Are you conscious of other people looking on?

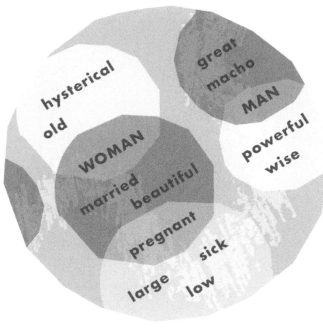

While it may be hard to define whether it is bias or not, you'll know how it makes you feel and that's enough to help you define it.

2. **Gauge your colleague's intention.** Was this comment intentional? Or was it a throw-away comment? This helps provide you with more context for understanding what has happened and what may be meant by the remark.

3. **Rise above the bias:** The bias says more about the other person than it does about you. Instead of reacting, take a moment to be fully mindful of the moment you find yourself in while you consider how you want to proceed (see the other flavour recipes for more on this). Consider the context (where you are, who else is there, age divide, closeness of work relationship, personality, hierarchy, etc.) as this will help you decide how to deal with it.

4. **Address the issue:** Make a decision to draw your colleague's attention to it immediately or wait until later when you can have a proper discussion. Humour is often useful in navigating potentially difficult situations as it de-escalates the threat of any confrontation while at the same time allowing you to navigate a potentially difficult situation with greater ease.

5. **Dealing with the outcome 1:** Your colleague may apologise for their insensitivity and the flippant comment, which was not ill-intentioned. Accept the apology and congratulate yourself for being linguistically aware enough to draw your colleague's attention to it. You'll have also done them a favour by perhaps making him more mindful of his language use in future.

6. **Dealing with the outcome 2:** However, your colleague may disagree that the comment was inappropriate. You may have a more complicated discussion on your hands. In this situation, you cannot force your colleague to understand your point if they fail to, or refuse to, but by addressing the issue, you'll have alerted them, on whatever level, to the fact that linguistic appropriateness exists whether or not they choose to accept it.

Cook's tip

If at all possible, it is best to avoid confrontation. By addressing the issue in a firm but respectful way, you are making your own point, and you are only responsible for you. You'll feel better having put your point across.

Warning

Your colleague may not take kindly to having their use of language highlighted. Be aware that you have the right to say how you feel whether they like it or not.

Challenging bias

Alison Williams

Implicit or unconscious bias happens by our brains making incredibly quick judgments and assessments of people and situations without us realising. Our biases are influenced by our background, cultural environment and personal experiences. We may not even be aware of these views and opinions, or be aware of their full impact and implications. (Equality Challenge Unit)

Apart from being struck by the many graffiti versions of: "A woman needs a man like a fish needs a bicycle", the feminist consciousness-raising 1970s completely passed me by. I understood the phrase 'unconscious bias' but never really applied it to myself. Then I had the great good fortune to hear Jesse Jackson speak on the evening he was awarded an honorary degree by the University of Edinburgh. He said, talking of racism: "I don't blame people for their unconscious bias. The people I do blame are those who become aware of their bias and do nothing about it."

The following week I attended a research seminar led by three young women researchers who had flown up from London for the day. My first thought as I walked into the room was: "What can these young slips-of-girls possibly know?" It became very clear very soon that with their two PhDs and a degree in neuroscience between them they knew a lot, and were generous in their sharing.

And it also became clear to me, with Jesse Jackson's words ringing in my ears, that I had become aware of two of my own hitherto unconscious biases, age and gender, mixed up together. This recipe sets out what I did, and continue to do, to challenge and change any personal biases as I become aware of them. As bell hooks says: "[T]he problem is sexism. [...] all of us, female and male, have been socialized from birth on to accept sexist thought and action. As a consequence, females can be just as sexist as men" (hooks 2000, p. viii).

Ingredients

- A powerful stimulus.
- A whoopsie moment.
- An unconscious bias (alive and kicking and very nasty).
- A notebook and pencil and lots of awkward questions.
- Laughter (fresh, not canned).
- The 3 As (Awareness – Acceptance – Action) and some awkward questions.

Method

1. **Awareness.** First catch your whoopsie moment. Whoopsie moments feel deeply uncomfortable. Everyone has their own set of awareness triggers, mental, physical and – most powerful – emotional. I know I'm having a whoopsie moment when I find myself

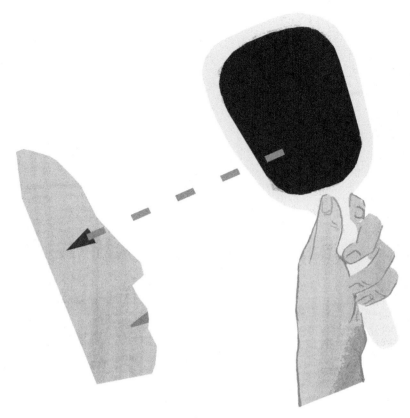

being critical, or defensive, or snippy, or using phrases like: "They make me feel/do/say". An unconscious bias can be slippery and devious when challenged.

Awkward question: What are your emotional/mental/physical responses to a whoopsie moment? Do you go red? Get aggressive? Point the finger? Stop collaborating? Do you try to prove that you are in every way superior to the person/people who are making you feel (watch out for that one – no one makes us feel, we do it all on our own) uncomfortable?

2. **Next, dissect your whoopsie:** lay it out on the kitchen table (or board room, or desk, or lab) and examine carefully. There will be an unconscious bias hiding in the middle of it. Now stop and ask yourself what it is that you feel uncomfortable about. Doing this is easier if you keep

your mouth shut and your ears open, and remember to breathe. And when you catch yourself at it, laugh!

Awkward question: What could you do to give yourself time and permission to look at your whoopsie and find the bias?

3. **Acceptance.** The next stage of this recipe is Acceptance. I can't do something about my bias and make changes to my own behaviour and responses until I accept that something is wrong. I need to mull things over: a good walk, or talking it over with a trusted friend or colleague really helps. And then I ask myself: "What can I do about it right now?" and "What can I do to make sure that it doesn't happen again?"

Awkward question: What's your process for accepting there's a bias in the centre of your whoopsie?

4. **Action.** Now your unconscious bias has been caught, laid out, examined and simmered for as long as it takes to be accepted, deal with it in the moment: keep your mouth shut and your mind open, keep breathing and keep smiling. Mentally challenge the bias – it isn't worthy of you. Resist any attempts that the bias makes to drag you into justifying it and prolonging its miserable life. Remember to laugh at it, and at yourself. Now, make sure it doesn't happen again.

5. **Take a small unused notebook (A6 conference freebie is ideal) that can tuck into a pocket or bag.** Start to record your whoopsie moments, and note how you respond, internally and externally. It's powerful to see it laid out on the page, and cathartic too. The funny thing about unconscious biases is that they hate the light. A good burst of exposure and they start to shrivel.

Cook's tips

This recipe is written from my IAD freebie notebook. I continue to use it to keep myself honest. Biases can take a while to exorcise and changing my thinking takes time. Now I have got to the stage when I mostly catch myself at it, and a few moments of laughing at myself helps the process along. Since starting my whoopsie journal, I have found myself making fewer and fewer entries. And having better and better conversations with more and more people that are nourishing, thought-provoking and keep us all coming back for more.

Unravelling rhetoric

Alison Williams & Derek Jones

There is a French phrase for that frustrating feeling you have upon realising what you should or could have said in a conversation: l'esprit d'escalier or 'staircase wit'. Very often you may (after the event, of course, on the way down the stairs) think of several things you could have said – each of which is most likely exceptionally witty and erudite. This feeling may go on for hours or even days, a constant replay of events with an ever-increasing list of Things I Should Have Said But Didn't.

But being able to respond quickly and confidently in the spur of the moment can be difficult – especially when responding to someone who appears exceptionally confident in what they are stating and the rhetoric they are using. The word rhetoric is important here because it is often this that convinces quickly rather than facts, information or critical dialogue. This is not to say that all rhetoric is a bad thing – we all use it. It's simply that it can do with a health check every now and again.

This recipe is not about giving the confidence or repartee to retort in any situation. It's about recognising some of the most common rhetorical devices used in place of knowledge – where opinion is very often passed off as knowledge and winning an argument is more important than exploring an issue.

By the way, we all do this. Humans are exceptional at 'lazy epistemology'. In other words, we don't have the energy to spend on thinking about everything all the time so we take shortcuts. And if those shortcuts get too short, we end up missing or distorting things.

So try this recipe as a grounded observational method the next time you find yourself in such a situation – keep an eye out: to ensure that opinion is not passed off as fact, and to ensure that ideas and thoughts are explored, not dismissed.

Ingredients

- Smile and pause.
- A few holding phrases.
- Carl Sagan's Baloney Detection Kit (Sagan, 1996). https://www. brainpickings.org/2014/01/03/ baloney-detection-kit-carl-sagan/
- A copy of the Thou Shalt Not Commit Logical Fallacies poster (Richardson, 2012).

Method

1. When you are confronted with that horrible situation of feeling the need to respond, think: "Do I have to respond at all?" Not everything demands an immediate response. Quickly scan the type of conversation it has been so far – if you count mostly Sagan 'baloney statements' then you

might want to think about whether there is any point in continuing. Look especially for the following:

- points that attack the person, not the argument or critique;
- argument that relies only on authority;
- extreme dualities and failure to recognise complexity (e.g. "You are either for this position or you're not");

- following quickly after a duality, some statement invoking 'normal', 'most' or 'average' people. Remember, 'normal' is simply a measure of statistical distribution of how far EVERYONE is away from an unattainable mathematical ideal;
- metaphorical arguments that assume a knowledge that is not necessarily valid (e.g. "We have to cut off this limb to save the patient");
- memes that may be compelling for no other reason than the perceptual appeal (e.g. "Better dead than red");
- lazy dismissal: "Oh that's just…", "Don't be like that…", "I was only…".

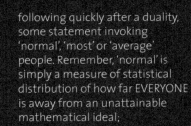

2. Have a few holding phrases you can use in situations where it is clear that rhetoric, not content, is being valued. For example:

    - "I think this issue would really benefit from..."
    - "An unusual point of view, I would like to ponder this at leisure..."
    - "Let me get back to you on this..."
    - "Mmm...interesting..."

3. Ask critical and rational questions (from Sagan's toolkit):

    - "Is there research into this?"
    - "What other ideas are there supported by the same evidence?"
    - "Has anyone considered this issue from the point of view of X?"
    - Ask a quantitative question: "How many...?", "How much...?", "When does...?"

4. You do not have to adopt the same pace, pitch and intensity of discussion as your discussant.

    - If you wish to talk slowly in response to someone talking too quickly then do that - if an idea is strong it will benefit from a measured and considered speed of consideration.
    - Talking quietly can be more effective than increasing volume.

- If you are interrupted without consideration or with disrespect, turn your body away slightly - show your shoulder. This can interrupt the interruption.

- If you are repeatedly interrupted then remember that you have already 'left' the conversation – it's OK to walk away from your time being wasted.

5. Remember that certain types of persuasion rely on drawing a discussant into the rhetoric itself, e.g. by making them appear a certain way or using their reaction as 'evidence' of something. As part of any conversation you should feel able to withdraw at any time - that's what discussion is. You may need a couple of phrases, rather than just: "Oh goodness, is that the time, I must fly, I can't keep [Nobel Prize-winner as appropriate] waiting any longer!" Adapt the holding phrases above to suit, or say that you are feeling...

- that this discussion has turned rhetorical and is no longer exploratory;
- that the discussion has reached an unhelpful circularity;
- browbeaten.

Damning with faint praise

Karen Chapman

Taking on a new role with considerable responsibility, a senior colleague (already on the management team) welcomed me with the comment: "I'm sure you will do a good job – you are very conscientious". Does he think I am not up to the job? How do I convey my acknowledgement of the "compliment" and agreement with the importance of so-called soft qualities like conscientiousness and integrity, while at the same time emphasising the other things I think I can contribute like leadership, vision, and innovative solutions?

There are layers of complexity in this single comment, contributing to what Savigny terms cultural sexism: "significant, invisible, [and] normalising" (2014, p. 796) cultural practices, norms and values that frame women's experience within the academy. Two strands in particular stand out: benevolent sexism, and the contrast between words used about women and those used about men.

Benevolent sexism can be insidious, portraying women as warm and supportive – as long as they conform to the roles assigned to them by men, and do not challenge men's authority (Dumont, et al., 2010). An integral part of benevolent sexism is its suggestion that women are less competent than men, and this can become, for a woman, a self-fulfilling prophecy. As Dumont et al. argue: Be too kind to a woman, she'll feel incompetent. Benevolent sexism is the obverse of hostile sexism and the two are closely related – see Glick & Fiske (1996; 2001) for discussion of ambivalent sexism theory – but benevolent sexism is often more difficult to spot, and less easy to counter, often because its language is complimentary.

"Very conscientious" is a 'grindstone' compliment. In their paper examining gender differences in recommendation letters, Dutt et al. demonstrate how:

> Implicit biases can surface via the way applicants are described in recommendation letters, with women being described as less confident and forceful, and more nurturing and helpful than men, and receiving fewer 'standout' adjectives such as superb and brilliant, and more 'grindstone' adjectives such as hardworking and diligent" (Dutt et al., 2016, p. 1).

They reference previous studies in fields including chemistry, psychology and medicine where similar biases have been identified, noting that these 'grindstone' adjectives are as likely to be used by women of other women, as by men.

Ingredients

- A slightly patronising male colleague, who is trying to be welcoming and friendly.

- A committee, management team or other senior group of people, in which men predominate.

Method

1. Take one moment to digest.

2. Accept compliment as it is: "Thank you".

3. Agree with the importance of being conscientious: "I hope that everyone on the committee/team is conscientious". Invite clarification: "I hope you invited

me to the committee to contribute more than just conscientiousness..." and wait expectantly for his reply. Give it a decent length of time. If he has any self-awareness, he will realise what he said and squirm a bit.

4. If he is suitably embarrassed and flounders a little, then offer help and an example of how you have already performed well in a leadership role: "I will also bring a different perspective, being female, as well as (for example) –

lateral thinking. When I was on the such-and-such committee, it was my idea to... (here, give an example) and I steered through... (give another example)."

5. Use the opportunity to demonstrate your anticipation of the role: "What do you see as the biggest challenges currently facing us?" and "What solutions do you envisage?", for example. Explore his willingness to credit others: "Are those your personal views or those of the committee as a whole?"

6. Finish up by emphasising your commitment and involvement: "Good. I think I will be able to contribute to that. I'm looking forward to joining the team" and move on.

Warning

If the recipient is completely lacking in self-awareness, a rather more blunt approach may be needed!

Cook's perspective

Interestingly, I haven't had a similar experience since. I think too, that gender equality is advancing rapidly (in the UK) as the person who made that comment last year moved from selecting all male nominees for awards a year ago, to having around 30% female this year. Amazing how much more aware people are of unconscious bias and the like!

Not just "a ladies' problem"

Jane Hilston

In my discipline of computer science (CS) the proportion of women is stubbornly low (Vardi, 2015). In the United States, according to the Taulbee Survey 2015, only 15.7% of the CS Bachelor's degrees awarded in 2015 went to women, and only 18.3% of CS PhDs went to women (Zweben & Bizot, 2016). In the UK in 2016, 18.7% of CS undergraduate degrees, and 39.8% of CS PhDs, were awarded to female students (HESA, 2017). This is despite at least two decades of efforts and initiatives to try and make the topic more attractive, particularly to female undergraduates (Vardi, 2015).

Sometimes male colleagues find themselves in a situation where the low female participation rate is strikingly obvious, for example teaching a first-year class and being confronted by a sea of male faces. They are shocked and outraged that this should still be the case and feel something should be done. And then take the first opportunity they can to hand the problem over to a female colleague.

In the UK, we have the Athena SWAN initiative which recognises departments which are able to demonstrate commitment and progress on supporting gender equality, through an extensive process of data collection and self-assessment. Many heads of department immediately assume that such a self-assessment team must be led by a woman.

There tends to be a societal norm which expects women to volunteer more. In What Works in Gender Equality By Design, Bohnet presents findings which show:

> When in same-sex groups, women and men were equally willing to volunteer. But when grouped with members of the opposite sex, the pattern suddenly changed. Women volunteered more and men less. Everyone, including the women, assumed women would volunteer more than men. Accordingly, men adjusted their behavior, expecting to benefit from the women, and women lived up to their expectations. (Bohnet, 2016, p. 196).

This is, she concludes, "a common pattern at universities [and] it is troubling that this pattern appears to be generalizable" (Bohnet, 2016, p. 196).

This is a recipe for trying to counteract the assumption that tackling gender equality is a problem that must be addressed by women. Make it clear that this is not your hobby, and that these roles should be regarded as academic administrative tasks like any others and should be allocated appropriately.

Ingredients

- An outraged male colleague who feels self-righteous for noticing the problem.
- A female colleague (you) who just happened to be the first he thought of, or the first he met, after the onset of his outrage.

Method

1. Bite your lip, count to ten and smile.

2. While counting to ten, try to think of male colleagues who could plausibly take on the role being thrust upon you – you're a woman, you should have no difficulty multi-tasking! For example, why shouldn't the colleague responsible for student admissions tackle the problem of female undergraduate recruitment. Of course, his unconscious bias may be the reason for the low numbers, but this is only an opening gambit.

3. When you reach ten, congratulate your colleague on his insight. Be careful with your use of language because you are aiming to be supportive without accepting ownership of the problem yourself. So, for example, do not thank him for bringing the situation to your attention. Instead ask what he plans to do about it, saying that you will be happy to support him, but making it clear that you expect him to take the lead.

4. He will almost certainly present a list of reasons why he doesn't have the time to take on this extra responsibility. Agree with him that yes, it is unreasonable to be expected to assume additional responsibility by a chance association

> At the time of writing, at the University of Edinburgh, seven of the twenty-two Athena SWAN teams are led by men.

with the problem, such as being the one to notice it or being a woman. This should make it difficult for him to pass the problem to you.

5. Now deploy your alternative suggestion and enter into a discussion of how the problem could be seen to fall within the remit of an existing administrative role. There are two alternatives here. Either the problem could be seen to fall within an existing role in which case the colleague responsible should be encouraged to broaden their perspective of the role to encompass this additional challenge. For example, this would be the case for female undergraduate recruitment. Alternatively, if it is a genuinely new role, such as coordinating an Athena SWAN self-assessment team, it should be allocated in the appropriate way, with appropriate recognition for the colleague who takes it on.

6. Aim to close the conversation with your colleague with a clear plan of action (on his part). This can be followed up later on with an email, saying you enjoyed your discussion and copying in the colleague that you jointly identified as being the most appropriate person to take action.

Cook's tips

Try to keep the tone throughout light-hearted and avoid confrontation. It's easy to feel annoyance at the assumption that gender problems need to be tackled by women, but keep this in check. Instead, try sympathy and encouragement.

Warning

Playing this game of academic administration hot potato is not for the faint-hearted or weak willed. Be careful to avoid being overly helpful. A firm hand and firm words are needed to return the potato to its originator.

Recognise your privilege

Pablo Schyfter

The history of scientific and engineering disciplines is one characterised by various forms of social inequity, including gender-based discrimination (for example: Rossiter, 1982; Oldenziel, 1999). Women have been characterised as hampered by their sex and thus unable to practise science and engineering properly (or at best, not as effectively as men). Some key figures during the scientific revolution even suggested that scientific enterprises could prove dangerous and damaging to women's fragile minds and bodies. Physician Thomas Willis argued that "Women before men are troubled with the Affects called hysterical" due to "Weaker Constitutions of the Brain and Genus Nervosum" (quoted in Easlea, 1981, p. 69). A contemporary of Willis, philosopher Nicolas Malecbranche, confidently claimed that women's minds display "insufficient strength and reach to penetrate to the core of problems" (Easlea, 1981, p. 69).

Most explicit misogyny of this kind may have been routed since then, but problems persist. For instance, in a famous incident in 2005, the then-president of Harvard, Lawrence Summers, postulated that men's innately superior proficiency for science and engineering might explain differences in participation. Because the statement caused great debate, it's worth the reader's time to make up his or her mind about Summers' claims. His remarks can be found at: http://www.harvard. edu/president/speeches/summers_2005/ nber.php. A subsequent letter he wrote concerning the lecture can be found at: http://www.harvard.edu/president/ speeches/summers_2005/facletter.php.

Moreover, a recent study by the European Commission demonstrates that women remain minorities in science and engineering professions, enjoy disproportionately fewer higher-grade jobs and leadership positions, and face greater challenges securing research funding (ECDGRI, 2013).

The issue of sexism in science and engineering is one broadly acknowledged – for examples, see the recent reports: Botcherby & Buckner (2012); Corbett & Hill (2015); Hill et al. (2010) – even though only limited action has been taken to address it. Some examples are: the WISE Campaign (https://www.wisecampaign.org.uk/); the Ada Awards (http://adaawards.com/); the European Centre for Women and Technology (http://www.ecwt.eu/en/home); 1,000 Girls, 1,000 Futures (https://www.nyas.org/ programs/global-stem-alliance/1000-girls- 1000-futures/); and Gender InSITE (https:// genderinsite.net/). Lagesen (2007) offers an accessible and insightful sociological analysis of a campaign to increase women's participation in science and engineering.

Crucially, few people recognise that gender discrimination doesn't just harm women; it also gives many types of privilege to men.

Male scientists and engineers tend to be more respected, paid higher salaries, promoted more easily, are more likely to be offered jobs, and more likely to have publications accepted and grants awarded (Hill et al., 2010). If we hope to combat gender discrimination, it isn't enough to lessen the harm done to women; we must also lessen the privilege given to men.

One way to do this involves encouraging men to recognise the benefits they have simply because they are men. That's why this recipe is for men. Recognise your privilege, and use that as a starting point to make a difference. This issue isn't about blame or guilt. Privilege isn't something that evil men conspire to achieve, nor is it something for which men should apologise. Privilege is something society as a whole produces, and it won't go away until people see that it exists and commit themselves to changing the situation. A necessary step is for men to realise that regardless of their personal attitudes, they have this benefit, and the benefit needs to go away.

Ingredients

- A field in science or engineering.
- An open mind.
- A commitment to equity.
- A desire to learn.
- Humility and tenacity.

Method

1. Learn about gender, science and engineering. Pick up a book, read a report, visit websites, get in touch with organisations. Here are two good places to start: read 'Why So Few?' and 'Solving the Equation' by the American Association of University Women (http://www.aauw.org/research/why-so-few/); and visit the WISE Campaign website (https://www.wisecampaign.org.uk/).

2. Make the lessons personal. Think back to your childhood, your school days, your years training in universities. Consider your work experience. Ask yourself questions like, "How many girls in my school took maths and science?" and "How many women are in my department?" Walk around your building and find portraits of celebrated scholars; how many are men? Wander around your campus and consider the names of buildings; how many of those names are masculine? Think back to the speakers you have seen at seminars, and the scholars who have been invited to the department; do men form a majority of them?

3. Talk to your women colleagues. Ask them if they have felt challenged by others' gender bias. Make sure that they know you are honestly interested.

If you run into hesitation, mention things you have learned about gender, science and engineering from your readings.

4. Recognise your privilege out loud. Don't make this something that sits inside your head. Tell others what you have learned, and what it makes you feel.

5. Find partners and start changing things. Maybe your university has support groups for women in science and engineering. Perhaps there is an ongoing effort to better the situation. Engage with them.

6. Identify goals to pursue right away. For example, make sure that there is a better gender distribution of invited speakers. Ask colleagues from the social and political sciences to deliver talks on these issues. Bring up and discuss these problems at your next laboratory meeting. Encourage others to read the same texts you did.

Cook's tips

You'll almost certainly run into resistance, and it may even come from women colleagues. You may be accused of trying to blame people, or of calling someone a sexist. Don't just give up. Explain as best you can: this isn't about blame; this is about changing things for the better. The goal is not to find villains, but to open eyes.

We need to recognise privilege out loud. An open mind does little good without an active voice.

Leadership styles and approaches in GeoSciences

Katriona Edlmann

In common with many of my academic colleagues, I entered the University to excel in my research and teaching rather than to become a leader; this article explores how senior academics often "learn as they go".

Excellent leadership within UK universities is more important than ever, as increasing fees, internationalisation and reducing research budgets lead to an ever more competitive research market. Current research indicates that successful leadership within an academic environment should be non-coercive, based on teamwork and relationships (Moss & Jensrud, 1995; McCafffery, 2004). Within the School of GeoSciences at the University of Edinburgh, the 2015 Athena SWAN statistics reveal that the school has 39% female staff at grade U09 and 15% female staff at grade U10, which is similar to the overall University female academic staff ratio (U09 35% and U10 22%).

Against this backdrop, this article presents my personal reflection on the leadership styles and approaches of four senior female academics within the School of GeoSciences. I review current definitions of leadership, their styles and context within the academic setting and the implications for female academic leaders. I then present the results of interviews and discussions I held with the senior female academics about their own leadership approaches and styles, and the article concludes with a personal reflection of how these practices can be adopted and adapted more widely, and their impact on my own academic leadership practice.

Successful academic leadership creates an environment that inspires and facilitates the achievement of shared goals; communicates a clear direction and vision; maintains a clear and level presence and ensures team unity/cohesion where the leader is accepted and respected (Adair, 2004; Heifetz & Laurie, 1997). A good leader will create the best environment for others to develop, but what makes someone a good leader? Defining leadership is complex, evolving and inherently subjective; not enough is known about what makes an individual an effective leader (Bryman, 2007; Bennis & Nanus, 1997). Current research on leadership combines defining the characteristics of successful leaders and their style or approach to leadership and includes the following areas of exploration:

- Trait theories – identifying the individual characteristics of successful leaders.

- Behavioural theories – identifying the actions and behaviours of successful leaders.

- Contingency theories – noting the influence of context and situation.

- Power and influence theories – identifying the leadership attributes that emerge as a result of positions of power and influence.

These combine to define the characteristics of successful leaders in terms of their personal attributes, interpersonal abilities and technical management skills. Personal attributes include: enthusiasm, confidence, initiative, intelligence (including emotional intelligence), warmth, humility, integrity, fairness, persistence and vision. Interpersonal abilities include: team building, outgoing personality and being compassionate. Technical management skills include analysing and evaluating problems, understanding a situation at different levels of detail, producing results, resolving

conflicts, and being goal orientated with an ability to enhance the work environment (Bensimon, et al., 2000). An ideal combination of these characteristics is an important contribution to being an effective leader.

Leadership style defines the approach to providing leadership. Goleman et al. (2002) have identified six leadership styles:

- Coercive – just get on and do what I say.

- Authoritative – gives clear messages on what needs to be done.

- Affiliative – puts people before the task.

- Democratic – gathers ideas and support from the team.

- Pace-setting – sets very high personal performance standards and expects the same from the team.

- Coaching – identifies strengths and weaknesses of each team member and links them to their goals.

Tucker (1984); Bensimon et al. (1989); Bensimon & Neumann (1993); Ramsden (1998); McCafffery (2004); Sapienza (2004); Bryman (2007); Robertson et al. (2009); and Middlehurst (2012) looked in particular at leadership in the context of higher education concluding that leadership styles need to be consultative and founded on strong teamwork and relationships. Bryman noted in his summary findings on leadership in higher education that "effective leaders create an environment or context for academics and others to fulfil their potential and interest in their work" (Bryman, 2007, p. 27) and "foster a collegial climate of mutual supportiveness and the maintenance of autonomy" (Bryman, 2007, p. 20). Sapienza notes in her Leadership Strategies in Scientific Research book that "an effective scientific leader is more likely to have an enthusiastic, energetic and passionately committed group working for them" (Sapienza. 2004, p. 3).

Carli & Eagly (1999) observe in their paper on the gender effects on leadership that research on gender stereotypes reveals that people consider men to have more agentic qualities (such as assertiveness and competitiveness) and women to have more communal qualities (such as being kind and supportive) (Broverman et al., 1972; Deaux & Kite, 1993; Williams & Best, 1990). This also extends to cognitive characteristics as well, with men perceived as more analytical and exact with women more imaginative and perceptive. This leads to an unconscious expectation that men are more likely to have an authoritative or coercive leadership style whereas women will have a more democratic or coaching leadership style which is ideally suited to the academic environment. Research by Helgesen (1990), Rosener (1990), and Glaser & Smalley (1995) reinforces the idea that women are particularly well equipped with the key personal characteristics that contribute to natural leadership in an academic environment. However, I feel it would be naive to assume that women are naturally more suited to academic leadership and new frames of reference are required. But it is worth highlighting the study by Zenger & Folkman (2012) for the Harvard Business Review which found that

women significantly outshone men in the positive leadership competencies of taking initiative, displaying integrity, honesty and driving results, and women rated higher than men in 12 out of 16 leadership attributes.

I used the Goleman et al. (2002) definition of leadership styles as the basis of my interviews with four senior female academic staff members from the School of GeoSciences to share their reflections on their personal leadership styles and approaches. We discussed a number of topics based around: How do they describe their leadership style? What personal characteristics do they believe contribute to their effective leadership? Has their leadership evolved or changed with time? Do they adopt a different leadership style with senior colleagues than they use with junior colleagues? Had they received training in leadership? Table 1 shows a summary of their answers when asked about their styles of leadership.

None of the interviewees identified with the coercive style of leadership; two interviewees felt that coaching was not a leadership style they used very often; one interviewee expressed a wish to add coaching to her leadership style more often, as she believed it "builds teams", and one

Leadership style	A	B	C	D
Coercive	●	●	●	●
Authoritative	■	60%	■	■
Affiliative	■	■	■	40%
Democratic	80%	20%	80%	40%
Pace-setting	20%	20%	20%	■
Coaching	✦	■	■	20%

● did not identify at all with this leadership style.   ■ occasionally used this leadership style.   ✦ would like to use this leadership style more.   % the proportion of time this leadership style is adopted.

Table 1. Results of the leadership styles interviews with four senior female academic staff members from the School of GeoSciences.

reported using coaching effectively with students. The predominance of democratic and pace-setting leadership styles with a coaching aspiration agrees with the gender stereotype of leadership. I feel this is most likely due to the fact that this style of leadership is the most successful in an academic setting and that this type of leadership is just as likely to be applied by male colleagues (future work might usefully run the same interview process with the male counterparts to see if this is the case).

All four interviewees felt that they used a mix of all the other leadership styles depending on the circumstances and individuals they were dealing with. There was a strong recognition among all interviewees that each individual they manage needs leadership styles tailored specifically to them. This is in line with the literature that indicates that the most effective leaders are those that adapt their leadership style to different circumstances and to different colleagues (Goleman et al., 2002).

Pace-setting leadership occurred in the majority of the critiques of their leadership style and from my personal observations this was something I was expecting to see with particular relevance to female leadership, as I often observe senior female academics setting themselves very high standards. All interviewees who do implement pace-setting leadership had an awareness that these high expectations needed careful monitoring so that the team is not overwhelmed by the pacesetter's demands.

The personality characteristics that led to their own leadership style that I observed in all interviewees centred on the excitement of doing innovative science, wanting to discover something new and making a difference. All interviewees felt it was important to "step up to the mark" to contribute and improve. They were all motivated by the environment of science and teaching in a multi-disciplinary international community.

A very descriptive analogy as to how the four interviewees undertake their successful leadership is the "galaxy-like spiral of change" described by Robertson & Cox (2009), where "leadership is energy-driven not just from the core, but with energy being generated by team members themselves, self-perpetuating and to some extent self-sustaining, though still benefiting from the momentum emanating from the core leadership". The leaders I spoke with certainly enthused and inspired their teams with their own excitement and love of their science and teaching; and carried their colleagues with them in that vision and adventure. I feel that this analogy goes hand in hand with the democratic and pace-setting leadership styles preferred by the female academic leaders interviewed.

The interviewees made a number of thought-provoking observations (all quotations are taken from interview notes) that provided some very important insights into successful leadership practices. These are grouped into the three main themes identified at the start of this article: personal and reflective attributes, interpersonal abilities and technical management skills:

- Have an awareness of how you behave and how that influences others; "notice when you make a difference". This was particularly pertinent to the interviewees who considered themselves pacesetters as they were aware that they needed to be careful to make sure other members of the team were not given unreasonable expectations.

- Develop a thick skin; sometimes you will make decisions that are not popular with everyone.

- Be a role model, be supportive of your team, involved and interested in their research, "attend presentations your students give" to show them that they and their work are a priority for you.

- All interviewees stated empathy as a great skill and this is especially relevant to the mathematical/applied

science discipline that we work within. They saw this as giving women a leadership edge as it helps to get the best out of all team members.

- Being a facilitator was a recurring idea during the interviews, which is in line with the idea of a good academic leader creating an environment for academics and others to fulfil their potential. This will often involve getting the resources and management right so there is the academic freedom in which to operate.

- Trust the students and academic teams that you lead to operate at their best and get on with it.

- "Support from colleagues makes you feel less exposed." Talking through complex matters with a senior colleague and getting them involved is a positive step and hugely valuable. Use support network groups and be open to new connections.

- Leadership skills evolve with time, experience and confidence. With maturity you are exposed to more experiences and ideas, take on more responsibility and become more aware of what you have to deliver.

- Communication is key to good leadership, especially modes of communication. If something important or sensitive needs to be discussed, do this in person; emails are an ineffective and troublesome way of communicating, and often open to misinterpretation.

- In meetings, it is hugely important to listen properly and leave a gap in the conversation for thought. This builds trust and improves communication.

- Prepare for meetings or important discussions. Have a plan of the outcomes you want to achieve in any meeting and try to make sure they are achieved. Be determined to achieve the outcomes that are really important to

you and don't worry about the ones that are not so important. Be really clear about your highest priorities for change and don't have too many of these.

- Be adaptable, don't be afraid to change leadership styles and even your own mindset; there is more than one way to tackle a problem.

- The democratic style of leadership was identified as particularly useful when dealing with senior male colleagues. The challenge of leading older male colleagues was raised by a few of the interviewees who were all extremely comfortable with leading students, postgraduates and peers, but felt less confident with older or dominating (and not always senior) male colleagues.

- Self-belief and confidence are very important. It was interesting to note that some of the interviewees who I regard as very confident, capable and exciting leaders often did not see that about themselves in every circumstance; personal perception is a very important part of leadership confidence. This is where the 3600 assessment (Johnson, 2004) would be a very interesting exercise and if a more in-depth analysis could be done on the results it would be fascinating to have each interviewee complete an assessment of each of the other interviewees' leadership styles and to see how their personal view of their own leadership style aligns with the external views of their leadership style.

All interviewees who had undertaken leadership training said they had benefited from it, primarily by exchanging experiences with their peers and gaining listening and problem-solving skills. It also helped in raising awareness of how their behaviour influences those around them. It was interesting to note that leadership training was offered the more senior they became, whereas on reflection some interviewees would have liked to have had this training and awareness earlier on in their careers.

The overall leadership approach adopted by everyone interviewed was that of a hand on the tiller for gentle guidance. Providing a well-defined vision, making the goals clear, enthusing the team to achieve these goals and giving each team member the resources and space to do it themselves. One interviewee emphasised the need to "make a clear statement; don't make assumptions". This is particularly relevant to PhD students where the recommendation given was that in year one the students will require significant leadership and guidance which gradually reduces as they take ownership of their research until you become more of a guide than a leader.

In addition to the very helpful insights into what makes for successful leadership in an academic environment described above, the key messages that I personally have taken on board are: enthuse and excite – if you excite your team they will be naturally motivated and passionate about their research and develop as valued independent researchers; listen effectively and implement fair and ethical leadership, particularly in areas such as paper co-authorship and the sharing of research ideas, areas which are easily open to abuse. I would also include as important but understated leadership skills, being patient, taking a considered approach to action, and keeping a level head. This must be underpinned with self-confidence so that I do not hang back and miss opportunities that, to quote Sheryl Sandberg (2013), I should have "leaned in" for.

And finally: to believe in yourself.

Acknowledgements

My thanks go to all the interviewees, in appreciation of their time and their insights.

Becoming visible in meetings

Silje Graffer & Alison Williams

A female colleague explained that when she was in a meeting and had raised an issue, people sort of nodded and half-agreed. However, when the same idea was raised later, and this time by a man (rephrased slightly), everyone was on board and gave him credit. She was left baffled. What was she to do – come off as 'bitter' or 'difficult' by speaking up and saying: 'Excuse me, but that's exactly what I said five minutes ago and you didn't seem so enthusiastic then'?

Or just silently assume that he probably was also simply thinking along the same lines and that the chair probably didn't mean to not listen. And then leave it. Yup, she went for the second option, because the first seemed too daunting. Incidentally, "judgements about whether an utterance counts as impolite may be informed by stereotypical beliefs about gender-appropriate behaviour" (Mills, 2005, p. 264).

'Leaving it' once because it seems inconsequential, as in the exchange above, can so quickly become the norm. When women attend meetings, the pressure is often to do as everyone else does, right? But this comfortable culture of conformity actually often comes with a bitter aftertaste of unconscious gender bias. Where there is a hierarchical structure and a leader present, women speak up, raise questions, but often feel like they are not being listened to.

The exchange above happened (not at Edinburgh University) within a highly androcentric department of clinical medical research. As Judith Butler observes, gender roles are often "an act that has been going on before one arrived on the scene [and] which has been rehearsed, much as a script survives the particular actors who make use of it, but which require individual actors in order to be actualised and reproduced as reality once again" (Butler, 1988, p. 526).

Other colleagues have spoken of their contributions – and indeed their very presence – going unrecorded in academic minutes or the meeting summary. McConnell-Ginet describes the "persisting under-evaluation of women's work and over-evaluation of men's" (2000, p. 127).

How can this change? Both the leader of the meeting, and the participants, can contribute to creating equal meetings. This recipe suggests what people – men as well as women – can do to ensure that everyone feels safe to contribute to whatever meeting they are at.

It is also helped when the leader of the meeting is aware that this is a present concern, and that there are very real issues of evaluative and unconscious bias. See *How to run more equal meetings* for some ideas on how the chair can foster a meeting environment where all the voices and contributions are heard and valued.

Ingredients

- Agreements/guidelines for meeting behaviour and a protocol for capturing outlier ideas.
- A cool head.
- Useful phrases, gathered from colleagues, observation, imagination, and practised out loud.
- A psychic mirror (or as the Americans put it: "You spot it, you got it") to be aware of your own behaviour and reactions.
- Daybook, pen, paper and ample space (for people to write stuff down if they want to raise something later in the meeting, but someone else is talking).
- Like-minded women for planning an amplification strategy with (see below).

Method

1. **Agree guidelines for the meeting.**
   Ask the chair – preferably beforehand – to start the meeting by inviting participants to co-create guidelines (this is relevant to both situations). These might include:

   - No interrupting (except by the chair if someone has spoken long enough).
   - No holding separate conversations during the meeting.

- Women should be respectful to other women too and not disregard them because of gender. Women can hold evaluative bias about other women too.

- Freedom to challenge inappropriate comments and non-verbal interjections such as sighs (which might occur when you go ahead with setting guidelines) with real concerns or facts. For example: "I think we should challenge the stereotype of women being quieter than men – actually take that a step further and ensure that the women contribute equally".

- Such examples work as positive interventions, and using positive language takes the conversation back to fact rather than putting the biased person in the limelight.

2. **Make notes** of every meeting in a daybook. Especially note who said what, and your own responses as well as other people's. Use the psychic mirror to become aware of your own biases (for help on this, see *Challenging bias*).

3. **Listen for themes and repeated behaviours.** Try calling it out with a useful phrase such as: "I am noticing that...", "What I am hearing is...", "How might we...?" or more specifically: "Interesting that Bill is feeling

Alice's behaviour is aggressive and unhelpful". Mills (2005) points out that what is heard as aggressive in women's language is often heard as assertive in men's.

4. **Claim the space.** If you are being ignored, cut-across or silenced, use a combination of body language and words. This method is offered by a consultant colleague: lean forward, put both arms onto the table from elbows to finger tips making a clear territory in front of you, and say: "I would like to make a contribution". Say it clearly and wait until everyone is attentive. Repeat until you are heard (this may take some time). Claim the space and hold it.

5. **Be authentic.** Resist the temptation to put on a fake smile. The fake smile is a warning sign for one of the authors that she is being 'a good girl' at the expense of the project, sanity and gender balance. And whenever you see it in someone else, they are definitely unhappy – check with them and maybe encourage them to speak up. In her essay Performative Acts & Gender Constitution, Judith Butler says: "gender is made to comply with a model of truth and falsity which [...] serves a social policy of gender regulation and control. Performing one's gender wrong initiates a set of punishments both obvious and indirect" (Butler, 1988, p. 528).

Thus the temptation to stay quiet and not be 'punished' can be very strong.

6. **Collaborate with your women colleagues.** Use amplification as described in this article from the Washington Post:

> When President Obama took office, two-thirds of his top aides were men. Women complained of having to elbow their way into important meetings. And when they got in, their voices were sometimes ignored. So female staffers adopted a meeting strategy they called "amplification": When a woman made a key point, other women would repeat it, giving credit to its author. This forced the men in the room to recognize the contribution – and denied them the chance to claim the idea as their own. "We just started doing it, and made a purpose of doing it. It was an everyday thing," said one former Obama aide who requested anonymity to speak frankly. Obama noticed, she and others said, and began calling more often on women and junior aides. (Eilperin, 2016)

Warning

Be aware of people who are biased (unconsciously or consciously); they sometimes don't like to have it pointed out to them. It never works to try to make a biased person change his (or her) mind just before a meeting. Do this in a private one-to-one meeting later. It's hard to argue with bias and prejudice – and before you know it you've lost your cool and are saying things that are inappropriate for a work meeting.

How to run more equal meetings

Silje Graffer, Nathalie Rochefort & Judy Robertson

In an executive or a scientific meeting, women are not only often under-represented but also not listened to, or their opinions not taken into account. Even worse, whether it is in academia or in the private sector, women often report that they said something at a meeting that was at first not noticed but later on, a male colleague suggested the same idea, sometimes word for word, and suddenly everybody listened and found it very relevant.

This situation is most of the time due to unconscious bias in attention and the way meetings are usually lead. The chair of the meeting is often not conscious of this bias and when a woman points out that her voice was not taken into account, she may be perceived as aggressive or 'over-sensitive' simply because the male participants are not aware of this issue.

Analysis of powerful men's and women's contributions to meetings from naturalistic data (such as transcripts from the US Senate) indicates there are distinct patterns in how often people contribute and for how long. Powerful men talk more in meetings, but equally-powerful women do not. Unfortunately, this may be because powerful women encounter backlash as a result of talking more than others – they are more likely to be perceived by both men and women as being less likeable, less efficient or too controlling (Brescoll, 2012). According to social norms, men leaders should display their power, but women leaders should not. This is yet another example of the "double bind" faced by women leaders, where they face the choice between being likeable and being competent (see *The double bind*).

A related issue is the style of the meeting, and the sorts of contribution which are routinely accepted. Academics often enjoy a nice robust debate. It can be a matter of pride to thrash issues out with a lively argument. Supervision meetings can degenerate into point-scoring matches between the supervisors with the student forced into the role of observer; exam boards can degenerate to the point where literally the loudest voice carries the decision; and supposedly consultative staff meetings can be entirely dominated by the most powerful. The drawback of this way of conducting business is that it disenfranchises those whose voices are quieter and roles are less powerful but who nevertheless have extremely useful contributions to make.

This recipe suggests some approaches which can overcome these problems and foster an environment where everyone feels safe to contribute in the knowledge that their views will be heard.

Ingredients

- A meeting with attendees of varying status, or a single member of a particular demographic group.

- Awareness of unconscious bias.
- Awareness of your own presence and that of others in this professional capacity; being conscious of how loud your own voice is, and the loudness of others' voices; and the emotional and physical comfort levels of the people around you.
- Preparation time.
- Patience and calm.

Method

1. **Have the meeting at a time which does not exclude people (inside core working hours).** Choose a time which does not clash with school drop-off and pick-up times. Try to rotate the days and times of regular meetings so that people who work part-time do not consistently experience scheduling conflicts.

2. **Pick the meeting chair carefully.** To make an inclusive meeting work, you need a resilient, firm chair who is willing to challenge irritating people even if they are senior to them, or higher in an unacknowledged power hierarchy.

3. **What to think about if you're the chair.** If you have been put in the role of the chair, you can acquire the skills you need with practice and deliberate planning before the meeting. It might also be helpful to have an ally who knows your goals in advance and can help you out in sticky patches. Often you will have to be far firmer and less polite than you would be comfortable with in normal conversation. Perhaps you might need to get over your worries about interrupting people who are older than you or higher up the pecking order. Don't worry about coming across as 'bossy' – this relates to women being perceived as strident or aggressive even when the content of their speech would not be considered in this way if a man said it.

In the end, it doesn't matter whether you are bossy or not. Your job when running a meeting is to cover the necessary ground, while ensuring that everyone who wishes to contribute can do so, and to get it all done before the end of the allocated time slot. If you have to seem bossy to achieve this, so be it. If you have a naturally quiet voice, you could tap a glass with a spoon (or bang your head off the desk!) to attract attention. If you think the meeting will be pressed for time, you could use a timer which everyone can see, and regularly draw attention to the time remaining to reduce waffle and get decisions made.

4. **Plan the meeting structure to avoid lengthy periods of verbal debate.** Academic meetings can bring out the worst in otherwise perfectly reasonable people. Academics often love to talk, and like to hold forth in lecture-sized chunks. This results in uneven participation because if a couple of people hog the floor, then other views go unheard. Sometimes it is best to disrupt the normal meeting pattern so as not to encourage them. For example, you could ask for email comments beforehand and summarise them, or use an online voting system live for voting during the meeting.

5. **Consider whether you can increase the proportion of women at the meeting (or members of a minority group).**

The dynamic of the meeting may change when more than one-third of attendees are women and critical mass is achieved (Bohnet, 2016).

6. **Deliberately and systematically consult everyone and ensure equal speaking time.** You need to strike a careful balance here between putting shy people on the spot and giving them the opportunity to speak. You might have to adopt different techniques depending on the size of the meeting. In small meetings, you could deliberately go round each person at the table in turn to ask them for their view, thanking each person respectfully for what they contributed regardless of their status. In large meetings, you could ask people to write down their views on a piece of paper (anonymously if you prefer) and pin them to the wall so that everyone may browse the views of their colleagues by reading them.

The advantage of this is that you have a record of the views to take away and think about afterwards. It may be necessary to explain why you are doing this to the senior people or the mouthy people who feel aggrieved that they are not getting a chance to hog the discussion as they normally would. You could do this publicly as you introduce the exercise to make the point that you want to hear from everyone.

7. **Ensure good quality listening in the room.** Do this by making sure there is no background noise or individual conversations when anyone is speaking, particularly if someone with a quieter voice is trying to contribute. For a big audience, take the time to set up the microphone right, especially for women.

8. **Keep track of who said what.** When making the summary of the meeting either orally or in writing, be sure to name equally the persons who suggested the different ideas or contributions. If you're not taking notes yourself, remember to brief the minute-taker at the start of the meeting to specifically include names for each contribution.

• **Call out bad behaviour.** As the leader of the meeting, it is your job to analyse your own unconscious gender bias (whether you identify as a woman, a man or as in-between or as neither gender) and strive to redirect this act of listening to the whole group as much as you can by intervening and calling it out when you can see it happening. From time to time your colleagues will misbehave by interrupting, dismissing their colleagues' contributions, ignoring or patronising junior people, hogging the floor or 'mansplaining'.

It's your job to civilly draw attention to this as an unacceptable behaviour by way of training the rest of the

participants on how to behave and reassuring the recipients of the behaviour that it is OK to speak. Here are some phrases you might find helpful:

• Thank you, Joe, but we have already heard from you and I would like to hear what other people think about this.

• I'll just stop you there because we need to move on to address X.

• [Bill] that's a great issue/ idea to raise, but I believe that [Alice] already raised it earlier. Thank [Alice] after it occurs.

9. **Deal fairly with confrontations.** If there is a confrontation, be sure that the arguments from a woman or a younger participant are not discarded simply because the other side speaks louder or is more confident.

10. **What not to do.** Do not make jokes or comments on physical aspects (clothes, hair style, and accessories) or on 'how kind' or 'how nice' women are. Do not assume that all women in the room are on the same side and share the same opinions just because they are women.

11. **Good luck.** It takes a while to change unconscious bias (it is unconscious after all), but the first step is to acknowledge that it's happening so that other people become aware of it and realise when it's happening and change behaviour accordingly.

What have you done to my squash courts!

Jon Turner

I'm a keen squash player. Some years ago, the University of Edinburgh Sport & Exercise Pleasance Complex closed four squash courts and replaced them with a gym full of running machines, training bikes, etc. I was very cross, as were lots of the folk I play squash with – lots of whom are male and heading towards middle age and beyond. Many of us made our displeasure known – something that must have been uncomfortable for Sport & Exercise as we were long-term members and several of us have managerial/leadership roles in different parts of the University.

Now, more than ten years later, the Sport & Exercise gym is usually pretty full and I've noticed that lots of the users (perhaps about half) are women and younger than the old squash demographic. There are also lots more people using the gym space than used to use the four squash courts.

The Sport & Exercise management were absolutely right in identifying that a change in space usage would have a profound positive impact on reaching more people and in reaching a group who, at that stage, were under-represented in their membership (female students). They were also absolutely right to ignore the representations of the older, predominantly male, previous users of that space. I don't know if Sport & Exercise were primarily motivated by gender equality, but this was certainly a positive result. And yes, I do still play squash at Sport & Exercise, and I now use the running machines and bike trainers as well!

Ingredients

- Indignation (use VERY sparingly).
- Persistence.
- Open-mindedness.
- Ability to see the bigger picture.

Method

This recipe is about change – reacting to it, understanding it (however reluctantly at first!) and embracing it. Seeing how it worked, not just for my own benefit, but for the benefit of the wider University community.

1. Take a large dollop of indignation, then discard all but a tiny pinch of it.

2. Take a deep breath, and then another, deeper one.

3. Persist in using the available facilities rather than going off in a huff.

The next method step is what I wish had happened, rather than what actually did:

4. Ask the management what their thinking is behind the proposed changes, and how they intend to manage the transition for existing and potential members.

And the last bit is what is happening now...

5. Enjoy the added facilities and carry on playing squash!

Exercise and sport for all

Jim Aitken

According to the annual Edinburgh University Sports Union Club Survey, the standard of its fitness facilities is a key factor for many potential students in choosing a university. University of Edinburgh Sport & Exercise, with Olympic medal-winning ambassadors such as Sir Chris Hoy (cycling) and Dame Katherine Grainger (rowing), contributes significantly to the University's reputation locally, nationally and internationally (see the University of Edinburgh's Strategic Plan 2016: Delivering Impact for Society).

In actual fact, sport has featured at the University for over 150 years. This was founded largely on traditional school sports played through a formal club structure, but not now. The University of Edinburgh's Scottish and UK pre-eminence (see The Times and Sunday Times: Good University Guide) has been built over the last 15 or so years, with the Director widening the focus from sport to health, fitness and exercise – 'modernising the offering' as he puts it. In the process he has radically changed and upgraded the physical facilities to enable and reflect this change and produce a better balance between 'sport' and personal 'health & well-being'.

In 2004 the University's sports offer had around 8,100 members from across the University and community. The focus was very much on supporting students who came into the University with a pre-existing interest in sport and encouraging them

to continue their involvement through the University's 50+ sports clubs or via the recreational 'Intra-Mural' programme. This was further swayed by the largely sports bias of the University's facility mix. At the time, around 6,500 students were involved in sport and gym activity, the majority of whom were male (56%).

For example, when members entered the University main sports centre at Pleasance, the first facilities they saw were eight squash courts, occupied – when they were at all – by (predominantly) male senior faculty "heading to middle age". Of course there was a modest gym provision that members could use – tucked away at the far side of the ground floor, about the size of one-and-a-half squash courts, in constant demand and cramped. This contrasted with the extensive provision for squash (800 square metres of space) supporting a maximum of 16 people at any one time.

This made a very poor impression on potential students and new members, especially young women, reinforcing the stereotype that the University was seemingly prioritising its recreational facilities for middle-aged men, not for them.

Responding to student feedback and the clear imbalance, University Sport & Exercise challenged this paradigm, rethought its core purpose, and drew up a change programme that moved the facility from a predominantly

sport-based focus to celebrating and promoting exercise, health and fitness, for all. The change was additionally underpinned by Sport England and Sport Scotland facility guides on ideal occupancy levels of squash courts, which suggested the University had more courts than it needed for the size of its squash community.

The new approach of supporting health, fitness and exercise was planned, the design for a new space was drawn up; half of the squash courts were closed and the refit started – to loud protests from the users (*see What have you done to my squash courts!*).

This transition process did create a very unsettling time for University Sport & Exercise's members and staff, but the results have been hugely positive. Within the first year, membership rose by 1,500, and gender balance approached 50:50 as more female students felt the sport & fitness offer contained something appealing for them. More, the new gym space boasted a stunning design, and was located immediately on arrival to Pleasance – this presented a very dynamic, attractive and relevant option for students, and encouraged them to be more physically active. Sport & Exercise has gone from strength to strength ever since, helped by the completion of an even more ambitious facilities extension plan in 2010. This has positioned the University as one of the UK's premier sport & fitness providers, which is hugely pleasing for everyone involved.

Now in 2017, its membership is 18,700 and in 2016 it had an annual footfall of 800,000. Its student membership is 43% male and 57% female. This is fuelled by state-of-the-art facilities, with a raft of contemporary gyms, supportive staff, about 100 group-exercise classes each week, and affordable pricing – all within easy walk of the University's main city centre campus, and with a superb marketing and communications plan. That's all quite a change from 2004! The good news is that squash is still booming at the University!

Initial Ingredients

This recipe has two sets of ingredients. The first set are the ones used in the first change programme (2004); and the second are additional ingredients being used now, as a direct result of learning from the first round of changes.

- A huge dollop of confidence in your conviction to see change through, backed up by a robust set of evidence and the justification for change, including:
    - Information and feedback from students;
    - Independent statistics (Sport England and Sport Scotland reports).
- Clear and expressed values.
- A lived passion for exercise, health and fitness.

- A visible way of tracking/ identifying impact.

Additional Ingredients

- Communication.
- Communication.
- Communication.
- Listening.

Method

1. Take the first three ingredients – conviction + evidence, clear values, and passion – mix together and live them in yourself. This way you attract other passionate people to work with you.

2. Provide great service in great facilities:

   a) Make the offering attractive to a diverse membership – gender, age, physical ability, status, ethnicity, locality. For example, there is a wide range of different interests, types of experience, levels of confidence, and current trends in fitness; and we need to cater for them all.

   b) Design the new facilities so that they clearly demonstrate your values the moment a member walks into the space:

   - A passion for exercise, health and fitness.
   - Healthy bodies support healthy

minds – and this is what the University is here to do.

- A safe and supportive space for all members to meet, mix, and learn.
- A place where everybody is welcome.

c) Deliver wide member choice, for example:

- Reaching inactive staff and students through the SPA programme (Support for Physical Activity) for people who want to become more active for their health. This may be achieved through a variety of activities including walking as well as gym and sport.
- Nurturing mind and body together through yoga and PIYO (pilates/yoga).
- Supporting all students through stress-buster activities around exam time, although we do lose the big hall to examinations!
- Fitness is personal. Everyone has individual tastes, needs and wants which are dynamic and ever-changing. So the offerings need to be regularly revisited to meet changing demands from customers: different times, types, lighter or more intense regimes.

d) Offer out-of-the-ordinary member services, for example Sport & Exercise has FASIC (Fitness Assessment and Sports Injuries Centre), a multi-disciplinary sports injuries clinic, with podiatry, physiotherapy, massage, a doctor service, workshops and training courses. It also has dedicated spaces for archery, grappling, climbing, rowing, boxing, specialist gym areas, and lots more besides, including stunning changing rooms, with saunas. Don't be scared to experiment with your exercise offerings.

e) Set (exercise) menus can prove tiresome, and remember there are new approaches and recipes being tried in exciting new restaurants all the time, so be mindful of complacency and competition.

3. Link into research – for example, through the Healthy University project, University of Edinburgh students have the opportunity to carry out research that has benefits for their own development and that of Sport and Exercise.

4. Measure the results.

We now regularly add the missing ingredient – communication, communication and even more communication:

5. Communicate what the change programme is offering – what it is, why it is important to the University and its students, staff and community, and why you are passionate about it. If we'd done this in the first place, we'd have avoided the recipe *What have you done to my squash courts!* ever needing to be written!

6. Communicate what any short-term discomfort might be, and communicate the long-term benefits.

7. Communicate to everyone and keep communicating: make no assumptions that they will have taken it on board and understood the first time they heard it.

8. Remember that communication is a two-way process, not just broadcast. Listen, and respond nimbly and speedily to feedback.

Reflections on exercise and sport in the University

Alison Williams

Perspectives from recipe writers and interviewees

Each person contributing their perspective on exercise and sport in the University, as a recipe author (see *What have you done to my squash courts!* and *Exercise and sport for all*) or an interviewee, shares the same passion. They agree that good health is everyone's right and should be in the University's DNA. Good health in study and work, and in a safe environment, is for everyone; it leads to better marks and academic performance, has clear productivity benefits and supports a healthier lifestyle and longevity. It is not just an aspiration for the few.

As well as interviewing the Director of Sport & Exercise, Jim Aitken, for his recipe *Exercise and sport for all*, I interviewed Dr Andrew Murray, FASIC (Fitness Assessment and Sports Injuries Centre) Sports Physician and Researcher; Helen Ryall, Healthy University Project Coordinator; two 3rd-year women student gym members; and Zach Murphy, male graduate student member. The discussions were wide-ranging, and highlighted the multiple readings of reality (Charmaz, 2000) that emerge from differing stakeholder perspectives: gender, professional staff and student.

Staff perspectives

Dr Murray emphasised how exercise can contribute to seven years' extra life and prevention of chronic disorders, while regular sport makes people happier. "Getting active, and staying active really is the best thing you can do for your health. Each step is a step to health." Dr Murray is aware of the barriers to people engaging in sport. He noted that: "We need to be more respectful of people who don't conform to stereotypes."

Helen Ryall, the coordinator of the Healthy University Project (HUP) prioritised supporting inactive people "who want to be a bit more active, a bit more often" and reach the recommended 150 minutes of physical activity a week. She noted that: "Women are more likely to have a conversation about health; the majority of people who engaged in conversations in the Freshers' Week health project were women."

She also observed that people very often need an impetus to make a life change; everything from, for example, having a heart attack, to having trouble keeping up with a friend while walking, or even seeing an unflattering photo of themselves. For students, who are at a key transition in their lives, there is usually an opportunity to intervene at an earlier point in the trajectory.

> The SPA programme (Support for Physical Activity) is a confidential non-judgemental service open to all staff and students at the University who need some support to make the changes they want to make to their lifestyle through physical activity. HUP offers workplace programmes for staff as well as support and opportunities to students to become more active (http://www.ed.ac.uk/sport-exercise/healthy-university).

Student perspectives

The female student member who said that the University gym is "definitely the best gym for students in Edinburgh" then went on to say: "I think as long as you know it well and begin to feel comfortable there it is a really good gym – just a question of getting used to it!"

This section examines what, for a young woman, "getting used to it" can mean, and what might be required for her to begin to feel comfortable, especially in some areas of the facility. For example:

> It took several months before I felt OK going in [to the Vault Room] on my own.

The interlinking themes that emerged from the interviews with the three student members and with University Sport & Exercise staff members are: the impact of the physical space, the sense of performance and being observed, perceptions and feelings of insider/outsider.

Physical Space

The article *Stereotype threat* explores how the women students may be hampered by their internalisation of societal stereotypes of what is and is not appropriate behaviour and activities for their own and other genders. There may also be a social price to pay for not conforming to gender stereotypes.

The two women students described how the different physical spaces in the gym were informally demarcated by gender. One of the students drew a 'snapshot' map (Figure 1) of the population by gender in each of the rooms during one visit to the gym:

Both women are very aware of how the different spaces within the Sport & Exercise Pleasance building impact them.

> The men dominate the space. For example, I'll wait [queue up] for a woman to finish on a bit of equipment but I wouldn't wait [queue up] for a man to be finished.

They talked of feeling intimidated in the rooms with more traditionally masculine activities (weights in particular):

There's a feeling that the space is primarily for men.

It was several months before one felt comfortable enough to go into the weights room on her own:

> The Olympic Room is male dominated. At first I wanted to be accompanied [by boyfriend or another woman] when I went in. You feel like you need permission to have access.

> It's off-putting – the guys are all kitted out with the gear – big belts and things – and I feel, well, who are meant to be there?

> Names make a difference. The Vault Room's name is SO masculine. It should really be called 'Intense Basement Situation'.

> [It] is very male dominated, and I've never seen more than three women (including myself) in it at

a time. Sometimes I'm the only woman in there to 20 guys. [...] The machines are arranged facing inwards, so that everyone is looking at each other, and there are no mirrors.

Incidentally, the Vault Room is so called because it used to be a vault in one of the old buildings in the Pleasance complex.

The Sport & Exercise staff are aware that women may feel intimidated by the weight-training facilities, and are now running workshops for "women who want to take up weight or strength training in a welcoming and understanding environment". The advert acknowledges that "free-weights gyms are some of the most intimidating and unwelcoming places for females due to requiring a level of competence to use and they are typically male-dominated places". Women's weightlifting workshops are selling out and encouraging more women to overcome negative perceptions surrounding strength training.

Being looked at

The issue, for young women, of feeling observed, introduces the further dynamic of performance.

> The other thing is make-up – I feel I need to go to the gym in full make-up, because when I exercise I get hot and sweaty – very red in the face with a ring of white round my mouth like a mask. I wouldn't want to be seen like that."

> Sometimes women go to be seen. Full make-up and just sauntering along on the treadmill very slowly...

One of the women students started sometimes going to a private central Edinburgh gym so that she can wear little or no make-up because:

> I'm less likely to see anyone I know.

The feeling of being observed – the 'male gaze' (Lacan 1988; Foucault 1977; Mulvey 1975) – can be restricting

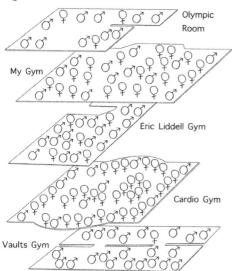

A map of men and women in the CSE during a session at the gym.
♀ = Women
♂ = Men

Olympic Room
My Gym
Eric Liddell Gym
Cardio Gym
Vaults Gym

Figure 1: University Gym population, 3pm Monday 27th March 2017, charted by female student member.

and uncomfortable. One of the female students said that:

> The guys will make snidey comments about underarm hair.

This theme also emerged in the Unapologetically Me photography exhibition.

It is not just the case in the gym, of course, as School of Education women students attending another workshop noted similar pressure at other buildings in the University:

> If you go to Potterrow [a student union venue] or the main library you can see it and like hear it and if I go to the main library I feel like I should wear something nice and put on make-up. More so than if I came here [to the Education satellite campus] because it is all girls here... It's the whole male gaze thing. If you go to the main library then you feel very looked at.

The female gym members I interviewed prefer spaces where the male gaze is least in evidence, for example in the MyGym or the Cardio Gym, borne out by the snapshot map (see Figure 1).

> MyGym is more female dominated. There are mirrors, and the machines face outward [away from each other] so you aren't being observed. And where there are mirrors you tend to be watching yourself to make sure you are doing things right.

The students noted that the equipment layout in MyGym and the Cardio Gym means the gender ratios in those spaces are more balanced. When designing the MyGym space, the University Sport & Exercise staff deliberately adopted a bright and light ambience, ensured the cardio kit faced outwards, and used contemporary and attractive loose equipment. The equipment was limited to 10kg to prevent 'macho' training, and there is a deliberate policy of no group or club training.

The same philosophy was adopted in the circuits and the Cardio Gym. Their aim of creating a welcoming space which was not intimidating has been successful in the sense that the gym is very popular, and 70% of those exercising there are women. It may still be the case that women prefer to exercise in proximity to other women; the students note that:

> [MyGym] tends to have an informal segregation, with women congregating together in one part of the space.

Fitting in

People can also feel like outsiders in a gym for reasons unrelated to gender; there are many cues which can subtly suggest that they are not part on an "in-group". They might feel self-conscious about their bodies, or because they do not feel fit enough, or because they feel "too old". For example, a woman might feel initially uncomfortable in a class with other women if she perceives her peers to be more fit. Indeed, some staff have commented that men may be intimidated by a majority female presence at an exercise class if they are self-conscious about their body condition.

The women student members commented:

> I don't see women in the gym who are any larger than a size 16, and yet it's a great way to lose weight.

> I can see that divide too; there are lots of sporty men and very few 'unfit' ones! However, interestingly, I see more older men using the University Sport & Exercise than older women although perhaps that's just the areas I frequent.

Reflecting on feelings of not fitting in, the male student member thought:

> People get into a bit of a bubble when they put their headphones on. It removes one of their senses, and increases their sense of isolation in the gym [which] increases their sense of "Do I fit in?"

The question is, how do we enhance the desirable benefits of inclusive behaviours in the gym?

Currently the Sport & Exercise membership statistics for non-students (who make up 20% of the total membership) show that in all categories (staff, associate, community and senior) the percentage of men is much greater than of women. The staff are consequently working hard to combat people's self-perceptions that they don't belong at the gym: a key value is that the facilities are open to everyone. There are gym staff on hand (70% female) to help orientate new members to the gym, and Sport & Exercise aims to extend this next year with a gym buddy scheme. They offer beginner programmes in most activities to help get people started and grow confidence. Staff are trained to be warm and engaged with all members, and the centre offers around 100 exercise classes per week with 85% women attendees. The classes cover a range of exercise options and social exercise opportunities.

Sport & Exercise has also invested heavily in improving the quality of changing provision (especially in the female areas, including saunas) to ensure the visitor has a positive experience before and after each exercise session (with attention to privacy). The cleaning staff also work to ensure a pleasant environment in the gym and changing areas to dispel myths about smelly or sweaty spaces. The staff want to ensure that people feel that they belong, and that they exercise in a pleasant environment.

In the future, it would be beneficial to conduct some further qualitative research to understand gym users' perspectives about the gym space, and gather some quantitative data on footfall in different facilities by gender, fitness level and ethnic group.

Reflections

It has been a fascinating and intriguing journey working on this article, and editing the two associated recipes (see *What have you done to my squash courts!* and *Exercise and sport for all*) which together make up this cluster about the University of Edinburgh Sport & Exercise Pleasance Sports Complex & Gym, evoking what Charmaz (2000) terms multiple readings of reality.

The iterative process of interviewing, writing, inviting and incorporating comments and contributions, reflection and response has brought about the "mutual creation of knowledge by the viewer and the viewed" (Charmaz, 2000, p. 510); with the addition of you, the reader, as creator of yet another reading of this reality that is the Pleasance Sports Complex.

The principal reflections arising from the recipes and interviews are, first, that Sport & Exercises' expansion from elite sports to health and exercise has had a noticeable positive impact on student and staff membership numbers and gender balance. The interviews and recipes acknowledge and celebrate this, and the value of the changes made.

The second is that for some young women, there are challenges associated with feeling comfortable within the physical spaces of gyms, being in these spaces if they are male dominated and coping with the male gaze. The gym is not the only place where women encounter these difficulties. Women students may also feel pressure relating to body image and male gaze in student social spaces; see also the student photographs and illustrations in this volume, and for a wider sample of students refer to Stanton (2014). Students in the School of Education focus group also believed that: "There continues to be a pervasive attitude of male superiority and female objectification within some of the University's male sports clubs/teams", and commented that: "While there are policies in place, lad culture is still very prevalent in sports societies". This is borne out by evidence of sexual harassment incidents at sports societies reported in Mehdi (2013).

These issues are also reflected more widely across the University in academic environments. In a conversation about gender equality, senior University leaders, (see *Leadership perspectives on gender equality*) when asked what they thought the key issues were, talked about how "there can be cultural problems". For example, one of the senior female professor's comments echo the women students' 'work-arounds' to deal with their feelings of intimidation in particular spaces:

> Women coming into this [male-dominated] field are more aware of the existing culture and you have to learn how to fit in. You often need to adapt. Men don't need to do this but persuading them of the value of being aware of the cultural norms and pressures can help people to see how hard it can be [if you're in the minority].

For example, during our writing workshops, a senior woman staff member told us she was intimidated by the "bear pit" atmosphere of academic meetings and a group of students explained how they found particular online learning environments hostile.

Another senior leader mentioned the "need to avoid outsider vs insider". In academic environments, stereotype threat (see *Stereotype threat*) can be triggered in students feeling outsiders because of their ethnicity, socio-economic status, native language or religion. In the Sport & Exercise facilities, insider and outsider groups may emerge not only from gender but from body image perceptions and the fit compared to the unfit. Staff are aware of this and actively working to tackle these issues.

The challenge is to strike a balance of belonging and culture, to work towards an environment where, as another senior leader described it:

> You want people to feel they can be themselves [...] to have their own cultures, [...] to create an environment where people can be honest, be open.

Asking for equitable buildings

Derek Jones

Our built environment is not simply the material stuff from which it is made – it depends entirely on its interaction with people to make it meaningful. Lefebvre considered space to be a continual construction of a society (Lefebvre, 1991); Weisman demonstrates that architecture is a cultural artefact (Weisman, 1981, 2000); and Rendell that the spaces we use in architecture are "used, occupied and transformed through everyday activities" (Rendell, 2000). Such constructions will necessarily reflect the biases identified elsewhere in this book.

In the architectural profession, only 25% women (ARB, 2015) and only 1 in 5 women architects would recommend architecture as a career (Tether, 2016). The latest results from the Architects' Journal Women in Architecture Survey (Architects' Journal, 2017) confirm that the glass ceiling is proving to be made of toughened glass. Such imbalances of gender representation in both buildings and the profession itself inevitably lead to imbalances in the design and provision of space and architecture. For Weisman it is clear: "Feminism implies that we fully recognize this environmental inadequacy and proceed to think and act out of that recognition" (Weisman, 1981).

In the spirit of EqualBITE, this extended recipe (banquet?) provides some guidance on how to make space a bit more equitable. Use this as a series of starting considerations whether you are evaluating your own working environment or particularly if you are responsible for procuring space for other people.

1. Be utterly and completely universally inclusive from the start.

Universal design automatically considers asymmetries. Universal design aims to design for the entire human population not some statistically normal standard in that population (Lidwell et al., 2010). This leads to wider inclusion in existing populations and extends the sustainability of use across all populations through time. And remember that the minimum standards are just that: minimum standards. Universal design goes way beyond what are usually the minimum legal requirements. For example, the Roslin Institute at the University of Edinburgh, has a dedicated breast feeding/expression room going beyond what is required or even recommended. This is not simply about putting a chair in the accessible WC (most people don't like to eat their dinner in a toilet...)

Think intersectionally and beyond conditions – people with particular needs are also individuals and very often have intersections with other requirements. By focusing on the issues that arise from individuals' lived experiences, a far greater empathy in design can be achieved – instead of medical conditions, focus on the consequences and the experiences of people. For example, instead of considering 'autism', talk with people on the autistic spectrum to find out about the effects of cognitive overload, panic, shifting mental states, fatigue, and identity. Chances are they intersect with many other users – and not only those with a 'condition'. Make this part of an inclusive design process involving users and stakeholders in an organisation – not simply a list of items.

Lots of little, practical ideas make a huge difference. Have a read through the guides in http://universaldesign.ie/Built-Environment/Building-for-Everyone/. For example: providing rest space in stairwells and larger circulation areas;

providing sanitary facilities and support appropriate to each gender (not just the minimum standards – ask what people might need); have a clearly communicated and suitable family policy for an estate, school or individual buildings; consider security beyond the building itself (of arriving and leaving work outside normal hours). As before, setting out issues such as these with stakeholders and users is often more effective and inclusive.

2. Surface bias and break assumptions to generate new ideas.

Bias and belief checking. Surfacing hidden gender representations of an organisation or design team can be a useful starting point that is easily achieved through planned methods and means. For example, Fraser (2014) outlines a process used by researchers discussing their subject beliefs at the start of a project. This can be extended to any project team considering new space requirements or building by testing the values and attitudes of the team – remember, this process is one of reflection and consideration, not categorisation.

Check your congruence and spatial assignments. As with bias checking, take a look at the assumptions being made about the spaces you are asking for. Are PhD students squashed into a cupboard while that named professor is in a corner office with windows? Out of these groups of people, who is actually in the building more? And when you look at the function names on a plan of your building (e.g. admin office, research office), which genders first come to mind? Surfacing the socio-political congruence we hold between roles and genders can have an impact on how we design and assign space to both roles and genders.

Share the design. Digital prototyping and building information modelling (BIM) can lead to significantly improved collaboration and design performance, but only if it is used in particular ways and with particular values applied (Jones & Dewberry, 2013). One significant advantage it offers in in surfacing 'hidden' assumptions in individual contributor's contributions – when these become shared, they become exposed to wider scrutiny. When this is accompanied by a shared attitude of critical thinking and a shared solution-driven attitude, significantly improved collaboration and inclusion can be achieved.

3. Ask for values as well as objects

Shift your perspective and aim beyond problems. Don't simply ask for things you think you can get now – try to consider what your future values might wish to express. For example, when specifying or designing, considering mental health as opposed to mental illness can help shift the attitudes we bring to activities. It's odd that we are good at specifying spaces for analysing our heads when things go 'wrong' but are pretty bad at asking for spaces that support cognitive well-being. In academia we work with our minds so why should we not take this seriously and realise that our physical and mental bodies are one and the same (Damasio, 2006).

It's OK to ask for dreams and conceptions as well as specifications. Instead of asking for a room with 60 lux, why not ask for light that inspires creative thinking? The minimum lighting level is precisely that – the minimum required for functional performance. It says nothing of spatial quality or the values behind the spaces being created. As Robert Venturi famously stated, it is not a case that we have to have 'either or' – 'both, and' is possible (Venturi, 1984).

Ask for flexibility and adaptability. One sad thing that accompanies traditional procurement is the myth that the building being designed will last forever or that we have to get it right when we imagine

how the building works. But designing for adaption and future change can allow far greater social and political change to take place in an organisation. The traditional ordering of space assumes some anterior (and better) knowledge of what people want and need and it is simply wrong. The best (and most sustainable) architecture is also responsive and adaptive to human needs – both predicted and unimagined.

4. Process matters more than product

Design the process as much as the object itself. We do not have to accept existing modes and methods of procurement and we particularly do not have to accept the habits and failures they have consistently brought to public procurement for many decades (e.g. Morrell, 2011; Egan, 1998; Latham, 1994). Reports on procurement of public buildings repeat the same point – the process of designing is far more important than the product. And this process can itself be designed – so recognise this in any appointments or contracts, both in terms of the individuals involved as well as the legal forms themselves.

Consider soft landings, not hard stage gates. Design processes require decisions to be made and how this is done can have a significant impact on the process itself. Hard stage gates are decision points that have to be met with a yes/no before proceeding (e.g. 'Is everything ready for us to start building?'). Mostly, these are very sensible questions but many buildings and spatial services are now procured using only these 'hard' criteria at all stages of the process, making it far less efficient and effective for longer or more complex projects. The soft landings approach in building procurement allows for extended, performance-based approaches to verification of key stages in the procurement process (British Standards Institution, 2013; Sinclair, 2012). The shift in processes and attitudes required also engenders a more inclusive approach within the design team and between them and stakeholders.

Include people in the process in a valuable way. The other observation made in Latham (1994) and Egan (1998) is that the relationships between stakeholders and professionals matter. Involving people can be difficult because there simply is no such thing as an objective reality when isolated subjectivities are involved (Hastorf & Cantril, 1954)! But reaching a consensus is not the only reason or goal for collaboration or co-design – think about capturing different stakeholder perspectives for future record or changes; look for opportunities to design in adaption and change; consider other opportunities for spatial (or even organisational) redesign that may be required.

And finally...

Remember that a building is not a static artefact. It changes, adapts, grows, ... lives.

How an organisation brings its built environment to life through its operation, organisation and use is just as important if not more so than the elements themselves.

Like gender equity, bringing a building to life is a process, not a product.

Leadership perspectives on gender equality

Editorial team

We asked two focus groups of senior leaders in the University what they thought the key issues were about gender equality, how they felt things had changed and what they felt the priorities were for the future. Some were from academic departments, others professional services. Just over half were women and most of the group had worked at the University for many years. The discussions were frank and wide-ranging.

There was consensus that achieving gender equality required organisational change.

Equality is not about attending some training courses; it is a change programme for the workplace.

Another added:

You need to tackle gender inequality at different levels. There are significant structural barriers [as well as] day-to-day interactions. You need a systems level change.

Recognising the problem

One of the first people to speak said:

The first step is to recognise that you have a problem.

This was not always straightforward. Several senior women spoke of their experience of gradually adapting to a challenging environment until they stopped noticing it.

I was the first woman appointed to chair in my department. There were the inevitable 'you only got the job because you are a woman' comments. There is a drip, drip, drip of undermining comments you face as a female academic. It just becomes normal.

Someone else said:

It can be hard to challenge behaviours that are so embedded that you stop noticing. Small everyday injustices... but tackling them is not only good for women but good for everyone.

The importance of workplace culture was mentioned again and again.

There can be cultural problems; you can have a macho culture and that is everything down to the way people talk, use their bodies, their sense of humour. You want to strike a balance, you want people to feel they can be themselves at work, and for different disciplines to have their own cultures but you need to be able to challenge stereotypes where they do exist and create an environment where people can be honest, be open. You need to avoid outsider vs insider.

A female professor in a male-dominated field said:

Women coming into this field are more aware of the existing culture and you have to learn how to fit in. You often need to adapt. Men don't need to do this but persuading them of the value of being aware of the cultural norms and pressures can help people to see how hard it can be [if you're in the minority].

There was an acknowledgement that men can also feel like outsiders.

One benefit of Athena SWAN was also to look at subjects where men are in the minority. Gender imbalances are a two-way street.

People also referenced the challenges of overcoming wider societal expectations around gender roles.

Societal expectations can affect who takes 'parental' or family policies. Championing a wide range of role models is important.

Another mentioned that:

It is often male students who need more encouragement or who are more reluctant to ask for help.

The role universities play in society in educating the next generation for a diverse range of careers was another area to explore. Curriculum design is clearly of vital importance and it is helpful to be aware of the gender dimensions:

There are issues with gender in the curriculum. Who teaches what, how teaching is perceived by students, what is taught.

There are also challenges for student recruitment:

It is important to reflect on the gender balance of different sectors. How do you bring men into female-dominated workforces as well as increase the number of women in more male-dominated areas?

Another person said:

It is important that the initiatives we put in place as an organisation support positive action. We have to give equal access to opportunities at all times. We must avoid positive discrimination, though – that's both unfair and potentially harmful.

Recognising your own biases

In addition to noticing the wider culture or working environment, several people stressed how important it is to be aware of your own biases.

In your head you have someone in your own likeness, or an idea of a typical person in that field. I was asked to give suggestions of people who could be on an advisory board. They got back in touch to say all the suggestions I had provided were all men and could I suggest any women. And I'm a woman and that was me doing that!

It's not that there aren't good women out there; it's just that [in] your mindset... they just haven't bubbled to the top.

Another person talked about bias in recruitment.

We were recruiting for an academic post. One candidate was a very eloquent man and you could hear comments from other panel members like: 'I could see myself working with him', 'He reminds me of colleague x'. There was a female candidate who was more softly spoken. The panel's comments were things like: 'She has a very quiet voice; she won't be able to teach'. It was a long day of interviewing and by the end I felt too tired to reach a final decision. Coming back to it fresh the next morning was a chance to have a broader perspective. When I looked again at the CVs, reviewed the experience of the candidates and thought about the answers to the interview questions, it was obvious that the 'quiet' woman was better qualified for the role.

External drivers

Culture change is complicated, particularly in the context of a large, devolved and ancient university with many different communities and subcultures. Several people spoke of the value Athena SWAN has of providing an external push for change.

External drivers can galvanise action; Athena SWAN is a good example of this.

Another added:

You need a baseline to track progress. Athena SWAN is helpful with this.

External accreditation like Athena SWAN can provide some structure for a systems level approach to change and is implemented alongside other HR (Human Resources) policies which aim to achieve a workplace which is fair to all. While everyone acknowledged the importance of fair processes for recruitment, workload allocation, promotion, performance management and reward, just adopting appropriate processes is not always enough.

Recruitment

Recruitment is crucial. We need to recruit for the right mindset, attitudes and ability. But how do you encourage people to apply in the first place?

The University launched the Chancellor's Fellowship scheme in 2012 to recruit 100 people who had the potential to be future research leaders in their fields. Two-thirds of the appointments were men. But two thirds of the people who applied were also men. It is very hard to address gender imbalances when the starting point is a very imbalanced pool of potential applicants.

This isn't limited to academic roles.

[The University is] a large tech employer and we compete for staff with other tech companies in Edinburgh. We have the same problems that they do in retaining women. Our career paths are not clear, we have no graduate recruitment programme and few visible women in senior management roles. We are working hard to get our job adverts seen by a more diverse set of people and rethinking recruitment strategies.

Promotion and reward

The gender imbalance of the applicant pool also applies to promotions.

The percentage of women and men who are successful in promotion is the same. The number of men and the number of women who put themselves forward is dramatically different.

Even once women do reach the senior grades, there can be very different salary levels. While people appointed externally rather than promoted internally can have more opportunity to negotiate salaries, there are clear gender imbalances in pay.

As a head of school, the thing which most shocked me is massive disparity in salary levels. Men have often demanded larger salary packages. Your salary is influenced by what you ask for when *you come in, what your previous salary was. All of this results in a big gap.*

University of Edinburgh salary gender figures can be found in: http://www. docs.csg.ed.ac.uk/EqualityDiversity/ Equal_Pay_Report_2015.pdf.

Another person added:

Women tend to be more modest – they don't know what others are on and what is reasonable to ask for. If you have different salary expectations early in your career and new job offers are based on previous salaries, there is a cumulative effect.

People are willing to take action to redress this:

We have tried to be proactive with this as much as the structures allow, particularly awarding additional increments.

But there are limits to how much a salary can be adjusted once someone is in post. It could take many years to reach parity.

It is also important that there is a sense of fairness to all members of staff.

There is also a disparity for reward processes for support staff. It can be very challenging to get even a small contribution award for junior admin staff members. Staff can feel like they aren't valued [if they aren't an academic].

Workload allocation and flexible working

Day to day working patterns and expectations around workload can be hard to balance.

How you use and what you do with your workload models are a double-edged sword. They can help but they can also hinder.

There were also reflections about the level of work staff were asked to do.

[We] need to look at workloads for everyone. Are we asking colleagues to do things which are just not possible in a 9-5 working week?

As managers, people found it hard to tackle a long-hours culture:

It is hard to prevent it as those who want to work long hours will. But they will probably do more stuff and will probably be promoted more quickly so in effect you are rewarding that behaviour.

This can put more pressure on people to feel that they have to also work very long hours. Not everyone can or wants to do this. The perceived costs of career progression can increase and in some cases outweigh the benefits. This may put talented and capable people off developing their careers further.

In addition to long hours, flexible working had its challenges.

Athena SWAN can be a double-edged sword. In my department, it has been quite divisive between female support staff and female academics. Flexible working arrangements are there for academics but what about for professional services staff?

In other sectors, men have faced stigma in requesting flexible working.

Even when flexible working or part-time requests are granted, they can be difficult to manage in practice. The nature of the work can be hard to adjust to part-time and expectations of colleagues (real or perceived) can mean people feel under significant pressure or that they are never quite doing 'enough'.

The challenges of reconciling long hours and flexibility was touched on several times and it came back to the wider point of rethinking what careers should look like:

We need to particularly look at career structures across the board. As long as we think about 'pipelines' as a vision of career, it's not particularly helpful. We need a different mindset which is more relevant to flexible careers – scale up, scale down, what happens outside work, what happens in work.

A broader view of careers is something which could benefit everyone.

Performance management

It is never enjoyable to tackle performance-related issues. However, several managers described the dilemma they felt in this aspect of their role.

It is a pressurised position. Challenging poor performance can take you into dangerous territory if the person not performing is a woman or from a minority group. There is a risk that your actions will be viewed as discrimination – and it can put you off tackling a performance issue.

There was also an acknowledgement that the level of support from HR had improved over the years and there was more confidence in handling these issues appropriately.

Internal drivers: creating a culture based on trust and respect

While establishing workplace policies and action plans to enhance equality are not in themselves sufficient to change the culture, they play a vital role in highlighting the issue and examples of acceptable and appropriate behaviour. This can help people to feel more confident to take action individually.

You need an environment where people feel safe to challenge inappropriate behaviour. You need trust. People need to feel they can talk about it and be listened to.

Creating an inclusive culture takes effort and courage.

[Where] there is a disparity of gender and power, if it is not called out, it sets the culture where that imbalance is OK.

However, it isn't easy to continually challenge seemingly minor incidents particularly:

To call out behaviours with colleagues who don't think they are like that.

Another person spoke of the security a more senior role provided:

There is a risk when you do call out bad behaviour – there is a backlash. I wouldn't be able to call out bad behaviour until I got to this level of seniority. And now I am at this level I feel I have a responsibility to.

Several people shared the sense of responsibility they felt they had in a leadership role.

The biggest thing I've learned as head of school, you have to lead by example. If you want something to be adopted, you have to do it and pay attention to it. People look to what you do, not what you say.

Another senior woman added:

Once you get to a certain level, there is much more support. You feel you have responsibilities to support junior colleagues.

Reflecting on the 'drip, drip, drip' of negative comments, one person stressed the need to:

Reflect on the automatic things you do. Once people are openly talking, senior managers set the tone, culture, everyone speaks out. It is about being human.

Another woman said it is about:

Giving back; what made a difference to you can help counter some of the other stuff. You need male role models too.

The importance of diverse role models and a positive attitude was mentioned several times.

There is a general forward direction of travel. We shouldn't beat ourselves up about apparent lack of progress. There is now, in my area, a critical mass and variation of female role models. It is good for students to see there are many ways to be a successful female scientist.

We always talk about the negative side of imbalances, there should be more focus on positive experiences – it is harder to get that out. We need to avoid shooting ourselves in the foot; we need to talk about what is positive.

In some areas there was a sense, several years on from the first Athena SWAN initiatives and other policies, that there had been a shift.

Coffee-room conversations can be dangerous ground. Now, discriminatory talk is called out and challenged by colleagues. You wouldn't have seen this 10 years ago. It is important that everyone does this, not just one person who is then seen as a nag.

Changing Expectations and Habits

People also provided examples of how some polices had become default habits. One person particularly stressed:

Email and the timing of email. We have a new email etiquette in the school – what is and what isn't appropriate. No expectation of emails between 5pm and then 9am the next morning.

Another head of school said:

I have a strapline on my email – I don't expect an answer outside normal working hours.

Reflecting on experiences of recruitment, another person added:

I've been more aware of obstacles people may have faced in their career... It is hard not to make assumptions. The weakness we have in the school is getting people not to make assumptions, everyone involved in recruitment has to have training regarding unconscious bias and E&D [equality and diversity].

Looking ahead

The sheer increase in numbers of women is helping. Not at senior levels yet but there is more awareness; it is talked about more often. There is more training on things you can do as a manager.

While there was a sense from most people that there had been positive change, this did come with some caveats.

Universities shouldn't be complacent. There is an absolute need for reflective practice.

Looking to the future, the priorities for senior leaders were to avoid complacency, protect progress made so far, appreciate and celebrate successes and continue to drive for change.

The world is changing but it takes time. We need to be careful we don't revert back, we need to look at long term effects.

Another person said:

We appointed over 100 Chancellor's Fellows. There was no gender pay gap when they were appointed. It would be interesting to see in five years and beyond if a gender pay gap opens up. It goes back to data: what you can put in place and then measure.

They went on to stress that:

Ownership is crucial. People need to take action. And to do that they need resources – money and time.

Gender inequality is pervasive [in our society] – in my view it's not really changing. The least we can do is work within the institution. But new power structures are fragile: you need to keep your foot on the pedal.

Focus group participants

Chris Breward is Professor of Cultural History, Principal of Edinburgh College of Art and Vice-Principal Creative Industries and Performing Arts.

Sarah Cunningham-Burley is Professor of Medical and Family Sociology and Assistant Principal Research-led Learning. Sarah is also Dean of Molecular, Genetic and Population Health Sciences, Edinburgh Medical School.

Shelagh Green is Director of Careers and Employability and President of the national Association of Graduate Careers Advisory Services (AGCAS).

Melissa Highton is Director of Learning, Teaching and Web Services and Assistant Principal Online Learning.

Alan Murray is Professor of Neural Electronics, Assistant Principal Academic Support and Head of the BioEngineering Research Institute. Alan is a former Head of School of Engineering.

Colin R Pulham is Professor of High-Pressure Chemistry and Head of School of Chemistry

Kathryn A Whaler is Professor of Geophysics and Deputy Head of School of GeoSciences. Kathy is a former Head of Department for Geology and Geophysics and a former Head of Institute of Earth and Planetary Sciences.

Lesley Yellowlees is Professor of Inorganic Electrochemistry and Vice-Principal and Head of the College of Science and Engineering. Lesley is a former Head of the School of Chemistry.

Emerging themes and recommendations

Editorial team

> Actions often ripple far beyond their immediate
> objective, and remembering this is reason
> to live by principle and act in hope that
> what you do matters, even when results are
> unlikely to be immediate or obvious.
>
> (Solnit, 2017)

In the *Introduction* we asked you to imagine working
and studying and researching and learning in a culture
where "mutuality is the ethos shaping our interaction
[...] where we can all be who we are [...] living the truth
that we are all 'created equal'" (bell hooks, 2000, p. x).

As the recipes and articles throughout the book
demonstrate, there are places within the University of
Edinburgh which have encouraged and enabled systemic
cultural change with the aim of embedding gender
equality in practice. In Lumby's (2009) terms, this is
when the institution is working with diversity, not just
for (or towards) diversity; and when people are internally
motivated to challenge and change biases in themselves
as well as in others and in the system (Carnes et al., 2012).

Based on reflection about our authors' contributions,
and our experience and learning during the project,
we present recommendations which we hope will
help University leaders, staff and students shape
a principled and equitable future for all.

What have our authors told us?

We examined the recipes and papers through two
main lenses: purpose and meta-theme. We asked what

the authors' underlying purposes were in writing their recipes and articles. As referenced in the *Introduction*, we found content that was:

- **Practical**: documenting steps which worked for real change on an institutional level (14); on a personal level (8) and across a group of people (4).

- **Informative**: exploring a topic in depth (23); introducing a topic (4) and providing illuminating facts (5).

- **Illuminating**: describing authors' pivotal moments (4), and other content that reveals what it feels like to be the author – giving an insight into other lives (27).

We looked for recurring themes across the different types and focuses of content and found the following:

- Responsibility: of individuals, groups, departments and the University to identify, challenge and change inequalities and biases wherever and whenever they are encountered.

- Reflection: as each author considered what they are documenting, and how and what their own contribution might have been to both the problem and the response.

- Challenging bias and denial (own and others'): a natural follow-on from reflection. We noted feelings expressed and honoured; courage; and emotional labour (paid) and emotional work (unpaid).

- Language: the importance of language – what is said, how it is said, and what is actually meant, and what is heard. The power of the 'paper-cut comment' to undermine and diminish – whether meant or not – should never be underestimated.

- Well-being: this theme was implicit in the central thesis that if it is better for women then it is better for everyone,

but emerged unexpectedly strongly across the different contributions as a desirable state worth striving for.

- Humour: often the recipes are funny – wryly, and ironically – giving a strong sense of the authors' voices. The humour in some of the proposed responses and solutions to difficulties makes the message easier to put across.

- Personal skills: the list of personal skills grew as we looked at the recipes in particular. Listening, appreciation, empathy, curiosity and imagination were especially noteworthy.

- Personal principles: congruence, integrity, sincerity, and again courage figured in many of the recipes, especially where the authors had had to make some kind of stand about poor, but long-accepted, practice.

- Processes: overlapping with the practical purposes above, many of the recipes described how the process of reflecting, identifying, changing, and sustaining that change was in and of itself as important as the change that was made.

The writers document how they, along with their colleagues and students, are quietly and firmly dismantling the stereotypes and inequities that have for so long got in the way of, as our initial statement affirmed, "embracing differences to create a more vibrant and rigorous intellectual, supportive and learning context for all our community". In doing so, they give us all practical guidance, ideas and a route map towards gender equality.

A colleague once exclaimed in exasperation at yet another organisational Grand Plan: "Milestones! I'm sick of milestones. I want inch pebbles!" The EqualBITE project in itself is a significant milestone on the University of Edinburgh's journey towards greater equality; this article sums up the inch pebbles that the authors – all of them – recommend.

Change for an equitable future

> The first step is to recognise that you have a problem.

The above quotation and others at the start of each subsection are by senior leaders in the University of Edinburgh (see *Leadership perspectives on gender equality*).

The model of change that we proposed at the start of this book notes that changes are driven from the inside out, and from the outside in: individual changes drive team changes, which in turn make shifts at a departmental and school level. And at the same time, societal changes drive policy changes which impact the institution and require change from institutional to individual level. The introduction of Athena SWAN has driven much of this change, but would not have worked had there not been substantial societal change to make it more than just a 'nice-to-have' tick-box exercise.

There is a Scottish phrase "It's aye been" which means things have always been that way, always will be that way, that's just how things are, and don't start rocking the boat now. This can be the most difficult aspect of culture to shift, especially in an institution with ancient and honourable traditions, but where tradition for its own sake can reinforce the blocks to healthy and necessary change. The authors recognise and challenge this: *Leadership styles and approaches in GeoSciences* recognises different professional and leadership styles – not just 'alpha male' research star professor; *The power of language: moving beyond past harms and present hurts* looks at how language can either reinforce or shift barriers; and *Women, competition and beliefs* and *Stereotype threat* explore external and personal/internal obstructions to change.

Once gender inequalities are seen, then they cannot – and should not – be unseen.

Our recommendations for action

EqualBITE is pragmatic as well as visionary. We propose a set of practical recommendations emerging from the meta-themes and the recipe purposes; taken together these recommendations are what our authors have found can create sustainable culture change in practice.

1. Close the gap between policy and practice.
2. Take a pragmatic, evidence-based approach to implementing equity.
3. Involve everyone to attain equity.
4. Insist upon and model open and honest awareness, reflection and action.
5. Know, develop and celebrate yourself.
6. Remove bias (conscious and unconscious) in learning and teaching.
7. Continuously balancing gender is the outcome.
8. Create an environment that enables people to flourish .
9. Recognise and honour the greater context.
10. Be a beacon.

1. Close the gap between policy and practice

> If you want something to be adopted, you have to do it and pay attention to it. People look to what you do, not what you say.

People believe what is done, not what is said. How values are implemented in practice really matters. Most people will say that being equal or fair is a good thing – this is a high-level value and few would disagree with it. But is there congruence between what you say you value, and what you do?

Which workplace policies and behaviours do you say are valuable and which do you reward? Much of this book documents the authors' experiences of messy bits between policy and action; for example, the recipe *Flexible working: being realistic* looks at what can happen when flexible hours and workload expectations do not match. This is a problem highlighted not just in the recipe, but also in *Leadership perspectives on gender equality*, and in *Gender in higher education: the current landscape in the UK*. Without congruence there can be a double problem – not only will some issues not be addressed, they will be actively suppressed because people believe that there is a system in place to prevent them.

Universities need to live up to their stated values if they want to earn and keep their students' respect. The two contributions about anti-harassment campaigns – one from a student representative, and one from the University – illustrate the importance of this (see *A reflection on EUSA sexual harassment campaigns* and *A reflection on the University of Edinburgh's policy on sexual harassment*).

The meta-themes crucial to doing what we say we do, are: responsibility of individuals, groups, departments and the institution to maintain and practise values-driven behaviours day by day; language – being aware of whether what is said, and what is meant, and what is heard are congruent and trustworthy; and maintaining our individual personal principles of integrity, sincerity and courage to stand up for what is valued regardless of pressure.

Linking the operational to the aims of an organisation requires significant effort and ongoing maintenance. Importantly, it requires a continuous process of review, reflection, and adjustment, paying attention to process as well as outcomes, to be enacted at all stages of aims, strategy, policy and operational design; regularly, efficiently and effectively. The Athena SWAN process of award renewal is a useful starting point.

There are recipes and content clusters that demonstrate excellent practice, and others that show what happens, and how to respond, when there is a mismatch between espoused values and actual practice. Among the many recipes and articles are: *Flexible working – being realistic, Gender balancing your seminar speakers, Advertise all opportunities large and small,*

What have you done to my squash courts!, How to run more equal meetings, How to become a better scientific evaluator.

2. Take a pragmatic, evidence-based approach to implementing equity

You need a baseline to track progress. Athena SWAN is helpful with this.

Nurturing and growing gender equality through a pragmatic evidence-based approach requires as much rigour as any other piece of research. Collect good data and regularly assess what is unknown. Where are the gaps? What might we not be seeing because of our own unconscious bias? Any enquiry into gender equity has to start with values, not data. What does the organisation and culture value? How might this value be measured? If it is done the other way around, data will drive culture and this will introduce unintended biases and assumptions. Data should be a way of checking and informing; not a way of driving and directing organisations; this is, perhaps, one of the key benefits of Athena SWAN.

There is much good research already out there that can be used to inform policy and processes – not just the data the organisation collects but the body of knowledge in other fields. We have, for example, used evidence-based research to inform our thinking in developing *A model for change*, in particular research on gender bias as a remediable habit (Carnes et al., 2012), and the review of evidence from a behavioural economics perspective (Bohnet, 2016).

Many of the required data sets relating to gender equality are now publicly available. This transparency makes the task of monitoring the impact of change easier. However, there are still areas which lack transparency. For example, the Guardian newspaper's report on sexual harassment in UK universities between 2011/12 and March 2017, characterised the level of staff-student harassment as an "epidemic".

The article was based on data from freedom of information requests to universities within the UK. Rachel Krys, co-director of the End Violence Against Women Coalition, quoted in the Guardian article said:

> We know that institutions which take tackling sexual harassment and violence seriously, and have policies and systems in place to encourage reporting and train staff to deal with complaints as they arise, report higher numbers. It's the universities which aren't dealing with this openly which perversely appear to have fewer problems. (Batty, et al., 2017)

The report raises a potentially troubling issue but it is difficult to accurately gauge the nature and the extent of the problem without more robust data and careful analysis. While these are delicate issues, universities do employ researchers with the requisite expertise to sensitively gather and sift the evidence.

Meta-themes here are responsibility, reflection, personal principles, and processes. Responsibility for determining and maintaining a good process for ongoing checking of data-informed decisions; processes for reporting data analysis conditions and contingencies as clearly as the results themselves (the conditions under which some data are valid, or not, matter just as much as those data themselves); reflection on possible biases; and principle in clearly communicating how decisions made relate to the data. Relevant recipes and papers include: *Sport and exercise for all*, *Challenging bias*, *A model for change*, *Gender and the Research Excellence Framework*, *Defining excellence*.

3. Involve everyone to attain equity

> Championing a wide range of role models is important.

Everyone can and should benefit from a more equitable working environment and culture. To achieve this, everyone has to contribute to its success. Without exception.

Carnes et al. (2012) identify the moment of real change in addressing and amending habits of gender bias when motivation switches from external to internal drivers. They observed people moving from "I don't want to appear prejudiced to my colleagues" to a realisation that "I can do it" and "I will benefit from doing it" as the advantages of rectifying bias became apparent. This is known informally as the WIIFM factor – What's In It For Me – and reframes old attitudes toward equality work ('making up', 'redressing') as 'great improvements'.

This can be a huge challenge when the wider, changing social and political context is considered. Athena SWAN, as Judy Robertson has observed in her paper *The current landscape at the University of Edinburgh* can sometimes be perceived as a duty rather than a wholeheartedly embraced opportunity for change. Our authors suggest that we should pay attention to our processes – how we recruit, interview, and take on staff and students; what language we use to do this; how we build diversity within groups, rather than between them. Be aware of critical mass – for example rather than distributing a small number of female students between groups so they end up as the only woman, make sure that one-third of students in a group are female, even if that means some male-only groups. Recipes and papers direct us to lead by example, supporting each other when we challenge inequitable behaviour and language, and demonstrating its opposite. This means being aware of one's own privilege – it is not the same as entitlement. With privilege comes a significant responsibility; acknowledge it and check it as the language of privilege can be unhelpful, even damaging.

Many of the recipes document steps that have worked for real personal and group change, pivotal moments, and a sense of what it is like to step into someone else's shoes. The meta-themes of personal principles and personal skills talk of courage: to refuse to accept 'bear-pit' behaviour, and to challenge it when it rears its ugly head.

One senior woman leader said: "There is a risk when you do call out bad behaviour – there is a backlash. I wouldn't be able to call out bad behaviour until I got to this level of seniority. And now I am at this level I feel I have a responsibility to". Another senior woman, talking about 'the bear-pit' in an EqualBITE workshop, insisted on anonymity as she was not comfortable raising the issue outside of a safe space. Men in the University are also aware of what it takes to speak up against unacceptable behaviour (see *Allies in the classroom*).

The relevant meta-themes also identify the importance of collaboration, language, respect; and reaching a point where everyone benefits – it is not just individual success that matters.

Related recipes and papers include: *Recognise your privilege, The power of language: moving beyond past harms and present hurts, The current landscape at the University of Edinburgh, Say something, Damning with faint praise, Not just "a ladies' problem", Tackling difficult situations – supporting your staff and students, Educated Pass: engaging young males from low socio-economic status backgrounds with learning, Support for students who report sexual harassment or assault.*

4. Insist upon and model open and honest awareness, reflection and action

> There is an absolute need for reflective practice.

All change starts with open and honest recognition and awareness, as so many of the recipes in this book demonstrate. Many of the recipes share their author's experience of developing a culture of open reflection and awareness for all members of staff and students.

Senior women leaders in GeoSciences prefer to lead with democratic and pace-setting styles rather than in coercive or authoritarian ways (see *Leadership styles and approaches in GeoSciences*) and senior leaders, discussing honest reflection and action (see *Leadership perspectives on gender equality*) acknowledged that creating an inclusive culture takes effort and courage.

A recent example of honest awareness from a UK university about equality issues comes from Imperial College which, acting on concern about sexism within university sports, commissioned and published some of the results from an independent research project about gender and culture within its organisation (Taylor, 2016). The report, which is published on the university's website, documents negative views of staff and students including the perception held by some that misogyny is "ingrained" at the institution. In an article in the Independent newspaper, the researcher Dr Phipps noted that: "Imperial College has shown tremendous courage in not just ticking the boxes, but appointing a feminist team to do in-depth research on its institutional culture. We feel confident that positive changes will take place because of our study." The Provost of Imperial commented that "we are committed to ensuring gender equality and eradicating sexist behaviour wherever we can, at all levels. These findings remind us that we cannot stand still. We must do better." This demonstrates awareness and reflection on the problems within a culture, which can be the first step to cultural change.

Having the tools to do this proactively and positively is important. Academic debate and workplace dialogue are not necessarily congruent and some types of academic discourse are just not suitable in normal working situations, for example argument based on authority of methods, models or even people; and on the assumption that there is some correct answer or way of doing something. Similarly, in those subjects where more complex answers exist, the arguments drag on and the literature expands to fill entire libraries. In equitable workplaces, dialogue, negotiation, collaboration and what Charles Handy calls 'decent doubt' should be the norm. Like any other academic process, applying an appropriate methodology as well as specific methods is vital!

Recipes and papers abound to support this recommendation. Here are just some of them: *Unravelling rhetoric, Grumpy, Say something, Be vigilant with your vocabulary, Challenging bias, Pause, Leadership styles and approaches in GeoSciences, Leadership perspectives on gender equality.*

5. Know, develop and celebrate yourself

> There is a drip, drip, drip of undermining comments you face as a female academic. It just becomes normal.

Authors – students and staff at all stages of their studies and their careers – wrote about the difficulty of developing and maintaining a healthy level of confidence and self-esteem in the face of the "drip, drip, drip" of an historically androcentric (and predominantly white, middle-class) context. See, for example, undermining comments that aren't even meant as such (see *Damning with faint praise*) and whose speaker would be – and is – horrified when confronted about them; and the choice between being perceived as competent or likeable (see *Likeability and the double bind*). There are many recipes where the author (often anonymously) tells us how she (and sometimes he) has encountered these societal pressures and dealt with them.

One of the most compelling personal accounts is Theresia Mina's story about how she – determinedly, assertively and respectfully – convinced her family to let her study. In doing so, she made her excellent academic record and letters from mentors part of the argument about why her academic future was worth investment. Theresia knew her

own potential even when those closest to her did not yet recognise it. (See *How to convince your family to let you study.*)

The recipes recount personal successes, and the satisfaction of seeing how many small triumphs of courage, wit and humour can help a whole culture begin to shift. Other recipes look at the opportunities there are for professional development in parallel with the personal journey; often the two are closely interlinked – learning how to talk about your achievements without feeling either an imposter or becoming a 'humble-bragger' takes courage as well. Making a choice to step outside of a research career, or to plan a career consciously and carefully rather than just falling into the next thing that presents itself, takes skill and support.

The titles speak for themselves: *Dealing with imposter syndrome, Becoming visible in meetings, Raising your profile within your organisation, Career coaching for individuals, Stereotype threat, Talking about your achievements, Likeability and the double bind, Research isn't the only route, Career progression on a shoestring, Planning your career, Defining excellence, How to convince your family to let you study.*

6. Remove bias (conscious and unconscious) in learning and teaching

> There are issues with gender in the curriculum. Who teaches what, how teaching is perceived by students, what is taught.

The authors are very aware that teaching practice, as well as curriculum content, influences young minds. How we approach pedagogy, opportunities, ideas, support, pastoral care, tolerance, attitudes, are all reflected in our teaching practice – both explicitly and implicitly. There are recipes written by students who have dealt with challenging classroom situations, and also by members of the academic staff who have faced similarly difficult circumstances. Curriculum content is flagged up by contributors, students as well as staff, with the challenge to consider whether the topics discussed in classrooms include the intellectual contributions of women and give due weight to issues affecting women in society.

In addition to attending to bias in curricular content across disciplines, serious attention should be paid to the study of gender equality itself. Although there are academic staff whose research areas (English, French, German, Film, Russian, Hispanic Studies, Education and others) encompass gender and feminism, there is no department of Gender Studies at the University of Edinburgh. In 2014 an Edinburgh University Students' Association (EUSA) 'academic campaign' to create a Gender Studies department at the University convened a working group of academics with the vision of creating a Gender Studies course which would be available to all students.

There is now a Masters by Research degree in Gender and Culture, based in the School of Social and Political Science. There is ongoing work with EUSA to extend the subject and make it available to all students. As we observed earlier, how values are implemented in practice really matters; and in an academic institution value is demonstrated by the attention paid to it – a degree is the ultimate value for students. Raising the status of gender as a subject of study at the University is a positive step.

The ideal of the University as a place of learning and teaching relies on an appropriate culture of self- and peer-reflection and critique. Being aware of the necessity of creating and maintaining a culture of support is vital. Here are a few of the recipes that do this: *Creating a safe space for classroom discussions, Allies in the classroom, Grow and succeed with fellow students, Gender balancing the curriculum, Show your daughters the joys of science, How to convince your family to let you study.*

7. Continuously balancing gender is the outcome

> It can be hard to challenge behaviours that are so embedded that you stop noticing. Small every day injustices... but tackling it is not only good for women but good for everyone.

It is the process of enabling equity that matters. The process of making changes, changes the people involved (see *Finding my voice*). As editors we have each responded to the challenges of the project by rethinking our ideas and preconceptions and often by learning new behaviours.

We have continuously thought that we had reached a final point, an outcome, in our exploration, only to find that there is always more to do. Closing down the content-gathering was painful! There are always other groups of people who would benefit from more equitable chances in higher education.

All of the recipes, case studies and evidence in this book, share a common idea – change can happen and it starts with identifying something, acting on it and then monitoring the changes. The recipes that describe their process, naturally extend that last step to checking that the intended effect was achieved as well as any potential unintended effects (see 2. Take a pragmatic, evidence based approach above).

They also all recognise that these matters are inherently social, emergent and complex. There are rarely any single solutions to any of the issues around gender equity in academia. They require a process of 'making equitable' to also be collectively engaging, continuous and nuanced. Reframing gender equity as a process, not just a set of policies and procedures or single activities, ensures that the balance between collective and individual responsibility can be developed and maintained. That is, each person has a responsibility within the culture to contribute to the process of equity in gender. Similarly, the institution or organisation itself must actively support such processes, and in no way impede or discourage the people engaged in them.

Emily Yarrow's article *Gender and the Research Excellence Framework* (REF) reminds us of what can happen when new inclusive processes are forgotten in a drive to meet governmental pressures. The high stakes of the REF apparently led to bias in selection of academics for inclusion in the REF itself, and biased REF-related hiring and salary decisions will have a lasting impact on equality across the UK higher education sector.

It is possible that processes designed through Athena SWAN action groups were not sufficiently well embedded within universities to withstand the fiercely competitive game of optimising REF returns. However, it shouldn't be that departments tick the boxes to get their Athena SWAN report submitted and then move on to sorting out their REF profile; departments should habitually use bias-reduction strategies to maintain gender equality (see *A model for change*).

The meta-themes are all relevant here: responsibility, reflection, challenging bias, language, well-being, humour, personal skills and principles and – of course – processes. Recipes and papers here include: *The power of language, Raising your profile within your organisation, Gender and the Research Excellence Framework, Finding my voice*.

8. Create an environment that enables people to flourish

> You need an environment where people feel safe to challenge inappropriate behaviour. You need trust. People need to feel they can talk about it and be listened to.

'Environment' encompasses social and physical spaces, people, resources and processes: they are deeply interlinked. The gendered nature of buildings (see *Asking for equitable buildings*) explores how our built environment is an operational as well as a fixed entity that meets some human need. Bringing the affordances (things that hold the possibility of an action) into alignment with a positive organisational culture is as important as the claimed values and practices. The University has policies intended to support physiological issues, and authors' recipes examine what happens when the physical and financial assets to support policy are provided generously (for example the Roslin Insitute's childcare provision).

The contributors also tell us about how protracted policy implementation affects them. The move toward gender-neutral toilets, for example, is slow. The impact of this can be read plainly in the Unapologetically Me piece (see *Perspectives from students*) where a student has to decide each morning whether they look feminine enough to get into the women's toilets without getting chucked out, a point reinforced by a student's illustration of a toilet gender guard. Student parents are also arguing for environmental changes to accommodate their needs.

The physical environment can also have a strong emotional impact, for example, crucial interviews, meetings and examinations held in rooms where every portrait on the walls is male (see *You can't be what you can't see*) – something that male visitors to the room don't notice and aren't affected by, but which triggers stereotype threat and imposter syndrome (see *Dealing with imposter syndrome*) in women; and the impact, reported by female students, that a very masculine gym environment can have on them (see *Reflections on exercise and sport in the University*).

Perhaps unsurprisingly, the learning and teaching spaces we create reflect the complex socio-political spaces the academy inhabits. The way a room is laid out can enhance or inhibit learning, especially collaborative practice; more than one of the editorial team is in the habit of arriving early in any seminar room to rearrange the furniture.

Recipes include: *Rose surprise - when your period comes early, You can't be what you can't see: visible celebration of notable women, Reflections on exercise and sport in the University, Exercise and sport for all, What have you done to my squash courts!, Asking for equitable buildings, Creating a safe space for classroom discussions.*

9. Recognise and honour the greater context

> We need a different mindset which is more relevant to flexible careers – […] what happens outside work, what happens in work.

The academy exists in, and is part of, society. Like any other employment space, the relationships between work, lifestyle, family, and society generally can be difficult.

Many of the recipes in this book discuss the difficulties of balancing academia with family commitments. That balancing should even be required shows that we have a long way to go before achieving any dream of socially sustainable employment. But at the very least, universities must take on board "Close the gap between policy and practice" and ensure that opportunities such as flexible working or part-time working are supported fully. Very often the implementation of these falls far short of the strategic aims or values set out. Staff deal with these shortfalls on a daily basis with significantly raised stress levels and high workloads; surveys of the academic workforce document lower than average well-being across a range of indicators (see *Gender in higher education: the current landscape in the UK*).

Hierarchical perception of disciplines and careers can be pernicious (as a pure physics

student was heard to say: "Art students are top of the heap, then pure maths and pure physics, then it's downhill from there"). Traditional linear career paths are not necessarily 'better', and 'leaky pipeline' discussions risk narrowing the focus and ignoring alternative approaches. Non-linear and alternative career directions already exist in academia and in other employment domains. The University of Edinburgh is beginning to support and develop such options, and some of the recipes recognise and celebrate this. Success is being redefined. Recipes include: *Raising your profile within your organisation, Career coaching for individuals, Advertise all opportunities large and small, The kids are alright, Flexible working: being realistic, Deadlines and diapers: being an academic dad, Career progression on a shoestring, Proactive promotion.*

10. Be a beacon

We know that the influence the academy has on knowledge, culture, policy, society, economics, etc. is significant. The minds being shaped in and by the academy will go on to shape and create society in turn. Similarly, the direct influence of the academy in policy and legislation is also significant. At these levels it is even more important to ensure that the principle of "closing the gap between policy and practice" is embedded in the culture. If the external actions of a university do not match their stated values, this is noticed by staff and students.

Part of achieving an Athena SWAN Gold award at institutional level is to be a beacon for gender equality, and to take responsibility for helping other universities to improve. Being a beacon also means more than aspiring to have slightly higher proportions of women students than the UK average for a specific discipline, particularly if the national average is in single digits. We can propose and achieve higher targets for the proportion of women who are included in the more senior levels of academia, as illustrated in the recipe about gender balancing seminar speakers in which the initial target of 30% women presenters was comfortably surpassed.

At the 'domestic' level, universities can influence neighbours in the academic ecology, such as academic publishing processes and publishers; and neighbours in the ecology of work practice, including quality approaches and standards agencies; policy advice and legislation representation; knowledge transfer and business interrelations. And the universities' influence on arts and culture, employment and work/life issues is also considerable.

Universities can support socio-political influence in an open way, recognising that the value of the academy is in its contribution to the society from/ within which it exists. The methods by which this is achieved are also open to creativity – how the University represents and embodies divergent views is of significant value to wider society.

The more difficult consideration is the incongruence of inaction – where Universities choose to make no responses, which may seem to contradict their stated values. The tensions here are clear, and the incongruence between stated values and actual practice can be damaging; but beyond any simple conceptualisation of these as power negotiations there is yet another way of looking at this. Universities are significant places of novelty and change and they cannot help but contribute to that change – positively or otherwise. The academy can reach out and be proud of this, taking a lead and demonstrating leadership rather than simply driving inevitable change.

The academy is a place within which the future is imagined and then created. When this becomes an equitably shared imagining, the future, too, becomes an equitably shared one. Margaret Mead wrote:

Never doubt that a small group of thoughtful, committed citizens can change the world; indeed, it's the only thing that ever has.

(http://www.interculturalstudies. org/faq.html)

While, as an editorial team, we would not claim to change the world, as a small group of thoughtful and committed citizens, we and all our contributors do not doubt that the writing of, illustrating, reading, reflecting on, and acting upon this book is part of creating an equitable academic world.

That is a most inspiring outcome.

Glossary

The EqualBITE project has been a journey of discovery for all the editors. We have encountered terms that we had never come across before, some that we thought we knew, but turned out to be wrong about, and others that were familiar to some but not to all of us.

As we went through the process, we captured all of these – and more – and it is this that, as we increasingly used it as a resource for ourselves, evolved over the months into the Glossary.

The entries are generally not our own definitions – rather they reflect the wide and sometimes idiosyncratic reading we have done. Many of the terms have different meanings or shades of meaning, depending on where they come from and who is using them; in these cases we have added contrasting quotations or positions. Some of the terms have been edited out of an article or recipe, but have been retained as part of the overall landscape of gender equality. Others are included simply because they are particular favourites of one or other editor.

Quite a few of the terms are neologisms or colloquialisms, showing how dynamic the topic is, but also meaning that the definitions here may not be what they become in even a few months time! There will also, inevitably, be terms that we have missed – so we have left space for you to add your own at the end.

We hope that you will find the Glossary a useful, thought-provoking, and absorbing resource for your own exploration of the territory.

Ally: someone (in this context usually a man) who seeks out information about marginalised people's experience, and as a result of listening and understanding, actively intervenes when becoming aware of sexist or other inappropriate behaviour. They no longer bystand (see below). Allies start to actively tackle gender inequalities wherever they see them. An ally will speak out when they notice gender inequalities and sexist attitudes and behaviours.

Androcentrism: a general bias applied to the study, design or activity around physical differences between the sexes (e.g. medical research; crash test dummies in engineering product design; designed objects such as pianos built for male hand dimensions). Androcentrism has also been argued to be a fallacy of argumentation e.g. by Hundleby & Duran (2011). See also **Phallogocentrism**.

Benevolent sexism (and hostile sexism): also known as 'patronising prejudice' by Fiske et al. (2002). Their four-box 'Model of (Often Mixed) Stereotype Content' proposes patronising prejudice (the equivalent of benevolent sexism) and envious prejudice (the equivalent of hostile sexism). "Ambivalent sexism theory, as stated by Glick & Fiske (1996, 2001), proposes that two components of sexism,

hostility and benevolence, are strongly interrelated but can nevertheless be conceptually distinguished. Hostile sexism (HS) is an obviously antagonistic negative attitude toward women that casts them as seeking to gain control over men. ...Benevolent sexism (BS), on the other hand, is a more positive attitude towards women that portrays them as warm but suggests that they are less competent than men. BS idealises women and suggests that they ought to be placed on a pedestal but only if they conform to the traditional roles men assign them and do not challenge men's authority (Glick et al., 1997)" (Dumont et al., 2010, p. 545).

Bias (implicit or explicit): cognitive bias can occur in any cognitive process relating to selection (including reasoning, evaluating, or judging), often affected by a range of embedded social norms. Implicit bias informs decisions in ways that we are largely unaware of; explicit bias affects decisions in ways that we are aware of. In terms of gender and sex, we prefer people who conform to our own expectations, preferences and values, hence the huge range of gender-biased terms in this glossary. See, for example, self-stereotyping, gender congruence and gender performance.

Bias literacy: Understanding bias by describing and labelling manifestations of stereotype-based gender bias, for example:

a) Expectancy bias: how group stereotypes lead to expectations about individual members of that group (Carnes et al., 2015).

b) Stereotype-based bias: "There is growing evidence that stereotype-based bias functions like a habit as an ingrained pattern of thoughts and behaviours" (Carnes et al., 2015, p. 221) Bias is then 'a remediable habit'.

Brilliance: Storage et al., in analysing over 14 million reviews on RateMyProfessors.com, found that "fields in which the words 'brilliant' and 'genius' were used more frequently also had fewer female and African American PhDs. Looking at an earlier stage in students' educational careers, we found that brilliance-focused fields also had fewer women and African Americans obtaining bachelor's degrees. These relationships held even when accounting for field-specific averages on standardized mathematics assessments, as well as several competing hypotheses concerning group differences in representation. The fact that this naturalistic measure of a field's focus on brilliance predicted the magnitude of its gender and race gaps speaks to the tight link between ability beliefs and diversity" (Storage et al., 2016). This effect is also in evidence in employment, where phrases such as "exceptional candidate" and "brilliant individual" increase bias towards male applicants, whereas straightforward skills-based descriptors lead to reduced bias (Castilla & Benard, 2010).

Bystanding: Not speaking up or acting when we notice something is wrong, or someone says something sexist or biased/stereotyped etc. Bystanding carries its own penalties, with women bystanders in the workplace more likely to develop depressive symptoms (Emdad et al., 2013). "The solutions are obvious. Stop making excuses.[...] Vigorously resist the urge to dismiss the gender problem. Make the effort and make the effort and make the effort until you no longer need to, until we don't need to keep having this conversation. Change requires intent and effort. It really is that simple" (Gay, 2014, pp. 172-173).

Centrism: A form of argumentation (and sometimes structure of knowledge) that assumes some standard, ideal identity (centrist) which is then compared, usually unfavourably, to others. For example, Hundleby & Duran refer to centrism as a fallacy of argumentation: "Centrism is treating

members of a privileged group of people as standard or ideal; it takes the forms of racism, heterosexism, and ableism, as well as other types of discrimination (Plumwood, 1996). [...] In the context of argumentation, centrism functions in argumentation schemes as an appeal to the standard, assuming an idealized social norm." (Hundleby & Duran, 2011, pp. 1-2). See also **Androcentrism** and **Phallogocentrism**.

Chilly climate: microaggressions, 'paper-cut comments', the 'drip, drip, drip of negative remarks' all serve to "highlight [...] the way in which seemingly inconsequential practices can become cumulative, failing to recognise women's contribution, devaluing their contribution resulting in loss of confidence and marginalisation" (Savigny, 2014). See also: Hall & Sandler (1982) and for a discussion of the contested nature of this phrase see Prentice (2000).

Cultural sexism: Savigny talks of "the cultural practices, norms and values which through their expression frame women's experiences within the academy [..] This cultural shaping of experience [...] provides a context which does not render it impossible for women to be as visible as their male colleagues, or as well-remunerated or promoted, but it does make it more difficult" (Savigny, 2014).

Divide and conquer (sometimes disarticulation): the process of ensuring that marginalised groups cease to talk to each other, collaborate or support each other. See McRobbie (2009).

Diversity: "The word diversity is slippery, used with increasing frequency but indicating a range of different conceptualizations. It appears to be used to indicate the presence within a group/population of whatever size of those deemed 'other'. Who makes judgments of otherness and on what basis renders diversity a concept which is contested, reflective of power relations, and socially constructed (Zanoni & Janssens, 2004). [...]Broad definitions incorporate a wide range of criteria, including age, disability, religion, sexual orientation, values, ethnic culture, national origin, education, lifestyle, beliefs, physical appearance, social class and economic status (Norton & Fox, 1997).

Do good, be good principle: the idea that enacting a target behaviour leads to subsequent changes in attitude. In some contexts, also known colloquially as "fake it till you make it".

Emotional labour: "The management of feeling to create a publicly observable facial and bodily display; emotional labor is sold for a wage and therefore has exchange value. [...] [It] requires one to induce or suppress feeling in order to sustain the outward countenance that produces the proper state of mind in others [...]" (Hochschild, 1983, p. 7). Hochschild noted that this was a particular issue for women, estimating that "roughly one-half have jobs that call for emotional labor" (Hochschild, 1983, p. 11).

Emotional work: Hochschild (1983) distinguishes between emotional labour which has exchange value and is therefore used in paid work, and emotional work which people use in private life and situations, regulating their emotions in interactions with family, friends, neighbours etc. As with emotional labour, emotional work involves both the suppression of emotion, and its evocation.

Equality and Equity: two strategies we can use in an effort to produce fairness. Equity is giving everyone what they need to be successful. Equality is treating everyone the same. Equality aims to promote fairness, but it can only work if everyone starts from the same place and needs the same help (see https://everydayfeminism. com/2014/09/equality- is-not-enough/).

Evaluative bias: how the contributions of one group (in this case women) are heard and evaluated by the dominant group (in this case men). Cecilia Ford (2008) writes: "In a contribution to a 1999 panel

discussion on language and gender in the workplace, linguist Sally McConnell-Ginet emphasised the importance of attending to evaluative bias. She insisted that: 'The major factor is not differences in women's and men's competence – including their communication competency. The big problem is people's attitudes towards women and men, their sharply differentiated expectations that lead, as psychologist Virginia Valain puts it, to persistent under- evaluation of women's work and over-evaluation of men's (McConnell-Ginet, 2000, p. 127)'" (quoted by Ford, 2008, pp. 1,2).

Feminism: there are many different definitions of feminism, and we offer some here for reference:

"Feminism is a movement to end sexism, sexist exploitation, and oppression" (hooks, 1984). "I love [this definition] because it so clearly states that the movement is not about being anti-male. It makes clear that the problem is sexism. And that clarity helps us to remember that all of us, female and male, have been socialized from birth on to accept sexist thought and action. As a consequence, females can be just as sexist as men" (hooks, 2000, p. viii).

"The core of feminism is a belief that all people deserve to be treated fairly

and justly regardless of gender identity" Marc Peters (MenEngage Alliance, http://menengage.org/).

Rebecca West said "I myself have never been able to find out precisely what feminism is: I only know that people call me a feminist whenever I express sentiments that differentiate me from a doormat". (Mind you, the original quotation went: "...differentiate me from a doormat or a prostitute".) West was referenced in Virginia Woolf A Room of One's Own: "..my astonishment [...] when Z, most humane, most modest of men, taking up some book by Rebecca West and reading a passage in it, exclaimed, "The arrant feminist! She says that men are snobs!" The exclamation, to me so surprising - for why was Miss West an arrant feminist for making a possibly true if uncomplimentary statement about the other sex? - was not merely the cry of wounded vanity; it was a protest against some infringement of his power to believe in himself" (Woolf, 1929, p. 53).

1. Feminism is a critical project:

"Feminists glimpse the world through a different lens and what they see usually requires a response. Feminism, in other words, follows a critical project with action to bring about social change." (Scholz, 2010, p. 2)

"If the future is anything like the past, we can be assured that feminism will continue to make a significant contribution to efforts to create positive social change and bring about social justice" (Scholz, 2010, p. 190).

2. Laughter is present in every form of feminism.

"Laughter is used as social critique of oppressive policies and actions, as political resistance to unjust treatment, and as social support for one another in the face of sometimes brutal dismissal. Laughter is a powerful tool against the serious and sometimes tragic force of sexism. As feminists, we also have to laugh at ourselves sometimes" (Scholz, 2010, p. 11).

William Thompson (1825). Appeal of One half of the Human Race, Women, against the Pretensions of the Other Half, Men, to Restrain them in Political and thence in Civil and Domestic Slavery. "As your bondage has chained down man to the ignorance and vices of despotism, so will your liberation reward him with knowledge, with freedom and happiness" (quoted by Walters, 2005, p. 45).

Gender: definition by Judith Butler, based on de Beauvoir (1949) and Merleau-Ponty (1962): "[G]ender is in no way a stable identity or locus of agency from which various acts proceed; rather,

it is an identity tenuously constituted in time – an identity instituted through a stylized repetition of acts. Further, gender is instituted through the stylization of the body and, hence, must be understood as the mundane way in which bodily gestures, movements, and enactments of various kinds constitute the illusion of an abiding gendered self" (Butler, 1988, p. 519).

(Prescriptive) Gender norms: cultural assumptions about how men and women should and should not behave and the social penalties of violating these norms (Carnes et al., 2015).

Gender congruence: similar to Gender norms, this is the association of gender with particular roles, traits, contexts, etc through social stereotyping, fixing, exposure, etc. For example, in the West, women tend to be 'congruent' with being primary school teachers; men tend to be congruent with leadership roles. (Conversely, male primary school teachers are perceived as incongruent in such roles.)

Gender performance: conforming to gender norms or congruence, particularly in terms of "... the idea that there is a right way to be a woman, a right way to be the most essential woman – is ongoing and pervasive" (Gay, 2014, p. 303). Also important in recognising the consequences of such

performance: "Performing one's gender wrong initiates a set of punishments both obvious and indirect, and performing it well provides the reassurance that there is an essentialism of gender identity after all" (Butler, 1988, p. 528).

Gender, sex and sexuality (EqualBITE definitions and disambiguation): recognising that gender and sex are often conflated or mixed up, the following definitions are provided as a reference point and to set out the definitions used by the EqualBITE editorial team:

	Sex	Gender
Definition (for EqualBITE)	Biological definition primarily based on reproductive characteristics at birth (chromosomes, differential gametes, reproductive organs).	Socially constructed, based on socio-cultural definitions and expectations of roles based on sex.
OED	Either of the two main categories (male and female) into which humans and many other living things are divided on the basis of their reproductive function.	The classes (typically masculine, feminine, neuter, common) of nouns and pronouns similarly applied to adjectives (and in some languages) verbs.
Binary (normative)	Male/Female	Man/Woman Girl/Boy Feminine/Masculine
Spectrum (relativist)	**Asexual** – scientific definition referring to reproduction which does not involve the use of gametes. **Intersex** – neologism used to describe (usually) an experienced conflict between sex and gender, such as being born with specific physiology that does not accord with an associated gender. **Transsexual** – someone transitioning from one sex to another.	**Cisgender** – self-identified gender that corresponds to the 'traditional' (normative) sex attribute. **Transgender** – like intersex, a gender identification that does not correspond to the physiology of the sex of the individual. May include also bigender, pangender, genderfluid, or agender. **Gender neutral** – identifies with neither 'traditional' genders or is specifically non-specific with respect to gender identity.
Other terms	**Androgynous** - can refer to sex, although this is a more historical usage, and in terms of physical characteristics associated with gender.	**Androgynous** – of both or neither gender in terms of appearance, attitudes, behaviours and other representations of gender. Indeterminate of sex and/or gender.

Gender pronouns: the use of gendered pronouns (she, he) to maintain stereotypes and cultural norms is an area of growing importance as the trans and non-binary LGBTQ+ community is more widely recognised and their status beyond a simple binary gender framework is appreciated. Alternative pronouns such as 'they' and 'them', or 'ze' or 'hir' (pronounced here), and their use, can be found at https://minus18. org.au/pronouns-app/.

Group (in and out): Socially constructed identities that permit individual associations with group characteristics - both positively and negatively.

Homo-negativism: **"is a fear** among heterosexuals that they may be perceived as homosexual. Women's sport (especially male-dominated sport such as football and rugby) is still regarded by some as fundamentally unfeminine. Lesbians are also regarded by some as fundamentally unfeminine" (Lindohf, 2005, p. 32).

Ivory basement: an informal term to refer to the range of gender biases, misogyny and sexism that exists and persists across all elements of higher education and which ensure that women do not have parity with men (i.e. keeps them in the ivory basement).

Identity contingency: "[I] dentity contingencies – the things you have to deal

with in a situation because you have a given social identity, because you are old, young, gay, a white male, a woman, a black, Latino, politically conservative or liberal, diagnosed with bipolar disorder, a cancer patient and so on. Generally speaking, contingencies are circumstances you have to deal with in order to get what you want or need in a situation" (Steele, 2010, p. 3).

Institutional misogyny: the use (implicit or explicit) of historical and societal contexts of the institute which safeguard androcentricity. Fiona Mackay (2014) argues that "institutions are not gender neutral but are actively constructing and reproducing gender relations and ideologies (see, for example: Acker, 1992; Duerst-Lahti, 2002; Duerst-Lahti & Kelly, 1995; Stivers, 2002)" (Mackay, 2014, p. 553), and moreover, that "[t]acit knowledge about what is valued, credible, authoritative, and strategic remains coded masculine and is widely shared among horizontal and vertical networks of power holders (Duerst-Lahti, 2002; 2008)" (Mackay, 2014, p. 556). In a societal context, including academia, Gay talks of "institutional sexism that consistently places women at a disadvantage" (Gay, 2014, p. 317) and the deeply embedded "trickle-down misogyny which starts with the legislature [and] reaches everywhere" (Gay, 2014, p. 171).

Intersubjectivity: "As Reinharz observes, the writing of women's biographical, oral history, is 'a circular process: the woman doing the study learns about herself as well as about the woman she is studying' (Reinharz, 1992, p. 127)" (in Savigny, 2014).

Intersectionality: "A foundational theory developed in the 60s and 70s by sociologists and multiracial feminists, maintaining that gender alone could not be representative of a woman's experience in the world [...] Intersectionality explores how biological, social and cultural identity factors like class, race, sexuality, gender, disability etc all intersect to mutually co-constitute an individual's experience, and how this overlaps with oppression, domination and discrimination" (Elisabeth Owuor, unpublished presentation, 2016). This was perhaps most famously articulated by Roxanne Gay: "On my more difficult days, I'm not sure what's more of a pain in my ass – being black or being a woman. I'm happy to be both of these things, but the world keeps intervening" (Gay, 2014, pp. 16-17).

The 'knower': [as in the production of knowledge] the significance of the sex of 'the knower': "Feminists start from a realisation that epistemologies, in their trickle down effects in the everyday world, play a part in sustaining patriarchal and other hierarchical social structures, both in the academy and throughout Western societies" (Code, 2000, p. 176).

Mansplaining: The phenomenon first described – but not named – by Rebecca Solnit, in her 2008 essay Men Explain Things To Me as: "Men explain things to me, and other women, whether or not they know what they are talking about". In an introduction to a reprint of the essay Solnit says: "Young women subsequently added the word 'mansplaining' to the lexicon. Though I hasten to add that the essay makes it clear mansplaining is not a universal flaw of the gender, just the intersection between overconfidence and cluelessness where some portion of that gender gets stuck. [...] Guys like this pick on other men's books too, [...] but the out-and-out confrontational confidence of the totally ignorant is, in my experience, gendered" (Solnit, 2012).

Moral licensing: when people respond to having done something good by doing more of something bad. The opposite is "do good, be good".

Normalisation: with respect to social/group behaviours, making some behaviours normal and acceptable to the majority of that society, even if these behaviours negatively or unequally affect that group or elements within that group.

Occupancy role congruity: the subtle advantage accrued to men being evaluated for roles that require traits more strongly linked to male stereotypes, such as scientist and leader (Carnes et al., 2015). (See Brilliance above.)

Paradox of visibility: the effect where women are perceived to be less employable, despite their over-representation, and higher achievements at undergraduate and graduate level Savigny (2014). See particularly van den Brink & Stobbe (2009).

Phallogocentrism: term used by Jaques Derrida in critical theory and deconstruction to refer to the privilege of men (originally the masculine) in knowledge production (androcentrism) and the gender bias in traditional structures of knowledge (Derrida, 2004).

Privilege: "Privilege is a right or immunity granted as a peculiar benefit, advantage or favour. There is racial privilege, gender (and identity) privilege, heterosexual privilege, economic privilege, able-bodied privilege, educational privilege, religious privilege, and the list goes on and on" (Gay, 2014, p. 16). In terms of gender privilege, this is considered to be sustained through "gender relations and rules and norms of masculinity and femininity [which] provide important mechanisms –

although often submerged and barely visible – by which wider particular arrangements and power asymmetries are naturalized and institutionalized or resisted and discarded" (Mackay, 2014, p. 553). David Foster Wallace likens the difficulty of becoming aware of privilege to telling a fish about water: "the most obvious, ubiquitous, important realities are often the ones that are the hardest to see and talk about" (Kenyon Commencement Address, Purdue University: May 21, 2005).

Redefining credentials: how the same credential can be valued differently depending on who has it (Carnes et al., 2015).

Role incongruity: "The damaging effects of stereotypes for women as leaders do not stem from beliefs about women that are mainly negative. On the contrary, consistent with the women-are-wonderful effect (Eagly & Mladinic, 1994; Langofrd & MacKinnon, 2000), women are regarded as the nicer, kinder sex and thus have a cultural stereotype that is in general more positive than that of men. [...] it is not the evaluative content of the stereotype of women but its mismatch with many desirable work roles that underlies biased evaluations in many employment settings (e.g. Hogue & Lord 2007; Lyness & Heilman 2006)" (Koenig et al., 2011, p. 617).

Self-affirmation theory:
"Self-affirmation theory begins with the premise that people are motivated to maintain the integrity of the self. Integrity can be defined as the sense that, on the whole, one is a good and appropriate person. [...] Threats to self-integrity may thus take many forms, but they will always involve real and perceived failures to meet culturally or socially significant standards (Leary & Baumeister, 2000)" (Sherman & Cohen, 2006, p. 8).

"There are four basic tenets that make up the self-affirmation framework:

1. People are motivated to protect the perceived integrity and worth of the self.

2. Motivations to protect self-integrity can result in defensive responses.

3. The self-system is flexible.

4. People can be affirmed by engaging in activities that remind them of 'who they are' (and doing so reduces the implications for self-integrity of threatening events)". (Sherman & Cohen, 2006, pp. 10-11).

Stereotype reactance: being aware of bias does in some cases overcome the need to conform to stereotype and increase performance in the domain in which one is negatively stereotyped.

Stereotype priming: ways in which even subtle reminders of male or female gender stereotypes bias one's subsequent judgement of an individual man or woman (Carnes et al., 2015).

Self-stereotyping: occurs when people apply their own implicit biases to themselves without necessarily being aware of it (see also Stereotype threat below).

Stereotype threat:
"Stereotype threat is a well-documented phenomenon by which individuals, fearful of confirming a negative stereotype about their group, display decreased performance on a task relevant to the negative stereotype (Steele & Aronson, 1995). For example, Steele and Aronson (1995) found that Black students performed worse on a test supposedly "diagnostic" of their intellectual ability than on a "non-diagnostic" test, even though the same test was used in both conditions". Similar underperformance can be seen in girls and women in maths tests (with a few notable exceptions, themselves racial stereotypes), or women in leadership (Carnes et al., 2015).

Stereotype counteracting (or reactance): ways of counteracting one's own stereotypes include (Carnes et al., 2015):

- **Stereotype replacement:** If, for example, girls are being portrayed as bad at math, identify this as a gender stereotype and consciously replace it with accurate information.

- **Positive counterstereotype imaging:** e.g. before evaluating job applicants for a position traditionally held by men, imagine in detail an effective woman leader or scientist.

- **Perspective taking:** imagine in detail what it is like to be a person in a stereotyped group.

- **Individuation:** gather specific information about a student, patient, or applicant to prevent group stereotypes from leading to potentially inaccurate assumptions.

- **Contact with counterstereotypic examplars:** e.g. meeting with senior women faculty to discuss their ideas and vision.

Counterproductive strategies: Strategies that do not work, and can even exacerbate the problem, include:

- **Stereotype suppression:** attempting to be 'gender blind' and 'Objective judgement' belief: a strong belief in one's ability to make objective judgments. "Both these have been shown to enhance the influence of stereotype-based bias on judgment" (Carnes et al., 2015).

- There is even a **bias against bias** (Moss-Racusin et al., 2015), where there is a denial that any bias exists, leading to an exacerbation of the bias.

The tone argument: dismissing a position/idea/argument simply because it has particular emotional content/position – in particular that a more positive emotional position would be preferable (regardless of truth or rational underpinning). This, along with certain other logical fallacies, tends to have a use-frequency affected by gender and sex. The choice of words matters, for example: 'coldly ambitious' instead of 'assertive' (Okimoto & Brescoll, 2010). (See also *Damning with faint praise*; and *Be vigilant with your vocabulary*.)

Trigger warnings: Originally used in treating war veterans with post-traumatic stress disorder, where something might trigger a memory and violent reaction. Now seen, ostensibly, as a way of protecting people from content (Internet, debate, classes, etc) that they may find distressing because "they trigger bad memories or reminders of traumatic or sensitive experiences" (Gay, 2014, p. 149). There is an ongoing debate about whether trigger warnings actually do protect people, and should protect people, rather than the position that "there is value in learning, where possible, how to deal with and respond to the triggers that cut you open [...] that remind you of painful history. It is untenable to go through life as an exposed wound. No matter how well intended, trigger warnings will not staunch the bleeding; trigger warnings will not harden into scabs over your wounds" (Gay, 2014, pp. 151-152).

The two-body problem: an informal term sometimes used to describe an academic couple or family during recruitment, where finding positions for both partners will affect the decision to take one or other position (and in some cases may affect the employing institution). Some institutions have proactive policies to address this; others are less aware of it as an issue and the associated tensions it can cause between partners.

Wise psychological interventions: Actions that address "specific underlying psychological processes that contribute to social problems... a wise intervention depends on a precise understanding of people's psychological reality – what it is like to be them and how they construe themselves and their social world" (Walton, 2014).

Editor
biographies
and
contributors

Judy Robertson is Professor of Digital Learning in the Moray House School of Education at the University of Edinburgh. Having spent twenty years learning and then teaching in computer science departments, she knows what it is like to be the only woman in the room a wearyingly large proportion of the time. Judy has experimented with various permutations of flexible working arrangements to fit around family life, and is grateful to work in the university sector where this is possible. She is married (to a man) and spends considerable time teaching her son not to blindly collude with the patriarchy by dropping his socks on the floor.

Alison Williams describes herself as a late-onset academic, awarded her PhD (on the impact of physical space on creativity) at 66. After a portfolio entrepreneurial career spanning sculpture and art teaching, co-founding a small company manufacturing specialist glass for large contracts, and consulting in creativity for multi-nationals, she has found in academia a challenging and stimulating community. Having completely failed to notice the 70s wave of feminism (apart from the slogan 'A woman needs a man like a fish needs a bicycle') Alison has embraced this project wholeheartedly, making up for lost time, and learning about herself and her place in the world, sometimes to the embarrassment of her partner and her grown-up children. Learning and growing never cease.

Derek Jones is a Senior Lecturer in Design with The Open University and part of the OU Design Group. He is currently chairing the course update to U101: Design Thinking, the award-winning Level 1 entry course for the university's Design and Innovation degree. His main research interests are: the pedagogy of design and creativity, embodied cognition in physical and virtual environments, and theories of design knowledge. Derek is a qualified architect with 15 years of experience in the construction design and procurement industries and is the Communications Officer for the Design Research Society.

Lara Isbel is the Head of Operations and Projects in the Institute for Academic Development at the University of Edinburgh. Part of her role is to provide coaching to staff and students within the University. Her interest in gender equality was partly sparked by a series of recurring themes in coaching conversations and the real, everyday challenges people face as they develop their careers. From her perspective, a more gender-equal workplace is about creating an organisational culture where everyone can thrive. Outside of work, Lara loves pretty much anything with a good story, particularly books, plays, films and ballet. She is married to an Australian and is usually saving for trips back to Australia to see family and experience the novelty of warm and sunny weather.

Daphne Loads is an academic developer at the University of Edinburgh, where she helps academics to survive, thrive, grow and develop in their teaching. Daphne studied English Literature, Life and Thought at Cambridge University, and has professional qualifications in social work, counselling, horticulture and education. She was awarded her EdD in higher education in 2012 by The Open University. She researches and publishes on academic identities and arts-enriched professional development. Daphne believes that gender equality in higher education is possible, but that we haven't achieved it yet. When she's not working, she loves gardening and travelling with her partner.

Contributors

Jim Aitken

Kathy Allnutt

Amy

Stuart Anderson

Arianna Andreangeli

Ros Attenborough

Graham Baker

Bella

Chris Belous

Noémi Berlin

Hope Bretscher

Amy Burge

Karen Chapman

Han Deacon

Gavin Douglas

Katriona Edlmann

Eli

Meriem El Karoui

Ester

Simon Fokt

Silje Graffer

Andy Hancock

Rosie Hawtin

Jonathan Hearn

Amalie Hjelm

Melissa Highton

Jane Hilston

Lara Isbel

Lindsay Jack

Derek Jones

Julia

Danai Korre

Daphne Loads

Lola

Barry Lovern

Gale MacLeod

Vicky MacRae

Alice McCall

Christine Meyer

Theresia Mina

Sarah Moffat

Brona Murphy

Zach Murphy

Jane Norman

Cael O'Sullivan

Martyn Pickersgill

Madeline Pinkerton

John Ravenscroft

Judy Robertson

Nathalie Rochefort

Rumana

Helen Sang

Pablo Schyfter

Sara Shinton

Neil Speirs

Jo Spiller

Stephanie

Jon Turner

Marissa Warner-Wu

Harry Whitelock

Alison Williams

Emily Yarrow

ECA students' digital portfolios:

Kathy Allnutt
http://cargocollective.com/kathyallnutt

Alice Griffin
http://alicemgriffin.com

Alice McCall
https://www.facebook.com/lcmcclldrws/

Madeline Pinkerton
http://madelinepinkerton.wixsite.com/madeline

References

AAUW (2016) At work, dads get a bonus, but moms get a penalty. What gives? http://www.aauw.org/2016/05/06/dads-get-a-bonus-but-moms-get-a-penalty/

Acker, J. (1992) From sex roles to gendered institutions *Contemporary Sociology*, 21(5), pp. 565-569

Adair, J. (2004) *The John Adair Handbook of Management and Leadership*. Thorogood.

Adichie, C.N. (2017) *Dear Ijeawele, or a feminist manifesto in fifteen suggestions*. London: 4th Estate.

Ahmed, S. (2017) *Living a Feminist Life*. Durham, NC: Duke University Press.

Aiston, S.J. & Jung, J. (2015) Women academics and research productivity: an international comparison. *Gender and Education*, 27(3), pp.205-220. doi:10.1080/09540253.2015.1024617

Aldrich, A.M., Connolly, S., Brien, M.O. & Speight, S. (2016) *Parental Working in Europe: working hours*. http://www.modernfatherhood.org/wp-content/uploads/2016/03/Parental-Working-in-Europe-Working-Hours-final_formatv3.pdf

Allen, G., Rhind, D. & Koshy, V. (2015) Enablers and barriers for male students transferring life skills from the sports hall into the classroom. *Qualitative Research in Sport, Exercise and Health*, 7(1), pp. 53-67.

Amabile, T.M. & Kramer, S. (2012) The progress principle: optimizing inner work life to create value. *Rotman Magazine*, Winter 2012. http://forimpact.org/downloads/blog_progressprinciple_011312.pdf

ARB (2015) *Architects Registration Board Annual Report 2015*. http://2015.arb.org.uk/facts-and-figures/registration/

Architects' Journal (2017) Women in Architecture survey reveals widening gender pay gap. https://www.architectsjournal.co.uk/news/women-in-architecture-survey-reveals-widening-gender-pay-gap/10017147.article

Ariely, D. (2012) *The (Honest) Truth About Dishonesty*. New York: HarperCollins.

Arnold, C. (2015) Countering gender bias at conferences. doi:10.1126/science.caredit.a1500189

Arshad, R., Wrigley, T. & Pratt, L. (eds.) (2012) *Social Justice Re-examined: dilemmas and solutions for the classroom teacher*. Stoke-on-Trent: Trentham Books.

Ayalon, H. (2003) Women and men go to university: mathematical background and gender differences in choice of field in higher education. *Sex Roles*, 48(5-6), pp. 277-290.

Baker, P. (2008) 'Eligible' bachelors and 'frustrated' spinsters: corpus linguistics, gender and language. In: Harrington, K., Litosseliti, L., Sauntson, H. & Sunderland, J. (eds.) *Gender and Language Research Methodologies*, pp. 73-84. London: Palgrave Macmillan.

Baker, P. (2014) *Using corpora to analyze gender*. London: Bloomsbury Academic.

Barnard, S., Hassan, T., Bagilhole, B. & Dainty, A. (2012) 'They're not girly girls': an exploration of quantitative and qualitative data on engineering and gender in higher education. *European Journal of Engineering Education*, 37(2), pp. 193-204.

Bateson, G. (1972) *Steps to an Ecology of Mind: a revolutionary approach to man's understanding of himself*. New York: Ballantine Books.

Bateson, G., Jackson, D., Haley, J. & Weakland, J. (1956) Towards a theory of schizophrenia. *Behavioural Science*, 1, pp. 251-254.

Batty, D., Weale, S. & Bannock, C. (2017) Sexual harassment 'at epidemic levels' in UK universities. *The Guardian*, 5 March 2017. https://www.theguardian.com/education/2017/mar/05/students-staff-uk-universities-sexual-harassment-epidemic

Bawden, A. (2014) Academia for women: short maternity leave, few part-time roles and lower pay. *The Guardian*,18 November 2014. https://www.theguardian.com/education/2014/nov/18/academia-for-women-short-maternity-leave

Beaman, L.A., Chattopadhyay, R., Duflo, E., Pande, R. & Topalova, P. (2008) Powerful Women: does exposure reduce bias? *NBER Working Paper Series*. doi:10.1017/CBO9781107415324.004.

Beckmann, D. & Menkhoff, L. (2008) Will women be women? Analyzing the gender difference among financial experts. *Kyklos*, 61, pp. 364-384.

Bedi, G., Van Dam, N.T. & Munafo, M. (2012) Gender inequality in awarded research grants. *The Lancet*, 380(9840), p. 474. doi:10.1016/S0140-6736(12)61292-6.

Beebee, H. & Saul, J. (2011) Women in philosophy in the UK - a report by the British Philosophical Association and the Society for Women in Philosophy UK. http://www.bpa.ac.uk/uploads/2011/02/BPA_Report_Women_In_Philosophy.pdf

Bennis, W. & Nanus, B. (1997) *Leaders: strategies for taking charge*. 2nd ed. New York: Harper Business.

Bensimon, E. & Neumann, A. (1993) *Redesigning Collegiate Leadership: teams and teamwork in higher education*. Baltimore, MD: Johns Hopkins University Press.

Bensimon, E.M., Neumann, A. & Birnbaum, R. (2000) Higher education and leadership theory. In: Brown, M.C. II, *Organization and Governance in Higher Education*, pp.241-231. 5th ed. Boston: Pearson Custom Publishing.

Bensimon, E.M., Neumann, A. & Birnbaum, R. (1989) Making sense of administrative leadership: the "L" word in higher education. *ASHE-ERIC Higher Education Report*. Washington DC: School of Education, George Washington University.

Berlin, N. & Dargnies, M.P. (2012) *Gender differences in reaction to feedback and willingness to compete*. CES Working Paper 2012.75. See also: *Journal of Economic Behavior and Organization*, (2016), 130, pp. 320-336. doi:10.1016/j.jebo.2016.08.002

Bettinger, E.P. & Long, B.T. (2005) Do faculty serve as role models? The impact of instructor gender on female students. *The American Economic Review*, 95(2), pp. 152-157.

Beyer, S. (1990) Gender differences in the accuracy of self-evaluations of performance. *Journal of Personality and Social Psychology*, LIX (1990), pp. 960-970.

Beyer, S. & Bowden, E.M. (1997) Gender differences in self-perceptions: convergent evidence from three measures of accuracy and bias. *Personality and Social Psychology Bulletin*, 23(2), pp. 157-172.

Bianchi, S.M. & Milkie, M.A. (2010) Work and family research in the first decade of the 21st century. *Journal of Marriage and Family*, 72(3), pp.705-725.

Bleach, K. (1998) *Raising Boys' Achievement in Schools*. Stoke-on-Trent: Trentham Books.

Bohnet, I. (2016) *What Works: gender equality by design*. Cambridge, MA: The Belknap Press of Harvard University Press.

Bohnet, I., van Geen, A. & Bazerman, M. (2012) When performance trumps gender bias: joint vs. separate evaluation. *Harvard Business School, Working Paper 12-083*. http://www.hbs.edu/faculty/Publication%20Files/12-083.pdf

Booth, A. & Nolen, P. (2012) Choosing to compete: how different are girls and boys? *Journal of Economic Behavior & Organization*, 81(2), pp. 542-555.

Boring, A. (2017) Gender biases in student evaluations of teaching. *Journal of Public Economics*, 145, pp. 27-41. doi.org/10.1016/j.jpubeco.2016.11.006

Botcherby, S. & Buckner, L. (2012) Women in science, technology, engineering and mathematics: from classroom to boardroom, UK statistics 2012. Bradford: WISE. http://www.raeng.org.uk/publications/other/wise-stats-document-final

Botting, N., Dipper, L. & Hilari, K. (2017) The effect of social media promotion on academic article uptake. *Journal of the Association for Information Science and Technology*, 68(3), pp. 795-800. doi:10.1002/asi.23704

Bourdieu, P. (1990) *The Logic of Practice*. (Trans. R. Nice). Cambridge: Polity.

Bourdieu, P. & Wacquant, L.J.D. (1992) *An Invitation to Reflexive Sociology*. Cambridge: Polity.

Bowles, H.R., Babcock, L. & Lai, L. (2007) Social incentives for gender differences in the propensity to initiate negotiations: sometimes it does hurt to ask. *Organizational Behavior and Human Decision Processes*, 103.1, pp. 84-103.

Bowles, H.R., Babcock, L. & McGinn, K.L. (2005) Constraints and triggers: situational mechanics of gender in negotiation. *Journal of Personality and Social Psychology*, 89(6), pp.951-965. doi:10.1037/0022-3514.89.6.951.

Braidotti, R. (2000) Sexual difference theory. In: Jaggar, A.M. & Young, I.M. (eds.) *A Companion to Feminist Philosophy*. Oxford UK: Blackwell, pp. 298-306.

Brescoll, V.L. (2012) Who takes the floor and why: gender, power, and volubility in organizations. *Adm Sci Q*. 2012:56, pp. 622-641. doi:10.1177/0001839212439994

Brescoll, V.L., Dawson, E. & Uhlmann, E.L. (2010) Hard won and easily lost: the fragile status of leaders in gender-stereotype-incongruent occupations. *Psychological Science*, 21(11), pp. 1640-1642. doi:10.1177/0956797610384744.

Brescoll, V.L., Uhlmann, E L., Moss-Racusin, C. & Sarnell, L. (2012) Masculinity, status, and subordination: why working for a gender stereotype violator causes men to lose status. *Journal of Experimental Social Psychology*, 48(1), pp. 354-357. doi:10.1016/j.jesp.2011.06.005.

British Standards Institution (2013) Specification for information management for the capital delivery phase of construction projects using building information modelling, PAS 1192-2: 2013, BSI Standards Limited.

Broverman, I.K., Vogel, S.R., Broverman, D.M., Clarkson, F.E. & Rosenkrantz, P.S. (1972) Sex-role stereotypes: a current appraisal. *Journal of Social Issues*, 28, pp. 59-78. doi:10.1111/j.1540-4560.1972.tb00018.x

Bryman, A. (2007) *Effective Leadership in Higher Education: final report*. London: Leadership Foundation for Higher Education.

Budden, A., Tregenza, T., Aarssen, L., Koricheva, J., Leimu, R. & Lortie, C. (2008) Double-blind review favours increased representation of female authors. *Trends in Ecology & Evolution*, 23(1), pp. 4-6.

Budig, M. & England, P. (2001) The wage penalty for motherhood. *American Sociological Review*, 66, pp.204-225. doi:10.1017/CBO9781107415324.004.

Burnhill, P., Garner, C. & McPherson, A. (1990) Parental education, social class and entry to higher education 1976-86. *Journal of the Royal Statistical Society*, 153, pp. 233-248.

Butler, J. (1988) Performative acts and gender constitution: an essay in phenomenology and feminist theory. *Theatre Journal*, 40(4), pp. 519-531.

Butler, J. (1993) *Bodies That Matter: on the discursive limits of "sex"*. New York: Routledge.

Caperton (2012) *Female Conference Speaker Bingo*. http://www.feministe.us/blog/archives/2012/09/24/why-arent-there-more-women-at-stem-conferences-this-time-its-statistical/female-conference-speaker-bingo/

Carli, L. & Eagly A.H. (1999) Gender effects on social influence and emergent leadership. In: Powell, G.N. (ed.) *Handbook of Gender and Work*. Sage.

Carnes, M., Devine, P.G., Isaac, C., Manwell, L.B., Ford, C.E., Byars-Winston, A., ... Sheridan, J. (2012). Promoting institutional change through bias literacy. *Journal of Diversity in Higher Education*, 5(2), pp. 63-77. doi:10.1037/a0028128.

Carnes, M. et al. (2015) The effect of an intervention to break the gender bias habit for faculty at one institution. *Academic Medicine*, 90(2), pp. 221-230. doi:10.1097/ACM.0000000000000552.

Carrel, S.E., Page, M.E. & West, J.E. (2010) Sex and science: how professor gender perpetuates the gender gap. *The Quarterly Journal of Economics*, 125(3), pp. 1101-1144.

Castilla, E.J. & Benard, S. (2010) The paradox of meritocracy in organizations. *Administrative Science Quarterly*, 55, pp. 543-576. doi:10.3905/JOI.2010.19.1.032.

Hundleby, C. & Duran, C. (2011) Androcentrism as a fallacy of argumentation. *OSSA Conference Archive*. Paper 14. http://scholar.uwindsor.ca/ossaarchive/OSSA9/papersandcommentaries/14

Charmaz, K. (2000) Grounded theory: objectivist and constructivist methods. In: Denzin, N.K. & Lincoln, Y. S. (eds.) *Handbook of Qualitative Research*. 2nd ed. London: Sage.

Cheryan, S., Plaut, V.C., Davies, P.G. & Steele, C.M. (2009) Ambient belonging: how stereotypical cues impact gender participation in computer science. *Journal of Personality and Social Psychology*, 97(6), pp. 1045-1060. doi:10.1037/a0016239

Chesterton (nd.) https://www.goodreads.com/quotes/328675-merely-having-an-open-mind-is-nothing-the-object-of

Cho, A.H., Johnson, S.A., Schuman, C.E., Adler, J.M., Gonzalez, O., Graves, S.J., ... Bruna, E.M. (2014) Women are underrepresented on the editorial boards of journals in environmental biology and natural resource management. *PeerJ*, 2, e542. doi:10.7717/peerj.542

Clayton, J.A. & Collins, F.S. (2014) NIH to balance sex in cell and animal studies. *Nature*, 509(7500), pp. 282-283. doi:10.1038/509282a.

Code, L. (2000) Epistemology. In: Jaggar, A.M. & Young, I.M. (eds.) *A Companion to Feminist Philosophy*. Oxford: Blackwell.

Cohen, G.L. (2006) Reducing the racial achievement gap: a social-psychological intervention. *Science*, 313(5791), pp. 1307-1310. doi:10.1126/science.1128317.

Cohen, G.L., Garcia, J., Purdie-Vaughns, V., Apfel, N. & Brzustoski, P. (2009) Recursive processes in self-affirmation: intervening to close the minority achievement gap. *Science*, 324(5925), pp. 400-403. doi:10.1126/science.1170769

Cohen, G.L., Steele, C.M. & Ross, L.D. (1999) The mentor's dilemma: providing critical feedback across the racial divide. *Personality and Social Psychology Bulletin*, 25(10), pp. 1302-1318. doi:10.1177/0146167299258011.

Cohen, J. (1992) A power primer. *Psychological Bulletin*. American Psychological Association, 112(1), pp. 155-159. http://psycnet.apa.org/journals/bul/112/1/155/

Coleman, J.S. (1961) *The Adolescent Society*. New York: Free Press.

Collins, C., Kenway, J. & McLeod, J. (2000) Factors influencing the educational performance of males and females in school and their initial destinations after leaving school. Australia: Deakin University, University of South Australia.

Collins, P.H. & Chepp, V. (2013) Intersectionality. In: Waylen, G., Celis, K., Kantola, J. & Weldon, S.L. (eds.) *The Oxford Handbook of Gender and Politics*. doi:10.1093/oxfordhb/9780199751457.013.0002

Connell, R.W. (2005) Change among the gatekeepers: men, masculinities, and gender equality in the global arena. *Signs*, 30(3), pp. 1801-1825.

Connolly, P. (2004) *Boys and Schooling in the Early Years*. London: RoutledgeFalmer.

Corbett, C. & Hill, C. (2015) Solving the equation: the variables for women's success in engineering and computing. Washington, DC: American Association of University Women.

Crenshaw, K. (1989) Demarginalizing the intersection of race and sex: a black feminist critique of antidiscrimination doctrine, feminist theory and antiracist policies. *The University of Chicago Legal Forum*, 1989(1), pp. 139-167. http://chicagounbound.uchicago.edu/cgi/viewcontent. cgi?article=1052&context=uclf

Crenshaw, K. (1991) Mapping the margins: intersectionality, identity politics, and violence against women of color. *Stanford Law Review*, 6, pp. 1241-1299.

Crenshaw, K. (2016) The urgency of intersectionality. TED talk (video). https://www.ted.com/talks/kimberle_crenshaw_the_urgency_of_intersectionality

Croson, R. & Gneezy, U. (2009) Gender differences in preferences. *Journal of Economic Literature*, 47, pp. 448-474.

Crozier, G., Reay, D. & James, D. (2011) Making it work for their children: white middle-class parents and working-class schools. *Int Stud Sociol Educ*, 21, pp.199-216. doi:10.1080/09620214.2011.616343.

Cumming, G. (2012) Understanding the New Statistics: effect sizes, confidence intervals, and meta-analysis. New York: Routledge.

Damasio, A. (2006) *Descartes' Error: emotion, reason, and the human brain*. London: Vintage.

Danziger, S., Levav, J. & Avnaim-Pesso, L. (2011) Extraneous factors in judicial decisions. *Proc Natl Acad Sci U S A*, 108, pp. 6889-92. doi:10.1073/pnas.1018033108.

Dargnies, M.P. (2012) Men too sometimes shy away from competition: the case of team competition. *Management Science,* 58(11), pp. 1982-2000.

Dasgupta, N. (2011) Ingroup experts and peers as social vaccines who inoculate the self-concept: the stereotype inoculation model. *Psychological Inquiry*, 22, pp. 231-246. doi:10.1080/104784 0X.2011.607313.

Datta Gupta, N., Poulsen, A. & Villeval, M.C. (2013) Gender matching and competitiveness: experimental evidence. *Economic Inquiry*, 51(1), pp. 816-835.

Davis, K. (2008) Intersectionality as buzzword: a sociology of science perspective on what makes a feminist theory successful. *Feminist Theory*, 9(1), pp. 67-85. doi:10.1177/1464700108086364.

Deaux, K. & Kite, M. (1993) Gender stereotypes. In: Denmark, F.I. & Lindzy, G. (eds.) *Psychology of women: a handbook of issues*, pp. 107-139. Westport CT: Greenwoods.

Deaux, K., Winton, W., Crowley, M. & Lewis, L.L. (1985) Level of categorization and content of gender stereotypes. *Social Cognition*, 3, pp. 145-167.

Deaves, R., Lüders, E. & Schröder, M. (2010) The dynamics of overconfidence: evidence from stock market forecasters. *Journal of Economic Behavior and Organization*, 17, pp. 402-412.

de Beauvoir, S. (1949) *Le deuxième sexe. NRF essais* (in French). 2 L'expérience vécue [Experience]. Gallimard.

Deem, R. (1998) 'New managerialism' and higher education: the management of performances and cultures in universities in the United Kingdom. *International Studies in Sociology of Education*, 8(1), pp. 47-70.

Derrida, J. (2004) *Dissemination*. London and New York: A&C Black.

Dissanayake, E. (2000) *Art and Intimacy: how the arts began*. Seattle: University of Washington Press.

Dohmen, T. & Falk, A. (2011) Performance pay and multidimensional sorting: productivity, preferences, and gender. *The American Economic Review*, pp. 556-590.

Dougherty, T., Baron, S. & Miller, K. (2015) Why do female students leave philosophy? The story from Sydney. *Hypatia*, 30(2), pp. 467-474.

Dragicevic, P. (2016) Fair Statistical Communication in HCI. In: Robertson, J. & Kaptein, M. (eds.) *Modern Statistical Methods in HCI*. Springer International Publishing.

Duerst-Lahti, G. (2002) Governing institutions, ideologies and gender: towards the possibility of equal political representation. *Sex Roles*, 47 (7/8), pp. 371–88.

Duerst-Lahti, G. (2008) Gender Ideology: masculinism and feminalism. In: Goertz, G. & Mazur, A.G. (eds) *Politics, Gender and Concepts: theory and methodology*, pp. 159-192. Cambridge: Cambridge University Press.

Duerst-Lahti, G. & Kelly, R.M. (eds.) (1995) Gender *Power, Leadership and Governance*. Ann Arbor: University of Michigan Press.

Dumont, M., Sarlet, M. & Dardenne, B. (2010) Be too kind to a woman, she'll feel incompetent: benevolent sexism shifts self-construal and autobiographical memories towards incompetence. *Sex Roles*, 62(7), pp. 545-553.

Dutt, K., Pfaff, D. L., Bernstein A.F., Dillard, J.S. & Block, C.J. (2016) Gender differences in recommendation letters for postdoctoral fellowships in geoscience. *Nature Geoscience*, 9, pp. 805-808.

DVSA (2015) Car driving test data by test centre. Driver and Vehicle Standards Agency. https://www.gov.uk/government/statistical-data-sets/car-driving-test-data-by-test-centre

Dweck, C.S. (2007) *Mindset: the new psychology of success*. Ballantine Books. http://search.ebscohost.com/login aspx?direct=true&db=psyh&AN=2006-08575-000&loginpage=login.asp&site=ehost-live.

DWP (2017) *Households below average income: an analysis of the income distribution 1994/95 to 2015/16*. UK Government. https://www.gov.uk/government/uploads/system/uploads/attachment_data/file/600091/households-below-average-income-1994-1995-2015-2016.pdf

Eagly, A.H. & Miller, D.I. (2016) Scientific eminence: where are the women? *Perspectives on Psychological Science*, 11(6), pp. 899-904. doi:10.1177/1745691616663918.

Eagly, A.H., & Mladinic, A. (1994). Are people prejudiced against women? Some answers from research on attitudes, gender stereotypes, and judgment of competence. In: Stroebe, W. & Hewstone, M. (eds.), *European Review of Social Psychology*, 5, pp. 1–35). New York, NY: Wiley.

Easlea, B. (1981) *Science and Sexual Oppression: patriarchy's confrontation with woman and nature.* London: Weidenfeld and Nicolson.

Easterly, D.M. & Ricard, C.S. (2011) Conscious efforts to end unconscious bias: why women leave academic research. *Journal of Research Administration*, 42(1), pp. 61-73.

ECDGRI (2013) S*he figures: gender in research and innovation.* European Commission Directorate-General for Research and Innovation.

Eckes, T. (1994) Features of men, features of women: assessing stereotypic beliefs about gender subtypes. *British Journal of Social Psychology*, 33, pp. 107-123.

ECU (2013) *Unconscious bias and higher education.* Equality Challenge Unit. http://www.ecu. ac.uk/wp-content/uploads/2014/07/unconscious-bias-and-higher-education.docx

ECU (2015) *Equality in higher education: statistical report 2015.* Equality Challenge Unit. http:// www.ecu.ac.uk/publications/equality-higher-education-statistical-report-2015/

Educated Pass (2015) *Tracking Report.* Edinburgh.

Egan, J. (1998) *Rethinking Construction.* London: Department of the Environment, Transport and the Regions.

Eilperin, J. (2016) White House women want to be in the room where it happens. *The Washington Post*, September 13, 2016. https://www.washingtonpost.com/news/powerpost/wp/2016/09/13/white-house-women-are-now-in-the-room-where-it-happens/

Emdad, R., Alipour, A., Hagberg, J. & Jensen, I.B. (2013) The impact of bystanding to workplace bullying on symptoms of depression among women and men in industry in Sweden: an empirical and theoretical longitudinal study. *International Archives of Occupational and Environmental Health*, 86(6), pp. 709-716. doi:10.1007/s00420-012-0813-1.

Equality Change Unit (nd.) http://www.ecu.ac.uk/guidance-resources/employment-and-careers/staff-recruitment/unconscious-bias/

ERC WGGB (nd.) *Working Group on Gender Balance.* European Research Council. https://erc. europa.eu/thematic-working-groups/working-group-gender-balance

Ertac, S. (2011) Does self-relevance affect information processing? Experimental evidence on the response to performance and non-performance feedback. *Journal of Economic Behavior and Organization*, 80(3), pp. 532-545.

Etz, A. & Vandekerckhove, J. (2016) A Bayesian perspective on the reproducibility project: psychology. *PLoS ONE*, 11(2), pp. 1-12. doi:10.1371/journal.pone.0149794.

Exemplars of Excellence (2015) *Exemplars of excellence in knowledge exchange (KE).* The University of Edinburgh. http://www.ed.ac.uk/files/atoms/files/exemplardocumentke_jul15.pdf

FIFA (2006) *The Big Count.* Nyon: Switzerland.

Fine, C. (2010) *Delusions of Gender: how our minds, society and neurosexism create difference.* New York: W.W. Norton.

Fine, C. (2017) *Testosterone Rex: myths of sex, science, and society.* New York: W.W. Norton.

Fiske, S.T., Cuddy, A.J.C., Glick, P. & Xu, J. (2002) A model of (often mixed) stereotype content: competence and warmth respectively follow from perceived status and competition. *Journal of Personality and Social Psychology*, 82(6), pp. 878-902.

Fletcher, C. (2007) Passing the buck: gender and management of research production in UK higher education. *Equal Opportunities International*, 26(4), pp. 269-286. doi:10.1108/02610150710749395.

Flinker, A., Korzeniewska, A., Shestyuk, A.Y., Franaszczuk, P.J., Dronkers, N.F., Knight, R.T. & Crone, N.E. (2015) Redefining the role of Broca's area in speech. *Proceedings of the National Academy of Sciences*. http://www.pnas.org/content/early/2015/02/09/1414491112.abstract

Ford, C. (2008). *Women Speaking Up: Getting and using turns in workplace meetings*. London: Palgrave Macmillan.

Forster, E.M. (1927) *Aspects of the novel*. New York: Harcourt, Brace and Company.

Foucault, M. (1977) *Discipline and Punish: the birth of the prison*. New York: Random House.

Fox, C. (2014) *The Athena Project Review: a report on the Athena Project's impact and learning for future diversity programmes*. https://www.athenaforum.org.uk/media/1088/athena-project-review-final-version-web.pdf

Fraser, M. (2014) How-What Space. In: Williams, A., Jones, D., & Robertson, J. (eds.) *BITE: Recipes for Remarkable Research*, pp. 170-175. Rotterdam: Sense Publishers.

Fullan, M. & Scott, G. (2009) *Turnaround leadership for higher education*. San Francisco: Jossey-Bass.

Gaio Santos, G. & Cabral-Cardoso, C. (2008) Work-family culture in academia: a gendered view of work-family conflict and coping strategies. *Gender in Management*, 23(6), pp. 442-457. doi:10.1108/17542410810897553.

Gaucher, D., Friesen, J. & Kay, A.C. (2011) Evidence that gendered wording in job advertisements exists and sustains gender inequality. *J Pers Soc Psychol*, 101(1), pp. 109-28.

Gay, R. (2014) *Bad Feminist*. New York: Corsair.

Gibney, P. (2006) The double-bind theory: still crazy-making after all these years. *Psychotherapy in Australia*, 12(3), pp. 48-55.

Gillborn, D. & Mirza, H.S. (2000) *Educational inequality: mapping race, class and gender*. London: OFSTED.

Gino, F., Wilmuth, C. A. & Brooks, A.W. (2015) Compared to men, women view professional advancement as equally attainable, but less desirable. *Proceedings of the National Academy of Sciences*, 112(40), 12354-12359. http://www.pnas.org/content/ 112/40/12354.short

Glaser, C. & Smalley, B.S. (1995) *Swim with the dolphins: how women can succeed in corporate America on their own terms*. New York: Warner Books.

Glick, P. & Fiske, S.T. (1996) The ambivalent sexism inventory: differentiating hostile and benevolent sexism. *Journal of Personality and Social Psychology*, 70, pp. 491-512.

Glick, P. & Fiske, S.T. (1997) Hostile and benevolent sexism: measuring ambivalent sexist attitudes toward women. *Psychology of Women Quarterly*, 21(1).

Glick, P. & Fiske, S.T. (2001) Ambivalent sexism. *Advances in Experimental Social Psychology*, 33, pp. 115-188.

Glick, P., Diebold, J., Bailey-Werner, B., & Zhu, L. (1997). The two faces of Adam: ambivalent sexism and polarized attitudes toward women. *Personality and Social Psychology Bulletin*, 23, 1323-1334.

Gneezy, U., Leonard, K.L. & List, J.A. (2009) Gender differences in competition: evidence from a matrilineal and a patriarchal society. *Econometrica*, 77(5), pp. 1637-1664.

Golding, C. & Rouse, C. (2000) Orchestrating impartiality: the impact of "blind" auditions on female musicians. *The American Economic Review*, 90(4), pp.715-741.

Goleman, D., Boyatzis, R. & McKee, A. (2002) *Primal leadership unleashing the power of emotional intelligence*. Harvard Business Review Press.

Good, C., Rattan, A. & Dweck, C.S. (2012) Why do women opt out? Sense of belonging and women's representation in mathematics. *Journal of Personality and Social Psychology*, 102(4), pp. 700-717. doi:10.1037/a0026659.

Good, J.J., Woodzicka, J.A. & Wingfield, L.C. (2010) The effects of gender stereotypic and counter-stereotypic textbook images on science performance. *The Journal of Social Psychology*, 150(2), pp. 132-47. doi:10.1080/00224540903366552.

Goodman, A. & Gregg, P. (eds.) (2010) *Poorer children's educational attainment: how important are attitudes and behaviour?* York: Joseph Rowntree Foundation.

Gordon, M. (2013) *Good boys and dead girls: and other essays*. New York: Open Road.

Greene, M.E. & Levack, A. (2010) Synchronising gender strategies: a cooperative model for improving reproductive health and transforming gender relations. http://www.prb.org/igwg_media/synchronizing-gender-strategies.pdf

Grove, J. (2012) Top university posts still elude female academics, study finds. *Times Higher Education*, London. https://www.timeshighereducation.com/news/top-university-posts-still-elude-female-academics-study-finds/419407.article

Grunspan, D.Z., Eddy, S.L., Brownell, S.E., Wiggins, B.L., Crowe, A.J. & Goodreau, S.M. (2016) Males under-estimate academic performance of their female peers in undergraduate biology classrooms. *PLoS ONE*, 11(2), pp. 1-16. doi:10.1371/journal.pone.0148405.

Haddock, G. & Zanna, M.P. (1994) Preferring "housewives" to "feminists": categorization and the favorability of attitudes toward women. *Psychology of Women Quarterly*, 18, pp. 25-52.

Hall, R. & Sandler, B. (1982) *The classroom climate: a chilly one for women*. Washington, DC. Project on the status and education of women. Association of American Colleges.

Harris, S., Wallace, G. & Ruddock, J. (1993) "It's not just that I haven't learnt much. It's just that I don't understand what I'm doing": metacognition and secondary school students. *Research Papers in Education: Policy and Practice*, 10, p. 254.

Hartley, E. (2015) Women fail driving tests far more than men – but are still safer drivers. *The Guardian*. https://www.theguardian.com/society/2015/nov/22/women-fail-driving-tests-far-more-than-men-but-are-still-safer-drivers

Hastorf, A.H. & Cantril, H. (1954) Case reports. They saw a game: a case study. *The Journal of Abnormal and Social Psychology*, 49(1), pp. 129-134.

Healy, A. & Pate, J. (2011) Can teams help to close the gender competition gap? *The Economic Journal*, 121(555), pp. 1192-1204.

HEFCE (2015) *Selection of staff for inclusion in the REF 2014*. Higher Education Funding Council for England. http://dera.ioe.ac.uk/23924/1/HEFCE2015_17.pdf

Heifetz, R. & Laurie, D. (1997) The work of leadership. *Harvard Business Review*, Feb. 1997, pp. 124-134.

Helgesen, S. (1990) *The female advantage: women's ways of leadership*. New York: Doubleday.

HESA (2015) *Academic staff (excluding atypical) at HE providers by terms of employment, mode of employment, academic employment function and sex (Table H)*. https://www.hesa.ac.uk/data-and-analysis/staff/overviews?breakdown%5B%5D=583&year=2

HESA (2017) *Higher education student enrolments and qualifications obtained at higher education providers in the United Kingdom 2015/16*. https://www.hesa.ac.uk/news/12-01-2017/sfr242-student-enrolments-and-qualifications

Heyder, A. & Kessels, U. (2015) Do teachers equate male and masculine with lower academic engagement? How students' gender enactment triggers gender stereotypes at school. *Social Psychology of Education*, 18, p. 467.

Hill, C., Corbett, C. & St. Rose, A. (2010) *Why So Few? Women in science, technology, engineering, and mathematics.* Washington, DC: American Association of University Women.

Hochschild, A. R. (1983) *The Managed Heart: the commercialization of human feeling.* Berkeley, CA: University of California Press.

Hogan, V., Hogan, M. & Hodgins, M. (2016) A study of workaholism in Irish academics. *Occupational Medicine*, 66(6), pp. 460-465. doi:10.1093/occmed/kqw032

Hogue, M., & Lord, R. G. (2007). A multilevel, complexity theory approach to understanding gender bias in leadership. *The Leadership Quarterly*, 18, pp. 370-390. doi:10.1016/j.leaqua.2007.04.006.

hooks, b. (1984) Feminist Theory: from margin to centre. Boston, MA: South End Press.

hooks, b. (2000) Feminism is for Everybody. London: Pluto Press.

Hoyt, C.L. & Simon, S. (2011) Female leaders: injurious or inspiring role models for women? *Psychology of Women Quarterly*, 35(1), pp. 143-157. doi:10.1177/0361684310385216.

Hundleby, C.E. & Duran, C. (2011) Androcentrism as a fallacy of argumentation. *Proceedings of the 9th International Conference of the Ontario Society for the Study of Argumentation (OSSA)*, pp. 1-8.

Hutchins, H.M. & Rainbolt, H. (2016) What triggers imposter phenomenon among academic faculty? A critical incident study exploring antecedents, coping, and development opportunities. *Human Resource Development International*, 20(3), pp. 194-214. doi:10.1080/13678868.2016.1248205.

Hyde, J.S. (2005) The gender similarities hypothesis. *The American Psychologist*, 60(6), pp. 581-592. doi:10.1037/0003-066X.60.6.581.

Hyde, J.S. (2014) Gender similarities and differences. *Annual Review of Psychology*, 65(1), pp. 373-398. doi:10.1146/annurev-psych-010213-115057.

Ignotofsky, R. (2017) *Women in Science: 50 fearless pioneers who changed the world.* Wren & Rook.

Ioannidis, J.P.A. (2005) Why most published research findings are false. *PLoS Med*, 2(8), e124. doi:10.1371/journal.pmed.0020124.

Jackson, C., Dempster, S. & Pollard, L. (2015) "They just don't seem to really care, they just think it's cool to sit there and talk": laddism in university teaching-learning contexts. *Educational Review*, 67(3), pp. 300-314. http://doi.org/10.1080/00131911.2014.910178.

Jagsi, R., Tarbell, N.J., Henault, L.E., Chang, Y. & Hylek, E.M. (2008) The representation of women on the editorial boards of major medical journals: a 35-year perspective. *Arch Intern Med*, 168(5), pp. 544-548. doi:10.1001/archinte.168.5.544.

Janis, I.L. (1972/1982) *Groupthink: psychological studies of policy decisions and fiascoes.* 2nd ed. New York: Houghton Mifflin.

Johnson, L.K. (2004). Retooling 360s for better performance. *Harvard Management Update*, 8(1). http://hbswk.hbs.edu/archive/3935.html

Jones, D. & Dewberry, E. (2013) Building information modelling design ecologies: a new model? *International Journal of 3-D Information Modeling, IGI Global*, 2(1), pp. 53-64.

Jones, S. & Myhill, D. (2004) 'Troublesome boys' and 'compliant girls': gender identity and perceptions of achievement and underachievement. *British Journal of Sociology of Education*, 25(5), pp. 547-561.

Kaatz, A., Gutierrez, B. & Carnes, M. (2014) Threats to objectivity in peer review: the case of gender. *Trends Pharmacol Sci.*, 35, pp. 371-373. doi:10.1016/j.tips.2014.06.005.

Kalladka, D., Sinden, J., Pollock, K., Haig, C., McLean, J., Smith, W. et al. (2016) Human neural stem cells in patients with chronic ischaemic stroke (PISCES): a phase 1, first-in-man study. *The Lancet*, 388,(10046), pp. 787-796.

Kamas, L. & Preston, A. (2009) *Social preferences, competitiveness and compensation: are there gender differences?* Working Paper, Santa Clara University.

Katz, J. (2006) *The Macho Paradox: why some men hurt women and how all men can help.* Illinois: Sourcebooks.

Kessels, U. & Steinmayr, R. (2013) Macho-man in school: toward the role of gender role self-concepts and help seeking in school performance. *Learning and Individual Differences*, 23, pp. 234-240.

Kim, D. (2003) Voluntary controllability of the Implicit Association Test (IAT). *Social Psychology Quarterly*, 66, pp. 83-96. doi:10.2307/3090143.

Kingsley, C. (1904) Poems of home: IV. Youth. A farewell. In: Carman, B. et al. (eds.) *The World's Best Poetry*. Philadelphia: John D. Morris & Co. http://www.bartleby.com/360/

Klinge, I. (2013) *Gendered Innovations: how gender analysis contributes to research*. European Commission, Directorate General for Research & Innovation.

Koellinger, P., Minniti, M. & Schade, C. (2007) "I think I can, I think I can": overconfidence and entrepreneurial behaviour. *Journal of Economic Psychology*, 28, pp. 502-527.

Koenig, A.M., Eagly, A.H., Mitchell, A.A. & Ristikari, T. (2011) Are leader stereotypes masculine? A meta-analysis of three research paradigms. *Psychological Bulletin*, 137(4), pp. 616-642.

Krawczyk, M. & Smyk, M. (2016) Author's gender affects rating of academic articles: evidence from an incentivized, deception-free laboratory experiment. *Eur Econ Rev*, 90, pp. 326-335. doi:10.1016/j.euroecorev.2016.02.017.

Kruschke, J.K. (2010) What to believe: Bayesian methods for data analysis. *Trends in cognitive sciences*, 14(7), pp. 293-300. doi:10.1016/j.tics.2010.05.001.

Kunda, Z. (1990) The case for motivated reasoning. *Psychological Bulletin*, 108(3), pp. 480-498.

Lacan, J. (1988) *Book One: Freud's Papers On Technique 1953-1954*. Miller, J-A. (ed.), (trans. J. Forrester). New York: W.W. Norton.

Lagesen, V.A. (2007) The strength of numbers: strategies to include women into computer science. *Social Studies of Science*, 37(1), pp. 67-92.

Lai, C.K., Hoffman, K.M., Nosek, B.A. (2013) Reducing implicit prejudice. *Social and Personality Psychology Compass*, 7, pp. 315-330. doi:10.1111/spc3.12023.

Lakoff, G. & Johnson, M. (1999) *Philosophy in the Flesh: the embodied mind and its challenge to Western thought*. New York: Basic Books.

Landsheer, H., Maassen, G., Bisschop, P. & Adema, L. (1998) Can higher grades result in fewer friends? A reexamination of the relation between academic and social competence. *Adolescence*, 33(129), pp. 185-191.

Langford, T., & MacKinnon, N. J. (2000). The affective bases for the gendering of traits: comparing the United States and Canada. *Social Psychology Quarterly*, 63, pp. 34-48. doi:10.2307/2695879.

Latham, M. (1994) *Constructing the Team*. London: HMSO.

Latu, I.M., Schmid Mast, M., Lammers, J. & Bomari, D. (2013) Successful female leaders empower women's behavior in leadership tasks. *Journal of Experimental Social Psychology*, 49(3), pp. 444-448.

Leary, M.R., & Baumeister, R.F. (2000) The nature and function of self-esteem: sociometer theory. In: Zanna, M.P. (ed.) *Advances in Experimental Social Psychology*, 32, pp. 1-62. San Diego: Academic Press.

Ledin, A., Bornman, L., Gannon, F. & Wallon, G. (2007) A persistent problem. Traditional gender roles hold back female scientists. *EMBO Reports*, 8(11), pp. 982-987. https://www.ncbi.nlm.nih.gov/pmc/articles/PMC2247380/

Lefebvre, H. (1991) *The Production of Space* (trans. D. Nicholson-Smith). Blackwell Publishers Ltd.

Lenton, A.P., Bruder, M. & Sedikides, C. (2009) A meta-analysis on the malleability of automatic gender stereotypes. *Psychology of Women Quarterly*, 33, pp. 183-196.

Lerback, J. (2017) Journals invite too few women to referee. *Nature*, 541, p. 455.

Leslie, S-J. (2017) The original sin of cognition: fear, prejudice, and generalisation. *Journal of Philosophy*.

Leslie, S-J., Cimpian, A., Meyer, M., Freeland, E. (2015) Expectations of brilliance underlie gender distributions across academic disciplines. *Science*, 347, pp. 262-265. doi:10.1126/science.1261375.

Lichtenstein, S., Fischhoff, B. & Phillips, L.D. (1982) Calibration of probabilities: the state of the art to 1980. In: Kahneman, D., Slovic, P. & Tversky, A. (eds.) *Judgment Under Uncertainty: heuristics and biases*, pp. 306-334. Cambridge, UK: Cambridge University Press.

Lidwell, W., Holden, K. & Butler, J. (2010) *Universal Principles of Design*. 2nd ed. Beverly, MA: Rockport Publishers.

Lindohf, J. (2005) *Making Women and Girls More Active*. SportScotland. https://sportscotland.org.uk/documents/resources/makingwomenandgirlsmoreactive.pdf

Lucey, H. & Walkerdine, V. (2000) Boys' underachievement: social class and changing masculinities. In: Cox, T. (ed.) *Combating Educational Disadvantage: meeting the needs of vulnerable children*, pp. 37-52. London: Falmer.

Lumby, J. (2009) Leaders' orientations to diversity: two cases from education. *Leadership*, 5(4), pp. 423-446.

Lyness, K.S., & Heilman, M.E. (2006) When fit is fundamental: performance evaluations and promotions of upper-level female and male managers. *Journal of Applied Psychology*, 91, pp. 777–785. doi:10.1037/ 0021-9010.91.4.777.

Mackay, F. (2014) Nested Newness, Institutional Innovation, and the Gendered Limits of Change. *Politics & Gender*, 10(4), pp. 549-571.

MacNell, L., Driscoll, A. & Hunt, A.N. (2014) What's in a name: exposing gender bias in student ratings of teaching. *Innovative Higher Education*, 40(4), pp. 291-303. doi:10.1007/s10755-014-9313-4.

Manca, S. & Ranieri, M. (2017) Networked scholarship and motivations for social media use in scholarly communication. *International Review of Research in Open and Distributed Learning*, 18(2). doi:10.19173/irrodl.v18i2.2859.

Maney, D.L. (2016) Perils and pitfalls of reporting sex differences. *Philosophical Transactions of the Royal Society B: Biological Sciences*, 371(1688). doi:10.1098/rstb.2015.0119.

Mangels, J.A., Good, C., Whiteman, R.C., Maniscalco, B. & Dweck, C.S. (2012) Emotion blocks the path to learning under stereotype threat. *Social Cognitive and Affective Neuroscience*, 7(2), pp. 230-241. doi:10.1093/scan/nsq100.

Martino, W. & Pallotta-Chiarolli, M. (2003) *So What's a Boy? Addressing issues of masculinity and schooling*. Buckingham: Open University Press.

Marton, F. & Hounsell, D. & Entwistle, N. (eds.) (1997) *The Experience of Learning*. Edinburgh: Scottish Academic Press.

Marton, F. & Saljo, R. (1976) On qualitative differences in learning - 1: outcome and process. *British Journal of Educational Psychology*, 46, pp. 4-11.

Marx, D.M. & Roman, J.S. (2002) Female role models: protecting women's math test performance. *Personality and Social Psychology Bulletin*, 28(9), pp. 1183-1193. doi:10.1177/01461672022812004.

May, R. (1975/1994) *The Courage to Create*. New York: W.W. Norton.

Mazei, J., Hüffmeier, J., Freund, P. & Stuhlmacher, A.F. (2015) A meta-analysis on gender differences in negotiation outcomes and their moderators. *Psychological Bulletin*, 141(1), p. 85-104.

McCafffery, P. (2004) *The Higher Education Manager's handbook: effective leadership and management in universities and colleges*. London: Routledge.

McCall, L. (2005) The complexity of intersectionality. *Signs*, 30(3), pp. 1771-1800.

McClelland, D.C. (1985) *Human Motivation*. New York: Cambridge University Press.

McConnell-Ginet, S. (2000) Breaking through the 'glass ceiling'. In: Holmes, J. (ed.) *Gendered Speech in Social Context: perspectives from gown and town*, pp. 259-282. Wellington: Victoria University Press.

McNutt, M. (2016) Implicit bias. *Science*, 352(6289), 1035. doi:10.1126/science.aag1695.

McRobbie, A. (2009) The Aftermath of Feminism: gender, culture and social change. Sage Publications.

Mediaworks (nd.) https://www.mediaworks.co.uk/news/visualising-the-gender-pay-gap-infographic-infographic/

Mehdi, N. & Moffat, S. (2013) Students' experience of sexual harassment in Edinburgh: a report. [Edinburgh University Students' Association internal report], pp. 1-30.

Merleau-Ponty, M. (1965) *Phenomenology of Perception*. (Trans: Colin Smith.) London: Routledge & Kegan Paul.

Merriam, E. (1974) Sex and semantics: some notes on BOMFOG. *New York University Education Quarterly*, 5(4), pp. 22-24.

Metz, I., Harzing, A-W. & Zyphur, M.J. (2015) Of journal editors and editorial boards: who are the trailblazers in increasing editorial board gender equality? *British Journal of Management*, 27, pp. 712-726. doi:10.1111/1467-8551.12133.

Middlehurst, R. (2012) *Leadership and Management in Higher Education: a research perspective*. Working Paper No. 2012/47. Maastricht School of Management. https://www.msm.nl/resources/uploads/2014/02/MSM-WP2012-47.pdf

Milkman, K., Akinola, M. & Chugh, D. (2015) What happens before? A field experiment exploring how pay and representation differentially shape bias on the pathway into organizations. *Journal of Applied Psychology*, 100(6), 1678-1712. doi:10.1037/apl0000022.

Miller, L. & Miller, J. (2011) *A woman's guide to successful negotiating: how to convince, collaborate and create your way to an agreement*. 2nd ed. New York: McGraw Hill.

Mills, S. (2005) Gender and impoliteness. *Journal of Politeness Research*, 1, pp. 263-280.

Miner, J.B. (1975) *The Challenge of Managing*. Philadelphia: W.B. Saunders.

Mitchell, G. (2012) Revisiting truth or triviality: the external validity of research in the psychological laboratory. *Perspectives on Psychological Science*, 7(2), pp. 109-117. doi:10.1177/1745691611432343.

Miyake, A., Kost-Smith, L.E., Finkelstein, N.D., Pollock, S.J., Cohen, G.L. & Ito, T.A. (2010) Reducing the gender achievement gap in college science: a classroom study of values affirmation. *Science*, 330(6008), pp. 1234-1237. doi:10.1126/science.1195996.

Mlodinow, L. (2012) *Subliminal: the new unconscious and what it teaches us*. London: Penguin Books.

Moore, A. & Malinowski, P. (2009) Meditation, mindfulness and cognitive flexibility. *Consciousness and Cognition*, 18(1), pp.176-186. doi:10.1016/j.concog.2008.12.008.

Moore, S.H. (2013) *Gender Equality Charter Mark: department analysis and action template*. The University of Edinburgh. http://www.docs.csg.ed.ac.uk/EqualityDiversity/Divinity.pdf

Morrell, P. (2011) BIM to be rolled out to all projects by 2016. *Architects' Journal*. http://www.architectsjournal.co.uk/news/daily-news/paul-morrell-bim-to-be-rolled-out-to-all-projects-by-2016/8616487.article

Moss, J. & Jensrud, Q. (1995) Gender leadership and vocational education. *Journal of Industrial Teacher Education,* 33(1), pp. 6-23.

Moss-Racusin, C.A., Molenda, A.K. & Cramer, C.R. (2015) Can evidence impact attitudes? Public reactions to evidence of gender bias in STEM fields. *Psychology of Women Quarterly*, 39, pp. 194-209. doi:10.1177/0361684314565777.

Mount, P. & Tardanico, S. (2016) *Beating the Impostor Syndrome*. Center for Creative Leadership.

Mulvey, L. (1975, 2003) Visual pleasure and narrative cinema. In: Jones, A. (ed.) The *Feminism and Visual Culture Reader*. London: Routledge.

Murphy, M.C., Steele, C.M. & Gross, J.J. (2007) Signaling threat. *Psychological Science*, 18(10), pp. 879-885. doi:10.1111/j.1467-9280.2007.01995.x.

Nature (2012) Nature's sexism. Editorial. *Nature*, 491(7425). doi:10.1038/491495a.

Nature (2016) Women need to be seen and heard at conferences. Editorial. *Nature*, 538, (7625). doi:10.1038/538290b.

Niederle, M. & Vesterlund, L. (2007) Do women shy away from competition? Do men compete too much? *The Quarterly Journal of Economics*, August, 2007, pp. 1067-1101.

Norlock, K.J. (2011) *Letter to Department of Philosophy*, Trent University, Ontario. https://drive.google.com/viewerng/viewer?a=v&pid=sites&srcid=ZGVmYXVsdGRvbWFpbnxhcGFjb21taXRoZWVvbnRoZXNoYXR1c29md29tZW58Z3g6NGQxNWNhYWIzNmExOWNhZg.

Norman, D.A. (2005) *Emotional Design - why we love (or hate) everyday things*. New York: Basic Books.

Norton, J.R., & Fox, R.E. (1997) *The Change Equation: capitalising on diversity for effective organisational change*. Washington, DC: American Psychological Association.

Noseworthy, C.M. & Lott, A.J. (1984) The cognitive organization of gender-stereotypic categories. *Personality and Social Psychology Bulletin*, 10, pp. 474-481.

NUS (2015) https://www.nusconnect.org.uk/articles/

O'Laughlin, E.M. & Bischoff, L.G. (2005) Balancing parenthood and academia: work/family stress as influenced by gender and tenure status. *Journal of Family Issues*, 26(1), pp. 79-106. doi:10.1177/0192513X04265942.

Okimoto, T.G. & Brescoll, V.L. (2010) The price of power: power seeking and backlash against female politicians. *Personality & Social Psychology Bulletin*, 36(7), pp. 923-36. doi:10.1177/0146167210371949.

Oldenziel, R. (1999) *Making Technology Masculine: men, women and machines in America*, 1870-1945. Amsterdam: Amsterdam University Press.

Olympic Charter (2016) International Olympic Committee. Lausanne: Switzerland.

Open Science Collaboration (2015) Estimating the reproducibility of psychological science. *Science*, 349(6251), aac4716. doi:10.1126/science.aac4716.

Özbilgin, M. F. (2009) From journal rankings to making sense of the world. *Academy of Management Learning and Education*, 8(1), pp. 113-121.

Pallasmaa, J. (2012) *The Eyes of the Skin: architecture and the senses*. 3rd ed. London: Wiley.

Paterson, L. (1991) Socio-economic status and educational attainment: a multi-dimensional and multi-level study. *Evaluation and Research in Education*, 5, p. 97.

Paxton, M., Figdor, C. & Tiberius, V. (2012) Quantifying the gender gap: an empirical study of the underrepresentation of women in philosophy. *Hypatia*, 27(4), pp. 949-957.

Perception Institute (2016) *Implicit Bias*. https://perception.org/research/implicit-bias/

Pinker, S. (2007) *The Stuff of Thought: language as a window into human nature*. New York: Penguin Books.

Prentice, S. (2000) The conceptual politics of chilly climate controversies. *Gender and Education*, 12(2), pp. 195-207.

Puar, J. (2011) *'I would rather be a cyborg than a goddess': intersectionality, assemblage, and affective politics*. http://eipcp.net/transversal/0811/puar/en

Pulford, B.D. & Colman, A.M. (1997) Overconfidence: feedback and item difficulty effects. *Personality and Individual Differences*, 23(1), pp. 125-133.

Ramsden, P. (1998) *Learning to Lead in Higher Education*. London: Routledge.

Rape Crisis Scotland (nd.) https://www.rapecrisisscotland.org.uk/

RCUK (2016) Research Councils Diversity Data (April 2016). HESA Data - estimating the diversity profile of the academic and studentship populations.

REF (2011) *Analysis of Panel Membership*. Research Excellence Framework. http://www.ref.ac.uk/media/ref/content/pub/analysisofpanelmembership/Analysispanelmembership.pdf

REF (2015) *Research Excellence Framework 2014: Manager's Report*. http://www.ref.ac.uk/media/ref/content/pub/REF_managers_report.pdf

Reinharz, S. (1992) *Feminist Methods in Social Research*. New York: Oxford University Press.

Rendell, J. (2000) Introduction: "Gender, Space". In: Rendell, J., Penner, B., & Borden, I. (eds.) *Gender Space Architecture: an interdisciplinary introduction*, pp. 101-111. New York: Routledge.

Reward Processes Timetable (2016). [University of Edinburgh internal document.] http://www.ed.ac.uk/files/atoms/files/reward_processes_timetable_16_17.pdf

Richardson, J. (2012) Get a free logical fallacy poster. https://yourlogicalfallacyis.com/poster

Richardson, J.T.E. (2005) Students' approaches to learning and teachers' approaches to teaching in higher education. *Educational Psychology*, 25(6), pp. 673-680.

Rippon, G., Jordan-Young, R., Kaiser, A. & Fine, C. (2014) Recommendations for sex/gender neuroimaging research: key principles and implications for research design, analysis, and interpretation. *Frontiers in Human Neuroscience*, 8(August), p. 650. doi:10.3389fnhum.2014.00650.

Roberts, T.A. & Nolen-Hoeksema, S. (1989) Sex differences in reactions to evaluative feedback. *Sex Roles*, 21(11-12), pp. 725-747.

Robertson, C. & Cox, R. (2009) *Challenging Culture and Managing Change in Higher Education*. Presentation to Leadership and Management Conference at the Institute of Education, University of Worcester, May 2009. https://eprints.worc.ac.uk/642/1/Chris_Robertson-Challenging_culture_and_managing_change.pdf

Robertson, C., Robins, A. & Cox, R. (2009) Co-constructing an academic community ethos – challenging culture and managing change in higher education: a case study undertaken over two years. *Management in Education*, 23(1).

Robertson, J. & Kaptein, M. (2016a) Improving statistical practice in HCI. In: Robertson, J. & Kaptein, M. (eds.) *Modern Statistical Methods in HCI*. Springer International Publishing.

Robertson, J. & Kaptein, M. (eds.) (2016b) *Modern Statistical Methods in HCI*. Springer International Publishing.

Robertson, J. (2014) Research group as extended family. In: Williams, A., Jones, D. & Robertson, J. (eds.) *BITE: Recipes for Remarkable Research*, pp. 116-119. Rotterdam: Sense Publishing.

Rogers, A., Bear, C., Hunt, M., Mills, S. & Sandover, R. (2014) Intervention: the impact agenda and human geography in UK higher education. *ACME*, 13(1), pp. 1-19.

Roos, P. (2008) Together but unequal: combating gender inequity in the academy. *Journal of Workplace Rights*, 13(2), pp. 185-199.

Roosevelt, E. (1958) Excerpt from a speech by Eleanor Roosevelt at the presentation of "In Your Hands: a guide for community action for the tenth anniversary of the Universal Declaration of Human Rights". Thursday, March 27, 1958. New York: United Nations.

Rosener, J. B. (1990) Ways women lead. *Harvard Business Review*, November-December, 1990. https://hbr.org/1990/11/ways-women-lead

Rossiter, M.W. (1982) *Women Scientists in America: struggles and strategies to 1940*. Baltimore, MD: The Johns Hopkins University Press.

Rudduck, J., Chaplain, R. & Wallace, G. (1996) *School Improvement: what can students tell us?* London: David Fulton.

Sagan, C. (1996) *The Demon-Haunted World: science as a candle in the dark*. New York: Ballantine Books.

Saini, A. (2017) Inferior: how science got women wrong. London, UK: Harper Collins.

Sammons, P. (1995) Gender, ethnic and socio-economic differences in attainment and progress: a longitudinal analysis of student achievement over 9 years. *British Educational Research Journal*, 21, p. 465.

Sandberg, S. (2013) *Lean In: women, work and the will to lead*. WH Allen.

Sapienza, A.M. (2004) *Managing Scientists: leadership strategies in scientific research*. John Wiley & Sons.

Savigny, H. (2014) Women, know your limits: cultural sexism in academia. *Gender and Education*, 26(7), pp. 794-809.

Schein, V.E. & Davidson, M.J. (1993) Think manager – think male: managerial sex typing among U.K. business students. *Management Development Review*, 6(3), pp. 24-28. doi:10.1108 EUM0000000000738.

Schmidt, F.L. & Hunter, J.E. (1998) The validity and utility of selection methods in personnel psychology: practical and theoretical implications of 85 years of research findings. *Psychological Bulletin*, 124(2), pp. 262-274. American Psychological Association.

Scholz, S.J. (2010) *Feminism: A Beginner's Guide*. Oxford: One World.

Schuh, S.C., Bark, A.S.H., Van Quaquebeke, N., Hossiep, R., Frieg, P. & Van Dick, R. (2014) Gender differences in leadership role occupancy: the mediating role of power motivation. *Journal of Business Ethics*, 120(3), pp. 363-379.

Sebald, H. (1981) Adolescents' concept of popularity and unpopularity, comparing 1960 with 1976. *Adolescence*, 16(61), pp. 187-193.

Sherman, D.K., & Cohen, G.L. (2006) The psychology of self-defense: self-affirmation theory. In: Zanna, M.P. (ed.) *Advances in Experimental Social Psychology*, 38, pp. 183-242). San Diego, CA: Academic Press.

Shih, M., Pittinsky, T.L. & Ambady, N. (1999) Stereotype susceptibility: identity salience and shifts in quantitative performance. *Psychological Science*, 10(1), pp. 80-83. doi:10.1111/1467-9280.00111.

Sigley, R. & Holmes, J. (2002) Looking at girls in corpora of English. *Journal of English Linguistics*, 30(2), pp. 138-157. SAGE Publications. doi:10.1177/007242030002004.

Simmons, J.P., Nelson, L.D. & Simonsohn, U. (2011) False-positive psychology: undisclosed flexibility in data collection and analysis allows presenting anything as significant. *Psychological Science*, 22(11), pp. 1359-66. doi:10.1177/0956797611417632.

Sinclair, D. (2012) *BIM Overlay to the RIBA Outline Plan of Work*. London: RIBA.

Six, B. & Eckes, T. (1991) A closer look at the complex structure of gender stereotypes. *Sex Roles*, 24, pp. 57-71.

Skelton, C. (2001) *Schooling the Boys: masculinities and primary education*. Buckingham: Open University Press.

Solnit, R. (2012) Men explain things to me. *Guernica*, August 20, 2012, reprint of 2008 article. https://www.guernicamag.com/rebecca-solnit-men-explain-things-to-me/. See also: http://www.tomdispatch.com/blog/175584/rebecca_solnit_the_archipelago_of_ignorance

Solnit, R. (2017) Protest and persist: why giving up hope is not an option. *The Guardian* newspaper, 13 March 2017. https://www.theguardian.com/world/2017/mar/13/protest-persist-hope-trump-activism-anti-nuclear-movement

Spencer, S.J., Steele, C.M. & Quinn, D.M. (1999) Stereotype threat and women's math performance. *Journal of Experimental Social Psychology*, 35(1), pp. 4-28.

Stanton, J. (2014) *Lad culture & sexism survey*. https://www.nus.org.uk/Global/20140911%20 Lad%20Culture FINAL.pdf

Steele, C. (2010) *Whistling Vivaldi: and other clues to how stereotypes affect us*. New York: W.W. Norton.

Steele, C.M. & Aronson, J. (1995) Contending with a stereotype: African-American intellectual test performance and stereotype threat. *Journal of Personality and Social Psychology*, 69, pp. 797-811.

Steffensmeier, D.J. & Terry, R.M. (2016) Deviance and respectability: an observational study of reactions to shoplifting. *Social Forces*, 51(4), pp. 417-426. doi:10.2307/2576686.

Stern, Lord N. (2016) *Building on success and learning from experience: an independent review of the Research Excellence Framework.* Government report. Ref: IND/16/9. https://www.gov.uk/government/publications/research-excellence-framework-review

Stivers, C.M. (2002) *Gender Images in Public Administration: legitimacy and the administrative state, 2nd ed.* Thousand Oaks, CA, and London: Sage.

Storage D., Horne Z., Cimpian A. & Leslie, S-J. (2016) The frequency of "brilliant" and "genius" in teaching evaluations predicts the representation of women and African Americans across fields. *PLoS ONE* 11(3): e0150194. doi:10.1371/journal.pone.0150194.

Stout, J.G. & Dasgupta, N. (2011) When he doesn't mean you: gender-exclusive language as ostracism. *Personality and Social Psychology Bulletin*, 37(6), pp. 757-769. doi:10.1177/0146167211406434.

Sutherland, K.A. (2017) Constructions of success in academia: an early career perspective. *Studies in Higher Education*, 42(4), pp. 743-759.

Svenson, O. (1981) Are we all less risky and more skillful than our fellow drivers? *Acta Psychologica*, 47, pp. 143-148.

Tapping all our Talents (2012) *Tapping all our Talents: women in science, technology, engineering and mathematics: a strategy for Scotland.* Royal Society of Edinburgh. https://www.rse.org.uk/cms/files/advice-papers/inquiry/women_in_stem/tapping_talents.pdf

Taylor, J. (2016) *A review of Imperial College's institutional culture and its impact on gender equality, 1-11.* https://www.imperial.ac.uk/media/imperial-college/staff/public/Institutional-culture-and-gender-equality.pdf

Tether, B. (2016) The Architectural Review - Results of the 2016 Women in Architecture Survey revealed. http://www.architectural-review.com/archive/results-of-the-2016-women-in-architecture-survey-revealed/10003314.fullarticle

Thompson, M., Adleberg, T., Sims, S. & Nahmias, E. (2016) Why do women leave philosophy? Surveying students at the introductory level. *Philosophers' Imprint*, 16(6), pp. 1-38.

Times HE (2016) University of Essex hikes salaries for female professors to eliminate pay gap. *Times Higher Education.* https://www.timeshighereducation.com/news/university-of-essex-hikes-salaries-for-female-professors-to-eliminate-pay-gap

Tinklin, T. (2003) Gender differences and high attainment. *British Educational Research Journal*, 29(3), pp. 307-325.

Tirrell, L. (2000) Language and power. In: Jaggar, A.M. & Young, I.M. (eds.) *A Companion to Feminist Philosophy*, pp. 139-152. Oxford UK: Blackwell.

Topaz, C.M. & Sen, S. (2016) Gender representation on journal editorial boards in the mathematical sciences. *PLoS ONE*, 11(8), e0161357. doi:10.1371/journal.pone.0161357.

Tucker, A. (1984) *Chairing the Academic Department: leadership among peers.* New York: ACE/Macmillan.

UCU (2016) Holding down women's pay. University and College Union. https://www.ucu.org.uk/media/7959/Holding-down-womens-pay-Feb-16/pdf/ucu_IWDpayreport_mar16.pdf

Uhlmann, E., Cohen, G.L. (2005) Constructed criteria: redefining merit to justify discrimination. *Psychol Sci*, 16, pp. 474-480.

UK House of Commons Science and Technology Committee (2014) *Women in Scientific Careers, Sixth Report of Session 2013-14.*

United Nations (2005) *Sport for Development and Peace: towards achieving the millennium development goals.* New York: United Nations.

UoE (2015) *Athena SWAN Silver University Award Application*. The University of Edinburgh.

UoE Exemplars (2015) *Exemplars of Excellence in Student Education*. University of Edinburgh internal document. http://www.docs.csg.ed.ac.uk/HumanResources/ExemplardocumentSE_Jul15.pdf

van den Brink, M. (2011) Scouting for talent: appointment practices of women professors in academic medicine. *Social Science & Medicine*, 72(12), pp. 2033-2040.

van den Brink, M. & Stobbe, L. (2009) Doing gender in academic education: the paradox of visibility. *Gender, Work and Organisation*, 16 (4) pp. 451-470.

van der Gaag, N. (2014) *Feminism and Men*. London: Zed Books

van der Lee, R. & Ellemers, N. (2015) Gender contributes to personal research funding success in the Netherlands. *Proceedings of the National Academy of Sciences*, 112(40), 12349-12353. doi:10.1073/pnas.1510159112.

van Tuijl, C. & van der Molen, J.H.W. (2016) Study choice and career development in STEM fields: an overview and integration of the research. *International Journal of Technology and Design Education*, 26(2), pp. 159-183. doi:10.1007/s10798-015-9308-1.

Vandegrift, D. & Yavas, A. (2009) Men, women, and competition: an experimental test of behavior. *Journal of Economic Behavior & Organization*, 72(1), pp. 554-570.

Vardi, M.Y. (2015) What can be done about gender diversity in computing? *Commun ACM*, 58, 5-5. doi:10.1145/2816937

Venturi, R. (1984) *Complexity and Contradiction in Architecture*. 2nd ed. Museum of Modern Art Papers on Architecture. New York: The Museum of Modern Art.

Walters, M. (2005) *Feminism: A very short introduction*. Oxford: Oxford University Press.

Walton, G. (2014) The new science of wise psychological interventions. *Current Directions in Psychological Science*, 23(1), pp. 73-82. doi:10.1177/0963721413512856.

Walton, G.M. & Cohen, G.L. (2007) A question of belonging: race, social fit, and achievement. *Journal of Personality and Social Psychology*, 92(1), pp. 82-96. doi:10.1037/0022-3514.92.1.82.

Warrington, M. & Younger, M. (1999) Perspectives on the gender gap in English secondary schools. *Research Papers in Education*, 14, p. 51.

Wasserstein, R.L. & Lazar, N.A. (2016) The ASA's statement on p-values: context, process, and purpose. *The American Statistician*, 70(2), pp. 129-133. doi:10.1080/00031305.2016.1154108.

Weisman, L.K. (1981) Women's environmental rights: a manifesto. *Heresies II: Making Room: Women and Architecture*, 3(3), pp. 6-8.

Weisman, L.K. (2000) Prologue. In: Rendell, J., Penner, B., & Borden, I. (eds.) *Gender Space Architecture: an interdisciplinary introduction*. New York: Routledge.

Whitley, L. & Page, T. (2015) Sexism at the centre: locating the problem of sexual harassment. *New Formations*, Issue 86: Sexism.

Williams, A. (2013) *A Grammar of Creative Workplaces*. PhD Thesis, University of East London.

Williams, J.E. & Best, D.L. (1990) *Measuring sex stereotypes: a multination study*. Newbury Park, CA: Sage.

Willmott, H. (1995) Managing the academics: commodification and control in the development of university education in the UK. *Human Relations*, 48(9), pp. 993-1027.

Willmott, H. (2003) Commercialising higher education in the UK: the state, industry and peer review. *Studies in Higher Education*, 28(2), 129-141.

Wilson, T.D. (2002) *Strangers to Ourselves: discovering the adaptive unconscious*. Cambridge, MA: Harvard University Press.

Wilson, T.D. (2011) *Redirect: the surprising new science of psychological change*. Penguin.

WISE PLM (nd.) *People like me*. WISE Campaign. https://www.wisecampaign.org.uk/uploads/wise/files/6pp_NFPLM_SUMMARY_v31.pdf

Woolcock, M. (2001) The place of social capital in understanding social and economic outcomes. *ISUMA: Canadian Journal of Policy Research*, 2(1), pp. 11-17.

Woolf, V. (1929) *A Room of One's Own*. London: The Hogarth Press.

Woolf, V. (1945) *A Room of One's Own*. 2nd ed. London: The Penguin Group.

Woolston, C. (2016) Faking it. *Nature*, 529, pp. 555-557.

Yarrow, E.L. (2016) National research evaluation and its effects on female academics' careers in the UK - a case study. (Unpublished PhD thesis, and subject to viva.) Queen Mary, University of London.

Yeager, D.S. & Dweck, C.S. (2012) Mindsets that promote resilience: when students believe that personal characteristics can be developed. *Educational Psychologist,* 47(4), pp. 302-314. doi:10.1080/00461520.2012.722805.

Younger, M. & Warrington, M. (1996) Differential achievement of girls and boys at GCSE: some observations from the perspective of one school. *British Journal of Sociology of Education*, 17, pp. 299-313.

Yousafzai, M. (2013) *I Am Malala: the story of the girl who stood up for education and was shot by the Taliban*. Little, Brown.

Zanoni, P., & Janssens, M. (2004) Deconstructing difference: the rhetoric of human resource managers' diversity discourses. *Organization Studies*, 25(1), pp. 55-74.

Zenger, J. & Folkman, J. (2012) Are women better leaders than men? *Harvard Business Review*. https://hbr.org/2012/03/a-study-in-leadership-women-do

Ziliak, S. & McCloskey, D. (2008) *The Cult of Statistical Significance: how the standard error costs us jobs, justice and lives*. Ann Arbor, MI: University of Michigan Press.

Zinovyeva, N. & Bagues, M. (2011) *Does gender matter for academic promotion? Evidence from a randomized natural experiment*. IZA Discussion Paper No. 5537. https://core.ac.uk/download/pdf/39371354.pdf

Zweben, S. & Bizot, B. (2016) CRA Taulbee Survey 2015. *Computing Research News*, May 2016, 28(5). http://cra.org/wp-content/uploads/2016/05/2015-Taulbee-Survey.pdf

Abbreviations, acronyms and initialisms

AAUW – American Association of University Women.

AHRC – Arts & Humanities Research Council.

AGCAS – Association of Graduate Careers Advisory Services.

AHSSBL – arts, humanities, social sciences, business and law.

AR – annual review.

BBSRC – Biotechnology and Biological Sciences Research Council.

BME – black and minority ethnic.

CTF – Career Track Fellowship.

DWP – Department for Work and Pensions, UK government department.

EBRC – Easter Bush Research Consortium.

ECA – Edinburgh College of Art.

ECR – early career researcher.

ECU – Equality Challenge Unit.

EPSRC – Engineering and Physical Sciences Research Council.

ESRC – Economic and Social Research Council.

EUSA – Edinburgh University Students' Association

FE college - further education college.

FASIC – Fitness Assessment and Sports Injuries Centre at the University of Edinburgh.

FIFA – Fédération Internationale de Football Association (International Federation of Association Football).

GH – guaranteed-hours (contracts of employment).

HEFCE – Higher Education Funding Council for England.

HESA – official agency for higher education statistics in the UK.

HR – Human Resources.

HUP – Healthy University Project.

IAD – Institute for Academic Development at the University of Edinburgh.

LGBTQ+ – lesbian, gay, bisexual, trans, queer/ questioning and other.

MRC – Medical Research Council.

NERC – Natural Environment Research Council

NUS – National Union of Students.

PDR – performance development review.

RCUK – Research Councils UK.

REF – Research Excellence Framework.

SPA – Support for Physical Activity programme.

STEM – science, technology, engineering and mathematics.

STEMM – science, technology, engineering, medicine and mathematics.

STFC – Science and Technology Facilities Council.

UCU – University and College Union.

UEFA – Union of European Football Associations.

UOA – unit of assessment, used by REF.

Index

Page references for glossary entries are in
bold; references for illustrations are in *italics*.